Artisans and Designers

COSTUME SOCIETY OF AMERICA

BOOK SERIES

The Costume Society of America book series includes works on all subjects related to the history and future of fashion, dress, costume, appearance and adornment, including historical research, current issues, curatorial topics, contemporary design and construction practices, and conservation techniques. These books range from scholarly to more general interest and vary widely in format as well, from primarily textual to heavily illustrated. The series embraces a variety of specialties, including anthropology and cross-cultural studies, contemporary fashion issues, textiles, museums and exhibits, research methods, performance, and craft or fashion design.

Artisans and Designers

American Fashion Through Elizabeth and William Phelps

REBECCA JUMPER MATHESON

THE KENT STATE UNIVERSITY PRESS Kent, Ohio

ISBN 978-1-60635-501-5
EISBN 978-1-63101-581-6
Published in the United States of America

Cataloging information for this title is available at the Library of Congress.

29 28 27 26 25 5 4 3 2 1

Contents

Selected Phelps Chronology

1890 William Drown Phelps born on September 20, in Laurel Run, Pennsylvania.

1909 Elizabeth Heintges Von Mevis born on November 27 in Germany.

1917 United States enters World War I.

William Phelps serves in the US Navy (through 1919).

1920 William Phelps marries Jean Marina True Ross on December 11.

1929 Stock market crash in October ushers in the Great Depression.

1932 William Phelps leaves his corporate career with General Motors and sets up woodworking business, initially in his mother's attic in Wilkes-Barre, Pennsylvania, then in New York City.

William and Elizabeth—"Jim and Elsie"—meet in New York City.

1933 Elizabeth studies at Art Students League.

1934 Divorce of William and Jean Phelps is finalized December 14.

William and Elizabeth Phelps marry in Wilkes-Barre on December 31.

1935 William Phelps begins teaching craft with the Civilian Conservation Corps on Governor's Island.

circa 1939 William and Elizabeth Phelps visit the Swamp leather district, purchase leather under the Brooklyn Bridge, and William makes the first wide leather belt for Elizabeth.

1940 At the request of fashion designer Clare Potter, the Phelpses set up Phelps Associates leather workshop at basement of 13 Washington Square. Phelpses focus on custom work.

1941 United States enters World War II on December 8, after Japanese attack on Pearl Harbor December 7.

1943 US rationing of leather shoes begins in February. Further leather restrictions in place through the M-310 basic leather conservation order by the end of the year.

Phelps Associates sell consignment of leather goods through Mark Cross store.

1944 Phelps Associates win a 1943 Coty Award and are honored at ceremony.

1945 VE (Victory in Europe) Day celebrated May 8; VJ (Victory over Japan) Day celebrated in the United States on September 12.

Phelps Associates' New York City workshop and showroom occupies three floors of 45 University Place.

William and Elizabeth Phelps purchase Joanna Furnace, an historic iron furnace property in Berks County, Pennsylvania, and make plans to move their residence and workshop there.

Simplified ready-to-wear leather goods production at Birdsboro, Pennsylvania workshop is set up in conjunction with department store investors.

1946 Lord & Taylor becomes a key retail outlet for Phelps Associates in New York City.

Phelps Associates receives a Neiman Marcus award.

1948 *Vogue*'s October 1 issue features Elizabeth Phelps's custom apron designs.

1949 June 4 fashion show at Joanna Furnace launches Phelps Deep Country Clothes ready-to-wear sportswear line.

Phelps New York showroom at 17 East 48th Street.

1950 Elizabeth Phelps participates in the Metropolitan Museum of Art's *Adam in the Looking Glass* exhibition.

Elizabeth Phelps receives honor scroll for outstanding achievement as a woman in business by the New York State Women's Council.

1951 Elizabeth Phelps designs leather and fabric sportswear for Sills (through 1953).

Sale of Joanna Furnace property to Bethlehem Steel is finalized in the summer.

In June, Phelpses move residence and workshops to North Carolina, purchasing Shadowlawn property in Skyland, outside of Asheville.

1952 Phelps Associates moves New York City showroom to 27 East Thirty-Seventh Street.

1953 Elizabeth Phelps Smart Togs for Action paper sewing pattern series in conjunction with *Woman's Day.*

1957 Phelps standalone retail shop opened near Sarasota, Florida. By the following year, the Phelpses would be operating four shops in North Carolina and Florida.

1959 Phelps Industries incorporated in North Carolina.

1960 Phelps New York City showroom is closed, and seasonal showings are held at Sheraton-Russell Hotel at Park Avenue and Thirty-Seventh Street (through 1969).

1961 Elizabeth Phelps receives Lord & Taylor American Design Award.

1962 William Drown Phelps dies on January 20 at the Phelpses' vacation home at Ormond Beach, Florida.

1964 Elizabeth Phelps applies for patent on convertible shorts to trousers.

1969 Hanes Corp. offers Elizabeth Phelps a consultant role, and she begins selling parts of Skyland property.

1973 Elizabeth Phelps sells additional acreage from Skyland property and has closeout sale of remaining Phelps stock and fabric, followed by auction of personal goods.

1978 Solo exhibition of Elizabeth Phelps's paintings in Ocean Springs, Mississippi, where she has relocated.

1981 Elizabeth Phelps wins prize in Seventeenth Annual LaFont Art Workshop exhibition in Pascagoula, Mississippi.

1987 Elizabeth Phelps dies on November 17.

Introduction

This book recovers the story of the life and work of husband-and-wife design team William Drown Phelps (1890–1962) and Elizabeth Heintges Phelps (1909–1987) and their contribution to American fashion through their leathergoods and sportswear firm, Phelps Associates. Researching the Phelpses' relationships with each other, American craft, and the American fashion industry and its related media and promotion also illuminates broader issues in American fashion, design, business, and manufacturing history, including gender roles, consumerism, reactions to industrialization, and articulation of American identity.[1] William and Elizabeth Phelps were critically acclaimed for accessories and sportswear that articulated American ideals from patriotism in wartime to simplicity and utility in the 1950s and 1960s. The Phelpses' accessories designs celebrated handcraft traditions that had persisted despite industrialization in the production of many types of leather goods, while both their accessories and sportswear combatted the consumerism of rapid fashion change by emphasizing long-term investment in quality goods. William and Elizabeth Phelps are significant in the history of American fashion for their leatherwork, which drew on American historical forms and craftsmanship, their experimentation with modes of making beyond mass production, their partnership as a husband-and-wife design team, their concern with the quality and functionality of materials and end products, their roster of clients that included many noncelebrities as well as fashion industry and media professionals, and Elizabeth Phelps's sportswear designs that gave a consumer base of primarily middle- and upper-class white women greater sartorial freedom without offending gender norms and notions of propriety.

Introductory Object: The Quintessential Phelps Postman Shoulder Bag

The bag was listed on the online auction site eBay.com in 2015 under the slightly inaccurate heading, "WW2 Era US Military Leather Doctor's Medical Bag With 'E Pluris Un Um' [*sic*] Emblem" (Fig. I.1). But of course, objects on eBay are not always what the seller claims or believes them to be. The seller was accurate in the dating (World War II–era), geographic region (United States), material (leather), general object type (bag), and—misspelling aside—inscription wording. However, the seller was mistaken as to the type and purpose of the bag; its actual story was something quite different. The eBay seller imagined the bag must have belonged to a military "Dr. Phelps" because of the

Fig. I.1. Phelps Associates, postman shoulder bag, leather, metal, circa 1945. (Author's collection. Photograph by the author.)

Fig. I.2. William and Elizabeth Phelps on the porch of their home at Joanna Furnace, Pennsylvania, 1945. (Walker Evans, [105 Views and Studies of Leather Craftsmen, Their Home in Birdsboro, Pennsylvania. and New York City Residence, Commissioned by *Fortune* Magazine for "The Small Shop," Published November 1945], film negative, Walker Evans Archive, 1994, 1994.252.3.1–.105. © Walker Evans Archive, The Metropolitan Museum of Art. Image source: Art Resource, NY.)

word *PHELPS* stamped into the leather. In fact, that mark indicates the bag was the work of American design team William and Elizabeth Phelps under their label, Phelps Associates (Fig. I.2). The design elements of this bag, now in the author's collection, exemplify the quintessential Phelps Associates leather bag: It is made from sturdy, plain leather; it is designed to be worn slung from the shoulder; its form is drawn from American history; and its metal ornament was already vintage when the bag was made and was repurposed from an actual or intended military use. Originally recognized in the 1940s for historicizing leather goods like this bag, the Phelpses went on to add sportswear to their offerings in the postwar period, while maintaining their emphasis on high-quality, functional style.

The bag in Fig. I.1 was a high-fashion item in the United States in the early 1940s and thus would have been worn with pride by the chic client who first owned it.[2] Due to similarities in style between military and civilian accessories of the period, this client might have been a socialite, despite the bag's similarity to shoulder bags worn by enlisted women such as the members of the Women's Army Auxiliary Corps. But when the war was over, perhaps the Phelps bag started to look less elegant. Eventually it was clearly dated, as is the nature of fashion cycles. Maybe the original wearer packed the bag away in her cedar chest or closet, or perhaps she gave it away. Perhaps after another twenty years had elapsed, the bag was found and worn while shoulder bags were again in style, enjoying a second fashionable life. In what limbo did the bag live for the next sixty or so years, until it passed into the hands of an eBay seller? By the time the bag was sold on eBay, it was no longer recognized as a woman's handbag. It was now a

Fig. I.3. Phelps Associates, postman shoulder bag, leather, metal. (Brooklyn Museum Costume Collection at The Metropolitan Museum of Art, Gift of the Brooklyn Museum, 2009; Gift of Mrs. Morehead Patterson, 1985, 2009.300.2632a–c. Image copyright © The Metropolitan Museum of Art. Image source: Art Resource, NY.)

collector's item. But when the bag did indeed enter a private collection, it was that of a fashion historian rather than a collector of military goods.

This bag, though now special to me, is actually very similar to others, including one in the collection of the Costume Institute at the Metropolitan Museum of Art (2009.300.262a-c) (Fig. I.3). It is not a one-off but part of a larger story of American fashion and craft production of accessories, how people interact with materials and the designed objects that surround them, and how fashion includes a range of everyday clothing and accessories, not just haute couture ballgowns.

Overview

In the 1940 US census, William and Elizabeth Phelps both listed their occupations as "artist—freelance."[3] Within the next two years, and with the encouragement of fashion designer Clare Potter, they would build William's hobby of leatherworking into a highly successful and recognized line of custom-made women's leather belts and handbags under the Phelps Associates label, while continuing to view themselves as artists and craftspeople. In their New York City workshop, the Phelpses created made-to-order belts as well as custom shoulder bags modeled on forms from American military history and adorned with Americana motifs, repurposed horse harness decorations, and other vintage metalwork. The Phelpses embraced modernist ideas such as truth to materials, but they also believed men's leather goods from the American colonial period were both beautiful and functional and could be successfully adapted to meet the needs of mid-twentieth-century women.[4]

The World War II–era designs of Phelps Associates were both modern and historicizing, forward-thinking while looking back to American history.[5] In arguing for this combination of elements in the work of William and Elizabeth Phelps, I am further developing ideas that I first applied to the work of Emily Wilkens, an American designer of ready-to-wear clothing for teenagers who also received critical acclaim during the 1940s. I first became interested in Phelps Associates while researching Wilkens, as their work showed a similar interest in Americana. While doing research for my book on Wilkens and her fashion designs for American teenage girls, I kept seeing the Phelpses' work everywhere in magazines, newspapers, and ephemera such as fashion show programs. They seemed to appear out of nowhere in the early 1940s and immediately started winning major awards, and I wanted to know why. What was so special about them? I wanted to recover the story of William and Elizabeth Phelps and to discover what made their leather goods so critically acclaimed during World War II, as well as to emphasize the importance of accessories to our understanding of a fashionable ensemble. As I continued research and learned more, my aims expanded to focus on how they worked together and then on the significance of Elizabeth Phelps's postwar sportswear designs.

The Phelpses' rapid critical success in the early 1940s stemmed from the ways their designs met wearers' needs, both aesthetic and practical, as well as suiting the narrative of craftsmanship and history that the American fashion industry was writing about itself. Phelps Associates entered the American fashion scene in the midst of the Second World War and the accompanying promotion of US fashion. The 1940 occupation of Paris disrupted the regular flow of fashion ideas and products from France to the United States that had begun in the nineteenth century and created both a dilemma and an opportunity for American fashion. The industry responded by addressing both the aesthetic concern of what constituted uniquely American style and the marketing need to promote American fashion to replace its longstanding reliance on Parisian haute couture. The media touted William Drown Phelps's New England genealogy; his identity as a craftsman—including that he was a descendant of the colonial-era Boston metalworker Shem Drowne (1683–1774), among other craftsmen—fit well with the industry's goals of creating an American design identity. In emphasizing handcraft, the Phelps label channeled both the mystique more usually associated with European luxury goods and a romantic view of the preindustrial American past. At the same time, Phelps Associates shoulder bags were an extremely practical design solution to the issue facing most American handbag manufacturers, which, once the government requisitioned metals for the war effort, could no longer rely on the metal frames that had been the mainstays of the bag industry.[6] Bernice Chambers of The Fashion Group, an organization dedicated to promoting American fashion and women's roles within the fashion industry, credited the Phelpses with starting the trend in the United States for shoulder bags, which also served a wartime need for female consumers to have handsfree mobility and to be able to carry their own packages.[7] William and Elizabeth Phelps quickly achieved critical acclaim within the fashion industry, receiving a Coty Award in 1944 as well as a Neiman Marcus award in 1946.[8]

Twentieth-century American fashion was dependent on accessories as well as main garments, yet many once well-known names of accessory designers are less familiar or forgotten today. New Yorker and novelist Mary Rodgers wrote humorously about her own struggles to look chic and the importance of accessories in 1970, advising readers, "Get the shoes and the bag to go with the dress; forgetting the accessories is a common frump failing."[9] Even the most fashionable dress would not have looked stylish without the correct accessories. My work here has both reinforced the importance of the etiquette of accessories and discovered ways individual wearers challenged or ignored the rules. In recent years, much of American fashion history has focused on designers of main garments and changes in silhouette over time, but there has also been increasing

Fig. I.4. "This Half Century," *Vogue*, January 1950, 93. (Irving Penn, *Vogue*, ©Condé Nast.)

interest in other aspects of the fashion system, from the process of design piracy to the "everyday" fashions worn by nonelites.[10] The Phelpses' early work falls within the under-researched but significant segment of the American fashion industry devoted to accessories, and even as they later added sportswear, accessories remained key to the full Phelps aesthetic.

By the end of the 1940s, *Vogue* magazine journalists chose a Phelps wide belt and shoulder bag paired with a dress by the successful designer Claire McCardell as the representative American look of the war years (Fig. I.4).[11] This editorial coverage of Phelps Associates is the most immediately recognizable image of the Phelpses' work. The photograph by Irving Penn (1917–2009) is the first thing that comes to mind when most fashion historians hear "Phelps." While the belt is more difficult to see, the camera's angle places the quintessential Phelps eagle postman bag as the focal point of the photograph and the page layout.

With fashions and fashionable ideals of femininity shifting in the postwar period, the Phelpses sought to expand their line beyond their signature rugged belts and shoulder bags. Phelps Associates' leather designs based on historic menswear pieces were less suited to accessorizing the traditional ladylike styles promoted after the war, so they sought growth by creating other—including nonfashion—products.[12] First, they added additional custom merchandise, such as a cow-horn salad fork and spoon in a leather case, featured in the Museum of Modern Art's *100 Useful Objects of Fine Design 1947 exhibition.*[13] As early as 1944, they had begun producing custom women's separates, including aprons and skirts, and in 1949 they introduced ready-to-wear, changing the name of their business to Phelps Industries by 1951. Fashion historians including Rebecca Arnold and Richard Martin have argued that inventiveness, utility, nonelitism, and practicality were key components of twentieth-century American sportswear.[14] The Phelpses' designs epitomized this combination of qualities. Elizabeth Phelps was credited in the media with most of the ready-to-wear design, and she worked within this American sportswear tradition. As in the case of the majority of American fashion designers of the mid-twentieth century, despite an emphasis on democratization of fashion, Elizabeth Phelps's unspoken target market was white and middle class.[15] She designed under the Phelps sublabel Phelps Deep Country Clothes to meet the casual clothing needs of these consumers, whether in the suburbs, in the country, or while traveling, with clothes that were easy to put on, fasten, wear, and wash, in practical fabrics such as denim, canvas, and corduroy (Fig. I.5).[16]

Fig. I.5. Phelps Deep Country Clothes label. Elizabeth Phelps for Phelps Deep Country Clothes, blouse, cotton, circa 1963. (Author's collection. Photograph by the author.)

One thread running throughout this narrative is the importance of the Phelpses and their workshop as being characterized as "American," both in how the Phelpses conceived their own work and how the fashion industry portrayed it. Between 1940 and 1952, the Phelpses moved from their original New York City workshop, first to historic Joanna Furnace (a nineteenth-century iron furnace) in Pennsylvania in 1945, then to a location outside of Asheville, North Carolina in 1951. Each of these locations affected their work and added to an aspect of their American story: fashion industry networking, materials, and skilled labor of immigrants are part of the New York City narrative; clothing forms and fastenings influenced by the needs of a rural lifestyle were added when they moved to Pennsylvania; and, later, the Phelpses consciously situated their work and workers as part of an Appalachian craft tradition in North Carolina.

Another thread is the relationship of William and Elizabeth Phelps as a husband-and-wife design team. A more typical scenario in the French fashion industry is the example of Madame Paquin, who designed while her husband ran the business. While husband-and-wife teams such as Charles Eames and Ray Eames and Florence Knoll and Hans Knoll achieved recognition in other areas of American design, such as furniture and textile design, the Phelpses' relationship as codesigners and makers was less usual in the arena of American fashion and was highlighted as one of the unique attributes of the Phelps company.[17]

A third thread of the Phelpses' work is its materiality—the physical properties and being of the objects and the relationships and interactions between people and things. The Phelpses cared deeply about the quality and functionality of the materials they used, whether working in leather or with textiles, and materials were an element they frequently discussed in interviews. They were also concerned with the way their designs functioned on and with the body—crafting, for example, a bag shaped to fit snugly on the wearer's shoulder. Further, they were also interested in materiality from the perspective of their workers and the process of creation and spoke about the importance of handwork to an artisan's well-being. In 2008, fashion and design studies scholar Hazel Clark defined *slow fashion* as "sustainable fashion solutions, based on the repositioning of strategies of design, production, consumption, use, and reuse, which are emerging. . . . [offering] more sustainable and ethical ways of being fashionable."[18] The Phelpses' oeuvre anticipates the twenty-first century's concern with sustainability and demonstrates the pair's passion for creating objects that align with many of the priorities of today's slow-fashion movement, particularly high-quality things with a long usable life.

Methods and Sources

Over the course of their lives, William and Elizabeth Phelps worked in several different areas of art, craft, and fashion, while resisting notions that these were entirely separate categories, but their longest and most recognized contributions were in fashion. This book takes a multifaceted approach to the definition of American fashion. The parameters of fashion as it applies to dress are debated, but most definitions involve a sense that the key to *fashion* is change (as opposed to the more all-encompassing term *dress,* which includes anything worn or done to adorn or modify the body). Fashion historian Lourdes M. Font's definition of *fashion* as "luxury and novelty combined into an irresistible force" captures a sense of Western fashion's power even in the mid-twentieth century and the luxury market that the American fashion industry was trying to replace domestically when Phelps Associates started (see chapter 2).[19] Cultural studies theorist Elizabeth Wilson also defines *fashion* as having to do with change—"dress in which the key feature is rapid and continual changing of styles"—and argues for a broad definition of *fashion* as a system: "in modern western societies no clothes are outside fashion; fashion sets the terms of all sartorial behavior." Wilson's example of even uniforms being designed by fashion designers is apropos for the World War II period and the overlap between accessories for women in the American armed forces and those for civilians, as exemplified in the Phelpses' leatherwork (see chapter 3).[20]

Yet, some aspects of Phelps Associates' work seem to defy fashion's change, or at least slow down the cycle; the company continued making some styles for decades, and clients who bought Phelps products continued to wear them for years. Cheryl Buckley and Hazel Clark's framework for considering everyday fashion "as a manifestation of routine daily lives that remains with people over time" and emphasizing the wearer's role in "the ordinary and mundane practices of wearing that draws items from the personal wardrobe in a routine manner" is helpful for understanding the ways that the genre of postwar "country clothes" sportswear, such as that produced by Phelps, was promoted even by fashion magazines and ultimately treasured by purchasers as a long-term investment.[21] Based in methodological models that seek to tell a story ranging from high fashion to everyday dress, this book takes a comprehensive view of fashion, treating all the work by William and Elizabeth Phelps as equally worthy of scholarly study, from the luxurious early custom leathergoods accessories to their later ready-to-wear sportswear and even home sewing patterns.

Jane Bradbury and Edward Maeder's *American Style and Spirit* demonstrates how synthesizing object-based, documentary, and visual source research gives a fuller picture of the people who wore the clothes, how they wore and interacted with these objects over time, as well as the history of fashion's changing silhouettes, consumption patterns, and social context. [22] In following this model, this book incorporates the stories of multiple women who wore the Phelpses' designs, starting with the objects they owned, and using other types of evidence to fill in the narrative of how they interacted with the Phelpses' creations and what these objects meant to them. Charlotte Niklas and Annebella Pollen's *Dress History: New Directions in Theory and Practice* also offers helpful examples of interdisciplinary dress research, which starts with the primary source object itself and moves outward.[23] In this book, each chapter similarly begins with an example object or objects that will form starting points for considering an aspect or period of William and Elizabeth Phelps's design.

Studying Phelps objects in museums has helped me gain a greater understanding of their construction methods, dimensions, materials, labeling, and overall appearance than it is possible to grasp from textual or visual sources and has prompted new questions. During museum research appointments, I have often sketched objects as a method of close looking, or the "slow approach to seeing" as Ingrid Mida advocates.[24] Object-based research methods have helped me understand more about the wide range of fashionable and fashion-industry or media connected women who bought, saved, and donated or passed down Phelps accessories and clothing. They used the belts so much that the leather is worn where they buckled them. They repaired the trousers so they could continue to wear them. Phelps garments and accessories had moments when they were highly fashionable and moments when they were just "classic," but their clients seemed to collect and treasure their things and keep them. I also incorporate objects in my own collection, which allow for handling not possible in museum collections and provide a haptic reference point for understanding the materiality and functionality of objects now singularized in a museum. For example, I can try on my Phelps shoulder bag on my own shoulder to see how it would have felt and how easy or difficult it would be to keep the bag in place.

I also use archival material to gain an understanding of what Phelps Associates made, precisely where they made it, what legal, historical, and economic constraints they were working under, and what level of financial and/or critical success they achieved. The archives consulted include those of the Fashion

Group at the New York Public Library (for content of their participation in industry meetings), of retail buyer Virginia "Jimmie" Booth at the National Museum of American History in Washington, DC (Booth was a friend and their contact at Lord & Taylor), and of publicist Eleanor Lambert at Special Collections and College Archives, Gladys Marcus Library, Fashion Institute of Technology, in New York (for information regarding the Coty Awards). Archival research, particularly in the Fashion Group archives helps me answer questions about why the Phelpses' accessories and their craft workshop production made them so critically acclaimed in the 1940s; the Fashion Group's archives reveal the US fashion industry's struggle to articulate what American fashion was all about, and the Phelpses' work was a tangible answer to this question.

I also use methods from art history to analyze visual sources such as photographs and newsreel film, relying on art and fashion historian Anne Hollander's theory that in each era the way clothing felt and looked to people was based on an ideal body that was most clearly expressed in visual art.[25] Phelps Associates' accessories and garments generally reinforced the fashionable ideal body in each decade of their production, yet their designs offered women slightly more freedom within those confines—for example, with a skirt that could be adjusted by wrapping and tying. Art historian Sally Stein's framework, which considers the intentional placement of both textual and visual content of magazines to sell more goods, is helpful for analyzing the Phelps Associates' magazine coverage.[26] I also consider how the Phelpses were influenced by larger movements in art and design, including the arts and crafts movement, modernism and the concept of the American folk, and the American colonial revival.[27]

Geographic Availability

Following one of dress historian Lou Taylor's key areas for object-based scholarship of dress—finding objects—part of this research focused on the geographic availability of extant Phelps objects (as well as their identification and interpretation).[28] It appears that Phelps leather goods and clothing were primarily sold on the US East Coast. One initial question was whether custom-made Phelps objects were disproportionally represented in museum collections, as opposed to the ready-to-wear, but it appears that both are present, with more early and custom work in New York City institutions, and later, mostly ready-to-wear work elsewhere. I have located Phelps objects in museums including the Costume Institute, Metropolitan Museum of Art, and the Museum at the Fashion Institute of Technology (FIT) in New York; the Wadsworth Atheneum in Hartford, Connecticut; the Valentine Richmond History Center in Richmond, Virginia; the North Carolina Museum of History, in Raleigh, North Carolina; and the Hay Creek Valley Historical Association, housed in the Phelpses' former workshop at Joanna Furnace, Pennsylvania. Although some crucial periods in my Phelps research coincided with the COVID-19 pandemic, and I faced the challenges of conducting in-person research during this time, I also had some wonderful experiences of serendipity. For example, when I planned a visit the Phelpses' Pennsylvania workshop location at Joanna Furnace, thinking I would just be seeing the space, I discovered that the Helen Hart accessory set had entered its collection. These accessories, together with an earlier published oral history and documents from Hart's personal files and from her funeral helped me tell a very different part of the Phelps story, from the perspective of workers.

I have not been able to find many Phelps pieces in collections in other parts of the United States, despite clues that they were marketed (even if to a limited degree) more broadly. For example, the Phelpses won a Neiman Marcus award from the store headquartered in Dallas, and a Phelps Deep Country Clothes skirt sold by the San Antonio vintage store Montage in 2016 contained both a Phelps and a "Neiman Marcus Trophy Room" label. Neiman Marcus was also involved as an investor in a postwar Phelps project.[29] This indicates that their work was sold in the Neiman Marcus store in Dallas and possibly other Neiman Marcus locations, and quite likely there are surviving Phelps pieces in Texas, but none are in the Texas Fashion Collection in Denton, Texas, a museum Neiman Marcus founded in the late 1930s.[30]

Review of the Literature and Contribution

This book is the first in-depth study of William and Elizabeth Phelps, and their business, Phelps Associates. Because so little has been previously published about the Phelpses, even constructing basic biographical information has been a careful stitching together of research from a wide range of sources, including official documents found through genealogical databases, such as marriage and divorce records and census records, as well as newspaper databases that cover newspapers of such small towns as Ocean Springs, Mississippi, where Elizabeth Phelps lived in the 1970s and 1980s. Elements of their lives still remain unknown and may continue to elude the researcher.

In the secondary literature, Phelps Associates is usually just mentioned in passing. For instance, in the context of her discussion of Claire McCardell, fashion historian and curator Valerie Steele quotes the text of *Vogue*'s reference to "her Phelps belt and bag bold" in the January 1950 "This Half Century" article (which accompanied the iconic Penn photograph, Fig. I.4), but does not elaborate on Phelps.[31] Secondary sources most often reference Phelps Associates within the context of lists of American fashion designers and award winners. For example, the fourth edition of Fairchild textbook author Annalee Gold's *One World of Fashion* includes William and Elizabeth Phelps on pages dedicated to "Coty Award Winners, 1943 to 1946" and notes that "Elizabeth and William Phelps combined leather with interesting hardware touches. Their stylish, oversized shoulder bags were an innovation."[32] Caroline Rennolds Milbank's 1989 *New York Fashion* contains a short profile of the Phelpses, contextualizing them in her chapter on New York fashion designers of the 1940s.[33] As I discovered during this research, Milbank's knowledge of Phelps is not just academic but also personal (see chapter 3).

When Phelps Associates accessories have been shown in exhibition catalogs, they have sometimes been uncredited. For example, in the catalog for the

Fig. I.6. Phelps Deep Country Clothes sportswear shown in the Museum at FIT catalog *Denim: Fashion's Frontier,* by Emma McClendon. Elizabeth Phelps for Phelps Deep Country Clothes blouses, skirt, and shorts, cotton, circa 1955, Museum at FIT. (Courtesy the Museum at FIT. Photograph by Eileen Costa.© The Museum at FIT.)

Museum at FIT's (MFIT) 1985 exhibition *All-American: A Sportswear Tradition,* fashion journalist (and Phelps client) Sally Kirkland's essay includes a paragraph on the relationship between Phelps accessories and horse harness. However, the only image of a Phelps accessory in the *All-American* catalog is, again, the famous Irving Penn photograph (Fig. I.4) showing a model with a Phelps eagle shoulder bag; the catalog caption lists only the designer of the model's dress, Claire McCardell.[34] Similarly, the Phelpses were not mentioned in MFIT's 1998 exhibition catalog, *Claire McCardell: Redefining Modernism,* with the same *Vogue*/Penn image, as well as other fashion photography and even an extant Phelps belt from the MFIT collection, used in garment photography to accessorize McCardell's dresses.[35] In a more recent MFIT exhibition catalog, *Denim: Fashion's Frontier,* extant Phelps garments and accessories are credited and shown together in the catalog, with an entry that highlights Phelps's use of denim in the Deep Country Clothes line (Fig. I.6).[36] The Wadsworth Atheneum's 1998 exhibition, *Designing Women: American Style 1940–1960,* included text about Phelps in the Labels and Gallery Guide, but unfortunately a catalog was not produced.[37]

The majority of available published information about Phelps Associates comes from fashion press and industry publications, which championed Phelps in the 1940s, at the height of their critical acclaim. Both *Harper's Bazaar* and *Vogue* included Phelps Associates' work in their pages, presenting it as simultaneously modern and historicizing. *Harper's* continued to cover the designs through the 1950s, and *Vogue* showed occasional Phelps accessories as late as 1970, perhaps due to specific fashion editors' preferences. The Phelpses were also profiled in fashion industry educational publications, such as *Fashion Fundamentals* by Bernice G. Chambers, of the Fashion Group.[38] Both the fashion industry newspaper *Women's Wear Daily* and newspapers for a general readership, such as *The New York Times,* ran stories that included information on Phelps Associates, more frequently in the 1940s and early 1950s, and slowly diminishing in the 1960s. A *Women's Wear Daily* journalist declared after they won a 1943 Coty Award, "There is a keen, alert, up-to-the-minute air of 1944 about Mr. and Mrs. Phelps which belies the fact that their impelling force, as far as handbag and belt design is concerned, should have derived from the days of the young American republic for inspiration. But it is evident that the revolutionary spirit of those pioneer days has cast a spell over them."[39] This combination of "up-to-the-minute air of 1944" alongside "the revolutionary spirit of those pioneer days" was key to the modern yet historicizing Phelps appeal, as an American story of a husband-and-wife team creating handcrafted leather goods for women.

This study of William and Elizabeth Phelps, and Phelps Associates, is important to several different fields of study and categories of reader. First, it is important to fashion and design historians because it recovers the story of a critically acclaimed yet understudied American fashion design team. It is also a designer-based study that goes beyond the great designer trope to consider many different aspects of what made a particular creator's work fashionable, including editorial coverage, publicity, retail stores, and resonance with the consumer. This book is valuable to women's studies scholars as a case study of one woman's path as an artist and craftsperson as well as an entrepreneur. It is also helpful for considering the way Elizabeth Phelps's designs benefited wearers. This work is of interest to business historians as a case study of the challenges for designers associated with trying different production methods for mid-twentieth-century fashion. The Phelpses experimented with unusual production methods—from the small, independent custom craft workshop; to a retail investor-backed shop making handmade models in limited designs to a very small-scale factory making limited runs of both their own and others' designs. When one experiment failed, they tried something else. Finally, this study is relevant to the general reader who is interested in fashion.

The book chapters are arranged in a generally chronological but also thematic order. For example, chapter 1, "Craft Connections and Early Careers," explores the beginnings of the Phelps Associates brand, from the early lives of William and Elizabeth Phelps, through the creation of the Phelps workshop. The Phelpses deliberately positioned themselves as artists and their work within a context of American history, casting themselves as heirs to both New England craft traditions and the history of the New York City leather industry. Their fashion industry connections were key to their transition into that market, and their working style as a husband-and-wife team was unusual within that field.

Chapter 2, "Workshop on Washington Square to University Place," examines the first two Phelps workshops in New York City, arguing that the Phelpses' emphasis on craft met the need of the American fashion industry for luxury and artisanship to replace the Paris couture, with a flair that expressed long-held American values. William and Elizabeth Phelps combined their interest in "honest" materials within a traditional of handcraftsmanship in leather that was related to that used in making ornamental horse harness. The workshops were sites for the Phelpses' own working relationship as a team and also shopping locations for custom clients. While I have not uncovered evidence that Phelps Associates' workshops were unionized, they were places for experimentation in modes of small-scale production that were more empowering and even healing for employees. This research suggests that Phelps was a modestly profitable enterprise in New York during World War II.

The demands of war led to shortages of materials such as metal and leather in the early 1940s, and chapter 3, "Shortages and Shapes," discusses these supply issues as well as the historically inspired shapes that Phelps Associates favored. William and Elizabeth Phelps crafted a careful design program incorporating Americana motifs based on historical forms and created a workshop that referenced historical production methods associated the Phelps name with American craftsmanship in a way that appealed to both consumers and tastemakers and went beyond the Americana gestures of other brands. Phelps Associates first received critical attention during World War II, as their products met wartime needs ranging from the aesthetic to the utilitarian.

William and Elizabeth Phelps relied on many channels to broaden awareness of Phelps Associates beyond the confines of New York–based fashion insiders, and these avenues are explored in chapter 4, "Promoting and Selling Phelps Associates' Products." The type of free news-making publicity, a public relations specialty, was one aspect of fashion promotion for brands like Phelps, through industry events like the Coty Awards. The Phelpses also participated in museum exhibitions, subsequently donating objects to institutions like the Museum of Costume Art. Magazines' editorial coverage of the Phelpses' work supported their goals of creating a brand image associated with patriotism and craftsmanship. These articles also instructed readers on the right places and times for wearing Phelps accessories, according to prevailing fashion etiquette. Retailers were the final bridge between Phelps and consumers, showing and selling their accessories to women who might not have ever entered their workshop.

Chapter 5, "Postwar Expansion: Joanna Furnace, Pennsylvania," follows William and Elizabeth Phelps's move from New York City to rural Pennsylvania as they sought to expand their business and experiment with a new, two-tiered production method. Their two Pennsylvania workshops would offer different types of making: a streamlined Birdsboro workshop attempted to meet the demands of large specialty stores by making fewer and simpler designs, while a Joanna Furnace workshop was the space for more detailed leathercraft. In the postwar period, with the Phelpses' own new lifestyle in the country, they also began producing garments: initially custom sportswear, with Elizabeth Phelps creating clothing that suited her lifestyle yet conformed to William's notions of gender roles and later making flattering, appropriate casual ready-to-wear sportswear for women.

Chapter 6, "'Mountain Craftsmen' and Ready-to-Wear: Skyland, North Carolina," considers the final Phelps workshop location in Skyland, just outside of Asheville, North Carolina. There, the Phelpses developed mutually beneficial relationships with textile manufacturers, which led to advertising and promotional opportunities greater than what Phelps could have undertaken alone. Elizabeth Phelps also broadened the audience for her designs by creating paper patterns, which allowed more women to experience Phelps design. This chapter applies notions of the everyday to Phelps Deep Country Clothes sportswear, arguing that Elizabeth Phelps's careful design details improved the lives of postwar women who were under pressure to fulfill multiple roles in their everyday lives.

Chapter 7, "Elizabeth Phelps Leads," discusses the end of the Phelps business and the final years of William and Elizabeth Phelps's lives. In this period, Elizabeth emerged as the head of the Phelps business when William retired, and then she ran the firm alone after his death. She continued to design in the same spirit of functionality for better living, even patenting her work. In her final years, Elizabeth Phelps closed the Phelps workshops and concentrated on her artistic first love: painting.

As the first extended scholarly treatment of William and Elizabeth Phelps, this book contributes to the growing body of knowledge about mid-twentieth-century American fashion designers. It adds to the literature of American fashion design and its production, from the search for inspiration in models from American history—also employed by other 1940s designers—to the forward-looking quest for different and more empowering structures of production, unusual among American fashion designers of the mid-twentieth century. Additionally, this book broadens the discussion of twentieth-century American fashion by considering the story of one fashion brand through the multiple lenses of those who made, designed, promoted, photographed, wrote about, sold, wore, passed down, and collected Phelps objects.

As this project has evolved, I have realized that it is special in the way that the object-based and lived experience research highlighted so many different wearers. I thank Meredith Linn for the suggestion about anchoring each chapter with an introductory object, because many of these also spotlighted individuals who wore Phelps: Phelps employee, fashion editor, fashion photographer, store buyer, fashionable teenager, and garden club president. While the Phelps wearers I have discovered in the course of this research were all white women, they represent people from different socioeconomic classes and regions. One of the primary scholarly contributions of this study is that it encompasses both high fashion and the everyday, the glamourous image of fashion and the day-to-day reality.

The significance of the Phelps Associates workshop and the designs of William and Elizabeth Phelps is threefold: first, in the innovative ways the Phelpses positioned themselves and their products to connect to American patriotism, history, and craft, which seem unique within the American fashion industry; second, in their concern about labor and artisanal making and their attempts to reimagine how American fashion was produced to be more empowering for the people creating it; and third, in the ways that the Phelpses' designs, particularly those attributed to Elizabeth Phelps, responded to the challenging demands placed on women and offered elegant and practical solutions. But the Phelpses did not set out with a grand plan to revolutionize American fashion; instead, their workshop began with the desire for one specific object, as they later reported: a wide leather belt for Elizabeth.

1

Craft Connections and Early Careers

This chapter considers aspects of the Phelpses' historicism relating to ways they and others promoted their work as heir to longstanding traditions of American craft, through a family history of New England craftsmanship on William Phelps's side and the connection of their work to New York's historic leather district, the Swamp. Biographical overviews demonstrate that the Phelpses were also involved with other fields of 1930s American craft, such as woodworking. Finally, this chapter introduces their intertwined personal and professional relationship, so important to the Phelps workshop and brand, and the challenges of discerning how gender roles shaped their work style or the way it was presented in the media.

Introductory Objects: Two Leather Belts

The Phelps Associates story began with a belt—specifically a wide leather belt that William made for Elizabeth.[1] Belts would remain a consistent part of the Phelps look, from the early leather goods offerings to later sportswear that was designed to allow for a belt to be worn. Two medium-width leather belts in the author's collection are of a basic, rugged type that Phelps produced over many years (Fig. 1.1). Both are made of brown leather, with brass buckles with two prongs, metal grommets over the belt notches, and metal end tips. Both are in ready-to-wear sizes in line with misses' dress sizes of the mid-twentieth century, one a size 10 and the other a size 12.[2] The size 12 belt has a metal Phelps trademark insignia just past the buckle. The other end of the belt would have overlapped the trademark symbol when worn. The size 10 is missing the

Fig. 1.1. Ready-to-wear belts with two-prong buckles. Phelps Associates, belts, leather, metal, 1940s to 1960s. (Author's collection. Photograph by the author.)

Fig. 1.2. Detail showing Phelps belt, ready-to-wear size 10, missing trademark symbol. Indentations in the leather show where symbol would have been attached. Phelps Associates, belt, leather, metal, 1940s to 1960s. (Author's collection. Photograph by the author.)

Phelps trademark, but indentations in the leather indicate where it would once have been attached (Fig. 1.2). In 1943 and 1944, the early years of Phelps Associates, a belt of this type was featured in *Harper's Bazaar* and in *Vogue*. In 1962, *Vogue* would show this style again, declaring, "The famous Phelps belt of the late forties, in its 1962 identity—and it's never looked newer (newest now with a multi-gored skirt). Brown cowhide by Phelps, $16, Lord & Taylor."[3] The Phelpses must have been very fond of this design to have produced it over so many years or revived it, and it must have continued to be a client favorite and good seller. Belts were the Phelps objects most often shown in magazines and among the things they were most known for.

In a 1947 interview, in answer to questions about the origin of the Phelps Associates business, Elizabeth Phelps recalled, "I just wanted a wide belt. We went to the leather market under Brooklyn Bridge and picked up a piece and my husband made it for me. Then he made me a few more."[4] This origin story reveals the importance of materials—here, leather—to the process. In telling how it all got started, Elizabeth Phelps does not describe sketching out a design first. While I have not been able to determine whether the Phelpses ever sketched, the materials drove the method. Therefore, they began with the search for the right piece of leather. Bernice Chambers, of the Fashion Group, wrote in 1947, "The manufacture of fine bags is so much a question of material and production that frequently the bag designer's name is lost in the process. The firms of Bieman-Davis, Inc., Koret, Josef, Evans Case Co., Phelps Associates, Pichel, Inc., Coblentz, and Eric DeKolb are all makers of fine bags in America."[5] This Phelps Associates origin story points to themes including the importance of materials, handcraft, historicism, and the working relationship of William and Elizabeth Phelps.

One of the key factors in Phelps Associates as a husband-and-wife team is that in their creative efforts, the partners sought to please each other, not just themselves, an outside muse, a known client, or even an imagined client. *Fortune* magazine later reported that this first belt was a Christmas present.[6] Although this was not exactly akin to the Romantic idea of love as artistic inspiration, the desire to please and be approved by the other spouse seems to have served as a vital motivation. Whether William sought to please Elizabeth through this first wide belt, or, later, Elizabeth sought to please William through the sportswear she designed, each spouse created with an eye to the aesthetic and social viewpoint of the other.

Fig. 1.3. Wide Phelps belts shown with swimwear by Claire McCardell, Joset Walker, and Carolyn Schnurer in *Harper's Bazaar,* January 1946, 80–81. (*Harper's BAZAAR,* Hearst Magazine Media, Inc. Photograph by Genevieve Naylor/Corbis via Getty Images.)

Fig. 1.4. Wide Phelps belt over Claire McCardell diaper bathing suit, *Harper's Bazaar,* May 1946, 99. (*Harper's BAZAAR,* Hearst Magazine Media, Inc. Photograph by Louise Dahl-Wolfe. © Center for Creative Photography, Arizona Board of Regents.)

The wide belt, one of the early Phelps Associates signatures, is found in several iconic fashion photographs of the 1940s. For example, *Harper's Bazaar* often showed wide Phelps belts over Claire McCardell swimsuits (Figs. 1.3 and 1.4). One of these well-known images was photographed by Louise Dahl-Wolfe, also a Phelps client (see chapter 2). While Phelps Associates would grow and expand into other product lines and materials, the original wide leather belt was significant both to the fashionable public and to the couple and became part of the origin story they repeated in multiple interviews.[7] This chapter will give biographical background on both William Drown Phelps and Elizabeth Heintges Phelps, as well as documenting the beginnings of their personal and professional life together. Although the Phelpses were not always equally credited as creators of Phelps objects, their relationship influenced the things they created; their connection to craft was important to the way they conceived of the Phelps workshop and themselves as artists; and they consciously positioned their work to connect with American history.

William Drown Phelps

William Drown Phelps was born on September 20, 1890, in the eastern Pennsylvania coalmining town of Laurel Run, near Wilkes-Barre.[8] He was the son of Francis Alexander Phelps, born in New York City, and Margaretta Drown Phelps, born in Philadelphia.[9] Francis Phelps had multiple business interests, including a local hardware firm, as well as work in the banking, coal, and paper industries in Pennsylvania, New York, Wyoming, and Canada.[10] Francis and Margaretta had three children: in addition to William, there were two girls, Alice Darling Phelps and Frances Slocum Phelps.[11] The Phelps family was wealthy, aligned with management in an atmosphere of sometimes confrontational labor relations. When William was nine, there was a strike riot at the Parish Coal Company in Wilkes-Barre, in which his father served as a director, and a supervisor was assaulted.[12] As an adult, William would strive to create a cooperative and egalitarian environment within his business.

William Drown Phelps's New England genealogy was emphasized in media coverage of Phelps Associates. His identity as a craftsman, descendent of American craftsmen, fit well with an American design identity. William Phelps had ancestry dating to the British colonial era on his father's side, and his paternal grandfather, father, and uncles were all members of the Pennsylvania Society of Sons of the Revolution.[13] However the equally long lineage of his mother, Margaretta Darling Drown, would furnish the ancestors aligned with craft and artisanship. Fashion journalist Virginia Pope wrote in 1944, "William Drown Phelps, skilled craftsman, inherits his taste for fine handicraft from a long line of New England ancestors, among whom were silversmiths and furniture makers."[14] Pope used Phelps's American craftsmanship pedigree to bolster the reputation of Phelps Associates' 1940s creations; here, not just products but also people are related to early American and colonial revival themes. Looking to an American past as a source for contemporary design was an idea popular in 1930s design circles, and in the 1940s this was overlaid with the urgency of wartime propaganda. The colonial period in New England was particularly linked with notions of democracy and a fight for freedom that resonated in wartime. *The New York Post* cited Shem Drowne (1683–1774) as "an ancestor on [William Phelps'] mother's side, [who] was Boston's chief silversmith before Paul Revere, and the first of four generations of silversmiths. Among his creations are the sacred codfish on Faneuil Hall and the golden cock on Old South Church."[15] Here, the *Post* distorts the facts a bit—the sacred codfish is a wooden statue inside the Massachusetts State House; tin- and copperworker Shem Drowne created the weathervane on the cupola of Faneuil Hall in 1742, but it is, in fact, a grasshopper. Drowne also created the swallowtail banner weathervane on Old *North* Church in 1740.[16]

This same ancestral artisan was introduced into the pages of American literature by Nathaniel Hawthorne (1804–1864), who fictionalized the craftsman as a woodworker rather than a metalworker, in his short story "Drowne's Wooden Image."[17] Hawthorne's tale is a fanciful meditation on what the author perceives to be the difference between fine art and craft, the "inspired hand" versus a "mechanical style."[18] Hawthorne imagines Boston painter John Singleton Copley (1738–1815) dropping into Drowne's workshop and holding forth as Drowne produces a ship's masthead in the form of a fashionable European woman—a work distinguished from all Drowne's previous efforts by its lifelike, spiritual qualities: "Who would have looked for a modern Pygmalion in the person of a yankee mechanic?"[19] Hawthorne ultimately argues that every human being has the potential for greatness, which circumstances can develop or inhibit. In the case of the fictional Drowne, romantic love is the catalyst for a new level of artistic achievement.[20] In studying design partnership of Phelps Associates, it is interesting to consider Hawthorne's theory regarding the potential of love to facilitate artistic production, even if we may take a more pragmatic and less romantic perspective the Phelpses' mutual love seems to have motivated them as they created new things. Hawthorne also references the historical Shem Drowne's copper *Native American Archer Weathervane* (now in the collection of the Massachusetts Historical Society), describing it as "an Indian chief gilded all over[, which] stood during the better part of a century on the cupola of the province house bedazzling the eyes of those who looked upward like an angel of the sun" (Fig. 1.5).[21] Nathaniel Hawthorne's story demonstrates that for about a century before Elizabeth and William Drown Phelps established Phelps Associates, William Phelps's ancestors were present in both American history and literary imagination as craftspeople and creators of American folk art. The Phelpses used William Phelps's Drown(e) family heritage to bolster their credentials and connect their twentieth-century craft with the past.

Fig. 1.5. *Native American Archer Weathervane*, made by William Drown Phelps's ancestor, Shem Drowne, hammered copper and glass, circa 1716, 136.8 cm x 118.2 cm x 4.3 cm. (Collection of the Massachusetts Historical Society.)

William Phelps also had an ancestor involved in the fashion industry, and even specifically in the production of accessories. William Drown Phelps was the namesake of his great-grandfather, William Drown, who manufactured parasols in Philadelphia in the nineteenth century (Figs. 1.6 and 1.7).[22] In 1887, the William A. Drown & Co. Umbrella and Parasol Factory was located in two separate facilities, a Stick Factory and a Finishing Works, on adjacent blocks of Gillingham Street. Together, the factories employed over 350 people (including 25 children) when running at full capacity.[23] The Costume Institute holds a collection of eleven nineteenth-century parasols and umbrellas, which William Drown Phelps donated in 1943. At least one of these parasols (C.I.43.29.15) is marked "Drown & Co. Makers," carved on the wooden handle. When William Phelps donated these accessories, he was acting consistently with his views on objects of American history as resources from which twentieth-century designers could draw inspiration; by donating these, he made it possible for other designers to study them.[24] The Drown & Co. Umbrella and Parasol Factory story did not fit as usefully into the Phelpses' public narrative of historic craft production, however, because it was a large factory rather than a small workshop. William Phelps's donated collection shows that he had some familiarity with his family history of mass-produced fashion accessories and was interested in making these available as inspiration for other designers.

William Phelps's early education began at the Hillman Academy in Wilkes-Barre, Pennsylvania, where he was an honor student in the primary department.[25] William's family was affluent enough to send him to St. Paul's School, and then to Yale, where he studied for three years.[26] However, on July 6, 1911, the front page of the Wilkes-Barre newspaper reported that fifty-two-year-old Francis Phelps had died that morning at 10:30, after a long illness, at the Phelps family's Laurel Run summer home.[27] William Phelps changed his plans.[28] He left Yale and went to work, first working in his father's wholesale mining supplies firm. At some point, he also worked for five years with Lee, Higginson as a bond salesman.[29]

William Phelps served in the navy during World War I, from 1917 to 1919. He attended training school in Philadelphia and spent a few months at Cape May, New Jersey, before serving on the USS *Aurora*. On a later veterans compensation application, Phelps stated that his active duty had included experiencing a submarine attack in the Irish Sea and mine laying in the North Sea.[30]

William Phelps's early working life was conventional: marriage, family, and a corporate career. On December 11, 1920, Phelps married a Scottish woman, Jean Marina True Ross, the oldest daughter of

Brigadier General Sir Walter Chartaris Ross of the British army and his wife, Lady Rosa Ross. They were married at the bride's home, Cromarty House, Scotland, with plans to settle back in Wilkes-Barre, Pennsylvania, by January 1921.[31] The couple's first son, Alexander Ross, was born in Wilkes-Barre a respectable nine months later, on August 21, 1921.[32] Their second son, Walter James, was born in Port Elizabeth, New Jersey, on January 9, 1927.[33] By 1927, William Phelps was working as a General Motors foreign manager. A 1927 incoming immigration card from a transatlantic sailing lists his address as care of General Motors on Broadway, New York City. Phelps sailed between Europe and the United States frequently, sometimes taking his family with him.[34] These frequent trips might have made it possible for Jean Ross to visit her family.

But even while William Phelps enjoyed outward signs of success, he was not entirely satisfied and longed for a different way of working and ultimate product. Many years later, *Harper's Bazaar* would report that although he was a General Motors branch manager in Europe and Africa, "he didn't cotton to mass production."[35] Automotive industry practice in the 1920s and 1930s was indebted to the ideas of Henry Ford and F. W. Taylor and involved each assembly-line worker doing only one task, in the most precisely time-efficient way possible, relying on motion study to plan employees' activity.[36] It is noteworthy that while working in the automotive business, one of the first industries to embrace assembly-line production, Phelps developed an interest in artisanal production. *Harper's Bazaar* also recounted that "everywhere he roamed, he always found himself seeking out the tucked-away places where things were made by hand—the leatherworkers, metalworkers, woodcarvers."[37] These are all crafts Phelps would experiment with in the 1930s. One of the places that inspired him was very likely Antwerp, Belgium, a city he sailed in and out of in his transatlantic voyages. Antwerp also was the historical leather market of Europe, dealing in some 900,000 hides per year in the mid-nineteenth century.[38] If

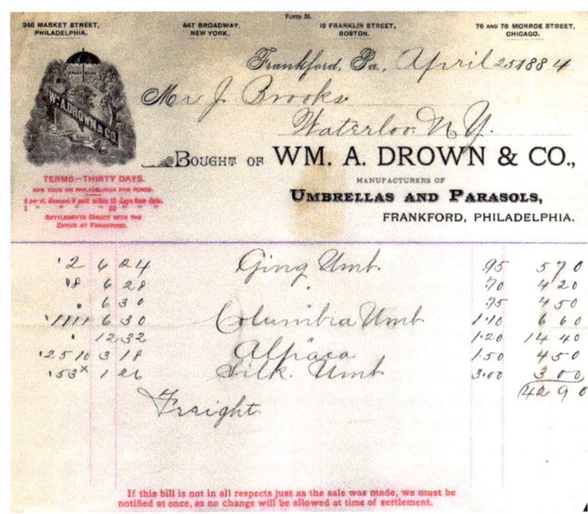
246 MARKET STREET, PHILADELPHIA. 447 BROADWAY, NEW YORK. 10 FRANKLIN STREET, BOSTON. 76 AND 78 MONROE STREET, CHICAGO.

Frankford, Pa., April 25 188

Mr J. Brooks
Waterloo N.Y.

Bought of WM. A. DROWN & CO.,
MANUFACTURERS OF
UMBRELLAS AND PARASOLS,
FRANKFORD, PHILADELPHIA.

TERMS—THIRTY DAYS.

Ging Umb. .95 5.70
.70 4.20
.75 4.50
Columbia Umb 1.10 6.60
1.20 14.40
Alpaca 1.50 4.50
Silk Umb 3.00 3.00
42.90
Freight

If this bill is not in all respects just as the sale was made, we must be notified at once, as no change will be allowed at time of settlement.

Fig. 1.6. A bill from the umbrella manufactory of William Drown Phelps's ancestor William A. Drown, April 25, 1886. (Author's collection.)

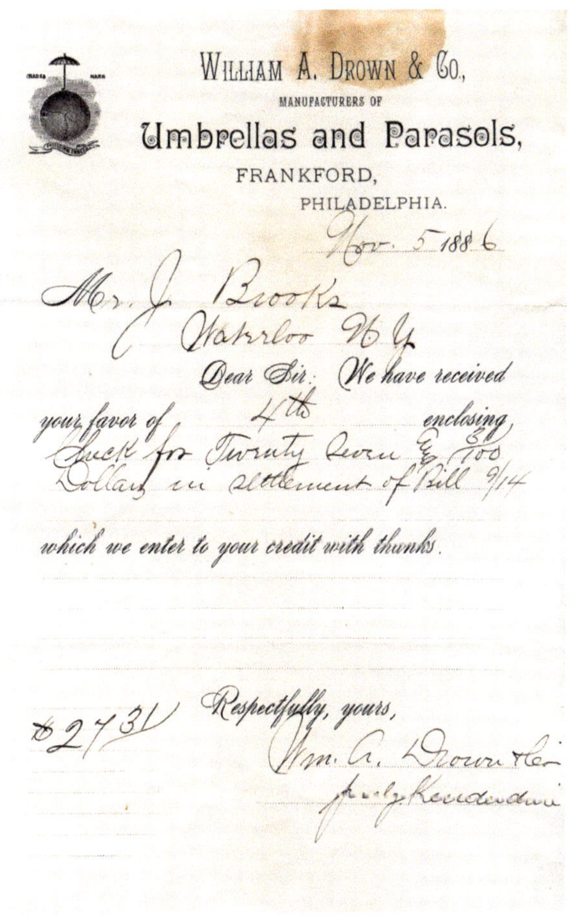
WILLIAM A. DROWN & CO.,
MANUFACTURERS OF
Umbrellas and Parasols,
FRANKFORD,
PHILADELPHIA.

Nov. 5 1886

Mr. J. Brooks
Waterloo N.Y.

Dear Sir: We have received your favor of 4th enclosing Check for Twenty Seven 31/100 Dollars in settlement of Bill 9/14 which we enter to your credit with thanks.

$27.31

Respectfully, yours,
Wm. A. Drown & Co.

Fig. 1.7. A receipt issued by William A. Drown & Co., November 5, 1886. (Author's collection.)

Phelps did, in fact, seek out makers and materials in his travels, it is quite likely that he had some contact with leather and leatherworking in his time there.

Whether William Phelps's discontent with the automotive industry would have ever been enough to push him to another career, we do not know; in any case, the Great Depression made the decision for him. In 1932, Phelps left General Motors.[39] He would later attribute his job loss to the Depression. He then started a woodworking business in his mother's Wilkes-Barre attic. He soon moved his woodworking business to New York City, where he made dower chests.[40] Given his location and interest in historic American craft, he likely made these chests in the Pennsylvania German style, but no surviving examples have been located. *Fortune* magazine later reported that William Phelps's income around this period was about $200 per month, above average for a man employed in hand-carving furniture.[41] It is possible that at least by the time of this move to New York, he and Jean were separated, because he soon met the woman who would be his wife and design partner for the rest of his life. For William Phelps, a job loss due to the Great Depression appears to have been a catalyst for personal change. Both his corporate career and his marriage had failed, but he found new interest and purpose in pursuing craft.

Elizabeth Heintges Phelps

Fig. 1.8. Publicity photograph of Elizabeth Phelps for the Coty Awards, 1944. (Photograph by ASCH. Image courtesy of FIT Library Special Collections and College Archives, Fashion Institute of Technology|SUNY.)

If William Drown Phelps represents the established New England strand of American national identity, Elizabeth Phelps represents a strand of American identity associated with first-generation immigration from Europe (Fig. 1.8). Elizabeth was born in Germany on November 27, 1909, the daughter of Herman and Anne (Kuhlen) Von Mevis.[42] Whereas William Phelps drew from a line of New England ancestors to support his craft credentials, Elizabeth's German heritage might have been a negative to the Phelps brand during World War II. Elizabeth had to search within her own memories to portray herself as a craftsperson: she recounted to *New York Post* journalist Mary Braggiotti that she had entertained herself as a baby by lacing and unlacing an old shoe, citing this as evidence of an early interest in handwork.[43] Design historians Pat Kirkham and Lynne Walker note, "In addition to formal education, early childhood activities and experience of 'doing' have been identified as central to design students' personal and professional identities, as well as their area of study and choice of career."[44] What does it mean that Elizabeth Phelps's childhood story was not one of making doll clothes, sculpting clay, or crafting alongside a parent or other mentor? The image of shoe-lacing evokes solitude but also privation and does not reveal much about Elizabeth Phelps's childhood or early relationship influences, perhaps because her German connection was not one she wanted to emphasize.

Elizabeth recounted a happier childhood memory—of a Christmas gingerbread house in her home in Germany. However, it is unclear whether she and her family made or purchased the gingerbread house. In the 1940s, Elizabeth made a gingerbread house similar to the one she recalled and displayed it as part of her Christmas celebrations.[45] This work was a wonder of detail: "On a table is another of her hobbies, a little house that for 10 years has had a place under the Phelps Christmas tree—a fairy tale house of cookies and marshmallows, gum drops and sugar, landscaped with snow and trees, furnished complete as an old-fashioned Mennonite kitchen."[46] This gingerbread house—possibly shellacked or stored in a freezer from year to year—is documented in both the Phelpses' Pennsylvania and North Carolina homes, showing that Elizabeth cared enough about her creation to move it interstate. Material-culture and design scholar Beverly Gordon, writing about women's domestic pastimes in the late nineteenth and early twentieth centuries, theorizes that these activities contained "a 'saturated' quality, a kind of heightened experience (state, reality) that was aesthetically and sensually charged and full." The construction of a gingerbread house would certainly lend itself to Gordon's conception of the satisfaction of projects activating multiple senses and channeling imagination. Gordon writes of miniature objects: "Miniature things of all kinds . . . give us a sense of power and protectiveness, magic and delight . . . they change our sense of time and space, creating and allowing us to experience the wide-eyed wonder of a child. When the miniature is a space that can be entered, at least in the imagination, its power is particularly potent."[47] Elizabeth Phelps's gingerbread house provided an opportunity for her, as an artist, to engage in playful aesthetic expression that also likely evoked memories of childhood, perhaps allowing her to reimagine it by savoring the positive and forgetting the negative, and invited her to project herself into a world of delights.

Not much is known about Elizabeth's childhood in Germany, but around 1918, Elizabeth's mother remarried. Elizabeth's stepfather was a US Army officer stationed in Germany after World War I. Before Elizabeth married William Phelps, her surname is listed as Heintges—it is unclear whether this was her father or stepfather's name. If the Herman Von Mevis listed in her records was Elizabeth's biological father, then perhaps a stepfather with the surname Heintges adopted her. At the age of nine, Elizabeth moved to the United States with her mother and stepfather, and she lived the army brat lifestyle in camps. Elizabeth had two brothers (or half brothers) who would later serve with US forces during World War II. A 1944 press release states that she also spent part of her childhood in Kentucky.[48]

Around 1930, Elizabeth Heintges reportedly left the "Chilkoot Barrier" (perhaps Chilkoot Pass), Alaska, where she had been living, and moved to New York

City.[49] Like much of Elizabeth Phelps's early life, the Alaska phase remains a bit mysterious. However, she would later reference Alaska and its Gold Rush by creating clothing using a gold-and-blue striped fabric called Klondike denim.[50]

"Jim and Elsie" Together

In New York, William pursued a life in artistic circles, and he met Elizabeth Heintges "at a literary tea in Greenwich Village." They soon became close, calling each other "Jim" and "Elsie." William and Elizabeth Phelps later claimed to have been married in 1932.[51] The relationship probably began then, but at that point William was still married to Jean.

During the early months of William and Elizabeth's relationship, Elizabeth pursued formal art education. In January 1933, she began to study at the Art Students League, which had been founded in 1875 by a breakaway group from the National Academy of Design, many of whom were women.[52] The main school's campus was—and remains—an 1892 building designed by Henry J. Hardenbergh, on Fifty-Seventh Street between Broadway and Seventh Avenue. As fashion historian Nancy Deihl notes, various American fashion designers of the twentieth century studied at the Art Students League and were able to "parlay . . . their 'good taste' or 'artistic upbringing' into a fashion career."[53] In the spring 1933 semester, Elizabeth, registered under the name Elsie Heintges and living at 8 Minetta Street (a few blocks southwest of Washington Square Park) began taking life drawing, painting, and composition classes with William Von Schlegell and Frank Vincent Dumond, later adding portrait painting with Ivan G. Olinsky.[54]

Fig. 1.9. William Phelps and Elizabeth Heintges's address on returning from Europe in 1933: 14 Minetta Street, Greenwich Village, New York City, as it looked March 19, 2021. (Photograph by the author.)

In the fall of 1933, Elizabeth Heintges only took one class at the league—a life drawing class with George B. Bridgman.[55] According to the school's records, this was her last class there.[56] Perhaps her new relationship with William Phelps was consuming more of her time: Phelps and Heintges went to Europe together for the first time that year. On September 3, 1933, they sailed from Cherbourg, and they arrived in New York City on September 8, on the ship *Europa*. They both gave their address as 14 Minetta Street, a three-story brick building just down the street from where Heintges had been living, so they appear to have moved in together prior to the trip (Fig. 1.9).[57]

William and Jean Phelps were in the process of divorcing by at least May 1934, when he filed for veterans compensation based on his World War I naval service. Phelps listed Jean, Alexander, and Walter as his dependents, with a note that he and his wife were "being divorced."[58] However, not until December 14, 1934, was the divorce finalized. Two weeks later, on New Year's Eve, William Drown Phelps married Elizabeth Heintges Von Mevis in Luzurne, Pennsylvania. He was forty-four, and she was twenty-five. On their marriage certificate, his address is given as 70 Horatio Street, his occupation as artist, as is Elizabeth's.

It is listed as her first marriage. The Rev. Paul S. Heath, pastor of First Presbyterian Church, Wilkes Barre, Pennsylvania, performed the ceremony.[59]
For the next few years, the Phelpses continued to try to find their place in the arts. While Elizabeth Phelps was focused on painting in these years, William Phelps was immersed in craft. He taught industrial arts at New York University and continued with his woodworking.[60] He served as president of the New York Society of Craftsmen.[61] Elizabeth worked as a mural painter and taught private students.[62] William worked in the Civilian Conservation Corps workshop on Governor's Island from 1935 to 1938, "with ten thousand young men in shops learning crafts of iron casting, etc."[63] The Phelpses also lived briefly in Woodstock, New York, before moving back to the city. In March 1939, the Junior League of nearby Kingston had to find a lastminute replacement speaker for the first in a series of art lectures: "Dr. Taylor addressed the group in the absence of William Drown Phelps of Woodstock, noted wood carver, who was to speak on 'Folk Lore.'"[64] Phelps's intended topic is an example of his interest in American history, craft, and popular traditions. The 1940 census shows the Phelpses were back in Manhattan and living at 42 Washington Square.[65]

The Phelpses' First Leather Belt and the Swamp Neighborhood

With their return to New York City, the Phelpses continued their commitment to craft and branched out in a new direction: leatherwork, which they would later carefully situate in the context of American history, specifically the history of leather production and leatherworking in New York City. Elizabeth Phelps recalled, "I just wanted a wide belt. We went to the leather market under Brooklyn Bridge and picked up a piece and my husband made it for me. Then he made me a few more." The leather market under Brooklyn Bridge, where Elizabeth Phelps recalled buying supplies, was the remnant of the Swamp, a formerly flourishing neighborhood where aspects of the leather trade had been carried out from the eighteenth to the mid-twentieth centuries. In the 1940s, the Swamp was invoked as part of the Phelps Associates origin story, as artisan-designers William and Elizabeth Phelps cited going to this neighborhood to purchase leather for their first belt.[66] This anecdote associated the Phelps name with the historicism of an old neighborhood and a long tradition of local American leather craftsmanship, in New York City. Celebrating US craft and craft history was key to both the Phelpses' design philosophy and their marketing strategy, which emphasized wartime patriotism. By calling out the Swamp neighborhood, the Phelpses placed a brand-new, startup workshop within a much longer tradition of leather production, leatherworking, and leather wholesaling.

The Swamp took its name from its natural topography: a swamp with an outlet into the East River. It had been known as Beekman's Swamp or simply the Swamp, and by the end of the eighteenth century, it had become the center of

Fig. 1.10. The approximate area of the original Swamp is the land directly above the word *Sound.* (George Hayward, *A Plan of the City of New York and Its Environs,* 1855, based on 1775 original. Courtesy of New York Public Library.)

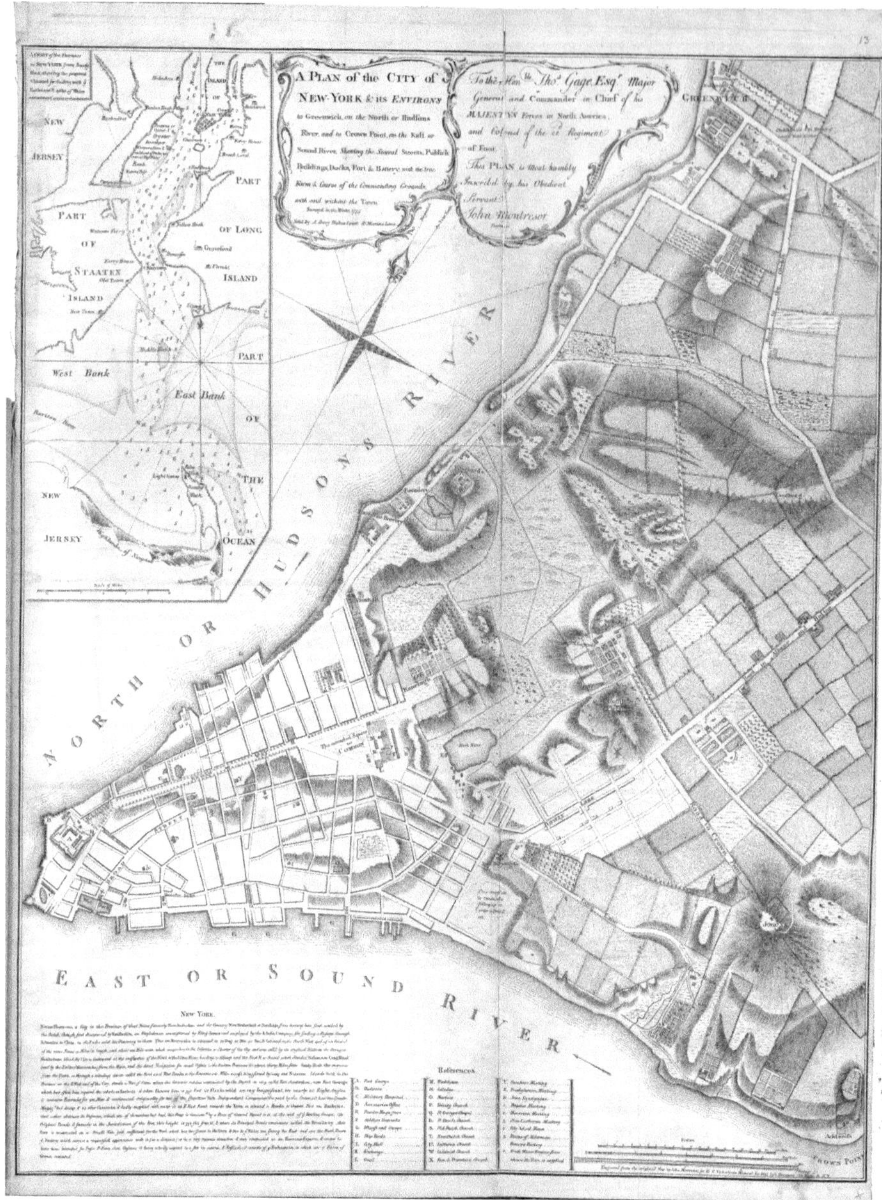

New York City's tanning and leatherworking (Fig. 1.10). Access to water, which the Swamp provided, was key to the manufacture of leather, a material that served many uses, including belts for machinery, before the introduction of synthetic materials.[67] Leather-industry journalist Frank W. Norcross stated that in the 1811 city directory, New York boasted twenty-four tanneries, all but two of which were in the Swamp.[68] However, over the next twenty years, tanning in Manhattan would steadily decrease. As the city grew northward and southern New York State's hemlock supply was depleted, many tanneries moved to areas upstate, including the Adirondacks, where an ample supply of hemlock trees provided the necessary tannic acid for the tanning process.[69]

Meanwhile, the Swamp remained dedicated to other aspects of the leather industry. Tan vats were filled in, and leather warehouses grew up in the place of the tanneries. In 1856, *The New York Times* reported that the tanneries had gradually disappeared, from the turn of the nineteenth century until around 1830, "when only a single one remained, which is still in operation in Frankfort-Street."[70] In the 1860s, labor disputes and riots, as well as the continued outbreak of epidemic disease among the rich as well as the poor (and sanitary discoveries that suggested the city might actually be able to halt disease) brought the attention of middle- and upper-class New York to the living conditions of their fellow New Yorkers in working-class and poorer neighborhoods, such as the Swamp. As a result, the Citizens' Association of New York, a philanthropic organization tasked its Council of Hygiene and Public Health with preparing a report on the health of New York City neighborhoods to bolster support for sanitary reform. Reformers highlighted the Swamp because it was particularly spectacular from a propaganda perspective due to the sensory aspects of the leather industry: the Swamp stood in for all the City's sanitary issues.[71]

Historian and urban studies scholar Gergely Baics observes that only after the Council on Hygiene and Public Health published its 1865 report was state legislation passed to establish the Metropolitan Board of Health.[72] This new interest in eradicating health nuisances also resulted in tanyards being removed from the crowded areas of the city. After the report was published, the tan vats of the Swamp's remaining tanyards were "indicted as a nuisance, and its historic vats were filled up."[73] Decades later, a concern about avoiding being deemed a neighborhood nuisance led the Phelpses to stop working with horn in their Washington Square location.

The Swamp was still noticeable for its smells, despite the tanning vats' closures. In an 1880 article titled "Relics of an Old Street," a *New York Times* writer asked, "Have you counted the smells down here in the Swamp? They would go somewhere up in the hundreds, and each one worse than the last. Above all, and swallowing them all, unless you stand very near a garbage box, is the smell of leather."[74] The volume of leather in the warehouses and shops was enough to fill the air with the pungent smell of leather, despite the decrease in heavy manufacture such as tanning.

By 1880, parts of the Swamp had been subsumed into the Brooklyn Bridge. On the south side of the Swamp's Frankfort Street, there were "leather stores and leather manufacturing places, reaching all the way to Franklin Square." On the north side, buildings had been replaced by the bridge approach, which on street level had a series of brick arches, planned as potential warehouse space.[75] These arches can still be seen on the north side of Frankfort Street today (Fig. 1.11). By May 1884, the warehouses in the arches underneath Brooklyn Bridge were ready for occupancy. Paper, fur, and leather merchants leased the five warehouses at numbers 12 to 16 for between $1,800 and $1,900 per year. The two-story, plus cellar, spaces were touted for their relative fire-resistance due

Fig. 1.11. Brooklyn Bridge arch warehouses undergoing repairs, March 19, 2021. (Photograph by the author.)

to their brick-and-iron construction and were equipped with modern conveniences such as elevators and steam heating.[76] These arched warehouses were likely still operating as the leather warehouses Elizabeth Phelps referred to when she and her husband first visited the Swamp.[77]

In the early years of the twentieth century, the Swamp still covered the same small area that it had after the encroachment of the Brooklyn Bridge approach. In 1934, *The New York Times* included Frankfort, Gold, and Cliff Streets as part of the Swamp.[78] In 1937, the Tanners' Council of America maintained its headquarters at 100 Gold Street, as it produced publicity materials promoting the American leather industry.[79] Twentieth-century media coverage of the Swamp was often tinged with nostalgia. In 1924, the area was described as having "an old world touch in the tangle of streets themselves, close by Brooklyn Bridge, and there is a bit of the old world, and of old America, too, in the men who have walked in them."[80] The Swamp neighborhood was thus a useful image for the Phelpses because it evoked the "old world" of European craftsmanship that William Phelps stated he had admired while working overseas, a positive view of the influence of immigrants (like Elizabeth Phelps herself) on New York, and a sense of the American history that they championed as inspiration for American fashion.

By the 1940s, when the Phelpses visited the Swamp, the Brooklyn Bridge leather area was far removed from the other main area of garment supply and production in the Midtown Garment District, clustered around Seventh Avenue. Throughout the nineteenth century, owners of leather producing, finishing, and wholesaling businesses chose not to move uptown. A 1930s experiment in which some leather firms moved uptown toward the Garment District, settling on Thirty-Fourth Street, concluded with many firms returning to the Swamp by 1936 due to "homesickness," according to *Vogue*.[81]

Today, the remnants of the Brooklyn Bridge arch warehouses are among the few visible traces left standing from the leather industry's many years of activity in the Swamp (Fig. 1.11). These former leather warehouses were bricked up when I first explored the Swamp neighborhood in 2017. When I visited again on a blustery March day in 2021, the site was under construction and the bricks had been removed from the windows and doors, offering a tantalizing glimpse of the dark, cavernous interior where hides were once stored, awaiting the touch of craftspeople like the Phelpses.

Connections to American history were important to the Phelps Associates image, so it is not surprising that in the origin story of the partnership, Elizabeth Phelps connected it with the Swamp, a neighborhood with two centuries of associations with the materiality of leather, artisans working in the trade of tanning, and the selling of leather. By invoking the Swamp as the source of their materials, the Phelpses placed themselves on the ongoing timeline of leather industries in New York City, as the 1940s heirs to the Swamp's past.

Connecting with the Fashion Industry

Elizabeth's request for the wide belt, the Phelpses' trip to the Swamp, and William's production of this first belt would change the pair's focus for the next decades. Journalist Elizabeth Harrison, writing later for *The New York Times,* stated that William Phelps had made additional belts for his wife, then went away on a survey of American crafts for the Carnegie Corporation just before they started Phelps Associates.[82] Successful womenswear designer Clare Potter, known for the simplicity of her garments and her use of color, admired one of the belts William Phelps had designed and made for Elizabeth, and wanted the Phelpses to make more.[83] Potter had been one of the designers retail executive Dorothy Shaver promoted as part of Lord & Taylor's 1933 American fashions campaign, and she was well established as an American fashion designer.[84] According to *The New York Times,* when William returned from his American craft survey "they were in the leather business. Clare Potter had seen the belts and wanted to use them with her next collection. She insisted [that] the Phelps set up a workshop. She also requested matching handbags, and the Phelps went immediately into that end of leathercraft."[85] It is likely that at least at first the Phelpses continued to source their leather from contacts in the Swamp. Harrison's version of the story definitely makes it sound as though it was Elizabeth who had the acquaintance with Clare Potter and made the connections that led to their breakthrough. Clare Potter and Elizabeth Phelps had both attended the Art Students League, but Potter was older and had attended the Art Students' League as a teenager, so they would not have been there at the same time.[86]

As a result of the Potter commission, William and Elizabeth Phelps set up a leatherworking shop in the basement of 43 Washington Square, next door to their residence at number 42 (Fig. 1.12).[87] Publicist Eleanor Lambert later reported that the Phelps Associates shop opened for business in 1940. Lambert later described the company's early belts as "'honest belts,' beautiful in themselves, yet part of the dress . . . heavy leather, marvelously handled, with old metal or stag horn decorations."[88] The Phelpses also could thank the *New York World-Telegram*'s editor Gertrude Bailey for calling attention to their workshop: "A neighbor, the fashion editor of the *New York World-Telegram,* sought out their

22 Harper's Bazaar, June 1942

MR. PHELPS, MRS. PHELPS, THEIR WORKERS, AND THEIR WORKS

WORKSHOP *on* WASHINGTON SQUARE

• It's a shop you might have stumbled on once in Paris, or in the back braes of Scotland, or somewhere in the Tirol A homespun, whitewashed workshop, converted from an 1834 cellar, with wooden tables and workbenches, and a handful of artisans who know the joy of making a thing from start to finish, complete. They make belts of fine leather; and bags—shoulder-strap bags, copies of old postilion bags, Civil War dispatch cases. They fasten them with old silver shell buckles and fantastic metal ornaments culled from bygone harness shops. They cut and polish cowhorn and staghorn from the stockyards, for fastenings, and necklaces, and buttons.

The workshop is William Drown Phelps's idea of success on his own terms. For many years he was a branch manager for General Motors in Europe and Africa. But he didn't like big business. He didn't cotton to mass production. Everywhere he roamed, he always found himself seeking out the tucked-away places where things were made by hand—the leather-workers, metal-workers, woodcarvers. In 1932 he quit big business forever He became an authority on industrial arts, and taught them in New York University But he still wanted to do it himself. A year and a half ago he rented the cellar at 43 Washington Square, put up the partitions with his own hands, slapped on the whitewash. And he's happy. He designs, instructs his four workers, goes down to the "swamp"—the old leather district under Brooklyn Bridge—to pick out skins. Besides, he serves his district as Sector Air Raid Warden—you'll see the sign on the door Mrs. Phelps, an artist, is his crack designer and cutter There's always coffee on call in the workshop kitchen: the whole shop lunches together daily in the wise tradition of the old guilds.

HANS JORGENSEN

Fig. 1.12. The first New York City Phelps Associates workshop, as featured in *Harper's Bazaar,* June 1942, 22. (*Harper's BAZAAR,* Hearst Magazine Media, Inc. Photograph by Hans Jorgensen.)

Fig. 1.13. Phelps-attributed belt with heart-shaped buckle. (Probably Phelps, leather, metal, circa 1944, Brooklyn Museum Costume Collection at the Metropolitan Museum of Art, Gift of the Brooklyn Museum, 2009; Gift of Mrs. Stanley Mortimer, 1972, 2009.300.7824. Image copyright © The Metropolitan Museum of Art. Image source: Art Resource, NY.)

tiny shop and ran a story on them, thus informing retail buyers about the excellence of their designs."[89]

Besides Clare Potter, the Phelpses would also later acknowledge the well-known dress designers Valentina and Adrian as well as custom tweed maker Arthur Falkenstein for supporting them in their first years of business.[90] The Phelpses praised Falkenstein for his business model of handcraftsmanship.[91] The Brooklyn Museum Costume Collection at the Metropolitan Museum of Art, in which there are both Phelps and Falkenstein items from the 1940s with the credit line, "Gift of Mrs. Stanley Mortimer," bears out the overlap in clientele between Falkenstein and Phelps Associates. These pieces include a Phelps-attributed belt (2009.300.7824, Fig. 1.13) with heart-shaped buckle, possibly made prior to adoption of a logo, and a circa 1942 Falkenstein brown plaid coat (2009.300.7803) that would coordinate well with the Phelps-attributed belt. Given the name and date of the accession, these objects were probably donated by Siri Larsen Mortimer (Mrs. Stanley Grafton Mortimer III), daughter-in-law of socialite Barbara "Babe" Cushing Mortimer Paley, but the original ownership of the objects is unclear. It is likely, however, that they were worn and used by someone within this socially prominent family, who could afford to purchase high-quality, custom-made American clothing and accessories.

Working Relationship

One of the crucial matters about the Phelpses' professional partnership is how they worked together. In their examination of twentieth-century wife–husband design partnerships, Pat Kirkham and Lynne Walker have observed: "The wife/husband partnership . . . was one of the ways women designers negotiated the dilemma of work after marriage . . . some of the most successful were between men and women free from childcare responsibilities. It is notoriously difficult to assess the particular nature of and individual contributions to collaborative work, particularly that between people who both live together and work together, not least because the best collaborations involve dialectic, dynamism, and telepathy."[92]

In her telling of the story of the first belt, Elizabeth Phelps sketched out some of the partnership's methods of creation, including the way they worked together on ideas, incorporating Elizabeth's opinions and desires regarding fashion. It is unclear how the Phelpses originally began learning their leatherworking skills, although they improved their skills by learning from one of the artisans they employed (see chapter 2). They may have initially experimented with leather through William Phelps's involvement with the Civilian Conservation Corps. In June 1942, *Harper's Bazaar* reported, "Mrs. Phelps, an artist, is his crack designer and cutter."[93] This characterizes William Phelps as head of Phelps Associates with Elizabeth Phelps "his" assistant, despite the importance of both design and cutting roles. British leatherworker Betty Dougherty believed cutting was "the most important stage in leatherwork. . . . If there is a mistake in measurement or angle, and the leather is cut to this incorrect line, the damage is often irreparable, especially when there is a shortage of leather."[94] However, it is surely a minimization of Elizabeth Phelps's contributions to characterize her as her husband's foreperson or assistant. Kirkham and Walker note that "in the 1940s and 1950s, women designers married to designers were often viewed as auxiliaries of their husbands and commonly featured as 'pretty girls' and faithful 'helpmates.'"[95] The 1942 *Harper's* characterization of the partnership may reveal more about the expectations of the journalist than the realities of the working relationship. Wilhela Cushman, fashion editor of the *Ladies' Home Journal,* went to the other extreme in a 1943 article that ignored William Phelps's part in the partnership and labeled a flat, envelope-style clutch bag as an "Elizabeth Phelps bag."[96] It is uncertain whether Cushman's attribution correctly identified which of the spouses had designed or made the bag.

A 1947 interview with the couple claimed they had a more equal role with tasks divided based on materials: "Both the Phelpses design and both make patterns and often models of the finished articles for their artisans to go by. . . . Mrs. Phelps creates the daintier bags and belts that lend themselves to lightweight leathers, while Mr. Phelps goes in for the heavier stuff."[97] This is still a highly gendered description of their work, with Elizabeth Phelps dealing with the "daintier" work while William Phelps took on the "heavier" materials more associated with masculinity. Pat Kirkham and Lynne Walker identify several mid-twentieth-century "markers of masculinity," including "size, strength, being allowed to dirty one's hands, and working in the public realm."[98] The 1947 newspaper article ascribes to the male member of the partnership the "heavier" leathers, which would presumably require more strength to manipulate in handwork. The description of Elizabeth's materials as daintier seems to reassure the reading public that although she was working with the male-associated material of leather, she remained feminine.

In 1955, *The New York Times* reported a stricter division of labor, with William the leather designer and Elizabeth the clothing designer.[99] Then, in 1958, *Women's Wear Daily* described Elizabeth Phelps as the separates designer and William Phelps as the accessories designer: "Though the Phelps are designers working in separate, though affiliated cooperating, fields, they get together to create a style as a unit. Mr. Phelps' bag and belt designs, for instance, with respect to material and color are created to complement Mrs. Phelps' designs in separates."[100] The way they worked together seems to have evolved over the years, as their interests and the physical workshop layout changed.

Conclusion

William and Elizabeth Phelps were from different backgrounds and different generations. In the first years of their marriage, they continued their separate creative interests—Elizabeth focusing on painting and William on handcraft, particularly woodworking. Elizabeth's desire for a specific type of leather belt and William's interest in crafting it led to the creation of the prototype Phelps wide leather belt. The way the Phelpses later described this new endeavor, linking the creation of the first belt to New York City's longtime leather district, the Swamp, shows them consciously positioning themselves within a story of historic leather and craft production. This first wide belt caught the eye of friends in the fashion industry, including Clare Potter, and led to a new working partnership between William and Elizabeth Phelps. Here again, the available sources for information on how the Phelpses worked together are written by journalists and require careful reading, as documents that reflect both how the husband-and-wife team wished to be seen by the public and the gendered expectations of the journalists and perhaps their readers. The Phelpses carefully crafted their public image to align with the Americana image of their new brand. Through all these sources, as well as through the official records that document their lives before and after their marriage, we see the coming together of two artists to create a new life as well as a line of leather goods characterized by craftsmanship, Americana historicism, and attention to materials. The Phelpses' artisanry showed the influence of an unexpected type of craft: handmade horse harness.

2

Workshop on Washington Square to University Place

William and Elizabeth Phelps emphasized handcraftsmanship and drew from the tradition of harness-making leathercraft in their early work, both in techniques and in materials. Their leather goods were handmade, and they created for both custom clients and ready-to-wear purchasers. This chapter argues that William and Elizabeth Phelps's emphasis on the importance of handcraft aligned with the early 1940s American fashion industry's desire for American-made craft as a replacement for, and even a challenge to, the craftsmanship of Parisian couture. To address the Phelpses' attitude about "honest" materials, and the types of leather with which they chose to work, this chapter also includes an overview of the tanning process. The Phelpses' two New York City workshops were sites for their experimentation with small-scale, artisanal production that aimed to empower the people who made Phelps accessories. William and Elizabeth Phelps's methods of working together most likely evolved as they moved from their first small workshop into a divided space with more square footage. Finally, this chapter details some of the Phelpses' early custom clients, who would also have visited the workshops. While these workshops gave the Phelpses access to fashion industry connections and skilled labor of artisans, they seem to have been only modestly profitable.

Introductory Objects: Two Belts Related to Horse Harness at the Museum at FIT

Seen from the front, as the wearers walked toward you, two belts in the collection of the Museum at FIT would have looked very similar. Both are black cowhide and have brass, heart-shaped buckle frames as well as heart-shaped brass end tips (Figs. 2.1, 2.2). Curiously, the hearts comprising the buckle frames on both belts lie horizontally when the belt is worn, most likely because the buckles are repurposed from ornamental horse harness. Decorative horse brass is often arranged on a strap called a martingale that hangs vertically on the horse (Fig. 2.3). When hung vertically on the horse, the buckle would have appeared right side up. (The belt in the Costume Institute shown in Fig. 1.13 also has a heart buckle, but the buckle in that example appears upright.)

When laid flat and viewed side by side, however, the differences between the two belts become apparent (Fig. 2.4). One (Fig. 2.1) is simple and straight cut, of even width along its entire length. The other (Fig. 2.2) is cut in undulating curves, narrower at the wearer's sides. The belt in Fig. 2.1 has metal grommets reinforcing the holes through which the buckle's single prong fastens, while the belt in Fig. 2.2 has holes that were simply punched, without reinforcing. This belt is decorated with four brass hearts, arranged in pairs, with a dangling chain below them, and has a brass shield shape at the wearer's center back (Fig. 2.5). The dangling chains likely provided a place for attaching a belt bag, another Phelps signature item, allowing for handsfree carrying of small essentials. The small decorative brass motifs on the belt in Fig. 2.2 are repurposed from horse harness, such as that shown in an extant harness (Fig. 2.6).

Top: **Fig. 2.1.** Phelps Associates, belt, leather, metal, circa 1943. (Museum at FIT, Gift of Sally Kirkland, 76.33.49. Courtesy the Museum at FIT.)

Above: **Fig. 2.2.** Phelps Associates, belt, leather, metal, circa 1945. (Museum at FIT, Gift of Louise Dahl-Wolfe, 74.157.2. Courtesy the Museum at FIT.)

Right: **Fig. 2.3.** Engraving showing how horses wore decorative harness with brass studs and decorative buckles. (Artist unknown, engraving, nineteenth century, 16.5" high x 10.5" wide. Victoria and Albert Museum. E.4014–1905.)

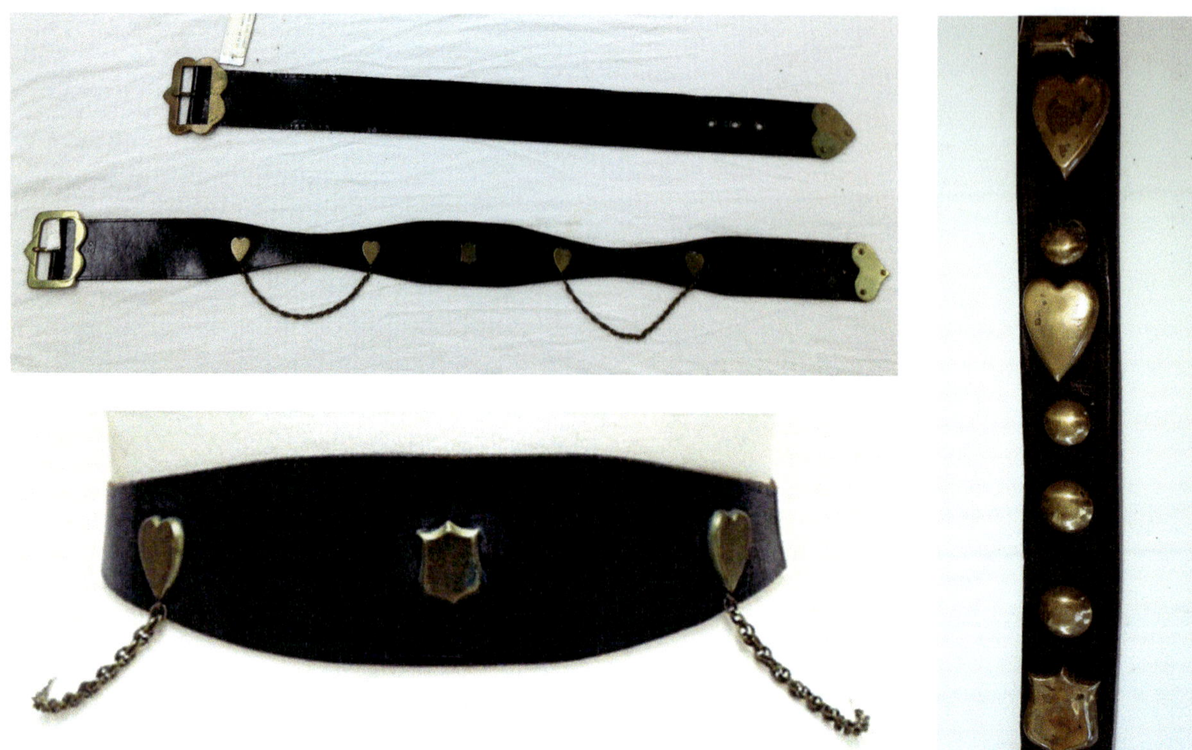

Top: **Fig. 2.4.** MFIT Sally Kirkland and Louise Dahl-Wolfe belts, side by side. (Photograph by the author. Courtesy the Museum at FIT.)

Above: **Fig. 2.5.** Reverse view of the Louise Dahl-Wolfe belt. Phelps Associates, belt, leather, metal, circa 1945. (Museum at FIT, Gift of Louise Dahl-Wolfe, 74.157.2. Courtesy the Museum at FIT.)

Right: **Fig. 2.6.** Detail of decorative horse harness strap. Leather, brass. (Author's collection. Photograph by the author.)

Taken together, these two belts point to several important aspects of Phelps Associates' workshop, design philosophy, and clientele. It is important to note that the company numbered among its clients many important figures in the American fashion media. The Museum at FIT acquired these two belts from women who were successful and influential in fashion print media in the years of Phelps Associates' beginning: fashion journalist Sally Kirkland (1912–1989, Fig. 2.1) and fashion photographer Louise Dahl-Wolfe (1895–1989, Fig. 2.2). Kirkland's belt is most likely an early custom-made piece, as it has no size markings or trademark markings. Instead, it is simply marked "Lele" on the reverse and is only 28 15⁄16" long from end to end, so when buckled it would have accommodated a very slim waist. Dahl-Wolfe's belt, one of two Phelps belts she gave to FIT, contains ready-to-wear waist size 32 markings on the front, just past the buckle. Kirkland and Dahl-Wolfe both wore Phelps accessories and were involved in promoting Phelps objects to the general public. Other Phelps clients in the fashion industry included designers (see chapter 1) and store buyers (see chapters 4 and 7).

Louise Dahl-Wolfe worked as a fashion photographer for *Harper's Bazaar* from 1936 to 1958. Photography curator Paul Martineau writes, "She understood the desires of the modern American woman and excelled at making her look relaxed, comfortable, and chic."[1] This aesthetic made her photography style an excellent fit for the work of the Phelpses.

Sally Kirkland was an assistant fashion editor at *Vogue* from 1939 to 1947, then the fashion editor of *Life* magazine until 1969.[2] Her *Vogue* years overlapped with the successful launch of Phelps Associates, and Kirkland embraced the look of a Phelps belt with a Claire McCardell jersey dress. At *Life* in 1949, she oversaw an article about Elizabeth Phelps's sportswear.[3] In 1985, Kirkland would recall, "Another unexpected source for a beloved fashion then and now were a retired professor and his wife, a Mr. and Mrs. Phelps. Saying that, 'humans should be as well-dressed as horses,' they used saddlery leathers and techniques for their handsome shoulder bags and belts (some with bags on them) often with glittering insignia added with great decorative effect."[4] Kirkland was probably referring to William Phelps's time as an NYU instructor; perhaps he also had a professorial manner, prompting her to remember him this way. Kirkland's characterization of the Phelpses' techniques and sources was probably based on her professional and personal knowledge of the couple and their work. The Phelpses became well-known among fashion industry insiders like Dahl-Wolfe and Kirkland in the 1940s, as Phelps Associates leather goods fit easily into the narrative the American fashion industry was creating about itself during World War II.

Fashion Industry's Push for Wartime Craftsmanship

A circa 1944 press release by publicist Eleanor Lambert proclaimed, "Elizabeth and William Phelps are, in addition to their standing as the finest designers of handbags and leather accessories in this country, the first exponents of a vital part of American fashion, the small craft shop."[5] For wartime promotional reasons, Lambert likely greatly exaggerated the vitality of the small craft shop in American fashion at the time. While locally produced custom clothing and accessories were certainly part of American fashion at the upper end of the price spectrum, American fashion was often acknowledged to be strongest in high-quality ready-to-wear items produced in factories, perceived as a democratizing influence.[6] However, this press release reveals the aspirations of the American fashion industry at the time; the Phelpses' craftsmanship fit well with the American fashion industry's surge of interest in craftsmanship and quality due to the war, as well as aligning with longstanding ideals of Americanness including practicality, simplicity, and democracy. After the fall of Paris, the American fashion industry could no longer rely on Parisian couture imports to set fashion direction and offer a model of aspirational luxury. Industry leaders looked to replace this tantalizing glow of luxury with American counterparts. At a meeting of the Fashion Group in California in 1941, "craftsmanship was the star of the show." The Fashion Group's members were influential women in the fashion industry, and their meetings were important in setting and reflecting the business's priorities. This meeting highlighted examples of sophisticated hand skills in garment production, such as an Adrian evening gown designed for Hedy Lamarr, adorned with "thousands of handmade loops decorating both yoke and skirt."[7] Appliqué, hand-painting, and block printing were also shown as examples of handcraft in fashion.

Alongside an interest in craftsmanship was a concern that for the duration of the war, the American fashion industry's previous championing of rapid obsolescence would have to give way to promoting fewer, higher quality purchases. In May 1941, Bonwit Teller advertising executive Sara Pennoyer (soon to be promoted to vice president) told the Fashion Group about the necessity of this change in focus: "Merchants must *do* something about selling the public on quality—Quality as the best economy."[8] To convince the American public to accept this new order in the consumer culture, the fashion industry deployed fashion itself as a tool, arguing that quality and durability were now in style.

Writing in spring 1942, Rachel Smith of Berkshire Knitting Mills agreed with Pennoyer about the importance of quality in wartime accessories and stated, "Three things will be demanded: Quality, because things must last; utility, because none of us can afford to buy things to decorate our closet shelves; and versatility, to give a lift to as many costumes as possible with combinations of the same accessories."[9] Speaking not long after Japan bombed Pearl Harbor, and the United States entered the war, *Vogue* editor-in-chief Edna Woolman Chase called for "fine workmanship" and quality as elements that went beyond fashion and economics to encompass the kind of moral fiber needed in wartime. Chase declared, "For in the days to come, we shall come more and more to demand quality not only in our material possessions, but also to demand it of ourselves and of our friends."[10] Chase made it clear that as the United States entered the war, objects were imbued with this symbolic meaning, reflecting expectations of the quality of character expected in its citizens.

Against this backdrop of fewer and higher quality purchases, accessories were accorded even more importance that usual. Sociologist Winifred Raushenbush, in her 1942 book *How to Dress in Wartime,* advised consumers on new government regulations such as the War Production Board's L-85 order governing permissible fabric allowances and the new price ceilings implemented by the Office of Price Administration. Government restrictions also affected the materials used by Phelps Associates (see chapter 4). Raushenbush also shared the Fashion Group's concern with quality and even argued that the government should implement a "floor," or minimum, quality level on consumer goods for the war's duration. In this context of concern with quality and what degree of consumption was patriotic, Raushenbush decreed: "Accessories are highly important, because it is through their use that American women are going to escape dowdiness. You may have to wear the same coat and dress year in and year out in wartime, but if you have individual, colorful, and amusing accessories your appearance will be morale-building for yourself and others."[11] Consumption of fewer, high-quality, unique accessories was in line with thinking within the fashion industry and expressed by government regulations and consumer-oriented groups.

Phelps Associates' work and design philosophy were also in accord with these currents of craft, quality, and investment purchasing. According to the Coty Awards program from 1944, the Phelpses' "inspiration has come from both sides of the Atlantic—from the native crafts of America in which they have deep faith and from the small artisans working in the Paris attics."[12] It is unclear the extent to which such associations of Phelps Associates with European, particularly Parisian, craft came from the Phelpses themselves, versus from journalists and press agents. In addition to the modernist concept of truth to materials, the Phelpses' design philosophy was also influenced by the idea of small workshops and traditional American crafts. As cultural studies and fashion theorist Elizabeth Wilson has observed, "the appearance of mass-produced artefacts opened a gap between art, including craftsmanship, on one side and machine-made imitations on the other. . . . The Artist found himself both more important and more threatened."[13] Decorative Arts scholar Edward S. Cooke Jr. credits William Morris with countering this industrialization in the 1870s and 1880s with a "concept of self-conscious craft" newly separate from the trades and manufacturing and notes that before this time "no specific cultural meaning attached to 'handcrafted' as a category of evaluation."[14] In framing their work as handcrafted, the Phelpses placed themselves squarely within a craft tradition that included reformers like Morris, European artisans (even as Elizabeth Phelps's German origins were publicly obscured), and American craftspeople. The Phelpses also viewed craft as art rather than a lesser form of aesthetic expression. One press release stated that William Phelps "deplored lack of understanding here [in the United States] which sharply divided 'art' from the creation of useful things."[15]

The Workshop: 43 Washington Square

The Phelpses' first New York workshop was located at 43 Washington Square in Greenwich Village, in 1940 a gritty and bohemian neighborhood where the pair probably interacted with other artists and could find relatively affordable space for their home and workshop (Fig. 1.12). Sociologist Richard Sennett, discussing workshops as far ranging as those used by medieval goldsmiths and science laboratories of the early twenty-first century, characterizes the craftsman's workshop as a home, either literally or metaphorically; in the Middle Ages these spaces were used for both work and sleep.[16] William and Elizabeth Phelps did not live in their workshop, but they did live next door.[17] To get to work each morning would have been the easiest commute imaginable—no subway, no bus, just a quick step out the front door, a view of Washington Square Park, and then back inside again next door.

The earliest mention of Phelps Associates in *Harper's Bazaar* is in a 1942 article, "Workshop on Washington Square," which described the space as "a homespun whitewashed workshop, converted from an 1834 cellar, with wooden tables and workbenches, and a handful of artisans who know the joy of making a thing from start to finish, complete" (Fig. 1.12).[18] While this building no longer exists, some similar New York architecture from the 1830s survives, such as the Merchant's House Museum on East Fourth Street, built in 1832, which gives some idea of what the basement-level rooms of the Phelps workshop might have been like.[19] To enter the workshop, one would have walked down steep, narrow stairs. The ceilings would have been low, and light would have only come in through the windows at certain times of day, so the whitewashed walls would brighten the room. It might have felt cool or slightly damp in summer, warm in winter.

Harper's portrays William Phelps looking like a businessman rather than at work as an artisan (Fig. 1.12). He is seated at a desk, his left arm resting comfortably while he does paperwork. He is holding a pen in his right hand, not writing but gripping it as one holds a pointer, while in the other hand he holds back the pages of a notepad—perhaps an order pad or receipt book. With no typewriter in sight, it is likely that the Phelpses carried on much of their business at this early stage through handwritten forms.

In the same article, Elizabeth Phelps is portrayed as a craftsperson rather than a businessperson. She is photographed with tools for cutting out the leather goods. She holds a square in her hands, aligning and preparing a corner on a small piece of leather. She is seated on a chair or perhaps a high stool, while the table is clearly visible. It is interesting to speculate whether William Phelps might have made this table or any of the other wooden furniture. Two other hand tools lie in front of her on the table—another ruler and the wooden handle of some sort of punch or stamp. *Harper's* contrasting portrayals of Elizabeth and William Phelps play into longstanding Western ideas about gender, with William shown as the rational businessperson and Elizabeth as his helpmate, the craftsperson under his direction. It is difficult to know whether this accurately represented their working arrangement or whether it reflected the views of the journalists who crafted the story.

As William transitioned from woodworking to leatherworking, and the Phelps Associates workshop was born, William and Elizabeth Phelps cared deeply about the materials with which they worked. A completed Phelps Associates belt or bag carried the history of the material, from animal skin to tanning technology and the Phelpses' philosophy of truth to materials in finishing. Additionally, in promotional interviews the Phelpses sought to connect their products with American history even in the procurement of the leather, by referencing the Swamp, New York City's historic leather district. Phelps Associates worked with a variety of leathers, selecting materials that would best serve the functional and aesthetic requirements of each design.

One journalist called William Phelps "an artist in leather."[20] To address the materiality of Phelps Associates leather goods, one must begin with this basic material. In photographs of the Phelpses' workshop, leather can be seen in various states: soft, tanned hides folded on the work table; pieces of leather being cut or sewn in the hands of the artisans; leather as finished shoulder bags hanging from nails on the wall (Fig. 1.12). Leather, which comes from an animal, is usually classed as a "natural" material in the context of fashion history, as opposed to synthetic fibers created by the chemical industries. 1940s American leather supplies were tied to the raising of cattle for meat, which came from the United States and Argentina, with skins as a byproduct. Supplies of leather were thus tied to demands and pricing for meat.[21]

The earliest mention of Phelps Associates in *Vogue,* however, was not for a leather good, but rather for an advertised necklace made of a different bovine byproduct—cow horn. The Phelpses polished horn into sports jewelry (casual costume jewelry), including necklaces and bracelets.[22] They also used cow horn and bone for fastenings on some of the early belts and bags and made it into buttons. "W. D. Phelps" was credited as the lender of Phelps bags, belts, jewelry, and buttons using bone and horn featured in the 1942 Museum of Costume Art exhibition *Fastenings and Embellishments,* which combined "some new creations by American designers illustrating closings under wartime regulations with a survey of fastening devices of the past."[23] However, the Phelpses apparently faced complaints from their neighbors about the smells from their experiments in horn work and thus decided to keep the focus on leather.[24]

The *Harper's Bazaar* article also gives clues as to the smells of the Phelpses' Washington Square workshop. A heavy-looking clear glass ashtray and two packs of cigarettes are shown at William Phelps's right side (Fig. 1.12). The article notes, "There's always coffee on call in the workshop kitchen," and one can imagine the heavy smells of leather, cigarettes, coffee, and the slightly musty old basement blending together.[25] There might have been other aromas as well: In the early days of Phelps Associates, there would have been the odors involved in working with cow horn.[26] Even without the horn products, the odors of the workshop were probably strong. American novelist Edna Ferber has described the pervasive aromas of a leather workshop: "The smell of leather, rich and oily, came to you even before you entered the shop."[27]

As a material, leather also makes strong impressions on the senses, and working with leather is a multisensory task. In Edna Ferber's novel *Fanny Herself,* a department store glove buyer describes how her childhood experience around her family's tannery prepared her for her later career: "I got so the smell and feel of leather and hides were part of me."[28] Ferber also evokes the sounds of leather in her 1952 novel, *Giant,* set in South Texas: "the creak of leather. Texas sounds. Everywhere the creak of leather."[29] There is something unsettling about humans wearing leather: the processed skin of another living creature brings to mind the death involved in object creation. When we put on leather, it becomes part of us, like a superpower second skin, even more than textiles do. The leather soles of my shoes substitute for feet calloused by walking barefoot. Leather is sympathetic to the human body in a way that a long chain of synthetic polymer is not. The smells, sounds, and textures of leather were just as much a part of the Phelpses' leather goods as were the visual elements.

The Tanning Process and the Phelpses' "Honest Leather"

Animal skins are transformed into leather through tanning. The word *tanning* derives from the traditional process of combining the tannic acids of plants with the protein-based collagens of hides to produce leather. Unprocessed hides are called green hides.[30] Yet even as leather is a natural product, the hides often a byproduct of agricultural meat production, leather used in mid-twentieth-century American was also a product of chemical processing in the tanning phase, whether bark- or chrome-based.[31] Chrome-tanned calf leather of 1940, like a chrome-plated cocktail shaker of the same year, holds a reference to scientific discovery and harnessing of natural minerals to redeploy them in a humanmade object—in the Phelps example through artisanal production, in the shaker example more likely through industrial mass-production.

The first step in tanning is curing the hide, soaking it in brine, applying salt and drying it, or just drying it. Salting is a temporary preservation that prevents skins from rotting while waiting to be tanned. Salted hides can be held three to five months without damage, although they do not keep as well in warm weather.[32] The next steps remove excess organic matter. The hides are soaked in water to remove the salt, blood, and dirt. Subsequent to the soaking, the hides are fleshed, a process that uses knives to remove any remaining fat and meat. After the fleshing comes the unhairing, which removes the animal's hairs and any remaining greasy particles.[33] In American colonial tanning, this process entailed a soak in a lime and water solution.[34] In the early nineteenth century, some American tanners instead began using a fermentation process called *sweating,* which created a slow decomposition on the surface of the hide, loosening the hair so it could be removed by a blunt knife. In the twentieth century, liming followed by dehairing in a special machine was the preferred method.[35] The next step in the process is *bating,* soaking the skins in an acidic solution to remove the lime used in the unhairing process.[36] Then the actual tanning can take place.

In the 1940s, the two most common types of tanning were chromium and vegetable. Each tanning process creates different properties in the finished leather. Chromium-tanned leathers are less susceptible to water and have greater elasticity. Vegetable-tanned leathers accept dyes and finish well. Some leatherworkers prefer these because they can be manipulated while wet and will retain this shape when they dry. Vegetable-tanned leathers are the only type that can be successfully tooled. They can also be molded, stretched, or stamped.[37] Oil-tanned leathers, while less common, are soft, supple, and stretchy.

In the twenty-first century, tanning is usually accomplished through vegetable or chromium tanning processes; prior to the mid-nineteenth century, it was all vegetable tanning. American colonial tanners filled wooden vats by alternating layers of hides with layers of sprinkled oak bark, filled the vats with water, then allowed them to soak for six months or more, sometimes replacing the bark with a fresh supply.[38] In the second half of the eighteenth century, New York tanners, looking for an alternative to oak, began experimenting with local hemlock bark.[39] In the early nineteenth century, research into the chemical basis for tanning was still new, and the existence of tannic acid had been discovered in 1793 by French chemist Nicolas Déyeux.[40] In the nineteenth century, the step called *handling* introduced the hide into a tannin solution. A quick tanning process might take three to four months for light sole leather or seven to eight months for heavy leather.[41] The base color of brown leather comes from the bark tanning process.[42] Chromium tanning was invented in the nineteenth century, and this process allowed for the production of lighter-weight and colored leathers. Chromium tanning relies on minerals that are mined, and then processed by the chemical industry into chrome salts: sodium bichromate or potassium bichromate.[43]

Throughout the tanning procedure, water is a key element of the chemical process. After leather is tanned, it is rinsed and dried. Some leathers are softened at this point. In the staking process, leather is rubbed back and forth over a hard surface to make it more pliable. Some leathers, such as sole leathers, are purposely not staked; hard and thick, and valued for these properties, sole leathers are left unstaked [44] During World War II, sole leather was set aside in greatest part for making boots for the armed forces.

The Phelpses embraced the modernist principle of truth to materials, and were quoted as saying they used "honest pieces of leather."[45] But what did they mean when they used the phrase *honest leather?* How can a piece of dead animal skin be honest? For the Phelpses, the term seems to indicate primarily a rejection of overdoing the last step in leather processing: finishing. A *Life* magazine article described the Phelpses' view: "Much fine leather, according to the Phelpses, is ruined by slick finishes which cover the natural markings and scars and take away some of the leather's character. The Phelpses clean their leather with mild soaps, finish it with waxes and dress it with milk and eggs."[46] Thus, they would presumably reject embossing that creates a faux reptilian look, for example. Additionally, the Phelpses decided as a matter of principle "to leave all fence scratches and other marks and scars of animal life on their leather."[47] Other common scars could be caused by such things as ticks, grubs, branding, or barbed wire.[48] Today's high-end leather goods manufacturers usually avoid these marks; for example, Louis Vuitton's chief executive, Michael Burke, stated in 2019 that while the company was opening a factory to manufacture bags in Texas, it would not use American leather unless it could persuade ranchers to stop fencing with barbed wire: "That typically makes it impossible for us to use the hides."[49] The Phelpses, in contrast, believed that allowing certain imperfections was more honest, gave a richer texture, and allowed the leather's character to shine through in the finished object.[50]

At the same time, one American leather manufacturer was described in this way in 1920: "He endeavored to make each skin a little better than ever it was made before. A leopard cannot change his spots. But the grain of many a skin, of a lamb, sheep, or goat was changed and improved through the efforts of Mr. Pearse."[51] The grain of a leather is the pattern on the hair side of the skin, determined by the spacing of the pores; fine-grained leather has small and close together pores while coarse-grained leather has large, widely spaced ones.[52] To what extent would the Phelpses have approved of enhancing a skin's grain? Their philosophy seems to have been to play up the leather's inherent qualities rather than create a too-perfect finish. The Phelpses' definition of *honesty* apparently did not preclude the use of showstopping colored leathers, however, as they frequently used reds and yellows (in addition to green seen on the introductory object green belt).

Leather Materials Used by Phelps Associates

In considering the materiality of Phelps Associates leather goods, it is also useful to think of the range of leathers that the Phelpses chose. Phelps Associates produced goods from many different varieties of leather, but the two types they used most commonly were cowhide and calfskin, which fit well with their discussions of honest leather. However, over the years the Phelpses also worked in suede, Morocco, goatskin, and deerskin, as well as more exotic skins and furs, due probably to both the suitability of the different types of leathers' properties and availability.

Cattlehide or cowhide leather was usually bark tanned. In the 1940s, contemporary splitting machines made it available in different thicknesses, usually one-twentieth to one-tenth an inch for bags and cases.[53] *Harper's Bazaar* describes a 1942 Phelps satchel as "cowhide, studded with a military ornament from the Spanish-American War."[54] Similarly, in a 1943 *Harper's Bazaar* article, a simple belt with a rectangular buckle, comparable to those in Fig. 1.1, is given a historical and military context: "a wide cowhide belt with an old Civil War brass buckle."[55]

Calf leather or calfskin was usually chromium tanned. This has a finer grain texture than cattlehide and, since it is scuff- and wear-resistant, is used in handbags, shoe uppers, gloves, garments, and bookbinding. According to the Tanner's Council of America, "besides the smooth or polished leathers which are made by dressing or glazing the grain side, a great quantity of suede leather is manufactured from calfskins."[56] *Harper's Bazaar*'s August 1943 issue shows a Phelps calfskin belt, which retailed for approximately $11 (Fig. 2.7).[57]

Suede is a leather, often calfskin, but also kid, sheep, and cattlehide upper, with a velvety soft, even nap raised by buffing the leather against an emery wheel. It remains strong because the flesh side rather than the grain side is surfaced. In the 1940s, suede was considered appropriate for women's belts, shoes, and handbags.[58] Phelps Associates sometimes used suede in combination with other leathers, as in a shoulder bag shown in *Harper's* in August 1943.[59] They also chose suede for a green evening belt-bag featured in *Life* magazine in 1945.[60] The Museum at FIT has in its collection a 2½"-wide black suede Phelps belt given by Despina Messinesi (1911–2003), American *Vogue*'s Paris fashion editor in the postwar period and later *Vogue*'s travel editor (Fig. 2.8).[61]

Around the time the Phelpses started their business, goatskin was favored for "the perfection of color obtainable," and it was produced by the chromium

Harper's Bazaar, August 1943 105

• Left: Navy blue wool jersey with umbrella gored skirt, about $23. Russeks. Phelps Associates calfskin belt, about $11.

• Right: A gold Botany flannel, about $15. Arnold Constable; Erlebacher, Washington. Phelps Associates leopard belt, about $19.

• Right: Gray wool designed by Mary Stevens, about $30. Lord and Taylor. Persian lamb belt, about $[illegible]. By Austein at Altman.

• Lifesize across the page: A Ben King original, two inches wide, in yellow fur, with a brown suede front and gilt buckle. About $15 at Lord and Taylor

• The big fur bags that will never spot or crock are made by Lesco—the dispatch case left, and a drawstring pouch above, both in brown and white pony skin.

Fig. 2.7. A calfskin belt in *Harper's Bazaar,* August 1943, 105. (*Harper's BAZAAR,* Hearst Magazine Media, Inc. Photograph by Plucer.)

Fig. 2.8. Phelps Associates, belt, leather, metal, circa 1945. (Museum at FIT, Gift of Despina Messinesi, 78.120.37. Courtesy the Museum at FIT.)

Fig. 2.9. A pair of children's shoes made of red Morocco leather. Shoes, leather, silver, made in England, 1750–1800. (Victoria and Albert Museum. Given by Mrs. Borough Johnson. T.23 to C-1956.)

tanning method.[62] In November 1942, *Harper's Bazaar* showed a Phelps Associates yellow goatskin bag: "they trim it with a gilt eagle, holding a ring in its beak."[63] The chromium tanning process facilitates goatskin's ability to accept dyes such as the Phelpses' chosen yellow. In 1943, *Women's Wear Daily* described a Phelps bag as "strong heavy goat with a pebbly grain."[64]

Morocco leather is a fancy, colored leather made from goatskins and for centuries associated with production in Morocco (Fig. 2.9). This leather was originally red, but by the late 1940s it was available in a variety of colors.[65] In Morocco leather, the grain is brought out by boarding, in which leather is folded over itself, grain surfaces together, and fold-pressed back and forth by a cork board.[66] *Harper's Bazaar*'s March 1943 issue showed a black-and-white photograph of a "bright red morocco bag, $35, Phelps Associates."[67]

In the 1940s, US deerskin (or buckskin) objects in were primarily made of skins imported from Canada or elsewhere in the Americas. Deerskin for gloves was usually tanned with oil or formaldehyde, with a different process employed for sport shoes. Real deerskin was much less common than faux and the imitation product was often created using cowhide upper leather with an "ooze" finish, in which the surface was buffed with an emery wheel.[68] *Harper's* March 1943 "Junior Bazaar" showed a photograph of a "drawstring bag in natural deerskin. $12.50. Phelps Associates" (Fig. 2.10).[69] The bag was presumably described as "natural" to emphasize that it was created with genuine deerskin rather than the cowhide simulation. The bag's drawstring form emphasizes the leather's pliability and softness, exploiting deerskin's properties and reinforcing that it was real. Deerskin was a much-needed material in World War II for some types of gloves and shoes for the army, and at one point even recreational hunters were asked to give their trophy deerskins for the war effort.[70]

126

Young Set Separates

Skinner's

Bright, light new separates to mix or match for spring. The fabric is Skinner's widely acclaimed Aralac and Spun Rayon blend. The tailoring—note the hip length pockets—is superb. The colors: Buttercup, Heaven Blue, Nude Beige, Cherry.
WILLIAM SKINNER & SONS, NEW YORK

FRANKLIN SIMON New York
JULIUS GARFINCKEL & CO., Washington, D. C.
G. FOX Hartford
STIX BAER FULLER St. Louis
RIKE KUMLER Dayton
J. L. HUDSON Detroit
FLINT & KENT Buffalo
THALHIMERS Richmond

1. A pink felt beret with an eight-section crown, two back-tabs, and a disposition to lend itself to suits, cottons, or city silks. **$1.95.** Year-ounder, at McCreery. **2.** An enormous plastic heart pin, **$1.95.** Dalsheim, at Franklin Simon. And a key pin in sterling gilt, with a padlocked heart locket, **$17.50.** Mermod-Jaccard-King, St. Louis. **3.** Three belts: One with genuine old sleigh bells and a brass harness buckle, on cowhide, **$8.50.** Phelps Associates. One with Good Luck in brass letters and two four-leaf clovers studded with green stones, on black patent leather, **$20.** And one with a giant bow, in chartreuse kid, **$9.95.** Both Midtown Belt Originals, at Jay Thorpe. **4.** A pump in brown kid with a stitched sole, **$8.95.** DeLiso Deb at O'Connor and Goldberg, Chicago. **5.** A suit pump in black or brown calf, with a little stitched scoop on the toe, **$8.95.** Kay's, Newport, R. I., which specializes in mail order. **6.** A wooden-sole sandal in elkhide, **$5.** Connie Cloppers, at Foley Brothers, Houston. **7.** A drawstring bag in natural deerskin, **$12.50.** Phelps Associates. And the new spun rayon scarves printed with love letters, **$1** each. By Glentex.

Fig. 2.10. A Phelps deerskin bag. *Harper's Bazaar,* March 1943, 126. (*Harper's BAZAAR,* Hearst Magazine Media, Inc. Photograph by Hans Jorgensen.)

Capeskin was a glove-quality leather made of sheepskins, sometimes sourced from South Africa.[71] *Women's Wear Daily* described capeskin as "a sturdy, medium to light leather that is fine-grained and pliable, soft and velvety."[72] The Phelpses worked with "fairly heavy capeskin" in their 1943 collection, retailed at the Mark Cross store.[73] The following year, they designed a "shoulder bag of navy capeskin and blue and yellow striped worsted webbing . . . lined in red capeskin."[74]

As these quotations from fashion magazines and newspapers demonstrate, the type of leather a bag or belt was made from was considered important enough to be included in editorial coverage. It is likely that the Phelpses would have shared information about the type of leather with the fashion journalists who were writing about the accessories, and consumers may have also been more familiar with varieties of leather and their properties, just as there was greater general knowledge about textiles than today. Unfortunately, information about the type of leather is not included anywhere on the leather goods themselves. Unlike textile products, subject to Federal Trade Commission laws governing labeling informing the consumer of the fabric's fiber content, even today "leather goods and trim" are not covered by these regulations.[75] Therefore, most material attributions of extant Phelps leather goods are made based on connoisseurship.

The Workshop: Connections to Horse Harness

Phelps Associates leather goods tell many stories, including that of the intersection of industrialization and handcraft and connections between two different aspects of the American leather industry—horse harness and fashion accessories. According to British engineer and hand-tool collector Raphael Arthur Salaman, "many handbags and purses are the modern descendants of the wallets, holsters, and riding accoutrements that were at one time an important sideline of the harness trade, and were made with the tools of that trade."[76] William and Elizabeth Phelps hired at least one experienced harness maker to work for Phelps Associates, and this influence of the worker's tools, technique, and familiar forms, coupled with their interest in repurposing metalwork, led to their belts and bags often showing the connections to horse harness quite literally and intentionally.

In the first years of the twentieth century, aspects of American life from agriculture to transportation were increasingly being mechanized. Yet, during William Phelps's childhood—and to a lesser extent Elizabeth's—horses were still a major labor force in both rural and urban settings. For this work, horses wore a wardrobe of harness, with both decorative and functional elements, ranging from practical simplicity for Midwestern farm horses to more decorative harness used in cities, for example by breweries. Decorative brewery harness remained a repository of handcraftsmanship, even while the harness-making industry as a whole faced pressure in the nineteenth century to move toward mass-production, as refinements to industrial sewing machines in the 1860s improved the quality of their output.[77]

The Phelpses' belief in artisanship ran counter to this dominant perspective, which favored industrialization and mass production for a wide range of leather products. For example, Charles H. McDermott's 1920 book, *History of the Shoe and Leather Industries of the United States,* celebrates the industrialization of the harness- and saddlery-making process in the second half of the nineteenth century: "The progress in the saddlery business at this time was phenomenal. . . . The apprentice system of turning out skilled mechanics seems to have been abolished, it no longer being the rule to serve long years at the bench. The work was now accomplished by division of labor. No single workman made a complete harness. He exercised his skill upon the production of single parts, and hence became proficient in turning out that subdivision for which he had special aptitude."[78]

For McDermott, movement to division of labor in leatherworking was a triumph of progress; for the Phelpses, this movement represented a loss both for the final product and for the maker. In contrast to the assembly-line approach of the major of American belt and handbag producers, and in contrast to McDermott, Elizabeth Phelps lauded the concept of the contented worker who is not alienated from his labor because he works in an artisanal context: "I think people are happier making a whole thing, whether it's whole stove lid or a handbag, than a piece of a thing."[79] The Phelpses did not go so far as to offer profit-sharing in their business, but within the context of wage labor, they did want their employees' experience of work to be positive. This concept of wholeness and one maker overseeing an object from start to finish was in direct opposition to William Phelps's experience as a foreign manager at General Motors, where the assembly line was the operating model.

McDermott approved that in the manufacture of horse collars, "large establishments absorbed the many small and insignificant collar shops. The old slow and laborious hand process gave way to the rapid machine method, its products being astonishingly smooth."[80] The small shops were "insignificant"; a rapid process of mechanized manufacture was preferable to handmaking not only for its speed and ease, but also precisely because the final product did not show the touch of the craftsman's hand—it was "astonishingly smooth." The Phelpses, in contrast, embraced the process of handmaking as well as the end product. It was also something they emphasized in their marketing to clients, stamping "Phelps handmade" on many of their belts, for example. The working methods the Phelpses employed in their original basement workshop also emphasized quality production over quantity. The Coty Awards program announced, "They make the first, second, and third samples of each item with their own hands."[81] These models were then added to the Phelpses' repertoire of styles and could be produced by other craftspeople in the workshop.

Despite the pressure to industrialize production, handcraftsmanship in harness-making did continue, at least for the most ornate and decorative elements, such as those used for brewery horses, perhaps because this work required greater skill and customers were willing to pay more for harness that created a stunning visual impression. In founding Phelps Associates, William and Elizabeth Phelps sought mentoring in this tradition. They hired an Austrian leather craftsman, who had originally immigrated to the United States to make horse harness for a brewery, to teach them more about the trade.[82] The craftsman left his hand tools to William Phelps when he died, and William was still using them in 1955.[83] Jennifer L. Roberts has noted that, as the intelligence of making is not just in the mind of the maker but in an interface of mind, body, tools, and materials, "the movement of object-knowledge around the world cannot be dissociated from the movement of makers, and objects can never be fully alienable from their makers."[84] The Phelpses' ability to find an experienced leather craftsman to help them improve their skills, and therefore the overall quality of Phelps Associates products, cannot be disassociated from the immigration of the craftsman who taught them. Their ability to offer "European-style" quality handcraft depended to some extent on US immigration. The story of the Phelpses' first New York City workshop is, in part, a story of the movement of the immigrants who brought their skills, interests, and abilities from Europe to the United States—both this unnamed horse harness maker and Elizabeth Phelps herself.

Phelps Associates belts particularly reflect the influence of horse harness, in both formal and ornamental elements (Figs. 2.1, 2.2, 2.4, 2.5). The Phelpses' creativity lies in translating these elements into a decoration for the human body and in making them appealing to the tastes of twentieth-century American female consumers. The small brass hearts were common decorations on the leading reins and rein hangers of horses in decorative harness, such as draft horses.[85] A nineteenth-century print from a catalogue of harness, saddlers' ironmongery, and bits in the Victoria and Albert Museum, for example, shows how a horse was arrayed in similar harness with brass-studded ornaments (Fig. 2.3). An extant example of British harness decorated with small brass studs has studs in motifs such as hearts, shields, ovals, stars, and moons (Fig. 2.6). The Louise Dahl-Wolfe Phelps Associates belt in the Museum at FIT collection uses four of these heart-shaped brass studs, with a shield-shaped brass stud in the center (Figs. 2.2, 2.4, 2.5). Hearts were some of the earliest decorative shapes for horse brass, along with crescents and stars.[86] William and Elizabeth Phelps later told an interviewer that during their New York City years, "a real find was an old harness shop, which they bought in its entirety to salvage the metal accoutrements" to ornament many of their leather pieces.[87]

A belt in the author's collection shows the same formal relationship to horse harness. This one has seven scallops, each of which is ornamented with a metal motif of pond life, which may have been produced for the belt rather than salvaged (Figs. 2.11, 2.12). The belt has a frog in the center back scallop, then has turtles in graduated sizes on the others. The two scallops flanking the frog each have clusters of three small (⅝" long) turtles, then the next scallops have single (1⅛") turtles, and the scallops closest to the front buckles have the largest single (1½") turtles. The metal ornaments are fastened through the leather of the belt strap, and the metal ends are covered on the reverse of the belt with small circles or ovals of leather.[88] When buckled in the middle of the five notches, the belt would accommodate a 26" waist, and it is marked with the ready-to-wear size 26. The ready-to-wear sizing indicates that it is slightly later than 1945, when the Phelpses were concentrating on custom work after selling two consignments through Mark Cross.[89] The belt buckle is etched on the reverse, "Phelps trademark." Unlike some earlier belts, in which the buckle is attached by stitching of the folded-over leather strap, here the leather folded over the buckle's bar is secured

Fig. 2.11. Phelps Associates, belt, leather, metal, circa 1947. (Author's collection. Photograph by the author.)

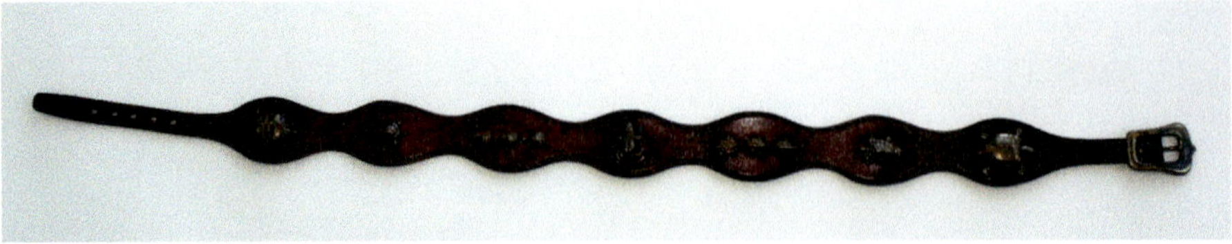

Fig. 2.12. Detail of belt with turtles and frogs. Phelps Associates, belt, leather, metal, circa 1947. (Author's collection. Photograph by the author.)

by a metal rivet. This belt is more daintily proportioned than many Phelps belts and is only $1\frac{11}{16}$" at the widest point of the center back scallop.

The Phelpses' interest in an egalitarian workplace was probably a factor in the inclusion of a photograph of their small team of workers in the *Harper's Bazaar* article. Phelps Associates' Washington Square workshop was set up to promote a feeling of respect within the shop; for example, everyone in the firm sat down together for lunch.[90] My research to date has not uncovered any evidence that the Phelpses actually introduced profit-sharing in their business or been able to confirm whether workers in any of their locations were unionized, but they did emphasize their concern with treating workers fairly, even as they struggled with how to implement best practices (see chapter 4).

In the *Harper's* photograph of the employee artisans, all four are shown using tools. While the photograph was no doubt carefully staged for the camera, it does give some idea of the kinds of tools and tasks that the artisans engaged with on a daily basis. Two people are hand-sewing with leather needles. To exactingly place stitch after stitch requires a confidence born of much practice. Richard Sennett has observed, "All craftsmanship is founded on skill developed to a high degree. . . . At its higher reaches, technique is no longer a mechanical activity; people can feel fully and think deeply what they are doing once they do it well." Sennett also notes that it is commonly suggested that ten thousand hours of practice are required to become a master musician or carpenter.[91] Each handsewn Phelps Associates leather accessory not only carries the connection to the artisan who made it but also bears the hours and years of training the artisan completed before even threading the needle for the particular piece. In each stitch is every stitch that has gone before it.

Today, the New York University Law School building takes up the entire block on Washington Square where the Phelpses lived and worked in the early 1940s (Fig. 2.13). The five-story building was built in 1950. However, the Phelpses moved their workshop well before the neighborhood was changing to increasingly be dominated by university architecture. The initial workshop was an intimate space well-suited to the Phelpses' early venture into leathercraft, but greater success and recognition meant they would need room to grow.

Fig. 2.13. The New York University Law School building at 40 Washington Square South covers the block that once held the Phelpses' home and workshop at 42 and 43 Washington Square, March 19, 2021. (Photograph by the author.)

The Workshop: 45 University Place

By 1945, Phelps Associates had outgrown the basement workshop and moved their New York City operations to 45 University Place, just a few blocks to the northeast (Fig. 2.14). In 2025, this building remains remarkably similar on the exterior, and it is still zoned for mixed use, including a deli/market at the ground level and residential apartments above (Fig. 2.15). On three floors, the Phelpses had both retail space and a workshop employing about twelve to fifteen artisans. Each worker singlehandedly produced about one bag per day, with very little division of labor.[92] While in the smaller basement Washington Square workshop, William and Elizabeth Phelps would have worked side by side and in close proximity to the whole team of artisans, in the larger workshop, operations were now divided over three floors. On the third floor, William supervised the work with hard leather used for more structured bags, assisted by two craftsmen, while on the fourth floor, Elizabeth Phelps directed a team of eight artisans (one man and seven women) in soft leather work, such as soft drawstring pouches.[93] Presumably, William and Elizabeth Phelps's working relationship changed when they were no longer in the same room. The physical separation would have meant they could no longer casually discuss the work while they were working; collaboration would have meant moving between their different work spaces.

Erving Goffman's understanding of regions and region behavior is helpful for imagining how the new workshop spaces—some designed for interactions with clients and some not—may have influenced the artisans' behavior. For Goffman, regions are places bounded by barriers to perception. A front region where a performance is given, governed by prescribed standards of behavior for a person's speech and behavior. The back region is where action related to the performance occurs, but the impression created by the performance is contradicted. The audience is expected not to intrude, and barriers are often put up to prevent the audience from doing so.[94] The original basement workshop was too small and open-plan for region behaviors. While workers might have been expected to put on their most polite behavior when clients called, the latter would have directly entered the workspace to order or make

Left: **Fig. 2.14**. Exterior of Phelps Associates workshop at 45 University Place, 1945. (*Fortune*. November 1945, 160. Walker Evans, [105 Views and Studies of Leather Craftsmen, Their Home in Birdsboro, Pennsylvania, and New York City Residence, Commissioned by *Fortune* Magazine for "The Small Shop," Published November 1945], film negative, Walker Evans Archive, 1994, 1994.252.3.1–.105. © Walker Evans Archive, The Metropolitan Museum of Art. Image source: Art Resource, NY.)

Right: **Fig. 2.15.** A contemporary view of the exterior of 45 University Place, March 19, 2021. (Photograph by the author.)

the final purchase of a belt or bag. The connection between client and artisan may have been stronger, then, in this first workshop than in the larger space where regions were established by the arrangement of different aspects of the Phelps business on different floors.

In the 45 University Place workshop, the showroom was dedicated to sales and showing of finished samples (Fig. 2.16). In 1945, this space included a wall of glass-fronted cabinets for displaying hanging shoulder bags; a wooden tree-type stand for belts; a tiered table; a tray table; and, in the center of the room, a low table with turned legs and storage drawers. The center table was the focal point of the room, and beneath a lush floral display it was draped heavy Phelps belts with multiple metal insignia. Many of these highly adorned belts were scalloped, with a different metal motif on each scallop section. The scalloped form is again connected to horse harness reminiscent of scalloped leather straps that hold larger horse brass ornaments. The turtle and frog belt shown in Figs. 2.11 and 2.12 is of the type pictured in the showroom photograph. The saleswoman showing this, or other Phelps belts, would have participated in the type of region behavior Goffman described.

Goffman cites the fashion saleswoman (his example is in a dress shop) as an example of a worker who engages in front region behavior and must hew to its standards of decorum: "She may be required to

Fig. 2.16. Phelps Associates showroom at 45 University Place. (*Fortune.* November 1945, 159. Photograph by André Kertész. © Estate of André Kertész. Courtesy of Estate of André Kertész.)

stand, keep alert, refrain from chewing gum, keep a fixed smile on her face even when not talking to anyone, and wear clothes she can ill afford." Goffman lists "behind the counter" and storerooms as back regions in stores; in the Phelps workshop building, the floors where leatherworking was carried on were the back regions where workers may have engaged in speech or behavior that would not have been formal, dignified, or conciliatory enough for the sales floor (Fig.2.17).[95] These new spatial divisions, a side effect of the business's growth, may have been a relief to workers who no longer had to maintain front region speech and behaviors, but they also separated artisans from direct contact with their clients.

A short clip from a 1947 newsreel *The March of Time: Fashion Means Business!* brought the front region of the Phelps showroom to an even wider audience and made the Phelpses' behavior in this area even more explicitly a performance.[96] *The March of Time* was a Time Inc. newsreel series that ran from 1935 to 1951 and aimed to create a film equivalent of print news magazines, covering current events.[97] *Women's Wear Daily* reported that the latest installment of *The March of Time* series, entitled *Fashion Means Business!* was planned for a February 21, 1947, release. The film showed aspects of the fashion industry from the shipping of raw cotton fiber to the work of fashion designers and fashion journalists. One section of the film focuses on Paris couturiers, including Christian Dior and Lucien Lelong, while another shows American custom designers including, Valentina, Charles James, and William and Elizabeth Phelps. *Women's Wear* reported that the film was likely to be seen by an estimated 27 million viewers.[98]

The scene featuring Phelps Associates opens with William Phelps, dressed in suit and bow tie, adjusting a display of shoulder bags. In the background,

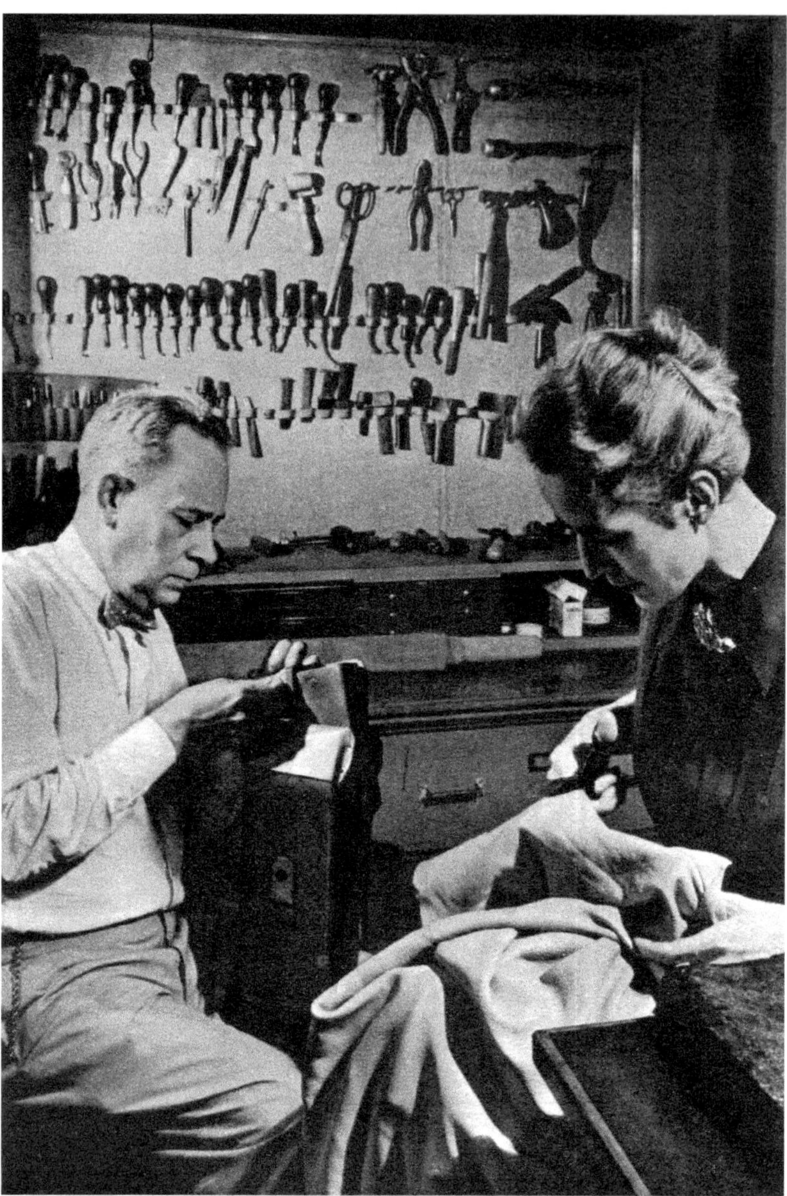

Fig. 2.17. William and Elizabeth Phelps at work. (*Fortune*. November 1945, 158. Photograph by André Kertész. Courtesy of Estate of André Kertész.)

Elizabeth Phelps's head is visible just over his shoulder. The bag that he touches is similar in form to an insect-adorned bag in the collection of the Costume Institute, but it has a shell-shaped decoration on the flap rather than the insect (Fig. 2.18). Instead of resting on shelves, as bags tend to be displayed in high-end specialty stores today, they hang from a series of metal S-shaped hooks on a wooden dowel, emphasizing the way they are meant to be worn.

A male narrator intones authoritatively, "Today's styles in handbags and leather goods can be traced to the designs of such craftsmen as William and Elizabeth Phelps, whose products, often made of rare and strange skins, carry the caché of the artisan."[99] As noted earlier in this chapter, most of the Phelpses' materials actually were from domesticated animals and a byproduct of meat production, but the newsreel's editors must have decided that "rare and strange skins" sounded more impressive. As the narrator speaks, William Phelps walks across the showroom, with the camera following him, then focusing on a closeup of Elizabeth Phelps assisting a "customer." The righthand wall of the showroom is lined with tall wooden cases, filled with wooden pegs at alternating heights, each peg suspending two to three hanging shoulder bags. In the foreground, a wooden fixture displays belts. The belts are primarily wide forms, some simply cut and others in scalloped shapes, some with brass decorations and others with only the functional hardware. Despite the limitations of black-and-white film, it is clear that the belts represent a wide variety of colors and shades of leather.

The final section of the clip shows Elizabeth Phelps working with a customer. (However, it is unclear who is portraying the customer—an actual customer? an employee, such as a salesperson? a model selected by the filmmakers?) Elizabeth wears her hair in a chignon and is dressed in one of her typical simple long-sleeved white blouses, worn with a modified dirndl skirt falling just below knee-length, with a wide belt of softly folding leather, which creates a waist-cinching silhouette.[100] As she confers with Phelps, the customer holds up the Phelps shoulder bag made of fur. In turn, Elizabeth Phelps shows the client a skirt identical to her own, holding it up as though for size, although the skirt would probably have been custom made, as the Phelpses had not yet started selling ready-to-wear clothing. In this closeup, the set-in hip pockets at the sides of the skirts are visible. A display with the words "Phelps Associates" is visible just behind the women in this scene.

The whole *March of Time* clip takes the Phelpses as designer-craftspeople out of the workshop and into the front region of the showroom. While the narration still emphasizes the artisanal creation process, this is not what is shown. Only the finished products, not the materials and labor, are displayed. While this scene is clearly staged for the camera, it does show how the new expanded workshop resulted in spatial divisions in the different aspects of the Phelps business. With the product and designers front and center, the other artisans are hidden in the back regions, away from clients and the filmmakers, giving them less credit for their contributions. In the newsreel, the filmmakers may have chosen not to show the artisans. However, the space itself demonstrates the challenges that the Phelpses faced as they balanced both a need to grow their business larger than what had been possible in the original basement workshop while still valuing and supporting the artisans with whom they worked.

Fig. 2.18. Phelps, shoulder bag, circa 1945, leather, metal. (Costume Institute, Metropolitan Museum of Art. Gift of Dorelle Moulton Tanner, 1983. 1983.484.1a, b. Image copyright © The Metropolitan Museum of Art. Image source: Art Resource, NY.)

Workers at Phelps Associates

Workers, often invisible in mid-twentieth American fashion media aimed at consumers, were frequently mentioned (and occasionally photographed) in articles about Phelps Associates. Because William and

Elizabeth Phelps wanted consumers to think about the process behind their products, the people whose hands and minds were so integral to the crafting of Phelps leather goods figured into the media discussion of the finished commodity. *Fortune* noted in 1945, "The Phelpses prefer to train their own craftsmen from the start rather than employ art-school graduates, who are all too apt to dote on design and neglect the manual effort so essential to quality craftsmanship."[101] The Phelpses wanted employees who would be artisans, first and foremost.

The Phelpses' fair treatment of the artisans was part of their workshop's reputation. A 1943 *Women's Wear Daily* article described Phelps Associates as "a group of workers assembled under the direction of William Drown Phelps and his wife."[102] This phrasing puts the workers first and has a collaborative, artistic ring: one might commonly say that a group of singers is assembled under the direction of a choirmaster, but one would not usually say that a mass-producing factory was a group of workers assembled under the direction of the CEO. Publicist Eleanor Lambert paid service to both labor concerns and the economic imperatives of operating a business when she informed the public in 1944, "Their craftsmen are paid much over the basic wage scale, and still it is profitable, because the things they make are needed."[103] In 1945, these wages for the New York workshop ranged from $27.50 to $45 per week.[104]

In a postwar *Harper's Bazaar* article, about the Phelpses' later workshop at Joanna Furnace, in Pennsylvania, the author reported that the Phelpses' workers were "craftsmen recruited from the countryside and from veterans' hospitals in the Philadelphia area."[105] There are two narratives present here: one of the rural American craftsperson, which the Phelpses also later used when discussing their North Carolina workshop (in the latter case, specifically the Appalachian mountain craftsperson); the second is that of employing veterans, particularly those who were disabled.

Craft was one avenue for the rehabilitation of veterans on both sides of the Atlantic; linking hand and mind was thought to produce beneficial effects to both the individual and society as a whole. Writing in 1947, British designer, leatherworker, and teacher Betty Dougherty stressed the benefits of handwork, arguing that craftspeople "become tidy, accurate, workmanlike and individual, their minds are trained in this way, and react unconsciously with clarity, decision, and promptitude. Rehabilitation centers are an excellent example of this."[106] However, the use of craft as rehabilitation for war veterans was not a new concept in the United States or Britain in the 1940s. As early as the arts and crafts movement, craft and therapy had been linked—for example, in potteries founded as sanatoriums.[107] Craft had also been had also been used as therapy in World War I. In Edna Ferber's 1919 short story "Long Distance," a shellshocked American veteran participates in craft training in the English countryside as part of his recovery: "They set him to weaving and painting as a means of soothing the shattered nerves. He had made everything from pottery jars to bead chains, from baskets to rugs. Slowly the tortured nerves healed." In Ferber's 1947 commentary on the story, she voiced sadness and shock that the story was again relevant to a new generation of veterans: "thousands and thousands, can now be found, almost thirty years later, still sitting in a hospital ward or garden, painting that wooden chicken yellow and waiting for the light to break."[108] In the United States in World War II, activities such as craft and theater arts were employed as paths to healing for soldiers with physical and/or psychiatric wounds.[109]

The Phelpses had been interested in participating in craft work programs for wounded veterans as early as 1944, when a press release at the time of the Coty Awards stated that they "would like to train wounded soldiers in their crafts, but have not climbed out of the red tape on that yet."[110] By the following year, William Phelps had hired two returned veterans, both of whom had experience in doing other types of skilled work with their hands. One had been an antique metal repairer but was wounded in the war and could no longer meet the physical demands of metalworking. The other, from rural Vermont, had previously trained as a barber.[111]

The veterans the Phelpses later recruited from Philadelphia-area hospitals may or may not have been physically wounded; they were probably participants in a Red Cross therapeutic craft program called "Arts and Skills." In 1942, weaver and textile designer Dorothy Liebes was appointed national director of the Red Cross Division of Arts and Skills, a project that gave war veterans in government hospitals across the United States the opportunity to learn hand skills and crafts. This program counteracted the boredom and sense of hopelessness that many veterans experienced in hospitals by bringing in skilled craftspeople—professionals volunteering their time—to teach and to design projects for the veterans to make.[112] "Portrait of America—No. 53," a typewritten document now in the Library of Congress, accompanying a group of photos of Arts and Skills participants, notes that the program was not to be confused with occupational therapy, "which retrains injured bones and muscles. Rather its aim is to retrain the mind."[113] Weaving and leatherwork were two of the thirty-two topics offered, as Liebes explained in a 1944 lecture titled "The Hand in Rehabilitation and in Industry," delivered before the Fashion Group.[114] The Phelpses believed in the importance of handwork to both the product and the workers' well-being, so Liebes's program was a good fit for them. Red Cross photos show male veterans in dressing gowns and trousers receiving instruction from female instructors in Red Cross uniforms (Fig. 2.19). A photograph from an American hospital in New Caledonia shows an integrated group of veterans learning how to make leather picture frames; other photos show veterans making purses (Fig. 2.20). According to the "Portrait of America" document, as a result of the Arts and Skills program, "Often when a soldier leaves the hospital he is equipped with at least a new hobby and sometimes with a new way for him to earn his living."[115] Veterans

Fig. 2.19. A returned serviceman is advised by a Red Cross worker about a purse he is making. (*Rehabilitation of American Servicemen of the Second World War, 1941–1945*, Lot 4801, Library of Congress, Prints and Photographs Division.)

who subsequently went to work for Phelps Associates were part of this latter category. The program proved popular enough to endure at least until the early 1970s, when the catalogue of a Dorothy Liebes retrospective exhibition noted her involvement in establishing the program, which was still in existence.[116]

Craft was offered as a path to healing for veterans who had experienced shell shock and other debilitating injuries during the war, and the Phelpses embraced this in their hiring practices. As a veteran of World War I, William Phelps probably was especially aware of these issues. Within the Phelps Associates workshop, William and Elizabeth coordinated their team of artisans to craft high-quality objects that would appeal to another group of people who also entered the site: their custom clients.

Custom Clients

Phelps Associates' New York City workshop was based on the idea that "maintaining their standards means to them the devoted kind of personal attention possible only in a small shop." A Phelps custom client entering the New York City showroom at 45 University Place in 1945 would find herself among the displays discussed above, all presenting a dizzying array of leather goods. By this time, there were about a hundred models of belts—would she choose one of the highly ornamented scalloped belts on the low table or one of the simpler belts hung on a stand? In the glass cases, samples of some of the seventy-five different models of Phelps bags were available, with shoulder bags hung from wall pegs and belt bags arranged flat on shelves. Custom clients paid from $14.50 to $85 for bags and from $3.50 to $35 for belts.[117] It is unclear whether the workshop was open to walk-in visitors or open only by appointment.

As producers of made-to-order products, the Phelpses created purses and belts for specific customers. A 1944 *Town and Country* article claimed that each of their shoulder bags was "individually designed and carefully fitted to its owner."[118] As early as 1943, however, Phelps Associates had also begun making ready-to-wear bags and belts, using the same artisanal techniques but in standard sizes and designs, rather than created to the specifications of a known client.[119] These could then be bought in large specialty or department stores, where the

Fig. 2.20. "Patients in this Army hospital are taught leather craft work by Dorothy Breitschadel . . . American Red Cross hospital recreation worker, in cooperation with an Army rehabilitation program." (Red Cross, PR06 CN 088, [HW] [Hospital Worker], Library of Congress, Prints and Photographs Division.)

eventual client might never actually meet William or Elizabeth Phelps. The purchaser of ready-to-wear would not have known the individual who made her accessory, but she would have known that it was made by an artisan in the Phelps Associates workshop. Thus, even with ready-to-wear items, the consumer would have a more specific idea about who made her accessory than if she had purchased a generic, mass-produced belt.

Society matron and clubwoman Dorelle Moulton Tanner was not just a Phelps client but a purchaser of some of their more expensive. When Tanner entered the Phelps showroom, she must have been attracted by the display in the center of the room. Tanner selected a matching Phelps accessory set of bag and scalloped belt ornamented with cicadas, which she gave to the Costume Institute in 1983, accession number 1983.484.1a,b (Figs. 2.18, 2.21). A similarly adorned insect belt was shown in *Vogue* in August 1944: "Buy it as a jewel—magnificent cowhide belt with antique brass bugs. $25—but divide its cost by five years' wear" (Fig. 2.22).[120] Phelps custom products were expensive, as this advice to amortize the cost of the bag suggests. However, this accorded with the wartime imperative to buy high quality items and use them for a long period. Other belts shown on the same page were more affordable; a Phelps belt in "red wool webbing with brass buckle" (the buckle with American bald eagle motif appears to be a repurposed vintage military buckle) sold for $9.50, and an even simpler red leather belt by Schaffer retailed for $1.50 at Saks Fifth Avenue.[121] The following month, *Vogue* showed a similar, but not exactly identical, bug belt, calling it "fit-for-an-heirloom."[122] Tanner not only bought the expensive belt but also the matching bag—evidence that Phelps accessories were sometimes bought and likely worn in sets.

Fig. 2.21. Phelps, belt, circa 1945, leather, metal. (Costume Institute, Metropolitan Museum of Art, Gift of Dorelle Moulton Tanner, 1983, 1983.484.1a, b. Image copyright © The Metropolitan Museum of Art. Image source: Art Resource, NY.)

Tanner, who lived in Greenwich, Connecticut, was "wife of the late Vincent D. Andrus and Frederick C. Tanner." She died on Friday, June 22, 2001, at the age of eighty-three.[123] She would have been in her twenties in the 1940s. Tanner was president of the Greenwich, Connecticut, Garden Club in 1957–58, active in historic preservation, including the Bush-Holley House restoration, and a president of the Historical Society of the Town of Greenwich. She was also on the board of the Bruce Museum in Greenwich, Connecticut, and on the Board of Regents for Historic Kenmore in Fredericksburg, Virginia.[124] It is worth considering that the historicism employed by Phelps Associates might appeal to individuals with an interest in historic preservation. Tanner also served as the national president of the Garden Clubs of America from 1971 to 1973, which accords with her interest in nature.[125]

Fig. 2.22. *Vogue* coverage of a Phelps insect-adorned belt. "Bold—Not Bitsy," *Vogue*, 15 August 1944, 120. (Irving Penn, *Vogue*, ©Condé Nast.)

Two life-sized metal (probably brass) cicadas crawl along the curving flap of Tanner's Phelps Associates pouch bag (Fig. 2.18).[126] The proper right cicada points vertically down toward the bag's turn-lock clasp. The proper left cicada scurries diagonally up and out. The cicadas are detailed, showing a trilobed shape just past the bugs' necks and striations and segmentation on the wings (Fig. 2.18).[127] The Phelps pieces followed just few years after the Schiaparelli insect necklace, from her 1938 Pagan collection, brought bugs into fashion accessories, using gold or colored insect ornaments in clear Rhodoid (cellulose acetate) collars (Fig. 2.23).[128]

Fig. 2.23. Elsa Schiaparelli (Italian, 1890–1973), Jean Clément (French, 1900–1949), necklace, Rhodoid (cellulose acetate) and metal, Fall 1938 Pagan Collection. (Brooklyn Museum Costume Collection at The Metropolitan Museum of Art, Gift of the Brooklyn Museum, 2009; Gift of Arturo and Paul Peralta-Ramos, 1955. 2009.300.1234. Image copyright © The Metropolitan Museum of Art. Image source: Art Resource, NY.)

The light-brown Tanner bag has a dull, rough texture, showing the leather's grain; it is pebbled and lightly crackled. The front flap is trimmed in a narrow band of the same leather, the edges left unfinished. The bag is constructed of three main pieces: the back, which folds over to create the front flap; a side band that joins front and back; and the front piece. Self-piping covers the join between the side band and the front. On the interior, a narrow leather thong on each side of the bag draws the pieces together and connects via a brass ring to the shoulder straps on each side. The biomorphic curves of the bag evoke saddlebags—yet another connection to saddlery.

Tanner's coordinating belt is of the same pebbled brown leather as the bag and is 29½" overall length x 2⅜" wide at the widest point (Fig. 2.21). Cut from a single piece of leather, the belt undulates in a series of seven scallops, each containing a metal decoration in the form of cicada or owl. Two of the four cicadas face the buckle, flanked by an owl on each side. In the back, an owl is centered with a cicada facing

Above: **Fig. 2.24.** Phelps, belt, leather, metal, circa 1946. (Author's collection. Photograph by the author.)

Left: **Fig. 2.25.** Detail of belt with insects and starbursts. Phelps, belt, leather, metal, circa 1946. (Author's collection. Photograph by the author.)

it on each side. These creatures are surreally out of proportion: the nocturnal predators, the owls, are small enough for the sap-munching cicadas to devour, should they become omnivores. Both insect and bird are flying creatures of the evening or night. Two wear lines around the second of five notches in the belt indicate where it was primarily worn. It is 25" from the end of the leather strap to this second notch, indicating that Tanner had a small waist when she wore this belt. There are no size markings, and this as well as the fact that it is cut from one piece of leather indicates that it is probably custom-made.

In the author's collection, there is a similar olive-to-light brown leather belt, 42¼" in overall length (Fig. 2.24). This belt has a pattern of four metal cicadas, five metal starbursts (cicada, star, cicada, three stars at back, cicada, star, cicada), also on scalloped segments of the belt (Fig. 2.25). The reverse of this belt, like most Phelps belts is unlined; it does, however, have small circular or teardrop-shaped leather patches on the back to cover the metal pieces used to attach the ornaments to the leather, so the belt would not snag the wearer's clothes. It also lacks size markings, so it might possibly have been custom-made. The belt measures 37" from the end of the strap to the belt notch with the most wear. However, unlike the Tanner belt, all cut in one piece, the author's is constructed with the scalloped, ornamented part in one piece and the two ends cut separately and then threaded through a slit and attached to the reverse. This may have allowed for faster production: the scalloped sections could be premade and the ends cut to measure and attached as orders came in. Like the Tanner belt, the author's has a metal Phelps trademark symbol attached near the buckle, and the reverse of the buckle has the words "Phelps TM" etched or stamped into the metal, while the Tanner belt's buckle simply reads "Phelps." This probably indicates that the author's belt was a later version. Phelps Associates continued producing belts with brass insect motifs at least into the mid-1950s.[129]

Another Phelps custom client was Margaret (Mrs. Morehead) Patterson, a society figure who also patronized Charles James. Patterson appears as a bridal attendant (already with her married name) in a 1922 wedding featured in *Harper's Bazaar,* so she was probably in her forties in the 1940s. The Smithsonian National Museum of American History has a Hattie Carnegie dress that Patterson wore and notes that she was "nee Margaret Tilt, the daughter of Charles A. Tilt of Chicago's Diamond T. Motor Car. She was at one time married to Moorehead [*sic*] Patterson, CEO of the American Foundry Machine Company (AMF),

Fig. 2.26. Phelps, shoulder bag, leather, metal, circa 1945. (Costume Institute, the Metropolitan Museum of Art; Gift of Mrs. Morehead Patterson, 1968. C.I.68.51.1. Image copyright © The Metropolitan Museum of Art. Image source: Art Resource, NY.)

New York City."[130] The Costume Institute currently holds a range of garments and accessories that once belonged to Patterson, some of which came directly to the Costume Institute, and some of which are part of the Brooklyn Museum Costume Collection at the Metropolitan Museum of Art, accessioned in 2009. In addition to a Charles James "Infanta" dress, there are garments and accessories by Balenciaga, Vivier, and Fontana. As of 2025, the Costume Institute collection has two Phelps objects that belonged to Patterson, an eagle-motif shoulder bag (2009.300.262, also mentioned in the introduction, Fig. I.3), and a shoulder bag with fern leaf motif (C.I.68.51.1, Fig. 2.26).

The quintessential bald-eagle postman shoulder bag, very similar to the bag in the author's collection, was given by Mrs. Morehead Patterson to the Brooklyn Museum in 1985 and is now part of the Brooklyn Museum Collection at the Costume Institute (Fig. I.3).[131] A bald eagle rises, phoenixlike, on the center-front flap of the bag, carrying a streaming banner in its beak, proclaiming "E pluribus unum." Two muskets are crossed behind the stars-and-stripes shield. In one (proper right) claw, the eagle clasps a branch laden with olives; in the proper left claw it holds three arrows. The eagle is on a curved patch pocket attached to the bag's front flap. The flap closes with a spherical, metal knob on the bottom on the body of the bag; a narrow strap at the end of the flap has a slit that the knob fits into. The word *PHELPS* is stamped on this end. The leather is a smooth, probably calf leather. Unlike the author's example, this bag does not have a back flap. When the front flap is opened, it reveals the bag's main compartment, as well as a small pocket of rougher grained leather with a flap and snap closure. Below this pocket is the metal belt-buckle-shaped Phelps insignia.

A metal insignia was also key to identifying the second shoulder bag, which Patterson donated directly to the Costume Institute in 1968 (Fig. 2.26).[132] This pouch-shaped bag has a metal foliate ornament on the exterior of its front flap. The ornament looks like a fern but has a pineapple or pinecone at the end point. Unlike many Phelps bags, this one is lined with suede. It is possible that the Phelpses added linings at the request of the client. The Costume Institute's catalog had previously listed this shoulder bag as "attributed to Phelps"; a metal Phelps trademark insignia on the interior, back side of the bag, stitched just below a seam, reveals that this bag is in fact a Phelps work, and the catalog now reflects this.

Business Philosophy and the Bottom Line

The craft and handwork philosophy of Phelps Associates, which led them to prefer to train their artisans rather than hire design school graduates, also came through in their handbag production. Within the context of larger mass production, there was a clear hierarchy of designer above craftsman/maker, and there was sometimes conflict between the dictates of the designer and the hands-on, bodily knowledge of the craftsman. For example, in her critique of the fashion industry, *Fashion Is Spinach,* designer and cultural critic Elizabeth Hawes described this conflict when she tried to persuade handbag makers to try a new folded form. She also identified the conflict's origin: "The craftsmen in the wholesale business in America have acquired a complete disrespect for a certain kind of people who call themselves designers and are only sketchers."[133] The craftspeople Hawes references were wary of designers who only designed on paper and did not understand the practical characteristics and demands of the material. Likewise, Claire McCardell described going to a craftsman like her local cobbler and ordering a design for leather bracelets, which the cobbler would simply carry out.[134]

In contrast, William Phelps believed design ideas should flow from craft, from craftsman to designer, with the designer's role as an editor, determining the best way to incorporate the ideas to appeal to consumers. I have not encountered any specific evidence of this being put into practice in the Phelpses' workshops, but if it was, the craftspeople did not receive credit for their designs. Phelps espoused this idea as early as 1944, when a press release stated that during his time in Europe, Phelps "became fascinated by the 'little craftsmen' [whose] creations added up to the wonders of the Paris couture. Believed that something of the sort should and could be developed in his own country. . . . Noticed that in Paris the top designers had a constant flow of things before their eyes every day, made by small craftsmen. 'They could pick and choose, pick and choose. I thought America could never develop a fashion force until something of the sort existed here.'"[135] He shared this philosophy with the Fashion Group in Philadelphia in 1950, in a program titled "Big Business Ahead for Hand-Crafted Fashions."[136] Although both William and Elizabeth Phelps took part in the program, William seems to have spoken on behalf of their design partnership, while Elizabeth ran a fashion show.[137] He urged stores to sponsor clinics "to develop and discover craftsmanship talents."[138] As an individual who came to leathercraft and design after a career in the automotive industry, Phelps was well aware that potentially talented workers might be currently employed in other fields. Without opportunities to discover their latent talents, these gifts might go unused—a loss for American design. William then described how the European system had worked in the 1920s and 1930s, with the named designers working "as 'editors' sorting out the flow of ideas submitted to them by various craftsmen and giving them the 'twist' necessary for successful fashion interpretation and exploitation." He also contrasted American and European designers, saying that the European designer started with the details, then moved to the designs, while the American designer started with the design, then tried to work out the details.[139]

William Phelps suggested that even within the American context, with its emphasis on mass-market volume, there was a need for craftsmanship, and custom work to "provide ideas which would be 'fuel for volume.'"[140] A few years before this, *Fortune* magazine had quoted him: "The U.S. needs plants whose production of any particular model lies between three and a thousand."[141] In other words, he saw a need for smaller-scale artisanal production that fell somewhere on the spectrum between the creation of completely unique, one-off objects and industrialized mass production.

So how financially successful were the Phelpses using this model of hand-craftsmanship in the expensive city of New York? Edward S. Cooke Jr., writing in 2007, proposed a number of key themes in the study of modern craft in the United States, including the tension between idealism and commerce.[142] Much of fashion industry media coverage of the Phelpses is concerned with image-making and idealism, but some sources deal with the commercial aspects of their workshop. *Fortune* reported in 1945, at the peak of Phelps Associates' critical success, that the firm's average retail prices represented 12 percent for materials, 30 percent for labor costs, 18 percent for overhead and 40 percent for profit. The article noted,

> They are satisfied with a profit of about $1,000 a month on a total investment of some $27,000. They are, indeed, among the most eloquent exponents of modesty with regard to profits. They feel sure that in many productive fields there is some point where small shop concentration on highest quality will pay off with comfortable profits and high working enthusiasm. In this connection, they think that thousands, perhaps tens of thousands of U. S. businessmen, caught in mass-production, maximum-profit psychology, do not know what pleasures they are missing.[143]

So, the answer seems that the Phelps Associates model was moderately profitable, at least as long as the objects they were creating fit the fashionable zeitgeist of the war years. Chapter 6 explores the ways the Phelps business evolved after World War II as fashions changed. The Phelpses also put a value on the intangible benefits of their working model and the positive atmosphere of the workshop. They were not producing high monthly profits by *Fortune*'s standard, but their income was higher than they had been accustomed to during the Depression. *Fortune* did note, however, that often the profits were reinvested in the business, so it is difficult to know how large a salary the Phelpses paid themselves.[144]

Conclusion

The Phelps Associates workshops in New York City were organized to put into practice William and Elizabeth Phelps's ideas about handcraft creation as valuable in and of itself but also as benefitting workers and society as a whole. The Phelpses were forward-thinking in desiring to reimagine the way American fashion could be produced outside of the mass-production, largescale factory model. The quality and properties of leather, the primary material in their early production, were important to the Phelpses. Drawing from the tradition of handmade leathercraft still in practice in ornamental horse harness, they made leather goods that explicitly referred to harness, both in forms and in some metal elements. The Phelpses' concern with workers and empowering working conditions meant that they encouraged artisans to make pieces from start to finish and actively sought to hire and train veterans, particularly those with disabilities. Custom clients visited the Phelps workshop, as objects were crafted with the specific individual and her body in mind. The Phelpses' design philosophy seems to have had moderate financial success in the New York context, although after the war they would seek other solutions to lower costs.

Shortages and Shapes

Phelps Associates' designs were particularly well-adapted to the constraints caused by shortages of materials as the United States entered World War II. The Phelpses incorporated vintage metal ornaments and hardware in bags that did not rely on metal frames, circumventing the problems other handbag manufacturers faced due to metal shortages. Phelps Associates' historicizing shoulder bags and belt bags enabled women on the go to have their hands free. American women, including servicewomen such as the Women's Army Auxiliary Corps (WAACs), learned new techniques of the body as they embraced these accessory styles. While handbags and belts were not rationed in the United States as shoes were, there were still shortages of leather; however, Phelps still managed to maintain a supply of leather adequate to the workshop's production needs.

Introductory Objects: The Seymour Laughon Rennolds Collection at the Valentine Richmond History Center

Many extant Phelps accessories in museum collections entered those museums as single objects, separated from the context of the original wearer's wardrobe. Quite a few Phelps accessories entered museum collections as part of an accessory set, such as the Dorelle Tanner bag and belt set adorned with cicadas (Figs. 2.18, 2.22). But the Valentine Richmond History Center is home to a collection of four leather accessories from the same original wearer. This grouping includes a bag that hangs from the shoulder, two bags that hang from a waist belt, and a belt (Fig. 3.1). The bags are objects made of leather, thread, and metal assembled into containers for carrying other objects. They are containers that

Fig. 3.1. The Seymour Rives Laughton Rennolds collection of Phelps leather goods in the collection of the Valentine Richmond History Center. (Gift of Caroline Rennolds Milbank, Amelie Rives Rennolds, and Margaret Rennolds Chace, in memory of Seymour Laughon Rennolds.)

could be strapped onto the body so the hands remained free; containers to meet the needs of women during one war, based on the gear of soldiers from past conflicts.[1] Although mostly dating from the immediate postwar period, the Phelps leather goods in the collection of the Valentine Richmond History Center illustrate many of the key elements of Phelps Associates' work that helped them achieve success during World War II, including the Phelpses' choice of shapes and strategies for coping with shortages.

These accessories were part of a collection of objects associated with the Rennolds family of Richmond. Most of the objects in the collection had belonged to Seymour Laughon Rennolds (1930–1995) and were donated in her memory in 1995 by Caroline Rennolds Milbank, Amelie Rives Rennolds, and Margaret Rennolds Chace. Seymour Laughon Rennolds grew up in southwest Virginia.[2] The 1940 US Census lists David C. Laughan and Alice T. Laughan both age forty-five, as the parents of David C. Laughan, age fifteen, and Ann Seymour Laughan age nine, all living in Pulaski, Virginia.[3] Seymour Laughon's father, David, was president of the Laughon Lumber Company.[4]

Seymour and her mother, Alice Laughon, shared a strong interest in American fashion and American fashion designers. Alice, for instance, had an outfit by Traina-Norell that also had the store label of Montaldo's, a specialty store in Richmond.[5] A 1980 article recalling the best retailers of Richmond's downtown shopping district noted that among the specialty stores, "Montaldo's, a women's boutique at Fifth and Grace, was the chicest."[6] The Laughons also sometimes traveled to Washington, DC, and New York City to shop.[7]

Seymour's daughter, fashion historian Caroline Rennolds Milbank, estimates that Seymour probably wore the Phelps leather accessories in the late 1940s and early 1950s, when Seymour was in her late teens and early twenties. Milbank notes that Seymour's wardrobe included clothes by Claire McCardell.[8] The pairing of McCardell garments with Phelps leather accessories would have aligned with the way the latter were often shown in fashion magazines. Seymour's 1947 school yearbook bears witness to her fashion-savvy reputation among her peers (Fig. 3.2). Alongside her elegant profile portrait (with very fashionable bangs) is the following description, written by a fellow student: "If it's talent you want, we've got it; if it's style you're seeking, you've come to the right place; if you're on the lookout for brains, looks, and a "bang"-up personality, tinged with a quality known as fey, we have your answer. It's all summed up in five-feet-four of terrific gal. Seymour is constantly mired in huge sheets of paper covered with creations which would make Adrian sit up and take notice."[9] Seymour Laughon's peer describes her talented and stylish and as the creator of fashion designs on par with celebrated American designers like Gilbert Adrian. Laughon was also the yearbook art director. While at first surprising that such a young woman would have assembled a collection of striking Phelps leather accessories, clearly Seymour Laughon was precociously fashionable.

Since Phelps Associates started with a belt, the first object from the collection to consider is a fairly simple brown leather belt, accession number V.95.46.1 (Fig. 3.3). It has a rectangular metal buckle, two prongs, a metal end tip on the opposite end of the belt, and metal grommets.[10] This belt is very similar to the two belts in the author's collection (Fig. 1.1). The belt is edged with two indented lines of an edge marker. The buckle end is turned over and secured with a single row of stitching.[11] The fastening end is finished with a metal piece 2½" high and has three columns/sets of two ⅝" grommets each in which the buckle's metal prongs could be inserted. Finishing of the leather is rubbed away on either side

SEYMOUR RIVES LAUGHON

(Two Years)

Usher: Betty Wellford

If it's talent you want, we've got it; if it's style you're seeking, you've come to the right place; if you're on the look-out for brains, looks, and a "bang"-up personality, tinged with a quality known as fey, we have your answer. It's all summed up in five-feet-four of terrific gal. Seymour is constantly mired in huge sheets of paper covered with creations which would make Adrian sit up and take notice. We have only one choice given us, to predict a star-spangled future for one of the best.

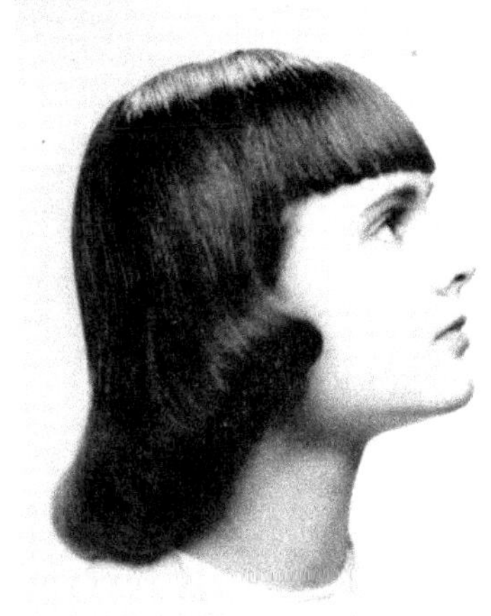

Fig. 3.2. Seymour Rives Laughon Rennolds's senior yearbook photo. (Stuart Hall School. *Inlook* Yearbook [*McClure,* 1947].)

Fig. 3.3. Phelps, belt, leather, metal, circa 1947. (Valentine Richmond History Center. Gift of Caroline Rennolds Milbank, Amelie Rives Rennolds, and Margaret Rennolds Chace, in memory of Seymour Laughon Rennolds. V.95.46.1.)

of the middle grommets, creating a worn area in the shape of the rectangular buckle. This wear pattern indicates that the belt was used and usually worn fastened to the center grommets. From this middle grommet set to the end of the belt is 26¼", suggesting the wearer's approximate waist size.

The Phelpses complimented their belt offerings with bags that could hang from the belts, much as soldiers' equipment might include cartridge boxes or holsters suspended from a waist belt. One of these bags (V.95.46.08) is black leather, with a prominent American eagle metal ornament and a holster-like shape (Fig. 3.4).[12] The bag's back flap is a separate parallelogram, and the bag's leather is fine grained and smooth, perhaps calfskin. The Valentine database estimates the date of this bag as circa 1945. However, I believe it might be earlier, as there is no belt-buckle trademark symbol (widely implemented in Phelps accessories by 1945), the shape is simple, and the construction is simple, with no piping—the leather is simply folded and stitched. There is no separate piece of leather to create the gusset—the front flap is simply folded in. The lower edge is stitched ⅛" from the bottom and extends all the way across the bag. The brass eagle ornament is similar to others—for example, the author's bag (Fig. I.1)—and measures 4½" high by 4¼" wide at the widest points. The top edge of the bag is decorated with two lines pressed into the leather with an edge marker.

The top of the bag has two tabs for suspending the bag from a belt. The tabs are 4½" overall length, with 2½" of this extending above the bag and 1¼" of this an active, usable loop. The Phelps belt included in the Valentine gift would have been too wide for this bag to attach directly. The two flaps curve inward toward each other and this shape, combined with the narrow amount of active loop, suggests that this bag would have hung from metal chains dangling on a belt. (See, for example, the chains hanging on the Louise Dahl-Wolfe belt in the MFIT collection, Figs. 2.2, 2.4, 2.5).

A second belt bag (V.95.46.09) is black leather with a brass leaf decoration; it is rounded and pouchlike, with self-piping and stitched in black thread to match the leather (Fig. 3.5).[13] The front flap is decorated with two brass leaves, 2¼" high by 1¾" wide. There are no fasteners visible on the flap's reverse side, so the bag is lined, unlike some Phelps designs, which have visible metal fasteners. There are wear patterns along the curves of the lower front, heaviest on the edges. The bag is meant to hang from a belt by a single, heavy tab, 7⅛" in overall length, with a line of stitching on the lower two inches to connect it to the rest of the bag. This stitch line runs parallel to the sides and bottom

Fig. 3.4. Phelps, belt bag, leather, metal, circa 1944. (Valentine Richmond History Center. Gift of Caroline Rennolds Milbank, Amelie Rives Rennolds, and Margaret Rennolds Chace, in memory of Seymour Laughon Rennolds. V.95.46.08.)

Fig. 3.5. Phelps, belt bag, leather, metal, circa 1945. (Valentine Richmond History Center. Gift of Caroline Rennolds Milbank, Amelie Rives Rennolds, and Margaret Rennolds Chace, in memory of Seymour Laughon Rennolds. V.95.46.09.)

Fig. 3.6. Phelps, shoulder bag, leather, metal, circa 1945. (Valentine Richmond History Center. Gift of Caroline Rennolds Milbank, Amelie Rives Rennolds, and Margaret Rennolds Chace, in memory of Seymour Laughon Rennolds. V.95.46.10.)

of the tab. The actual available active loop is approximately 5", which would allow for the belt bag to hang directly on a fairly wide belt. The bag's 6⅜" front flap opens to reveal a metal Phelps trademark belt-buckle symbol on the center front of the pouch, and the metal has created an impression on the flap's reverse side.[14]

Finally, the collection includes a rounded shoulder bag (V.95.46.10) with an interior leather drawstring system (Fig. 3.6).[15] Its exterior flap closure is decorated with a metal shell that is 1⅛" high by 2⅞" wide. This flap opens to reveal the drawstring system, in which a leather drawstring is threaded through a series of ten ¾" metal grommets, organized in pairs along the bag's inside top edge. A metal Phelps trademark belt-buckle symbol is on the center front of the bag, just below the grommets. The bag's smooth leather interior has two patch pockets on the side closest to the wearer's body.

The shoulder strap is connected to the rest of the bag with two round, metal rings. The leather shoulder strap is approximately 17½" long, and 1" wide, with decorative stitching on either side. Its metal buckle, 2⅜" high by 1¾" wide, would have allowed the strap to be adjusted. On the bag's proper right side, there are some conservation issues, as the bag has come unstitched and it is possible now to see the piece of leather that was folded over, covering

Fig. 3.7. Detail of shoulder bag with shell ornament, showing strap damage. Phelps, shoulder bag, leather, metal, circa 1945. (Valentine Richmond History Center. Gift of Caroline Rennolds Milbank, Amelie Rives Rennolds, and Margaret Rennolds Chace, in memory of Seymour Laughon Rennolds. V.95.46.10.)

leather of the other side (Fig. 3.7). The shoulder strap is two thicknesses of leather, increasing its strength.

Thanks to Caroline Rennolds Milbank's generous sharing of her memories, I also learned about what is missing from the Seymour Laughon Rennolds collection at the Valentine: a Phelps shoulder bag with a metal eagle ornament. Milbank recalls that her mother owned one of these shoulder bags, now lost. She also stated that the antique eagle became detached from the bag. It is worth considering the implications of this known absence: some donors of Phelps accessories might have owned additional Phelps pieces that museums did not acquire; some Phelps objects might have lost parts; some Phelps pieces might be unidentified because of having lost metal parts such as trademark symbols or decorative elements.

The leather goods in the Valentine's collection illustrate the Phelpses' creativity in dealing with shortages and exploring handsfree shapes. World War II brought shortages in both metal and leather, key elements of handbag manufacture. At the same time, women busy with war work and carrying their own packages needed handsfree convenience in their bag designs. Phelps leather goods, such as those in the Valentine's collection, were well adapted to deal with the materials shortages and to suit wartime lifestyle needs.

Rationing Regulations

The Phelpses' emphasis on craft and making as a design philosophy helped Phelps Associates rise to the challenges that World War II rationing and shortages presented, particularly to the handbag business. Boosters throughout the fashion industry encouraged designers and consumers to view these wartime difficulties as a spur to creativity. In February 1942, *Vogue* editor in chief Edna Woolman Chase declared to fashion insiders who were members of the Fashion Group, "Fashions do not die because of wars; many of the best of them are created by war's necessities."[16] Similarly, *Harper's Bazaar* brought this view to its readers in March 1942, in an article inspired by a speech H. Stanley Marcus, of Neiman Marcus gave to the Fashion Group in his new capacity as apparel consultant to the War Production Board's Textile, Clothing, and Leather Division. Marcus predicted: "The Government shortages will stimulate American ingenuity to real creation."[17] Phelps Associates accessories represent a convergence of many factors, including the Phelpses' design philosophy with the necessities brought about by the war. Whether the war spurred them to creative solutions they would not have considered otherwise or—more likely—simply engendered a receptive atmosphere in the fashion industry for what the Phelpses wanted to make, the fledgling Phelps Associates label became a critical success during the war. Phelps became best-known for beginning the US fashion for shoulder bags, in forms inspired by American military history.

Shortages: Metal

One of the first issues the war presented to the American handbag industry was a metal shortage, as new metal materials were funneled directly into the war effort. While scarcity of chemicals, such as dyestuffs, had been a major concern in the United States during World War I, sociologist Winifred Raushenbush informed consumers in World War II, "Much more severe than any of the chemical shortages is the shortage of metal."[18] Ruth Kerr, style analyst for the Calf Tanners' Association, told the Fashion Group in 1943, "Handbags are not controlled by government directives, except those which use slide fasteners, metal frames, etc., and the diversion of leathers for the war effort"; however, these directives would have affected many handbag producers.[19] At the onset of the war, many women's handbags were designed to incorporate metal frames. For example, in 1939, *Vogue* featured a full-page advertisement for Evans Fitted Handbags, which featured interior fittings that matched the bags' metal frames: "You'll find them in the better stores, in the smartest of leathers, their sleek lines clasped with Evans frames" (Fig. 3.8).[20] Evans's competitor Rolfs LaGarde Originals also frequently advertised their handbags in *Vogue*, such as one in calfskin with a "polished gold ornamental frame."[21] Without metal, many mass-market handbag manufacturers were at a loss for design direction.[22] Phelps Associates had begun making bags from the perspective of leathercraft, and so they were already designing soft, unframed bags that did not depend on a metal frame for their shape, and with the only metal hardware in rings, occasional fasteners, and decoration. The shoulder bag and the two belt bags in the Valentine Rennolds collection demonstrate this type of construction, and the shoulder bag in particular shows the softer shape (Fig. 3.1).

Fig. 3.8. Evans handbag, built on a metal frame. Evans Case Company, bag, fabric, metal, circa 1930s–1950s. (Author's collection. Photograph by the author.)

For decorative elements, Phelps recycled vintage and antique metal pieces. In addition to the horse harness elements discussed in chapter 2, the Phelpses were drawn to military insignia, which they sourced from antique, junk, and military-surplus stores. Phelps Associates were ahead of their time in the concept of upcycling of vintage metal. This seems to have been done for both design and practical reasons—antique and vintage metal pieces supported the historicism of their designs, and on a practical level, recycling was a way to deal with metal shortages.

William and Elizabeth Phelps's choice to work with repurposed metal drew positive media attention and was one of the reasons for their critical acclaim during World War II. *Harper's Bazaar* noted in an early (1942) article on Phelps Associates that they were using "old silver shell buckles" as well as repurposed horse harness ornaments.[23] Seymour Laughon Rennolds's shoulder bag shows an example of a repurposed shell-shape decoration (Fig. 3.6).

A 1943 *Women's Wear Daily* article about Phelps bags being sold through the Mark Cross retail store in New York City noted that many of the metal ornaments were authentic—implying that at that point many, but not all, were actual historical pieces. "Cross permits selection of individual ornaments for many bags—some of them are enormous size, six inches or so across."[24] These large ornaments mentioned in the *Women's Wear* article included the large American bald eagle details such as those on the author's eagle shoulder bag or the Rennolds belt bag (both of these eagles are 4¼" wide) (Figs. I.1, 3.4). *Women's Wear* also described some of the smaller ornaments as "brass or silver crests and insignia from the blinkers of carriage horses, buffed to give a gleaming finish."[25] Ready-to-wear bag customers purchasing through Mark Cross were able to personalize their bags with a choice of metal ornament that was then applied, adding an appealing level of customization. By the following year, Phelps Associates seem to have moved to using only vintage metal, and they were praised at the Coty Awards for their "creative work in the use of metals for accessories. During the war they are restricting this to the reconstruction of antique metals, such as regimental and civilian guard insignia and heraldic crests."[26] In an article on their Coty Awards win, *Women's Wear Daily* reported that Phelps Associates sourced insignia in harness shops and secondhand shops.[27] In 1945, *Life* magazine informed readers that Phelps Associates had a dedicated traveling shopper who went to pawn shops, antique stores, junk shops, et cetera, to collect "old medals, bits of harness, regimental insignia, drawer pulls" for decorations.[28] It appears that by this point even vintage metalwork was becoming scarce, and by November the Phelpses were encouraging customers to supply their own vintage insignia.[29]

A 1945 *Fortune* magazine article of states that an important local source for Phelps Associates' vintage metalwork was Francis Bannerman Sons, at 501 Broadway in New York (Fig. 3.9).[30] The five-story building housed Francis Bannerman Sons' army and navy surplus store as well as Bannerman's Military Museum.[31] In 1955, the company's own materials described the store as "the original Army Navy Goods House. We own all the buildings and warehouses we use including Bannerman Island in the Hudson River near West Point. We have been over 57 years on Broadway."[32] Francis Bannerman Sons were just as emphatic in describing what they were not: "We do not now and never did handle 'sporting goods.' We do not have any sporting rifles and no ammunition for them."[33] The store sold vintage and antique military goods from all over the world, including firearms, shields, swords, knives, as well as other military goods—including regimental ornaments, medals, and horse tack. Many items from their extensive stock were on display in their showroom, a tight and eclectic jumble of tall shelves, glass showcases with narrow aisles in between, and flags hanging near the ceiling (Fig. 3.10).

Fig. 3.9. Exterior of Francis Bannerman Sons, from *Francis Bannerman Sons, 84th Anniversary January 1949 De Luxe Edition Military Goods Catalogue* (Francis Bannerman Sons, 1949), 108. (Author's collection.)

Francis Bannerman Sons also sold through bound mail order catalogues, supplemented with regular flyers. The January 1949 "De Luxe Edition" of the bound catalogue ("$3.50, mailed in the United States) was 286 pages, plus appendixes, and contained short reference articles, historical illustrations, and

Fig. 3.10. Francis Bannerman Sons showroom interior, from *Francis Bannerman Sons, January 1955 Circular,* 1. (Patricia D. Klingenstein Library, New-York Historical Society Museum and Library.)

patent sketches, as well as the inventory currently for sale.[34] The company informed catalog customers, "TERMS are the same as we have to comply with when purchasing Government Auction Goods, viz. FIRST YOU PAY, THEN YOU GET THE GOODS."[35]

Because they bought some items at government auction, Francis Bannerman Sons often had bulk quantities of products and resold them at bulk prices. For example, immediately after World War II, ten thousand black halters for horses were available for ninety cents each, or nine dollars per dozen.[36] In the 1950s, the store sold "BRASS DEE RINGS, as used on harness, bags, and shoulder slings. Width, ¾ inch. Price, 10 cents each; $1.00 per dozen" (Fig. 3.11).[37] Phelps Associates probably took advantage of some of these bulk buys. The quintessential Phelps eagle shoulder bag from the author's collection, the first object in the Introduction, incorporates ⅞" dee rings (Fig. 3.12).

The metalwork ornaments that the Phelpses used employed many motifs, but because they were often from vintage American military insignia, Americana motifs predominated. Phelps Associates were not the first accessory designers to use motifs such as the bald eagle—for example, John-Fredericks produced an American bald eagle motif brooch in 1939.[38] However, Phelpses' systematic design program incorporating Americana motifs on bags and belts based on historical forms, and creating in a workshop that referenced historical production methods associated the Phelps name with historical American craftsmanship in a manner that appealed to consumers and went beyond other designers' Americana gestures—such as a red, white, and blue color palette.[39]

The Phelpses found that more common Americana pieces such as firemen's shields and state crests were just as popular with clients as rarer British regi-

SADDLERY 247

10444. U. S. ARMY PICKET PIN. With double swivels and adjustable shakle, steel forged, with solid hammer head. Full length 18 inches, diameter ⅝ inch, weight 21 ounces. Made at the Government Rock Island Arsenal, 1903. A necessity on every farm. Price, 45 cents.

10032. U. S. A. SNAP HOOKS. 14,000 IN STOCK. Loop takes ¾-inch strap. Steel springs. From the Rock Island Arsenal auction. Price, 5 cents each; 30 cents per dozen; $2.85 per gross.

A. 3,000 NEW U. S. CAVALRY TIE STRAPS; best bridle leather, hand sewed; full length, 25 inches; with snap hook, with brass link for adjusting length. All horsemen should have this handy strap. Price, 18 cents.

10204. SADDLERY HARDWARE FROM U. S. GOVERNMENT ROCK ISLAND AUCTION—

24684. Roller buckles 1½ inches, new, doz. 35 cents, gross $3.00.

1957. Roller buckles 1⅛ inches, new, doz. 30 cents, gross $2.40.

59525. Roller buckles 1 inch, new, doz. 25 cents, gross $2.00.

26936. Roller buckles ¾ inch, new, doz. 20 cents, gross $1.50.

72000. Roller buckles ⅝ inch, new, doz. 15 cents, gross $1.20.

31392. Bar buckles ¾ inch, new, doz. 20 cents, gross $1.50.

1330B. U. S. CAVALRY CARBINE BOOTS, old regulation, black leather with 2 straps for attaching to saddle. Made for use with Remington and Springfield cal. 45 single shot carbines. Will NOT hold bolt action guns. Second hand, much used, need oiling and some minor repairs. Length 31 inches, mouth 7 inches, tip 2 inches, all outside measurements. Price, 75 cents each, postage extra.

10200. U. S. A. HARNESS RINGS. Size 1¾-inch, 9,000 in stock. New blue steel color. Price, 25 cents per dozen.

10024. U. S. ARMY MODEL 92 BIT. Guaranteed forged steel, not to be compared with the cheap malleable cast iron style usually for sale. These bits are offered in cleaned, serviceable order. Used; our bargain price, 40 cents each.

We have now no complete sets of harness, no black or russet leather bridles.

U. S. CIVIL WAR CAVALRY BITS, without brass U. S. side pieces, old bits, regalvanized like new. Price, 30 cents each, $3.00 per dozen.

Set of U. S. ARMY GAUGES for Officer's Bits, made of fine polished steel; complete set gauges with sample bit in mahogany case, lined with velvet; size 20 inches long, 11 inches wide, 3 inches deep. Price, $5.00.

S-I HORSE COLLARS, leather, snap bottom, open throat, wood hames and short tugs attached. Heavy duty. Used. Price, $5.00 each.

ARMY COVERED STIRRUPS. Black leather, much used, in fair condition, need cleaning and oiling. Price, $1.75 per pair.

10286.—STEEL TRACE CLIPS. From Rock Island Arsenal for connecting chain to the trace; new, four rivet holes. Price, 18 cents each.

1678. — U. S. A. CURB STRAPS. Late regulation, new, in black leather, ⅝ in. wide, full length 18 in., with buckles and keepers; doubled for use as curb strap, useful for any purpose requiring good leather strap. Price, 8 cents each.

36-C-105. LOT U. S. A. COMBINATION FARRIER'S HAMMERS-TENT-PICKET PINS. Made of iron in one piece, with hammer head claw, pointed tip to drive in ground to picket horses, or may be used as pin for tent ropes. Weighs 2½ pounds. A very handy camp instrument. Price, 26 cents each.

17A. CARBINE SWIVEL SNAPS, for use on tethers, halters, etc., new, rusty, 20c. each or $2.00 for 12.

10294.—CIVIL WAR BRIDOON BIT. Kind used by Union Cavalry on watering bridle, made of forged steel with rings for reins and three link chain toggles for hooking into the ring of the halter, connecting the halter with bridle. Called watering bridle from the fact that it was quickly attached to the halter, the soldiers using it when watering horses. 25 cents each.

U. S. CIVIL WAR CARBINE SOCKET, attached to the saddle strap to hold the cavalrymen's carbine; new. Relics of 1861 to 1865. Price, 15 cents each.

10293. U. S. GUNNER'S POUCH. With shoulder sling strap; fine soft new russet leather, hand sewed. Length of the pouch 10 inches, width 2½ inches. Shoulder sling 40 inches, ½ inch wide. Price, 35 cents.

10037. U. S. A. BRIDLE CURB CHAIN AND RUSSET STRAP. Made of non-corrosive white metal with army circle curb locking hooks, which lie flat against the horse's lower jaws. Price, 48 cents. Price of chain and hooks, without the leather strap, 25 cents.

BRASS DEE RINGS, as used on harness. Have sold many to bag makers for use with shoulder slings. Diameter ¾ inch. Price, 10 cents each.

10117. PAIR OLD SADDLE PISTOL HOLSTERS. Officers. Price, $4.50.

2417. 24 PAIRS OF ANTIQUE METAL STIRRUPS. With stirrup irons, ornamented swivel loops, length 18 inches, stirrups 3¼ inches. The stirrup rods have three ornamented brass bands. Will make fine decoration for den. Price, $1.75 each stirrup.

3. 2,700 new U. S. ARMY ROCK ISLAND ARSENAL-MADE HAIR CINCHES; dark colored horse hair; bronze cinch rings, with dark colored russet leather covered safes, stamped in each cinch "Rock Island Arsenal," with the initials of the Government inspecting officer. Hand stitched 4½-inch bronze ring, new, perfect goods, superior to any cinch usually made by saddle manufacturers. Width, 8 inches. Price, $2.00.

800 NEW U. S. ARMY HAMES STRAPS, 23 inches long, 2¼ inches wide; best quality bridle leather. Price, 25 cents each.

Fig. 3.11. Dee rings shown in lower left corner of Bannerman catalog page. *Francis Bannerman Sons, 84th Anniversary January 1949 De Luxe Edition Military Goods Catalogue* (Francis Bannerman Sons, 1949), 247. (Author's collection.)

mental buckles.[40] Francis Bannerman Sons was a potential source for both domestic and international ornaments. For example, a January 1947 store circular included both a "British Army Irish Regiment Ornament of Harp, in Bronze," available for twenty cents each, and "United States Civil War Soldiers' Belt Buckles; brass, lead backs; serviceable order; fine relic. Price $1.50 each."[41] The Phelpses used similar ornaments and buckles, and the historical significance was a part of the editorial coverage of the accessories in fashion print media. A *Harper's Bazaar* article, "Add a Belt," devoted a full-page photograph to a blouse and slacks ensemble punctuated with a Phelps belt with vintage military buckle. "The stunning leather belt . . . has a bold brass buckle, relic of the Washington Greys. About $13" (Fig. 3.13).[42] In 1949, Francis Bannerman Sons sold a similar Washington Greys buckle for $3.75 (Fig. 3.14). The store kept its supply of badges, belt buckles, and other ornaments in labeled storage boxes set into vast shelving units. Many of these boxes displayed samples of the contents for easy reference.[43] In a 1949 catalog photo, the type of brass eagle used for Fig. I.1, as well as the Rennolds belt bag (Fig. 3.4), can be seen on the outside of a storage box labeled "U.S. Buckles" (Fig. 3.15).

Fig. 3.12. Detail of Fig. I.1., eagle shoulder bag, reverse, showing dee ring (⅞"). Phelps Associates, shoulder bag, circa 1945, leather, metal. (Author's collection. Photograph by the author.)

Fashion journalist Virginia Pope remarked of the Phelpses: "Eagles, crests, and belt buckles dating to Revolutionary days are frequently used for ornamentations by these artists to give individual interest to their models."[44] Here, Pope calls the Phelps artists and emphasizes the individuality of each bag as evidence that they are artists. *Women's Wear Daily* listed motifs as "knight's Heads, many American eagle motifs, Engineer's insignia, National or State Guard emblems."[45] "Engineer's Devices" is marked on another storage box on the shelves pictured in Fig. 3.15. Other metalwork pointed to its origin in

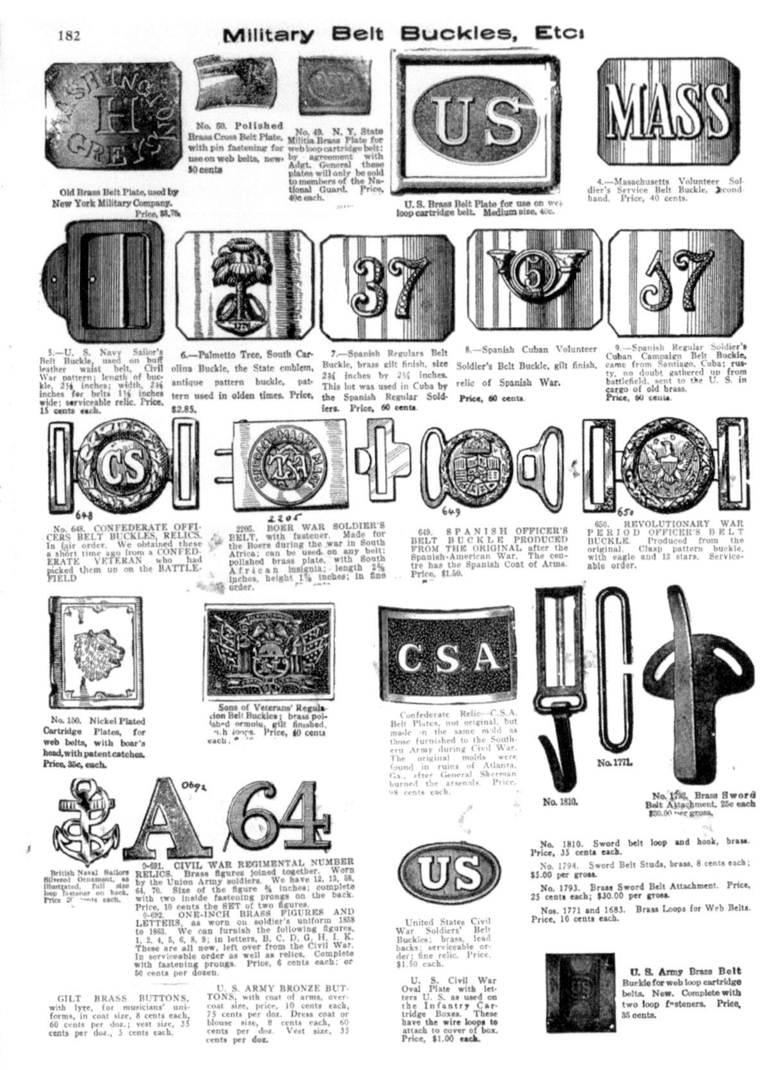

182

Military Belt Buckles, Etc.

Old Brass Belt Plate, used by New York Military Company. Price, $8.75.

No. 50. Polished Brass Cross Belt Plate, with pin fastening for use on web belts, new. 50 cents

No. 49. N. Y. State Militia Brass Plate for web loop cartridge belt; by agreement with Adgt. General these plates will only be sold to members of the National Guard. Price, 40c each.

U. S. Brass Belt Plate for use on web loop cartridge belt. Medium size, 40c.

4.—Massachusetts Volunteer Soldier's Service Belt Buckle, second hand. Price, 40 cents.

5.—U. S. Navy Sailor's Belt Buckle, used on buff leather waist belt, Civil War pattern; length of buckle, 2¼ inches; width, 2¼ inches for belts 1½ inches wide; serviceable relic. Price, 15 cents each.

6.—Palmetto Tree, South Carolina Buckle, the State emblem, antique pattern buckle, pattern used in olden times. Price, $2.85.

7.—Spanish Regulars Belt Buckle, brass gilt finish, size 2¼ inches by 2¼ inches. This lot was used in Cuba by the Spanish Regular Soldiers. Price, 60 cents.

8.—Spanish Cuban Volunteer Soldier's Belt Buckle, gilt finish, relic of Spanish War. Price, 60 cents.

9.—Spanish Regular Soldier's Cuban Campaign Belt Buckle, came from Santiago, Cuba; rusty, no doubt gathered up from battlefield, sent to the U. S. in cargo of old brass. Price, 60 cents.

648

No. 648. CONFEDERATE OFFICERS BELT BUCKLES, RELICS. In fair order. We obtained these a short time ago from a CONFEDERATE VETERAN who had picked them up on the BATTLEFIELD

2205

2205. BOER WAR SOLDIER'S BELT, with fastener. Made for the Boers during the war in South Africa; can be used on any belt; polished brass plate, with South African insignia; length 2⅝ inches, height 1⅞ inches; in fine order.

649

649. SPANISH OFFICER'S BELT BUCKLE PRODUCED FROM THE ORIGINAL after the Spanish-American War. The centre has the Spanish Coat of Arms. Price, $1.50.

650

650. REVOLUTIONARY WAR PERIOD OFFICER'S BELT BUCKLE. Produced from the original. Clasp pattern buckle, with eagle and 13 stars. Serviceable order.

No. 150. Nickel Plated Cartridge Plates, for web belts, with boar's head, with patent catches. Price, 35c, each.

Sons of Veterans' Regulation Belt Buckles; brass polished ormolu, gilt finished, with loops. Price, 40 cents each.

Confederate Relic—C.S.A. Belt Plates, not original, but made in the same mold as those furnished to the Southern Army during Civil War. The original molds were found in ruins of Atlanta, Ga., after General Sherman burned the arsenals. Price, 98 cents each.

No. 1771.

No. 1810.

No. 1793. Brass Sword Belt Attachment, 25c each $30.00 per gross.

0692

British Naval Sailors Silvered Ornament, as illustrated, full size loop fastener on back. Price 20 cents each.

0-691. CIVIL WAR REGIMENTAL NUMBER RELICS. Brass figures joined together. Worn by the Union Army soldiers. We have 12, 13, 58, 64, 70. Size of the figure ¾ inches; complete with two inside fastening prongs on the back. Price, 10 cents the SET of two figures.

0-692. ONE-INCH BRASS FIGURES AND LETTERS, as worn on soldier's uniform 1858 to 1863. We can furnish the following figures, 1, 2, 4, 5, 6, 8, 9; in letters, B, C, D, G, H, I, K. These are all new, left over from the Civil War. In serviceable order as well as relics. Complete with fastening prongs. Price, 6 cents each; or 50 cents per dozen.

GILT BRASS BUTTONS, with lyre, for musicians' uniforms, in coat size, 8 cents each, 60 cents per doz.; vest size, 35 cents per doz., 5 cents each.

U. S. ARMY BRONZE BUTTONS, with coat of arms, overcoat size, price, 10 cents each, 75 cents per doz. Dress coat or blouse size, 8 cents each, 60 cents per doz. Vest size, 35 cents per doz.

United States Civil War Soldiers' Belt Buckles; brass, lead backs; serviceable order; fine relic. Price, $1.50 each.

U. S. Civil War Oval Plate with letters U. S. as used on the Infantry Cartridge Boxes. These have the wire loops to attach to cover of box. Price, $1.00 each.

No. 1810. Sword belt loop and hook, brass. Price, 35 cents each.

No. 1794. Sword Belt Studs, brass, 8 cents each; $5.00 per gross.

No. 1793. Brass Sword Belt Attachment. Price, 25 cents each; $30.00 per gross.

Nos. 1771 and 1683. Brass Loops for Web Belts. Price, 10 cents each.

U. S. Army Brass Belt Buckle for web loop cartridge belts. New. Complete with two loop fasteners. Price, 35 cents.

Top: **Fig. 3.13.** Model wearing a Phelps belt with a Washington Greys belt buckle. "Add a Belt," *Harper's Bazaar,* November 1943, "Junior Bazaar" section, 104. (*Harper's BAZAAR,* Hearst Magazine Media, Inc. Photograph by Anne Simpkins.)

Right: **Fig. 3.14.** Francis Bannerman Sons catalog page, showing Washington Greys belt buckle in upper left corner. *Francis Bannerman Sons, 84th Anniversary January 1949 De Luxe Edition Military Goods Catalogue* (Francis Bannerman Sons, 1949), 182. (Author's collection.)

Above: **Fig. 3.15.** Storage boxes at Francis Bannerman Sons, showing various metal ornaments of the type Phelps used, including the brass American eagle. *Francis Bannerman Sons, 84th Anniversary January 1949 De Luxe Edition Military Goods Catalogue* (Francis Bannerman Sons, 1949), 108. (Author's collection.)

horse harness, such as a belt "with genuine old sleigh bells and a brass harness buckle, on cowhide."[46]

The Phelpses' interest in unique metalwork was immortalized in the trademark they had adopted by 1945. *Women's Wear Daily* reported early in 1944, "So devoted are the Phelps to unusual and authentic buckle and metal ornament ideas that they have worked out their own trademark, a shield-shaped version of a buckle, which eventually will appear in one form or another on every piece they create" (Fig. 3.16).[47] This buckle also probably references their origin story, of the wide belt that launched their leatherworking careers. Over the course of 1944, the Phelpses applied for and received three trademarks for Phelps Associates: one for bags and two for belts. The trademark for bags was granted to "Phelps Associates, New York, N.Y. Handbags and haversacks. 407, 823; June 27; Serial No. 467,465; published Apr. 18, 1944. Class 3." They received the "Garment belts" trademarks on June 27 and October 17, 1944.[48] The shield shape is found after this date in forms from a metal ornament on bags to a stamped impression in the belts' leather to a woven tag inside later sportswear. A metal Phelps trademark ornament inside a leather bag with fern motif in the collection of the Costume Institute C.I.68.51.1 allowed me to give a positive identification of this bag, previously listed in the catalogue as "attributed to Phelps" (Fig. 2.26).

Fig. 3.16. Detail of Fig. I.1., eagle shoulder bag, interior pocket, showing oxidized metal Phelps trademark symbol in the shape of a belt buckle. Phelps Associates, shoulder bag, circa 1945, leather, metal. (Author's collection. Photograph by the author.)

Modern and Historicizing Shapes of Phelps Bags

The types of twentieth-century main garments that fashion historians usually class as "modern" are those that hang from the shoulder and rely on the body underneath for their shape.[49] Instead of shaping the body through restricting or exaggerating elements in the garment and undergarments, modern garments require that the body itself be molded through exercise and diet to reach the ideal.[50] Similarly, Phelps bags were modern in that they did not rely on a metal frame structure to give them form. Many bag styles were soft and pouchlike, shaping themselves to their contents. Others were flat envelopes of folded leather.

While Phelps bags were modern, at the same time they were historicizing: they drew on forms from the past, many from American history. In the first decades of the twentieth century, American designers in various fields pondered what might constitute uniquely American design and what an American design vocabulary might be. Americana, such as the historical forms Phelps Associates used, was one proposed answer. As scholars including dress and textile historians Lauren D. Whitley and Ann Marguerite Tartsinis have demonstrated, during World War I, the American design community's desire for an American design vocabulary was largely focused on museum-based research of nonwestern objects, particularly ethnographic pieces from the Americas.[51] Individuals such as textile scholar and Fairchild journalist M. D. C. Crawford (1882–1949) continued to promote cooperation between the fashion industry and museums into the Second World War period, Crawford asserting: "Museums cannot create style; they can only offer inspiration to those who do create style."[52] During World War II, the American fashion industry's interest in museum research was in not only indigenous arts of the Americas but also US history. William Phelps's 1930s woodwork in forms influenced by historical American design, as well as his interest in traditional craft practices more generally, prepared the Phelpses to join in this movement in American fashion of the 1940s. Many of Phelps Associates' initial bag shapes were influenced by American menswear and military uniforms of the past.

Elizabeth Phelps would later recall that she and William first created shoulder bags in 1941. "My husband didn't like to see me clutching my pocketbook

Fig. 3.17. Cartridge box, leather, wood, circa 1775. 1976.05.003. (Fraunces Tavern® Museum, New York City.)

20 Handbags Women's Wear Daily, Friday, May 7, 1943

Historic Sources Inspire Bags

MONOCRAFT Fashion COLUMN

Mark Cross Presents Collection Stemming From U. S. Revolution

"A Tremendous Fabric Season for Fall," Forecasts Volume Buyer

Noah Bag Re-Vamped

Documentary Types

Saddlery Trims

STITCHED EFFECTS PROVE GOOD IN PATENT

Plastic Bags Selling In Summer Colors

Muff Bag and Shoulder Strap Are Style Leaders

Wood Frames Sell Best At High Price Levels

SYDNEY BAG CO. NEW FIRM SUCCEEDING MAURICE

American History as Resource For Modern Handbag Design

FAILLE 'N LEATHER . . .

MOM, MOTHER, MATER

BIG BLACK FELT . . .

MONOCRAFT INITIALS

Ration Book Cover Sells

Failles Register in Better Grade Bags Selling in Springfield Shops

How . . .

MABEN Bags 14 EAST 32nd ST. NEW YORK

Handbag Buyer

LADIES' HANDBAGS SAMPLE MAKER & PRODUCTION MAN

SELTZER & SELTZER, Inc.

Starlight FABRICS, INC. HEADQUARTERS FOR BENGALINES MADE OF RAYON-AND-COTTON

Fig. 3.18. Phelps shooting pouch, 1943. "Historic Sources Inspire Bags," *Women's Wear Daily*, 7 May 1943, 20. (Copyright © 1943, WWD. All rights reserved.)

. . . and so he developed a shoulder bag. We made it in cowhide, and, later on, in suede and fur."[53] One of the most common Phelps bag shapes among extant accessories is the shoulder bag known as the postman's bag, satchel, or dispatch bag (Fig. I.1).[54] A 1945 *Life* article called it a "postman's bag of cowhide has front pocket with American eagle."[55] Hung from the shoulder rather than the waist, this folded envelope shape is also very similar to that of a cartridge case, such as one on display at the Fraunces Tavern Museum (Fig. 3.17). While the postman bags generally only offered a small amount of interior space, Elizabeth Phelps advanced the idea that a small bag could hold more when equipped with a matching cigarette case, makeup kit, and change purse.[56] Presumably a well-organized bag could hold more than one that was a jumble of items, but it is difficult to imagine how this would have worked in practice, with the smaller interior bags each taking up some of the storage space.

Several other extant bags fit within the category of rounded pouch, or "shooting pouch." A "Shooting Pouch" illustrated in *Women's Wear Daily* was "designed to carry packages as well as serving as a handbag . . . with a drawstring front, a decorative motif from harness blinkers; it is done in sturdy goat" (Fig. 3.18).[57] The Valentine's shoulder bag with shell ornament fits into this group (Fig. 3.6). *Harper's* March 1943 issue shows a red Morocco pouch similar in form to that of the Valentine's bag, but with a star insignia.[58]

Some Phelps shoulder bags were cut in extremely large sizes, although I have not seen any extant examples in museum collections. These were termed *hunting bags* or *parachute bags*. *The New York Times* reported in October 1945 that Phelps Associates were offering a "Polish hunting bag": "The pouch of suede is on a drawstring; the top, of polished leather, fits snugly over the opening. A wide piece of suede fits over the shoulder."[59] A bag shaped similarly to the Polish hunting bag, but without the cover, was described in the November 19, 1945, issue of *Life:*

"Parachute bag of crushable shoe-calf leather is biggest in Phelps line."[60] According to Bernice Chambers of the Fashion Group, the trend for extremely large bags—"nearly like a weekend case"—was at its height in 1943: these "bags looked wonderful with boxy jackets and slim skirts and the bag had increased in size and importance as a daylong carryall for the busy woman."[61]

Phelps Associates also created waist or belt bags, such as those in the Valentine group, that allowed women to carry small necessities while keeping hands free (Figs. 3.4, 3.5). Even when the bags took shapes different from the cartridge case, the principle of hanging a bag from the waist for easy access is similar to that of belt-and-waist-bag combinations soldiers used for carrying ammunition.[62] In 1944, *The New York Times* described one of these bags: "Medieval-inspired pouch bag of polished leather worn on narrow belt and attached to wider belt by a metal clip."[63] *Life* showed two pouch-shaped belt bags and explained the appropriate time of day for wearing them. There was a daywear belt bag of light calfskin and dark buckskin and then a green suede belt-pouch bag with fireman's badge insignia for evening. The *Life* journalist warned the reader, "Only the slim-waisted should wear belt-bags like this."[64] There is no evidence that the Phelpses would have restricted their products to women with certain figure types, and in fact in 1951 they would offer ready-to-wear sportswear in extended sizes, 18 to 44, at the request of retailer Altman's.[65]

From shoulder-slung bags, such as postman's bags and shooting pouches, to belt bags hung from the wearer's waist, Phelps Associates crafted bags in practical forms that had historically been carried by men. These were helpful for American women in wartime, but the new fashions also required new ways of managing one's ensemble.

Techniques of the Body

Phelps Associates' frameless bags appealed to women for utilitarian and aesthetic reasons. Shoulder bags without metal frames also allowed and required American women of the 1940s to interact with their bags in new ways. Sociologist Marcel Mauss's ideas about "techniques of the body" help to analyze this.[66] Mauss defined *body techniques* as "the ways in which, from society to society, men [humans] know how to use their bodies." Mauss acknowledged that the ways people use their bodies are both consciously and unconsciously learned "physio-psycho-sociological assemblages of series of actions," and this is true of activities ranging from giving birth to sleeping, resting at table to walking or dancing.[67] Mauss gives an example of seeing hospital nurses in both the United States and France copying techniques of walking from Hollywood movies; this relates to art historian Anne Hollander's theory that fashion is a visual art that involves people more consciously internalizing and copying with their bodies the visual ideal of their time, including what was expressed through twentieth-century film.[68] Mauss also points out that there are learned techniques positioning the hands, whether walking or at rest. He contrasts English table manners of keeping elbows close to the body to French manners of holding elbows out or placing them on the table.[69]

During World War II, American women learned new techniques of the body, including walking and hand positioning, as handheld metal-framed bags gave way to frameless shoulder bags, such as those made by Phelps Associates. Bernice Chambers of the Fashion Group attributed the frameless Phelps design, along with the needs of female consumers doing war work and carrying packages for the increasing fashion for Phelps Associates' shoulder bags.[70] These new techniques of the body began as the Phelpses planned and designed their bags. A 1947 leatherworking guide for amateurs counseled, "Let us begin with the deciding factor in any design—the purpose and use of the article to be made. Has it to be roomy, or flat, large or small, to be carried under the arm, in the hand, or in the pocket?"[71] The techniques of the body required to wear or carry leather goods are built into the object from its conception.

The word *engineering* was used in both press releases and newspaper articles to describe the way Phelps Associates bags were designed to work on the body. A 1944 *Women's Wear Daily* article with the byline DLW, written about Phelps shoulder bags, noted that the designers "consider them an all-age fashion, excellent for travel, planes, general knockabout use. They work on engineering principles, believe the bag should be built to the figure so that as the wearer moves the bag fits snugly to her hip, just long enough so that her left hand can grip it conveniently. No hiking up the shoulder to hold the strap in place with Phelps bags."[72] As DLW makes clear, one of the techniques of the body required by a shoulder bag was the way to hold it on the shoulder: Would the wearer have to learn lift the shoulder slightly to hold the bag in place? Would she have to hold it in place with her hands, or just occasionally rest them on the bag? Phelps Associates used what Eleanor Lambert called "an entirely new kind of engineering to make the bag hang neatly and comfortably from the shoulder, they introduced not just a new tren[d] in handbags, but an entirely new article. Mrs. Phelps describes it as 'a change as sharp as the change from high to low shoe styles.'"[73] DLW's article on the Phelpses' shoulder bags makes it clear that one practical problem with a shoulder bag design is how to keep the bag from falling off the shoulder. DLW argues that the Phelpses designed the bag on "engineering principles" to ensure it conforms to the body—specifically the hip—rather than tending to fall off.[74] The *Brooklyn Eagle* echoed this, describing the Phelpses' "entirely new kind of engineering to make the bag hang neatly and comfortably from the shoulder."[75] While none of these sources describe the special engineering that helped keep Phelps bags on the shoulder, in the case of the Phelps postman-style bags it appears that William and Elizabeth Phelps placed the shoulder-strap attachment on the back rather than the sides of the bag, which might have helped push the bag against the wearer's body (see, e.g., Figs. I.1, I.3, I.4).

Many 1940s shoulder bags lacked the Phelps "engineering" and were difficult for the wearer to keep in place. For example, the relatively inexpensive mass-produced utility bags procured for WAACS by the Office of the Quartermaster General (OQMG) were not easy to maintain on the shoulder. These bags were originally designed to be worn crossbody-style, with the strap on the right shoulder and crossing the body so the bag rested on the left side. However, regulations were changed in June 1943 so that WAACs were required to wear the bag hanging straight down from the left shoulder. The bag slipped off the shoulder when worn this way, so the OQMG designed a device to keep it in place: "a small leather piece lined with brown cotton corduroy. The rough surface of the latter prevented any slipping of the shoulder strap, which was inserted through two slots cut in the device."[76] By November 1943, the regulations changed again, back to wearing the bag crossbody-style, due to concerns that the single-side wearing pattern would give the WACs bad posture.[77] As a result, the OQMG's device was no longer needed.[78] Photographs in the published memoir and archival scrapbook of WAC Clarice F. Pollard show the evolving regulations for the shoulder bags. In a May 1943 scrapbook photograph from the East Texas Research Center, Pollard poses outside of Neiman Marcus in Dallas, wearing the bag on her left shoulder (Fig. 3.19). Photographs from 1944, in contrast, show Pollard wearing her bag crossbody-style. A photo taken in Aberdeen, Washington, indicates that the bag's narrow strap was worn tucked into the notch of the jacket's lapel and under

Fig. 3.19. Auxiliary First Class Clarice M. Fortgang (later Pollard) wearing her shoulder bag on the left shoulder outside of Neiman Marcus in Dallas, Texas. May 27, 1943. (The East Texas Research Center, R. W. Steen Library, Stephen F. Austin State University, Nacogdoches, Texas.)

Fig. 3.20. WAAC Clarice (Pollard) Fortgang wearing her shoulder bag crossbody style, Aberdeen, Washington, 1944. (The East Texas Research Center, R. W. Steen Library, Stephen F. Austin State University, Nacogdoches, Texas.)

Fig. 3.21. WAAC Clarice (Pollard) Fortgang wearing her shoulder bag crossbody style, New Orleans, Louisiana, 1944. (The East Texas Research Center, R. W. Steen Library, Stephen F. Austin State University, Nacogdoches, Texas.)

the lower section of the collar, crossing the body on the chest (Fig. 3.20). A picture taken at New Orleans's Maison Blanche Department Store shows Pollard in a summer-weight uniform without a jacket, and the narrow bag strap sits mid-shoulder and crosses the body closer to the waist (Fig. 3.21).[79]

Writing later about the shoulder bags of the 1940s, Claire McCardell acknowledged the interplay between shoulder-bag design and the wearer's body. McCardell, thinking from the perspective of a main garment designer, added another layer to the interactions of objects and women's bodies. She suggested that main garment and accessory design worked together in alleviating this problem: the padding in the shoulders of dresses and suit jackets in the 1940s helped hold the bag in place (although I have not found any evidence that garment designers did this intentionally).[80] Presumably, this padding also made wearing a shoulder bag more comfortable, preventing the wearer from suffering red lines and broken blood vessels in the wake of a heavy shoulder strap. Ultimately, these objects of fashionable dress, from dress or suit to the accompanying Phelps bag, while requiring their own techniques of the body, also allowed women adopt new techniques, of the body such as elegantly using two hands to carry their own packages home, as stores curtailed delivery services due to the war effort.[81]

Whatever utilitarian or symbolic reasons women initially were drawn to Phelps Associates bags, they were also clearly part of the fashion cycle. Phelps bags followed a trajectory—from looking fresh and new in 1941, to being an accepted fashion in 1946, to no being longer attractive in the wake of Dior's 1947 New Look. Fashion historian James Laver argued in his 1945 second edition of *Taste and Fashion* that fashion "filters slowly down in the social scale. The actual garments which express it become less and less attractive, owing to the use of poorer material and because they are less skillfully made. A fashion, therefore, very quickly becomes dowdy . . . After a while it becomes worse than dowdy: it becomes hideous."[82] Laver's theory, while not universally applicable, does seem to have held true for the American fashion system of the 1940s. Early in the decade, newly fashionable Phelps shoulder bags represented high-quality material and handcraft, but eventually shoulder styles would be made at lower price points and the Phelps originals would become less fashionable.

Phelps leather bags suited the fashion for casual bags in the early 1940s. Ruth Kerr informed the Accessories Section of the Fashion Group in February 1941 in a discussion of "Casual Versus Dressy Fashions" that while some consumers still wanted more formal styles, the "new trend . . . is toward the casual feeling." Kerr noted that this trend took many manufacturers by surprise: "The handbag manufacturers are just beginning to get over the shock that tailored saddle bags and saddle colors are selling as well as the dressy types."[83] Thus, many handbag manufacturers of longer standing were unprepared for changes in metal availability, women's lifestyles, and fashionable bag silhouettes. Phelps Associates, though, offered products that met all of these criteria. Bernice Chambers noted that other manufacturers soon began to produce shoulder-bag styles, following Phelps Associates' lead.[84] By June 1942, Rachel Smith of Berkshire Knitting Mills told the Fashion Group to expect more of the bag types Phelps made: "We will have bicycle belts with attached purses, and over-the-shoulder bags, the newest of which have short straps and hang just over the armpit."[85]

In January 1946, Richard Koret of Phelps competitor Koret Handbags was quoted in the *Fashion Group Bulletin* declaring the fashionability of shoulder bags: "Shoulder strap bags have outgrown their utilitarian uses and definitely have a high-fashion place. . . . Drawstrings are in the same class."[86] On the front cover of this same issue of the bulletin, in an article about fashion editors' choices for spring looks, both *Harper's Bazaar* and *Vogue* representatives selected Phelps accessories. These ensembles were shown at the Fashion Group's Annual Meeting and Fashion Show at the Baltimore Hotel on November 26, 1945. For the *Harper's Bazaar* "Casual Country Look," a wide, tan leather Phelps belt was paired with garments by B. H. Wragge. *Vogue*'s "Daytime Look" consisted of "suit, hat, bag, all one color—'new penny'" including an oversized Phelps leather drawstring bag, worn slung over the arm of a Ben Gershel suit.[87] A photograph of the *Vogue* ensemble including the Phelps bag was also prominently displayed on the front page of the *Fashion Group Bulletin*. This appears to have been the first time that Phelps Associates was mentioned by name in the bulletin.[88] By March 1946, riding on this peak of fashionability, Elizabeth Phelps had been granted membership in the Fashion Group.[89] Just a few months later, Esther Lyman, the merchandise editor of *Harper's Bazaar* noted that for autumn, "the shoulder bag will go right on; it has hit the lower-priced market but has certainly not run its course."[90] By autumn of 1947, Lyman and I. Miller's accessory buyer, Regina Hellman, pronounced, "Bags with frames are best, not a squashy bag or gathered one. Most beautiful of all, the frame crocodile bag in black or golden brown, and that same look, too, in other fine leathers . . . The vanity case makers have been doing beautiful things with metal: marvelous reproductions of eighteenth- and nineteenth-century gold and silver boxes, which look as if a fine goldsmith or silversmith had made them by hand."[91] After Dior's New Look, American fashion still embraced both craftsmanship and historicism; however the ideal was no longer rustic, practical, menswear-inspired, or Americana, but now refined, indulgent, feminine, and with a European-inflected sophistication, as fashion catered to consumers' desires to move on and forget the war, embracing something fresh and new.[92] Laver's trickledown theory of fashion seems to have been applicable to the way the fashion industry worked at the time he wrote, and Phelps Associates bags were subject to this cycle.

Shortages: Leather

Phelps Associates seem to have weathered the leather shortages caused by World War II thanks to emphasis on quality rather than volume and to good business planning in finding the right wartime market for their products. Ruth Kerr told the Fashion Group in 1943, "Fundamentally, all the trades connected with leather pivot around one critical material—cattlehide in weights for sole leathers. Only threequarters of our needs come from native cattlehides . . . and there are numerous rulings, allocations and priorities that govern imports from other countries."[93] Historian Mary Ellen Snodgrass writes, "During World War II, rationing in the United States limited plain and exotic leather for belts and handbags; galoshes and cloth bags and belts were available, but sports shoes, dancing shoes, leather jackets, and hunting boots went out of production."[94] Even as the United States entered the war, and throughout the war's duration, Phelps Associates would continue creating leather goods such as bags and leather belts that had been their first product offering. The latter demonstrates one aspect of the difference in wartime materials experience between the United States and, for example, occupied France, where starting in January 1941, women's leather belts could be no more than 1⅝" wide.[95] Phelps Associates were able to begin their business with a wide choice of materials, and even leather shortages a few years later were not so dire as those in some other countries.

To conserve leather for troops, shoes were coupon-rationed, the only clothing item restricted thus in the United States.[96] This was in contrast, for example, to other Allied nations, such as Britain, where clothes rationing was introduced in June 1941, using a coupon system.[97] When in February 1943 it was announced that American civilians would be limited to three pairs of shoes per year, the most immediate result was a consumer buying frenzy. Shoe departments closed on Monday, February 8, to prepare for the new rationing system, and women started buying handbags, particularly practical bags in longwearing calfskin.[98] On Tuesday, when shoe selling began again, women rushed to purchase either sturdy leather or high fashion shoes, both of which were expected to become scarce. Retailers were surprised by the dramatic increase in handbag sales, also. *Women's Wear Daily* reported, "Women are convinced that if leather shortages cause rationing of shoes, the same condition will prevail in bags, and good leather bags were selling in a landslide with many departments."[99] As this statement suggests, consumer reactions to wartime scarcity were based on a combination of facts, perceptions, and speculations.

During the rationing period, shoe manufacturers were limited in the colors of leather they could use, to encourage consumers toward utility rather than novelty in purchases. However, colored leathers remained in the stocks of handbags manufacturers. Some of these came from tree-based dyes, but the majority were made using coal-tar aniline dyes, a product of modern chemistry.[100] In 1944, there was discussion of channeling these colored leathers into shoe manufacturing, but some retailers opposed this suggestion for fear of confusing customers, since there were restrictions in place generally limiting leather colors.[101] This probably allowed for handbag creators like Phelps to continue using the colored leathers.

Accessory producers had to keep pace with continually changing regulations and material availability. Ruth Kerr informed the Fashion Group in July 1943 that production of gloves was government-controlled "only indirectly because of the diversion of skilled labor and shortages of leathers and fabrics. These conditions apply also to leather belts."[102] By the end of the year, the M-310 basic leather conservation order, which contained restrictions that affected the leather industry far beyond shoe rationing, went into effect. Under this order, cattle hides and calfskins were specifically earmarked for production of handbags for the women's armed services.[103]

Fortunately for Phelps Associates, as early as July 1943, they had had the foresight to begin creating a line of made-to-order sling bags—"of brown or navy capeskin, leather-lined, and as per GI requirements. It sells for $32.50 at Mark Cross, and is a practical splurge for a soldier or sailor in skirts who needs a good duration bag."[104] At least some servicewomen probably purchased their own, better-quality bags. While the 1942 government-issued WAAC wardrobe included undergarments and some accessory items such as cotton and silk or rayon stockings (eight each), galoshes (one pair), fabric gloves (five) and Oxford shoes (three pairs), the OQMG seems to have had a difficult time in the designing and procuring a standard-issue shoulder bag.[105] In this struggle, there also appears to have been tension between the WAAC leadership's desire for smart attire and the OQMG's purse strings. Fashion leaders like Lord & Taylor executive Dorothy Shaver (1893–1959) were involved in discussions about American servicewomen's uniform design, and fashion historian and journalist Colin McDowell argues that the results were ultimately much more attractive than the uniforms provided for their British counterparts.[106] In the spring of 1942, Phelps competitor Richard Koret, of the Koret bag company, produced designs for a WAAC utility bag made of tackle twill, which would have been much cheaper than leather. However, WAAC headquarters disapproved of this design, and by summer the OQMG turned to manufacturers of synthetic leather bags for design alternatives. It is unlikely that the synthetic materials available would have been a satisfactory substitute for natural leather. In fall 1942, the WAAC director of sent the OQMG a leather Koret sample bag, which she wanted to be adopted for the WAAC uniform. Erna Risch, writing on behalf of the Historical Section of the OQMG, demonstrated the OQMG's hostility to the WAACs' desire for style and quality: "It was apparently immaterial that the bag was expensive and that it used calfskin leather, a critical material."[107] The OQMG would not agree to such a high-quality, expensive bag. However, by October 1942, the WAAC and the OQMG came to an agreement to have bags made by "medium-priced, high quality" mass-manufacturer Lesco, first in Arctic sealskin, and when that supply was exhausted, in "East-India tanned goatskin and genuine water buffalo."[108] The Army Nurse Corps also approved an oblong-shaped bag, with detachable strap, made of the same grade of sealskin as the WAAC utility bag.[109] Largescale procurement of quality leather and well-made bags was a major challenge, and servicewomen may not have been pleased with the bags they received in the meantime.

Women who joined the WAACs later did not necessarily receive the full complement of regulation wardrobe and had to find alternatives. Clarice F. Pollard, who joined in 1943, recalled, "The earliest enlistees received everything from inside out, which included girdles, brassieres and bathrobes, but we of the 'second wave' were not issued those forementioned parts of the wardrobe."[110] Pollard was told that some missing items would be issued at the next post, but these never materialized.[111] She also noted other procurement issues, such as the fact that uniform garment elements were produced from the same patterns by different manufacturers, so navigating the piles and racks of clothing at the Quartermaster Department in search of a jacket and skirt that both matched each other and fit the servicewoman was a challenge.[112] When WAACs left the service, they were allowed to take only one full government-issued uniform ensemble, the other items being put back into circulation for currently serving soldiers, who would eagerly search these hand-me-downs for their sizes and missing pieces.[113] Pollard recalled that she additionally supplemented the government-issued uniform wardrobe she received from the Quartermaster Depot with items she requested from home (Brooklyn), including undergarments and even a "well-tailored summer uniform" which she believed her mother would be more easily able to obtain in the New York City area.[114] If Pollard's experiences in procurement difficulties were representative of those of other WAACs in 1943, then likely many other servicewomen were seeking to supplement their uniform wardrobes with commercially available garments and accessories, such as those of Phelps Associates.

Phelps Associates were astute in producing bags which fit the armed forces' requirements and would provide an alternative to the standard-issue utility bag. The cheaper materials that the OQMG experimented with created functional problems: synthetic leather chipped, fabric frayed.[115] It is not surprising that servicewomen who could afford it would augment their wardrobes with a good Phelps Associates shoulder bag. A journalist writing later in the decade reported, "The Waves and WACs gave them a big push."[116] That Phelps shoulder bags were acceptable as women's military uniform accessories also demonstrates the clear connection to militarism in Phelps' general offerings. Additionally, the Phelps shoulder bag's connection to women's military uniforms was also held up as a selling point for nonmilitary customers. In April 1944, *Women's Wear Daily* encouraged handbag salespeople, "When you show shoulder strap styles add to their interest by reminding your customers that this style was the choice for women in the armed service and in civilian service."[117] With female military personnel able to exercise 1choice of vendor in their procurement of certain uniform elements such as handbags, the Phelpses had positioned themselves well as a military supplier in New York, a major port city and point of departure for those making the transatlantic crossing. During the period when handbag manufacturers were most affected by wartime restrictions, the Phelps had already mapped out an area of sales growth with a product that fit both their aesthetic and the need of the times.

In summer of 1944, even as the stocks of hides and skins for the making of leather returned, and restrictions on tanning and civilian leather consumption were lifted, the Federal Reserve Bank of Chicago predicted that a shortfall of finished leather would persist for some time, due to a lack of labor to run tanneries.[118] On Wednesday, August 28, 1945, the War Production Board (WPB) announced it was removing restrictions on the use of leather for goods including handbags as well as luggage, slippers, upholstery, jackets, and wallets. The move was made as an amendment to Order M-310, the basic leather conservation order. The amendment removed restrictions on the cutting of sole leather and raised from one hundred to five hundred per month the number of hides a manufacturer could buy from a tanner without WPB authorization.[119]

The ending of curbs on leather (other than shoe-rationing) in August 1945 presented dilemmas for handbag manufacturers: How much leather was available, and who would get it? *Women's Wear Daily* reported that a number of handbag manufacturers had a stockpile of calf leather they had been unable to use during the M-310 order period starting in late 1943.[120] Whether Phelps Associates were among the fortunate businesses with stockpiles to draw from, they must have welcomed the easing of restrictions and the possibility of postwar growth.

Conclusion

William and Elizabeth Phelps's leather goods designs for Phelps Associates were well-suited to dealing with the shortages of metal and leather caused by the diversion of materials to the war effort. The Phelpses' handbag designs drew from leathercraft traditions and therefore did not incorporate the metal frames that most mass-manufactured bags used at the start of the war.

William and Elizabeth Phelps repurposed vintage metalwork in their bags, from vintage military insignias used as decoration to vintage dee rings attaching their shoulder straps. This symbolism was particularly appealing to American consumers during the war. Army-navy surplus store Francis Bannerman Sons was a key bulk supplier of these metal materials. The Phelpses' reuse of vintage metalwork resonated with the fashion consumer, and their frameless designs reduced the amount of metal required to make a bag. This proved a great boon to their business, as it circumvented the metal shortages faced by most handbag makers, and the bags were recognized for their creative use of materials.

The Phelpses also appealed to wartime American tastes through their bag shapes, based on historical American forms including menswear and military uniform. In wearing fashionable shoulder bags, American women—both civilians and those in the armed forces—learned new techniques of the body, as they struggled to keep a shoulder bag in place on the shoulder, but journalists proclaimed Phelps bags easier to wear because of their engineering.

Leather shortages were another materials problem, but bags and belts were not coupon-rationed in the United States. The Phelps Associates business model of selling fewer, higher-quality items meant that they needed less leather in reserve to continue producing, and their bags that met military standards opened a key consumer demographic. While sustainability was not yet a fashion industry buzzword in the 1940s, Phelps Associates' practices offer a model for responding to today's environmental concerns about fashion consumption as well.

Promoting and Selling Phelps Associates' Products

Publicity and retail sales were both important factors in building Phelps Associates as a brand. William and Elizabeth Phelps took part in fashion industry–backed promotional activities such as the American Fashion Critics (Coty) Awards, as well as museum exhibitions. The Coty Awards, created by Eleanor Lambert, promoted both individual designers and the American fashion industry as a whole. In the 1940s, the Phelpses also received editorial coverage in fashion magazines, and fashion editors often connected their work with themes of craftsmanship, patriotism, and the pastoral. Magazine articles also educated readers about the "correct" etiquette for wearing Phelps accessories. Retail stores, including Lord & Taylor, were a vital link in connecting consumers with Phelps leather goods.

Introductory Objects: Lion Rampant Bag and Belt at the Costume Institute

The first example of Phelps Associates' work to be accessioned by a museum appears to be a leather shoulder bag and belt set now in the collection of the Costume Institute, the Metropolitan Museum of Art, with the credit line, "Gift of Mr. William Drown Phelps, 1944" (Figs. 4.1, 4.2). Unlike Phelps work that draws on American history, these objects reference heraldry traditions: a metal lion rampant roars across both the center front of the belt and the center front closure flap of the pouch-style bag. The pouch is rounded and large, with adjustable leather drawstrings on the bag's interior.[1] The Phelpses made the bag with two different leathers—a medium-brown for the body and strap of the bag, with the drawstrings and trim edging the curved closure flap in a lighter colored (and probably originally more supple) leather. The belt's length is constructed from one piece of leather, but the look of a center-front panel is created by overlapping a small section of leather on each side and topstitching it down.[2] In both the bag and the belt, the lion rampant ornament is stitched down with thread. It would be the late 1960s before Phelps clients began donating pieces to the Costume Institute—so why did the Phelpses donate this bag and belt set in 1944, at this early stage of their production?

The answer lies in the complex web of publicity and image production, cultural capital, and retail sales involved in the system of selling American fashion in the mid-twentieth century. William and Elizabeth Phelps won a 1944 Coty award for their accessory designs (in the 1943 year), and Coty Award winners seem to have been encouraged to donate examples of their work to the Museum of Costume Art (which became the Costume Institute of the Metropolitan Museum of Art in 1946).[3] Cultural theorist Elizabeth Wilson writes that capitalism "manufactures dreams and images as well as things, and fashion is as much a part of the dream world of capitalism as of its economy."[4] To sell products, Phelps Associates had to do more than simply make beautiful, useful things; they also had to communicate their message to the buying public and create a compelling brand image. They

Fig. 4.1. Phelps Associates, pouch-style shoulder bag, leather, metal, 1944. (Costume Institute, Metropolitan Museum of Art. Gift of Mr. William Drown Phelps, 1944. C.I.44.126.1. Image copyright © The Metropolitan Museum of Art. Image source: Art Resource, NY.)

Fig. 4.2. Phelps Associates, belt, leather, metal, 1944. (Costume Institute, Metropolitan Museum of Art. Gift of Mr. William Drown Phelps, 1944. C.I.44.126.2. Image copyright © The Metropolitan Museum of Art. Image source: Art Resource, NY.)

did so through public relations activities—from awards programs to museum exhibitions, media promotion of their image and products, and education of consumers as to how best to wear their pieces, leading, ultimately, to the purchase of Phelps Associates leather goods at retail stores.

Public Relations

Public relations (PR) was a key component in selling twentieth-century fashion. In her 1941 memoir *Publicity Is Broccoli,* publicist Constance Hope (1908–1977) defined publicity as "making news."[5] Hope worked primarily with classical musicians, but she also had clients who were restauranteurs or worked in the fashion industry. Her fashion-related clients included milliners Helen Liebert and Marion Vallé, specialty stores like Jay Thorpe, and even fashion prognosticator Tobé.[6] Since Hope worked with some individuals in the fashion industry, her memoir is a useful source of insights into how publicity was used to shape public opinion of fashion personalities and institutions. Hope's memoir reveals the complicated web of promotion in mid-twentieth-century America, especially New York. Paid advertising was an important component of promotion, and particularly within department stores it was a field that offered opportunities for women to advance in their careers, as advertising executives Estelle Hamburger (circa 1898–1983), Bernice Fitzsimmons (1894–1982), and Sara Pennoyer (1900–1985) all demonstrated.[7] But publicity involved all the ways to get a client into the newspaper (or other media outlet) apart from paid advertisements. Hope argued that in 1941 "a goodly percentage of the news stories and pictures in the daily press still reflect the skilled hand of the publicity agent. . . . Analyze the stories you read—look for the motive behind them. It may be a labor crisis, a startling medical discovery, a report from a government agency—all legitimate news. But nine chances in ten it was a publicity agent who got the story into the paper, either by writing it himself or notifying the papers that something hot was about to break."[8]

Getting a fashion designer's name before the public for free could involve anything from a mention in the social pages for an event he or she attended to a full-blown publicity stunt covered in the city news and intended to provoke controversy, such as Lilly Daché's enclosure of a good-luck horned toad in the cornerstone of her townhouse at the groundbreaking ceremony.[9] In the first years of Phelps Associates, during the war, William and Elizabeth Phelps did not pay for advertising, but they did rely on fashion industry connections and events for free publicity.[10]

Eleanor Lambert (1903–2003) was an extremely influential publicist who focused on the fashion industry. According to Lambert's 1976 biographical listing under "Fashion Influentials" in her own book, *World of Fashion,* she was involved with the founding of the Fashion Group International and the Costume Institute at the Metropolitan Museum of Art, running the International Best Dressed Poll as well as conceiving and coordinating the American Fashion Critics' Awards, beginning with awards for the year 1942.[11] The Phelpses were involved with several of these institutions and events, including donating to the Costume Institute (1944, under William's name), Elizabeth joining the Fashion Group (1946), and jointly winning the 1944 Coty Award. This led me to ask whether perhaps the Phelps Associates business was a Lambert client.

My research indicates that the Phelpses were not Lambert clients, despite their many overlaps with Lambert's activities.[12] The Eleanor Lambert collection at the Fashion Institute of Technology's Special Collections and College Archives of the Gladys Marcus Library contains extensive designer files, which Lambert maintained on both clients and nonclients; Phelps Associates are not represented in this series of files, SC.214.2, Eleanor Lambert Designer Files, 1942–2002. If Phelps Associates had been Lambert's clients, they most likely would have been represented in her designer files. Phelps Associates do appear in series SC.214.3 in Lambert's files, in reference to the Coty Awards, particularly the 1944 ceremony.

The Coty Awards provided multiple layers of promotion: first, it promoted the Coty cosmetics company as its named sponsor; second, it gave the American fashion industry an opportunity to promote the prestige of American fashion to the American public; and third, all involved individuals and companies had a chance at receiving their share of the publicity—from jury members in the media who were listed on the program to the designers who received awards. The first purpose—promoting Coty—was obvious in the naming rights. Fashion historian Sandra Stansbery Buckland argues that in the early 1940s Coty was also working from more altruistic motives, with the war effort in mind, and used the award "to encourage designers to work toward a unified style instead of following their own interests."[13] Fashion industry leaders made it clear that the Coty Awards were intended to promote American fashion as a viable alternative to European centers, particularly Paris. In 1976, when the awards had become a tradition of over thirty years' standing, Eleanor Lambert (clearly serving as her own publicist) wrote that "the purpose of the Awards, as they were conceived by Eleanor Lambert . . . was to draw attention to the originality, scope, and power of American fashion and bring it to equal prominence with European fashion."[14] Similarly, Lambert paraphrased the New York City mayor's speech at the 1944 award ceremony: "Mayor F. H. La Guardia presented the awards, and spoke of his conviction that that American fashions, particularly New York fashions, are second to none in the modern world."[15] In a 1944 press release, Lambert called the awards an "annual prize for excellence in the world of style" and described their importance to the war effort, thanks to Coty's allowing for independent judges to make the award selections: "This, in wartime, makes it possible to 'give credit where credit is due' to designers who show the greatest ingenuity in the face of difficulties and the greatest sensitivity to the psychological trend which fashion must always reflect."[16] Despite Lambert's trumpeting of the judges' independence, the New York City fashion world was a small one, and connections must have played at least some part in the jurors' selections. For example, one of the special award winners in the first year was milliner Lilly Daché, whose husband was Coty executive Jean Despres.

Although the Phelpses were most likely not Lambert clients, they probably did have a champion among the Coty jurors in the jury's vice chair, Gertrude Bailey of the *New York World-Telegram.* Bailey was a neighbor of the Phelpses and an early visitor to their workshop; she wrote an article about them that spread the news of their work to retail store buyers—a very successful bit of publicity.[17] Bailey's PR prowess was great enough that in 1945 she left the *World-Telegram* to become the PR representative for National Carbon Company's Krene film plastic.[18] By the end of the decade, Bailey was representing Monsanto Chemical Company, where she would go on to a long career as a PR manager.[19]

For William and Elizabeth Phelps, like other individuals involved in the Coty Awards program, the awards represented a significant opportunity for personal and professional publicity. The honorees at the 1944 ceremony were women's clothing designer Claire McCardell, milliner Sally Victor, and the Phelpses. Over two thousand invited guests attended the presentation and fashion show at the Hunter College Assembly Hall, at Sixty-Ninth Street and Park Avenue.[20] Most of these guests would have been involved in the fashion industry, so winning an award alerted the broader American fashion world to Phelps Associates' accessories and their historically influenced and Americana design direction. After the award ceremony, articles followed in a variety of industry and consumer publications, spreading the news to an even wider audience.

The program for the 1944 Coty Awards presentation visually announces the ceremony's patriotic emphasis. The front cover has a fashion illustration by Eric (Carl Erickson, 1891–1958) in the center, showing a fashionable woman's head and shoulders as she looks off into the distance, counterbalanced with large blocks of red, white, and blue space. The third page, listing the order of ceremonies, is topped with a large, stylized American bald eagle in gold and has each item on the program listed beneath a gold star. The list of the jury members, on page four, also features a line of gold stars, and it reads like a who's who of American fashion journalism in 1944: Edna Woolman Chase of *Vogue;* Virginia Pope of *The New York Times,* Carmel Snow and Diana Vreeland of *Harper's Bazaar.* The list of periodicals includes many that would feature Phelps Associates on their pages or had already done so.[21] The prizes were geared toward the war effort, and winners were presented with war bonds rather than cash: a $1,000 "G" bond to Claire McCardell, a $750 "E" bond to Sally Victor, and a $500 "G" bond to the Phelpses.[22]

The ordering of the awards also represents the hierarchy of fashion trades at the time: women's main garments at the top, millinery in second place, and leather goods less highly placed. The second page of the program was topped by a photograph of the award trophy—the "Winnie" statue created by sculptor Malvina Hoffman—with photographs and small blurbs for each of the award winners below (Fig. 4.3). McCardell received the "Winnie" trophy; the jurors selected her based on her denim suits, dresses, and coats, as well as her bestselling "Popover" dress. The jury praised Victor's Curvette hats as well as her designs for the war effort, such as the beret for cadet nurses and work hats for women working in General Electric factories. Both McCardell and Victor are photographed in head-and-shoulders views, wearing simple, dark clothing, with their gazes turned to a point off to the viewer's right. The Phelpses are photographed together, in three-quarter view, squarely facing the camera. William wears a three-piece pinstriped suit with a jaunty bow tie and has his hands in his pockets. Elizabeth stands slightly in front of her husband, with her arms crossed in front of her, wearing a plain, long-sleeved white blouse and a skirt. The program text honored them: "America's finest designers of handbags and leather accessories. They invented the modern use of the over-shoulder bag which is both functional and dramatic as it frees a woman's hands and provides an accent for a simple costume."[23] While the statement that the Phelpses "invented" the women's shoulder bag is hyperbole, it does indicate that their work was viewed as innovative as well as functional—a winning combination for American wartime fashion.

The Coty Award event included a fashion show, with actress Constance Bennett as commentator. The Phelps Associates objects displayed in the fashion show included bags that hung from various places on the body. As noted in the previous chapter, if one of the elements of modernism in main dress is that garments hang from the shoulders rather than containing stiff body-molding sculptural structures, the Phelpses' bags of the early 1940s are a modernist parallel in accessories. Their pieces shown in the 1944 Coty Award ceremony included pouch bags that hung from the arm; saddle bags and postman bags that hung from the shoulder; and belt pouches that hung from a waist belt, both for day and evening. Lambert's Coty Award press release noted that some of the cowhide leather the Phelpses used for their cowhide overarm pouches was material "including government rejects," emphasizing responsible wartime use of goods.[24] Their saddle bag "of worsted surcingle webbing with llama hide gussets" also used a leather not in demand for military purposes, paired with a woolen textile used in horse harness (a surcingle, a strap that goes around a horse's girth).[25]

The Coty Awards publicized that Phelps Associates actively sought the business of women in the military by providing bags that fit the required specifications to be worn with in uniform. Lambert's press release noted that the fashion show "included a WAC, WAVE, SPAR, and woman Marine" wearing bags that showed the Phelpses' influential style.[26] The Coty Awards continued to be a source of

Designed and executed by Malvina Hoffman

The 1942 Presentation at the Metropolitan Museum of Art

CLAIRE McCARDELL, Casual Clothes Designer

Exponent of young and thoroughly American fashions, Miss McCardell is looked to by the entire industry for inspiration in this field. She designs for the American woman whether at work or at play.

Miss McCardell introduced the blue denim suit, dress and coat: the bareback mode stems from her collection and the "popover" dress, designed in 1942, remains a national best seller. The "popover" influence set the trend for the shirt-sleeve shoulder for women as well as the rolled-up sleeve and wrap-and-tied dresses. The wide use of cottons has been the direct result of her styling of this material.

Miss McCardell also originated the wide-shouldered jumper dress which may be worn with or without a blouse. Her designs are widely copied.

SALLY VICTOR, Millinery Designer

One of our foremost millinery designers, Mrs. Victor is the originator of the Chetnik and the Curvette—both outstanding in 1943. Other important contributions are the side-draped hat and the cloche, as well as the beret for the Cadet Nurses and the work hats worn in the General Electric plants. She has played an important part in making women in the armed services and in the war plants functionally attractive.

Mrs. Victor has always stood for craft development in millinery design and has done a great deal to train young designers.

PHELPS ASSOCIATES, Accessory Designers

Elizabeth and William Phelps are America's finest designers of handbags and leather accessories. They invented the modern use of the over-shoulder bag which is both functional and dramatic as it frees a woman's hands and provides an accent for a simple costume. They also introduced important variations such as the postman bag, the postillion bag, the leather drawstring bag and the haversack.

Mr. and Mrs. Phelps have done much creative work in the use of metals for accessories. During the war they are restricting this to the reconstruction of antique metals such as regimental and civilian guard insignia and heraldic crests. Their inspiration has come from both sides of the Atlantic — from the native crafts of America in which they have deep faith and from the small artisans working in the Paris attics. They make the first, second and third samples of each item with their own hands.

These Awards are made to the most outstanding American fashion designers who, in the opinion of the Jury, have best interpreted the fashion trend in 1943, under the restrictive influences of war-time economy.

Fig. 4.3. Page from the 1944 American Fashion Critics (Coty) Awards ceremony showing honorees for the year 1943. (Image courtesy of Coty Archives, Coty, Inc. and FIT Library Special Collections and College Archives, Fashion Institute of Technology|SUNY.)

Fig. 4.4. Installation view of the Museum of Costume Art's *Seven American Wars* exhibition, showing the display containing Phelps Associates' lion rampant bag and belt. (Special exhibition, *Seven American Wars,* Museum of Costume Art, 1943–1944. View of World War Two. Image copyright © The Metropolitan Museum of Art. Image source: Art Resource, NY.)

publicity for the Phelpses. For the following year's ceremony and fashion show, Phelps Associates provided the bags used to accessorize the ensembles.[27]

The Coty Awards also led to Phelps Associates receiving further publicity through museum collecting and exhibition practices. The Phelpses garnered publicity while working to establish their legacy within American fashion history by donating examples of their work to the Museum of Costume Art at the Metropolitan Museum of Art, as mentioned. These pieces had been featured in the 1943–44 exhibition *Seven American Wars* (Fig. 4.4). An exhibition photograph shows the belt and bag mounted on a board between two dressed mannequins and over a bust-length mannequin, in a section of the exhibition focused on the seventh war of the title, World War II. This display featured 1942 and 1943 Coty Award winners. According to text supplied by Lambert, and now in the Metropolitan Museum's Watson Library Digital Collections, the playsuit on the left was by Claire McCardell (1943), and the dinner dress on the right was by Norman Norell (1942), with millinery by Lilly Daché (1942, left), John Frederics (1942, center), and Sally Victor (1943, right).[28]

Publicity offered by the Coty Awards and the Museum of Costume Art's *Seven American Wars* exhibition was important to raising the profile of Phelps Associates among tastemakers and fashion industry insiders. This publicity in turn helped increase coverage of Phelps leather goods in fashion media directed toward consumers.

Brand Perception and Media Coverage

Another key part of Phelps Associates' image-building and publicity was editorial coverage in fashion magazines. In analyzing Phelps Associates' work as covered in the 1940s by *Vogue* and *Harper's Bazaar,* several themes emerge, most notably patriotism, craftsmanship, and the pastoral. Roland Barthes theorized that fashion exists as three structures: technological (actual objects), iconic (fashion photography), and verbal (text in fashion magazines and newspapers).[29] Barthes's theory is helpful for understanding the ways themes can be conveyed to the fashion magazine consumer, who browses text and image together. When the theme is clearly present in the underlying object, this is the technical level. In other cases, fashion photographs are staged or sketches are drawn to bring out the theme—the iconic level. In other examples, the words describing the fashion evoke the theme, introducing it at the verbal level. In some magazine issues, themes may be present in overlapping technical, iconic, and verbal contexts.

The first theme that appears frequently is craftsmanship. *Vogue* sometimes mentioned the craftsmanship of Phelps Associates from the consumer angle, that much of their work was custom-made for the individual consumer, as in an article titled, "Made for You." Here, *Vogue* employs the theme through verbal structures, assuring the reader of what is difficult to convey through iconic structures—that the Phelps skirt and belt are unique and custom-made: "no two ever precisely alike."[30] *Harper's Bazaar* also verbally addressed intertwined themes of craftsmanship and patriotism in an 1945 editorial spread, "Custom-Made for American Women," which included independent American couturiers like Valentina, inhouse custom salons at stores like Bergdorf Goodman, and custom accessory suppliers like Phelps Associates.[31] By promoting the upper echelons of the American fashion industry and emphasizing craftsmanship, *Harper's Bazaar* and *Vogue* sought to elevate the status of the fashion industry as a whole. Small producers like Phelps Associates needed this type of luxurious image creation, as their output was necessarily limited by their design philosophy of handmade, and in many cases custom, production.

Another common theme in Phelps Associates media coverage is patriotism. Their products were represented as patriotic, with ties to both historical and current military efforts. *Harper's Bazaar* emphasized Phelps' patriotism and tied these accessories to the current war effort through both verbal and iconic structures. If the military detailing of an accessory might not be immediately clear to the viewer of an editorial photograph, *Harper's* made sure to point it out in the text. For example, in its November 1942 issue *Harper's Bazaar* describes a barely visible bag in a black-and-white photograph as a yellow goatskin from Phelps Associates: "They trim it with a gilt eagle, holding a ring in its beak."[32] The reader might easily have missed the bag's Americana motif if this were not pointed out through the verbal structure. A satchel dimly visible across the page in chiaroscuro lighting is described as "cowhide, studded with a military ornament from the Spanish-American War."[33] Similarly, in another article, what appears a fairly simple belt, with a rectangular buckle, is given a historical and military context: "a wide cowhide belt with an old Civil War brass buckle."[34]

In an April 1943 *Harper's Bazaar* editorial fashion spread, "See That You're Born in Texas," patriotism is introduced as a theme in technical, iconic, and verbal structures. Both the text and the photographs refer to the Randolph Field military training location, outside of San Antonio, where the photo shoot was conducted. A model carrying a Phelps Associates junior postman bag is described as wearing an outfit appropriate for work, travel, "or for that date with your Army or Navy beau."[35]

Another important theme in the fashion media's presentation of Phelps Associates' products was the pastoral. This was often presented via iconic structures, with Phelps leather goods shown in openair settings, as in *Harper's Bazaar* photographs of the country and smalltown life. This imagery relates to long-held ideas of the city as dangerous and the country as safe and wholesome and would have linked Phelps products with a sense of peace and safety. After the war, this theme also would tie to demographic and settlement changes, as many white families moved out of dense urban areas and into suburbs, changing shopping patterns and ushering in new needs for sportswear (see also chapter 6). The theme of the country, or pastoral, takes shape within a broader dialogue about the etiquette of accessories and where Phelps Associates accessories could properly be worn.

Etiquette of Accessories: Town and Country

Lesley Ellis Miller has observed that in the Paris couture of the 1950s, "not only was there a 'hierarchy of textiles' but there was also an 'etiquette of textiles.' That etiquette observed the season (autumn–winter, spring–summer), the time of day (morning, afternoon, evening) and the wearer's age, as well as the nature of the event."[36] This etiquette was true in 1940s America as well and also accurate for accessories. Caroline Rennolds Milbank wrote in her *New York Fashion* profile of Phelps Associates, "With the tweeds and wool jerseys of the 1940s, the most appropriate accessories were Phelps pocketbooks and belts, which, since they were handmade, had a roughhewn look that was suitable for country clothes."[37] Location also mattered, with different clothes considered appropriate for city versus country or suburban use.

Country clothes may have been more casual, but they were not always cheaper. African American novelist Ann Petry, in her 1946 *The Street,* contrasts the inexpensive city clothes worn by Black maid Lutie Johnson with the luxurious sportswear of the country clothes worn by her employer, Mrs. Chandler. While Johnson arrives in a tightly fitted black coat with velvet collar, thin stockings, and high heels, Chandler comes to meet her train in "a loose-fitting tweed coat," ribbed cotton stockings, and flat-heeled, red-brown leather moccasins.[38] Johnson mentally notes that every piece of Chandler's ensemble is expensive.

To achieve the fashionable look, both main garments and accessories had to be correct for the place and time they were worn. Periodicals educated women about the etiquette of fashion, as Petry narrates through the perspective of her character Johnson: "For in those two years with the Chandlers she learned all about Country Living. She learned about it from the pages of the fat sleek magazines Mrs. Chandler subscribed for and never read. *Vogue, Town and Country, Harper's Bazaar, House and Garden, House Beautiful.*"[39] Similarly, a 1939 advice book for women aspiring to fashion industry jobs informed the reader, "There are four different types of accessories to be worn with the four main classifications of clothes, i.e. 1) sports, 2) daytime, 3) late afternoon, and 4) evening. These are clearly separated in style and characteristics and should never be combined. For example, it is unsmart to wear a velvet hat and carry a saddle leather bag, just as it is to wear satin shoes with a tweed coat. . . . Sports accessories are hardy, classic, or imaginative. Frequently they are smartest when they have handwork on them, i.e. hand-stitching."[40] Most Phelps Associates accessories would have been classified as "sports" accessories.

During the years of World War II, the strict division of city versus country clothes and accessories was blurred, along with some loosening of the hierarchies based on the time of day, allowing Phelps accessories like shoulder bags to be worn in more contexts in urban settings. *Harper's Bazaar* for September 1942 shows a Phelps pouch as an acceptable accessory for town (the model is pushing an elevator button) worn with a wool day suit and leather gloves.[41] In October1942, *Harper's* showed a Phelps shoulder bag, "a dispatch bag in mahogany leather," accessorizing a "city-country suit" in oatmeal-color tweed.[42] Tweed was traditionally a country fabric, but *Harper's* assured its readers that this suit would work for both town and country. With fabric scarcity during the war, it was important for clothing to be multipurpose, and fashion accommodated this, with more flexibility in the rules as to which items belonged in country versus city settings. In August 1943, *Harper's* showed a model in a tweed suit with a Phelps shoulder bag in mocha leather and suede with a horn decoration, beside a window that overlooks a city scene including what appears to be a three-story building across the street—perhaps she is getting ready to leave a city apartment—showing that Phelps bags are appropriate for the urban lifestyle.[43] In October 1945, Phelps shoulder bags were shown with tweeds at the fourth edition of the Fashions of the Times fashion show at Times Hall.[44]

Vogue seems to have maintained firmer divisions of town versus country clothing even during the war. At least in some instances, the accessories determined the tenor of the whole outfit. The accessories were the deciding factor in whether a suit looked appropriate for a given setting and whether the wearer appeared overdressed, underdressed, or just right. Within the hierarchy of fashion etiquette, *Vogue* deemed Phelps accessories correct for the countryside, evoking the pastoral theme, and sometimes bridging the town or country divide. For example, in a January 1944 *Vogue* article, "Suits with Two Lives," a grey flannel suit was labeled as appropriate for the country when paired with a sweater and a Phelps drawstring "double over-the-shoulder buckskin moneybag," but for town when paired with a more structured handbag.[45] Similarly, a yellow gabardine suit was shown with a Phelps shoulder bag of worsted webbing for the country but an alligator handbag for town.[46]

It is important to note that while magazines and other media advocated for a specific fashion etiquette, women made their own decisions about whether to follow fashion dictates. Petry's *The Street* offers a fictional example of women's agency in choosing how or whether to follow fashion etiquette. While country clothes were often marketed as classics to keep long-term (see chapter 6), Mrs. Chandler is a compulsive shopper who buys new clothes, wears them a few times, then gives them to Lutie Johnson, following the longstanding perquisite of a maid to receive her employer's hand-me-downs.[47] Johnson refuses to wear these garments, instead giving them to a woman who lives in Harlem, "taking an ironic pleasure in the thought that Mrs. Chandler's beautiful clothes Designed for Country Living would be showing up nightly in the gin mill at the corner of Seventh Avenue and 110th Street."[48] Petry's character, an urban-dwelling Black woman, incorporates the clothing into her own lifestyle, wearing the clothes in the city rather than the country and at night rather than during the day, in defiance of the fashion etiquette promoted by magazines like *Vogue*. Chapter 5 further develops this theme of clothing and accessories such as Phelps pieces being worn by women outside the target audience of middle- to upper-class white women and offers a real-life example of how one woman wore items in ways that were different from the etiquette promoted by the fashion media.

After World War II, the divisions between city and country (or suburban) clothing again became more pronounced. Phelps accessories were shown in an October 1947 *Vogue* article, "Long Island Autumn," the title of the article making it clear that the clothes shown were intended for suburban or rural rather than city wear. Phelps shoulder bags were shown alongside main garments of tweed, suede, and jersey, and with "crocheted cotton string gloves by Smart Set."[49] Even fashion designer Anne Fogarty, who urged wives of the late 1950s to break the "fashion rules" by wearing tweed in the city, still proclaimed the importance of "a collection of tweeds, wools, leathers, and cashmeres for the country or suburban life" and discussed the pairing of string gloves with tweeds.[50] The Irving Penn photograph of the Phelps quintessential eagle bag also shows a pair of string gloves peeking out from the front pocket (Fig. I.4). This understanding of fashion etiquette as to correct clothes and accessories for country versus city would be implicit even in the naming of the Phelpses' sportswear line, starting in 1949: Phelps Deep Country Clothes. In the postwar period, the Phelpses expanded their line to include first custom sportswear and

Fig. 4.5. Detail, Phelps Associates, Phelps Vogue belt, leather, metal, circa 1951. (Author's collection. Photograph by the author.)

Fig. 4.6. Phelps Associates, Phelps Vogue belt, leather, metal, circa 1951. (Author's collection. Photograph by the author.)

then ready-to-wear, in easy-care, practical designs responding to the needs of women in the country and in the suburbs (see chapter 5).

In September 1951, Phelps ran an advertisement for their Deep Country Clothes, "For Country and Suburban Living," in *The New York Times*. This ad emphasized that Phelps clothes and accessories, including the "Phelps Vogue Belt," were proper for wear outside the city limits. The Phelps Vogue Belt was available either 1½" or 1¾" wide, in black or brown leather, for "about $5.00."[51] An extant belt in the author's collection is an example of the Phelps Vogue Belt in brown leather and the 1¾" width and is 31¼" from end to end (Fig. 4.5). Unlike the majority of Phelps belts, which have straps cut as completely straight lines, the strap of this belt arcs with a slightly curved line, the center back lower than the ends (Fig. 4.6). Stamped into the leather at the buckle end of the strap are the words "Phelps-Handmade," with the Phelps trademark buckle symbol stamped into the leather rather than present as a metal attachment. The metal belt buckle is etched with the words "PHELPS" at the pointed end and "VOGUE" at the squared-off end. It is unclear whether the Vogue name was one Phelps gave to this particular style of belt, or whether it was associated with or distributed through the Vogue Belt Company, a manufacturer of belts incorporated since 1928, whose belts were also featured in fashion magazines . . . such as *Vogue*.[52]

In the 1940s, fashion magazines were an important part of Phelps Associates' publicity, helping to market Phelps leather goods under themes of patriotism, craftsmanship, and the pastoral. Magazines were also a key element of consumer education as to how, when, and where these accessories should be worn and how they could transform an outfit for different occasions.

Retailers

Fashion industry and consumer knowledge of Phelps Associates was translated into sales via the retailers that sold their products. Phelps Associates initially offered their accessories only through their own workshop. In 1943, Phelps Associates sold a consignment of leather goods through the Mark Cross leather-

Fig. 4.7. A Phelps bag sold at Lord & Taylor in the 1950s. Phelps Associates, bag, cotton, leather, 1950s. (Costume Institute, Metropolitan Museum of Art, Gift of Elizabeth M. Riley, 1990, 1990.158. Image copyright © The Metropolitan Museum of Art. Image source: Art Resource, NY.)

Fig. 4.8. A Phelps leather belt owned by Lord & Taylor buyer and executive Virginia "Jimmie" Booth. Phelps Associates, belt, leather, brass, 1950s. (Costume Institute, Metropolitan Museum of Art, Gift of Virginia Wagoner Booth, 2000, 2000.475.8. Image copyright © The Metropolitan Museum of Art. Image source: Art Resource, NY.)

goods store on Fifth Avenue.[53] This retail effort was a success. and Phelps went on to sell a second consignment through Mark Cross, which also sold out immediately. However, the Phelpses could not come to an agreement with Mark Cross about production schedules, so this did not become an ongoing relationship. It is likely Mark Cross wanted the Phelpses to speed up their production—something they were not willing or able to do in their workshop arrangement. Instead, in 1945, for a time the Phelpses went back to a completely custom-order business sold only through their own shop at 45 University Place.[54]

Phelps Associates built a more successful long-term retail relationship with Lord & Taylor. Lord & Taylor was technically a large specialty store rather than a department store, as it focused on selling fashionable apparel rather than fitting the Census Bureau definition of a department store—a company selling a full range of household goods as well as clothing and dry goods.[55] However, historian Susan Porter Benson argues that large specialty stores such as Lord & Taylor were viewed by their management as part of the department-store industry. Departments were administrative units within a store, usually run by a buyer in charge of buying and selling in that department.[56]

Lord & Taylor's department-based selling techniques meant that in different decades, Phelps products were sold in different areas of the store. By May 1946, Lord & Taylor had become the only New York City store "handling regular stock models of the Phelps bags and belts, and Phelps still maintains its own retail stop where custom work is done."[57] Accessories departments had grown over the 1920s and 1930s to take over more of the prime retail space on the ground floor of department stores, and this is where Phelps objects initially were showcased.[58] According to Benson, items sold at street level were usually "glamour and impulse items to waylay women on their way to the upper floors."[59] In 1946, Phelps bags and belts were sold in a special section on the Lord & Taylor main floor, both in plaid wool-lined cases and on black racks against the wall.[60]

In 1955, Lord & Taylor was still the New York franchise holder—under this agreement, it was the only store allowed to sell Phelps goods in that city.[61] Phelps goods were also sold in the Lord & Taylor store in Philadelphia in the 1950s, and the Phelpses also maintained direct contact with that location. In 1956, Elizabeth Phelps made a two-day instore appearance at the Philadelphia location to promote the fall line.[62]

The Costume Institute has two objects that demonstrate the longstanding connection between Phelps Associates and the Lord & Taylor store. The first is a striped canvas bag with leather trim and lined in a solid mustard yellow canvas, sold at Lord & Taylor in the 1950s, accession number 1990.158 (Fig. 4.7). The second is a leather belt, accession number 2000.475.8, composed of three pieces of leather joined by brass rings: a curved center section and straight cut side sections (Fig. 4.8). This belt is of note because it was given to the Costume Institute by Lord & Taylor buyer and executive Virginia "Jimmie" Booth (1922–2011), another fashion industry insider who was also a Phelps client.

In the 1950s and 1960s, Lord & Taylor would spotlight the Phelps sportswear line, Phelps Deep Country Clothes, in a department headed by Jimmie Booth and dedicated to clothes deemed appropriate for wear in the country, the Country Clothes Shop. Fashion historian Tiffany Webber-Hanchett credits retail executive Dorothy Shaver for Lord & Taylor's promotions of American designers, starting with her 1932 "American Fashions for American Women" campaign, and also notes that beginning in the 1930s while Shaver was vice president, "the specialty department store also was known for its individual boutiques, stores within the store that sold fashions for petites, brides, mothers-to-be and mature women, as well as specific types of clothing such as sportswear in the Sports Shop and the Country Clothes Shop."[63] By 1949, Shaver was president of Lord & Taylor, and experts in the field singled it out by as an exemplary model of retail public relations work for its PR department, run by Alieda van Wesep, with biweekly meetings usually attended by Shaver herself.[64] Lord & Taylor hired Jimmie Booth in 1952, and she worked as buyer for the Fifth Avenue Country Clothes Shop, where the clothes of American designers like Clare Potter and Claire McCardell shared space with the designs of Phelps.[65] In the 1998 exhibition *Designing Women: American Style, 1940–60*, the Wadsworth Atheneum in Hartford, Connecticut, displayed Phelps outfits from Booth's personal wardrobe that came from Lord & Taylor's Country Clothes Shop, including a reversible evening dress (1998.14.1) and an apricot-toned ensemble of coat, shirt, and skirt (1998.14.17a–c).

From the author's collection, a two-piece ensemble of plaid blouse with a matching reversible wrap skirt embodies Lord & Taylor's promotion of American designers, long-term relationship with Phelps, and boutique-style merchandising of American sportswear (Figs. 4.9, 4.10). The origins and significance of Phelps sportswear will be discussed in chapter 6, but this ensemble is best considered here, in the context of the relationship between Phelps and retailers like Lord & Taylor. The outfit bears both the standard Phelps Deep Country

Fig. 4.9. Phelps Deep Country Clothes ensemble sold in Lord & Taylor's Country Clothes Shop. Elizabeth Phelps for Phelps Deep Country Clothes, skirt and blouse ensemble, cotton, early 1960s. (Author's collection. Photograph by the author.)

Fig. 4.10. Phelps Deep Country Clothes ensemble sold in Lord & Taylor's Country Clothes Shop, shown with wrap skirt reversed to solid. Elizabeth Phelps for Phelps Deep Country Clothes, skirt and blouse ensemble, cotton, early 1960s. (Author's collection. Photograph by the author.)

Fig. 4.11. Detail of Phelps Deep Country Clothes ensemble showing Lord & Taylor's Country Clothes Shop label. Elizabeth Phelps for Phelps Deep Country Clothes, skirt and blouse ensemble, cotton, early 1960s. (Author's collection. Photograph by the author.)

Clothes labels (brand label, fiber content, ready-to-wear size) as well as the label of the Lord & Taylor Country Clothes Shop (Fig. 4.11).

Elizabeth Phelps debuted reversible separates in her spring–summer 1956 "Tradewinds" collection and made an instore appearance at the New York City Lord & Taylor's Country Clothes Shop to promote the line. *The New York Times* reported, "Core of the collection is that hallmark of Phelps designing: the easy, pocket-trimmed wraparound skirt. Right side and reverse side blaze in contrasting colors that glow under the sun."[66] This collection, in a mauve and turquoise colorway, was also featured in *Vogue* that May.[67] American fashion designers had been creating mix-and-match collections of sportswear suitable for travel, and often conceptualized as weekend wardrobes or beachwear separates, since the 1930s.[68] For her 1956 line, Elizabeth contributed to this American sportswear tradition, choosing cottons or Dacron-and-rayon fabrics with antiwrinkle properties, which she offered in a blouse, halter top, shorts, and wrap skirts of both day and evening lengths.[69] The daytime wrap skirts photographed for *Vogue* are shown in a midcalf length, which is longer than the reversible wrap skirt in the author's collection, and the author's extant ensemble probably dates to the 1960s. In the mid-1960s, Phelps was still advertising "PHELPS REVERSIBLES . . . Wraparound skirts and matching shirts," along with other reversible items from shorts to hooded coats.[70] This surviving skirt and shirt ensemble, with the two pieces fortunately saved together, demonstrates how the long-term relationship between Phelps Associates and retailer Lord & Taylor came together in its Country Clothes Shop.

A 1951 advertisement lists other department and specialty stores across the country that were carrying Phelps Deep Country Clothes and some leather goods: four stores in Pennsylvania; three in Connecticut, Ohio, and New York State (outside of the city); two in Texas; and one store in each of California, Indiana, Massachusetts, New Jersey, and Oklahoma.[71] By 1958, William and Elizabeth were operating four Phelps retail stores of their own, and Phelps clothing and accessories were sold in forty-eight department stores and specialty stores in the United States and Canada. The Phelpses operated freestanding Phelps stores in Asheville and Charlotte, North Carolina, and in Ormond Beach and Sarasota, Florida. Phelps products were principally sold in stores east of the Mississippi.[72]

Conclusion

Like most mid-twentieth-century fashion companies, Phelps Associates relied on publicity and retail outlets to help sell their products. Public relations, the art of making news, was important to building the Phelps brand. Through events like the Coty Awards and placement in cultural venues like the Metropolitan Museum of Art, the Phelpses received free publicity that helped raise consumer awareness of their work. Being recognized for the quality of their work rather than paying for advertisements was something that the Phelpses would probably have considered desirable on ideal and practical levels. This type of publicity would have avoided both outright self-promotion and expense that could little be spared in a small startup business. Editorial coverage in fashion media, such as newspapers and magazines, was also important to the Phelpses' ongoing project to position themselves and their products as connected to US patriotism, craft, and folk life, and these themes, as well as the theme of the pastoral, were some of the most commonly evoked in magazine articles featuring their work. William and Elizabeth Phelps seem to have been successful in presenting their work in these terms to journalists, who shared these connotations with their readers. Magazine journalists also portrayed the Phelpses' work in terms of the etiquette of accessories, teaching consumers when and where Phelps accessories could be properly worn. During World War II, these strictures were somewhat relaxed in some media portrayals, but with increasing formality after the war, the Phelpses' work was primarily seen as suitable for country and suburban life. Retail stores, including Lord & Taylor, with which Phelps maintained an ongoing and special relationship, were also key to selling Phelps goods. Women who might never visit the Phelps workshop could instead discover a Phelps bag or belt on a ground-floor display or in a specialty department within a large store, where the quality of the materials in innovative forms could be seen and touched. Public relations, museums, fashion journalism, and retail were all means of establishing the Phelps image as patriotic and defined by a rugged aesthetic tied to a rural lifestyle and excellent craftsmanship.

Postwar Expansion: Joanna Furnace, Pennsylvania

After World War II, William and Elizabeth Phelps moved the center of their operations to rural Pennsylvania, where they experimented with two different workshop models, in an attempt to increase production. The Phelpses also introduced sportswear to their offerings, with Elizabeth Phelps creating clothes that were suitable for her country lifestyle but also conformed to William Phelps's ideas that women should dress in a traditionally feminine way. Originally, these garments were custom made, but in 1949 the Phelpses launched a ready-to-wear line, Phelps Deep Country Clothes. These, along with Elizabeth Phelps's side projects designing menswear prototypes and leather-based clothing for manufacturer Sills, gave Elizabeth Phelps an opportunity to showcase her talent for problem-solving and elegant designs.

Introductory Objects: The Helen L. Hart Accessory Set, Joanna Furnace

In the collection of the Hay Creek Valley Historical Association (HCVHA), located at Joanna Furnace, a nineteenth-century iron furnace near Morgantown, Pennsylvania, there is a recently acquired set of three accessories, two of which are Phelps. There is a simple scalloped leather Phelps belt and one of the quintessential Phelps eagle motif postman shoulder bags; a pair of white leather gloves was found tucked into the purse (Figs. 5.1, 5.2). Local resident Helen L. Hart (1930–2020) owned these accessories, used them, and kept them for a lifetime. Hart's estate donated this set after her death on New Year's Day 2020.[1]

A single woman, Hart had been predeceased by parents and siblings.[2] The text of a eulogy read at her funeral reveals Hart as remembered by her many nieces and nephews: her Methodist Christian faith; her appreciation for the beauty of creation, including birdwatching and wildflowers; her travel to Yellowstone Park; her care for objects with family provenance; and her powder-blue Indian motorcycle. This text also reveals Hart as someone who kept her clothing and accessories from year to year rather than discarding them: "She still had clothing in her closet from the '50s. She took care of it so it lasted, and it still fit, so why buy new ones!"[3] To find Hart's connection to the Phelps accessory set requires looking back to when she was a young woman in her teens and early twenties. Unlike more affluent and socially prominent Phelps clients, such as Mrs. Morehead Patterson, who donated a similar eagle shoulder bag to the Brooklyn Museum (Fig. I.2), Hart's relationship with the Phelpses was not of custom client but that of employee.

Hart's belt is cut from three pieces of leather.[4] The first and largest piece forms the main segment of the belt and has four scalloped shapes: two in back and two slightly larger that wrap around the wearer's sides to the front. Unlike the scalloped Phelps belts discussed in previous chapters, this one has no decorative metalwork on the scallops. The design is also simplified to contain fewer scallops. The edge stitching is brown and appears to have been done by machine. The stitching is not completely straight but sometimes meanders away from the curve of the belt. The second piece of leather is an end piece attached to the belt buckle.[5] The buckle itself appears to be brass and has the peaked shape

Fig. 5.1. Phelps Associates, shoulder bag, leather, metal, circa 1948. (Joanna Furnace, Hay Creek Valley Historical Association, Gift of the Estate of Helen L. Hart, 2020. Photograph by the author.)

Fig. 5.2. Phelps Associates, belt, leather, metal, circa 1948. (Joanna Furnace, Hay Creek Valley Historical Association, Gift of the Estate of Helen L. Hart, 2020. Photograph by the author.)

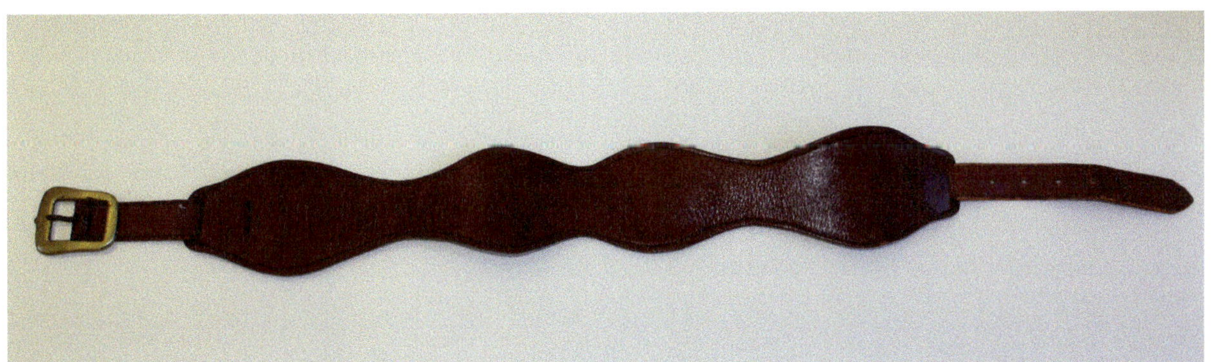

echoed in the Phelps trademark symbol. The reverse of the buckle frame has the mark "PHELPS TM" etched into the metal (Fig. 5.3). Leather is wrapped around the bar of the buckle and stitched down, with a hole cut for the prong. A third piece of leather, at the opposite end, is punched with five holes into which the buckle prong could be inserted. There is no metal end tip. The belt bends at the second from the last hole. This section of the belt shows wear, with areas of vertical cracking and loss of finish at the edges. The belt does not lay completely; the donor perhaps stored it rolled up.

Hart's Phelps shoulder bag is one of the quintessential eagle motif postman-style bags, with a short strap that would keep it close to the body.[6] Given the strap's short length, this bag (like the author's collection bag, in Fig. I.1) would have probably been worn close to the body on one side, rather than crossbody. The bag is made of a smooth, probably calf leather in a medium-brown color, between the light brown of the Costume Institute bag (Fig. I.3) and the darker brown of the author's collection bag (Fig. I.1). The main body of the bag is constructed of a piece of leather folded like an envelope, with side gussets to give the bag's two-inch depth. The front flap has a decorative line pressed in to follow the curves of the bag. It has a small strap that extends under the bag to close over a brass ball. On this strap, there is

Fig. 5.3. Detail showing reverse of belt buckle with Phelps trademark. Phelps Associates, belt, leather, metal, circa 1948. (Joanna Furnace, Hay Creek Valley Historical Association, Gift of the Estate of Helen L. Hart, 2020. Photograph by the author.)

a circular hole and a slit large enough to allow the brass knob to slip into the circle, in keeping with the designs of the other, similar bags. This strap also has the mark "PHELPS," in capital letters, stamped (slightly askew) into the leather.

The bag's most noticeable feature is the shield-shaped front patch pocket, with a brass American eagle motif, 4⅝" high and 4⅛" wide. The eagle is secured to the leather of the pocket via five metal fasteners that pierce the leather to the pocket's reverse side. The pocket has decorative white thread top-stitching on three sides and is open on the top.

On the interior, there is a small pocket, sewn onto the back of the bag's front edge (Fig. 5.4). This also closes with a flap; the part of the original snap is still in place on the flap, but the counterpart is missing. The interior metal hardware shows oxidation with green residue where the snap part would have been, as well as a remaining impression in the leather in the shape of the missing snap, and green tarnish on the remaining snap part. Significantly, there is also green tarnish and two small metal pieces at the top edge of the pocket opening, which indicates where the Phelps brass belt buckle-shaped trademark symbol was once attached (Fig. 5.5). In examining the bag, I discovered the heavily tarnished, crumbling, and disintegrating trademark symbol carefully wrapped in plastic (presumably by the late owner) inside the pocket (Fig. 5.6). Helen Hart must have known the importance of symbol and wanted to make sure that it stayed with the bag. I alerted the HCVHA director to this detached piece and its conservation issues.[7] Even apart from environment issues, like relative humidity, Phelps bags are likely to show this type of decay because metal and leather are reactive materials. From a conservation perspective, a Phelps bag is afflicted with inherent vice because the tannins in leather can corrode metals like brass.[8]

The reverse of the bag has two brass dee rings to which the shoulder strap attaches using clip-type hooks. Small leather straps hold the dee rings to the bag and are attached with two metal rivets each.

The strap has a buckle in the slightly pointed shape that is similar to the Phelps trademark symbol.

As mentioned, the shoulder bag contained a pair of c.1950 topstitched white gloves, which Hart most likely wore at the same time as the bag. The gloves, stained brown from extended contact with the bag, were most likely left inside after being worn together. Despite not being Phelps accessories, they add to our knowledge about how the set was worn. As discussed in chapter 4, the fashion etiquette of town and country as promulgated by fashion magazines such as *Vogue* dictated that Phelps shoulder bags were increasingly presented as a casual suburban or country style in the postwar period. However, the association of this bag with the white gloves suggests that at least one rural Pennsylvania woman wore her Phelps items not with the more casual string gloves suggested by fashion magazines and newspaper articles but with more formal white gloves for daytime.[9] Did she perhaps wear this bag, belt, and gloves to attend worship at Harmony United Methodist Church in Morgantown, where her obituary and eulogy note she was an active member?[10] Hart was known for "dressing nicely with a perky scarf and matching gloves."[11] The gloves suggest that perhaps Hart wore her Phelps items for "best" rather than casualwear. This is consistent with an introductory remark from a 1981 Hart interview that notes that the Phelps brand was "well known and popular with 'wealthy' people."[12] For someone who was not "wealthy," the Phelps accessories might well have been treasured items to be worn carefully rather than casually.

Helen Hart was born in 1930, in the early years of the Great Depression, when William Phelps was still working for General Motors and his meeting with Elizabeth "Elsie" Heintges was still a few years away. Hart's family lived on a farm when she was growing up, and her father also did plastering and woodworking.[13] Hart was a young teenager when the local historic iron furnace, Joanna, was sold by the last ironmaster's family to a couple from New York: William and Elizabeth Phelps.[14] The Phelpses moved into the Ironmaster's Mansion at Joanna Furnace, and the teenage Helen Hart was hired as parttime help to

Fig. 5.4. Helen L. Hart bag with top flap open. Phelps Associates, belt, leather, metal, circa 1948. Joanna Furnace, Hay Creek Valley Historical Association, Gift of the Estate of Helen L. Hart, 2020. Photograph by the author.)

Fig. 5.5. Helen L. Hart bag with interior pocket flap open, showing prior location of the metal Phelps trademark symbol. Phelps Associates, belt, leather, metal, circa 1948. (Joanna Furnace, Hay Creek Valley Historical Association, Gift of the Estate of Helen L. Hart, 2020. Photograph by the author.)

Fig. 5.6. Detached Phelps metal trademark symbol from the Helen L. Hart bag. Phelps Associates, belt, leather, metal, circa 1948. (Joanna Furnace, Hay Creek Valley Historical Association, Gift of the Estate of Helen L. Hart, 2020. Photograph by the author.)

serve meals at the mansion, working after school and on Saturdays. Hart's duties did not involve cleaning or cooking, which seem to have been done by a fulltime employee; she recalled that at one point the Phelpses employed a Chinese American man as cook and at another time a woman named Mrs. Kutz, from the nearby town of Birdsboro, was employed as cook.[15] Mrs. Kutz appears to have been a live-in staff member, Hart rarely stayed overnight at the mansion, labelling on her circa 2019 diagram of the mansion, "I slept there one night," indicating an upstairs guest bedroom.[16] Hart recalled that when the Phelpses had company for dinner, Elizabeth would help Hart clear the table before moving into the living room to have coffee with the guests.[17]

Hart was also an accomplished seamstress and patternmaker and made her living doing piecework for during periods of her adult life.[18] It is unclear whether she transitioned from parttime domestic work for the Phelpses to working in their business. The Phelps shoulder bag and belt she kept for the rest of her life most likely came into her possession while she was employed by the Phelpses. Perhaps she purchased them with an employee discount, or perhaps they were even a gift from her employers. The slight flaws on this set might have meant they were "seconds," which would not have been sold through the regular retail stores. Her time working closely with the Phelpses, particularly Elizabeth, in a domestic setting means that her memories of the Phelpses include personal glimpses of the family and a perspective that is valuable and different from the public, published interviews that appeared in newspapers and magazines.

Hart, with her father, Elmer Hart, was interviewed by members of the HCVHA History Committee on June 22, 1981, and the edited interview was published in the HCVHA *Journal* in 2010.[19] This interview, along with Hart's own clippings of newspaper articles about the Phelpses, her schematic plan of the Ironmaster's Mansion, and documents related to her death in early 2020, help fill in a picture of one Phelps employee who also owned and used Phelps leather goods. Helen Hart's memories and insights will be interwoven throughout this chapter, which considers the next stage of the Phelps Associates story: the workshop's move to rural Pennsylvania.

Birdsboro and Joanna Furnace

The Phelpses' critical success during the war years placed extra pressure on their business model, with its emphasis on quality rather than speed, and the well-being of the artisans rather than quantity of production. High-end department and specialty stores around the country were eager to stock Phelps Associates leather goods, but the New York workshop could not meet the demand. Rather than attempting to expand their workshop again, the Phelpses looked to William's home state of Pennsylvania for a potential new location with lower overhead and a lower cost of living, which would allow them to pay lower wages.[20]

A new phase in William and Elizabeth Phelps's working partnership came in 1945, when they purchased a historic iron furnace property in Berks County, Pennsylvania, from some of William's relatives and began planning to move their leathergoods workshop and residence there. The Phelpses paid $24,600 for the iron furnace and its nearly four thousand–acre tract of land.[21] The property had reportedly been in the possession of some part of William's family on the Drown side since the 1790s, and the *New York Post* reported that the surrounding acreage was 3,925.[22] They initially hoped to sell most of this land to the state for conservation purposes and retain some 800 acres for themselves and their business.[23] Joanna Furnace was named for the wife of Samuel Potts, who, along with Thomas Rutter II, Thomas May, and Thomas Bull, founded the furnace in 1791. The furnace produced iron throughout the nineteenth century.[24] William Phelps's ancestor William Darling had been an owner and operator of Joanna in the nineteenth century, and Phelps was also distantly related to the Smiths who were the last ironmasters of the working furnace. The final iron-producing blast at Joanna Furnace had occurred in 1898, and in the years between the last blast and the Phelpses' purchase, the buildings other than the Ironmaster's Mansion had fallen into disrepair and decay.[25]

Before completing the move to Joanna Furnace, the Phelpses set up a second, different kind of workshop in nearby Birdsboro, Pennsylvania, about nine and a half miles northeast of Joanna, and hired local labor (Fig. 5.7).[26] The Phelpses founded this initial Pennsylvania workshop with the financial backing of five big stores: Bonwit Teller of Philadelphia, Neusteter of Denver, Neiman Marcus of Dallas, Harzfeld's of Kansas City, and L. S. Ayers of Indianapolis.[27] These stores all wanted to guarantee that they would receive Phelps leather goods. The Birdsboro workshop appears to have been an incorporated entity with four of the stores investing $5,000 each and one investing $2,500, in exchange for shares of noncumulative preferred stock, while the Phelpses owned all of the $2,400 of common stock.[28] This arrangement absolved the Phelpses from having to pay dividends to their shareholders. It was also important because generally in corporations, the first duty is to maximize shareholders' profits, which would have fundamentally conflicted with the Phelpses' production philosophy.[29] If the venture was a success, the Phelpses hoped to eventually take full control of the enterprise by calling in the outside investors' shares at par.[30] It seems a wise choice for them to have set up this separate vehicle for their collaboration with the large specialty stores, rather than take the risks—including loss of artistic control—that might have resulted from allowing the stores to take stakes in Phelps Associates. This is quite likely an area in which William Phelps put his experience in the corporate realm to good use in service of their artistic goals.

The Birdsboro workshop, housed in an abandoned church, differed from the primary Phelps Associates business in production method as well as in business structure. Edward S. Cooke Jr. writes, "The romantic notion of the solitary craftsman lovingly making single objects one at a time remains central to our understanding, but it is ultimately a myth—a fiction that denies the economic realities of craft practice."[31] The Birdsboro space challenges the image of Phelps Associates as the small workshop, run by artisans content with modest profits. In contrast to the one-bag-per-worker-per-day method of the New York workshop, at the Birdsboro workshop the Phelpses aimed to "by working 'runs' on not more than five of the Phelps seventy-five standard-bag models . . . produce fifty bags in a day—two and one-half per worker."[32] This would be a significant increase in speed over the production of their University Place workshop, as noted in chapter 2. While

Fig. 5.7. The Phelps workshop in Birdsboro, Pennsylvania. (*Fortune,* November 1945, 160. Walker Evans, [105 Views and Studies of Leather Craftsmen, Their Home in Birdsboro, Pennsylvania, and New York City Residence, Commissioned by *Fortune* Magazine for "The Small Shop," Published November 1945], film negative, Walker Evans Archive, 1994, 1994.252.3.1–.105. © Walker Evans Archive, The Metropolitan Museum of Art. Image source: Art Resource, NY.)

artisans of the University Place workshop created a wide range of models and enjoyed the intellectual challenge of a constant variety of work, Birdsboro employees would make the same design repeatedly. The caveat, of course, was that by doing so they could not sacrifice quality. The gains in speed would have result from workers getting faster as they produced the same bag or belt multiple times; yet it would still be produced not by assembly line but by each worker making a whole item from start to finish by hand. Could the slightly askew Phelps stamp on the Hart eagle shoulder bag closure be the result of this pressure to speed up production?

The Birdsboro model was also a far cry from the original cozy Washington Square workshop, where the Phelpses and their employees all sat down to a communal table for lunch each day. How often would William and Elizabeth Phelps have been physically in the Birdsboro site working? Between the New York City workshop and showroom and the planned move to Joanna Furnace, it seems reasonable to speculate that they would not have been at Birdsboro very regularly. The move to speed up and increase production almost certainly resulted in a greater divide between the Phelpses as designers and master craftspeople and their employees, at least in Birdsboro. The Phelps invested $2,000 in equipment for the Birdsboro location and invested their time in training new employees, who would be paid at the local wage scale of $16 to $25 per week, well below the salaries earned in New York City of $27.50 to $45.[33] While the Phelpses did plan to keep their production at a modest scale, they were willing to experiment with different production models in an effort to reach a wider client base.

The Joanna Furnace property contained several buildings, including an 1847 Gothic-style engine house; the Ironmaster's Mansion, constructed of local red sandstone and converted from Federal to mansard style in 1877; and a mule stable that had once sheltered the animals that worked at the furnace.[34] The Phelpses planned to live in the Ironmaster's Mansion, and they purchased it with much of the furniture from the previous residents, the Smiths, still in place (Fig. 5.8).[35] William and Elizabeth undertook renovations themselves, including curing wood for the sandstone house floors themselves by boiling it so it turned black.[36] They also hired local workers to install electricity, update plumbing, and add stone fences to the property.[37]

Helen Hart remembered many details of the renovated mansion as it was during the years the Phelpses lived there. Downstairs, Hart would maneuver her way from the kitchen, with its black woodburning stove and rag rugs, to the dining room, where placemats were set to allow the wood of the Phelpses' carefully waxed oak dining table to be on display. The house had two front parlors, one of which contained a piano and was used by the family as a living room, and the other as a workspace for Elizabeth Phelps.[38]

The Joanna Furnace property had included at least seventeen tenant houses in the nineteenth century, and some of these were still standing when the Phelpses purchased it.[39] The Phelpses also initially planned to offer optional,

Fig. 5.8. The Ironmaster's Mansion, Joanna Furnace. (*Fortune*. November 1945, 161. Walker Evans, [105 Views and Studies of Leather Craftsmen, Their Home in Birdsboro, Pennsylvania, and New York City Residence, Commissioned by *Fortune* Magazine for "The Small Shop," Published November 1945], film negative, Walker Evans Archive, 1994, 1994.252.3.1–.105. © Walker Evans Archive, The Metropolitan Museum of Art. Image source: Art Resource, NY.)

low-cost ($6 to $20 per month) onsite rental housing for their workers, but it is unclear whether this was ever implemented or whether this was an option in which workers were interested.[40] It is also unclear whether any of their New York City employees moved to Pennsylvania to continue working for them. The Phelpses did at one stage provide daily transportation for their workers. Jane S. McIlvanie of the *Philadelphia Inquirer* reported in 1949 that William Phelps himself did the daily pickups and drop-offs, in an old school bus.[41]

One existing tenant, William Moore, was granted a life estate in his house and a lifetime paid caretaker's position, as part of the sale agreement when the Phelpses purchased the property. Moore's granddaughter, Anita Boyer Turner, grew up in this house and later recorded her impressions of both Phelpses. Turner recalled William Phelps as "a no-nonsense person who always wore pressed trousers and a dress shirt."[42] She remembered Elizabeth Phelps as "a tall, thin, refined lady with lots of energy who always spoke to my brother and me in a way that made us think she really liked us. She sometimes brought us gifts from New York such as art supplies, sketchbooks and children's novels."[43] Turner also remembered Elizabeth Phelps as having "a good sense of humor" and enjoying sledding and skiing with Turner and Turner's father "until Mr. Phelps came outside and yelled to his wife that she should come in and 'stop acting foolish.' Perhaps he did not like her having a good time with my dad."[44]

Fig. 5.9. The Joanna Furnace Mule Stable, west side, September 21, 2020. (Photograph by the author.)

Fig. 5.10. One of the windows the Phelpses had installed in the Mule Stable at Joanna Furnace, September 21, 2020. (Photograph by the author.)

Turner's memories of Elizabeth Phelps seem more positive than of the more reserved William Phelps. She also leveled a more serious charge: during the electrical wiring of the Joanna Furnace property, undertaken by Turner's father, "I heard Mr. Phelps trying to convince daddy to take shortcuts. Daddy insisted he would do it correctly or not at all. He kept working so, apparently, he won the discussion."[45] Whether Turner fully understood the particulars of the exchange, she was aware of tension between her father and his employer, perhaps heightened by Turner's family's position as tenants, next-door neighbors, and employees who contractually could not be removed or discharged.

By September 1947, when Mary Braggiotti of the *New York Post* interviewed the Phelpses, they were well on their way in the process of moving their personal and professional lives to Joanna Furnace. Braggiotti reported, "They hope eventually to have just a showroom and rush order workshop in New York." Her article offered such personal details as that "they are both Protestants, no political party affiliation. Regarding alcohol, they prefer hard cider, sherry, vermouth."[46]

William and Elizabeth Phelps chose the Mule Stable as the location for their new main workshop (Fig. 5.9).[47] According to the HCVHA's didactic labels in place at the Joanna Furnace site in 2019, the Phelpses modified the mule barn "by adding 19 windows with four panes over two sashes to bring extra light into the stable for their sewing crew." The Mule Stable has thick stone walls; the window sills at ground level are nineteen inches deep.[48] It is sited running north to south, with the long walls facing east and west. When the Phelpses remodeled the building, they added a series of large windows near the ceiling on the eastern wall. In 2020, these windows were covered by roller shades. The effect of opening even one of the shades is a vista of pure open blue sky (Fig. 5.10). Together, they would have provided ample natural light, especially in the morning.

The larger spaces at Joanna Furnace and in Birdsboro would allow Phelps Associates' business to grow beyond the capacity of the University Place workshop in New York. *Life* reported that by 1945 fifteen craftsmen worked in the New York location, with sixty more in the new Pennsylvania facility.[49]

Changes in Bag Styles

The popularity of shoulder bags and large, menswear-inspired belts waned in the 1950s, with the return to more feminine and formal fashions. This shift underscored Phelps Associates' need for to diversify their offerings. The fashionable postwar bag was unlike the classic Phelps shoulder bag in aesthetic, materials, and form. As discussed in chapter 3, Phelps-style shoulder and belt bags went through the full cycle of fashion over the decade of the 1940s, from being new, different, and highly fashionable; to popular and widely copied; to going out of style. In 1947, *Vogue* celebrated "the prim, new look of handbags; they're pocketbooks again. The Duchess of Windsor's is a prissy little bag of black calf on a stiff, almost stuffy gilt frame."[50] With metal again available for handbag frames, the all-leather structure of Phelps bags was no longer in demand. This rapid pace of fashion change left the classic Phelps bag and belt of the 1940s, studded with vintage metalwork, trailing behind. In 1954, the Phelpses' New York City metalwork supplier, Francis Bannerman Sons, advertised in its circular, "British Coat of Arms, brass with studs on the back for attaching. Size 5 inches wide, 3½ inches high. Fine decoration for hand bag, door, etc. Price, $2.50 each" (Fig. 5.11).[51] Ironically, by the time Francis Bannerman Sons actively marketed their products for handbags, fashion had already moved on. Fashion's constant demand for change conflicted with the Phelpses' craft model of production, in which similar styles were produced for years rather than changing dramatically with each season.

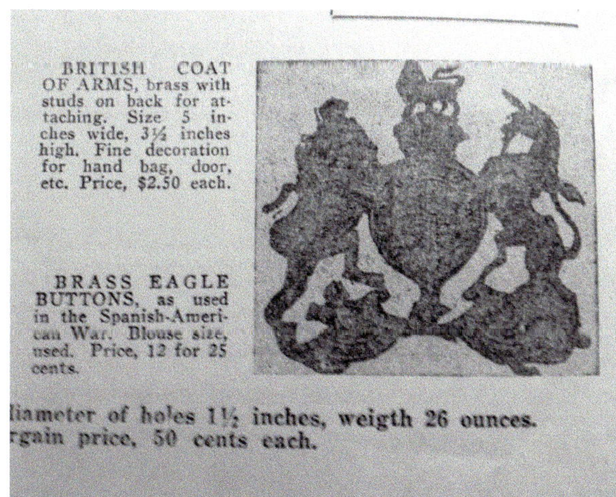
BRITISH COAT OF ARMS, brass with studs on back for attaching. Size 5 inches wide, 3½ inches high. Fine decoration for hand bag, door, etc. Price, $2.50 each.

BRASS EAGLE BUTTONS, as used in the Spanish-American War. Blouse size, used. Price, 12 for 25 cents.

liameter of holes 1½ inches, weigth 26 ounces.
rgain price, 50 cents each.

Fig. 5.11. Francis Bannerman Sons, January 1954 circular, 14. (Patricia D. Klingenstein Library, New-York Historical Society Museum and Library.)

In 1956, when Claire McCardell published her book of fashion advice, *What Shall I Wear?,* she included a section that critiqued the shoulder bag as an item thoroughly out of fashion, in contrast to her own clothing designs, which she promoted as timeless. McCardell presumably worked with a ghostwriter, so it is difficult to know precisely which ideas in the book are hers and which were the product of collaborators or editors. A letter tucked into the author's copy of the book from Brook Kindred of *McCall's* states, "*McCall's* fashion editor, Estelle Brent, had a little finger in this book—being somewhat of an expert."[52] It is possible that Brent worked with McCardell and some of the criticism of the Phelpses' work is attributable to her.

McCardell begins mildly: "Sometimes times change, and what Fashion said was good for *then* isn't good for *now*. The wartime shoulder-bag is an example."[53] She then details the practical benefits of shoulder bags: They allowed women to have two hands free, and they sat well on the padded shoulders of 1940s jackets. "It came, quite naturally, into the city in the early forties. Every woman had more errands to do, more carrying because deliveries were spasmodic and there were fewer taxis on the street. It was wonderful to have two free hands to shop with, to pull yourself on a bus or to hang onto a subway strap. Besides at the time, shoulders were padded and good for holding those big straps in place.[54] She explains that shoulder bags were "dreamed up imaginatively in all kinds of shapes—the pouch, the postilion, the knapsack. And the important point is, it could go to the Plaza at noon or at five or even after the theater."[55] The references to particular shapes, sometimes specifically used in reference to the Phelpses' work in the 1940s, implies that she was thinking of them. McCardell argues that during the war, the shoulder bag was appropriate for formal daywear, cocktail attire, even evening after the theater. The etiquette of fashion in the 1940s allowed for shoulder bags to be used in the city and at multiple times of day, but at the time of her writing, in the mid-fifties, fashion etiquette demanded more strict delineation between town and country and for different times of day. With the increasing formality and specificity of 1950s fashion etiquette, there was no longer room for the shoulder bag in the city at all—McCardell argues that in 1956 shoulder bags belonged in the suburbs, no longer at the Plaza, but rather the local grocery store or elementary school: "Today, the shoulder-strap bag stays in the country. . . . You seldom see it in a truly urban setting. Somehow it has become too *emphatic* a bag. Once it looked sophisticated and right with town clothes. Now it either looks military or too casual."[56] An illustration by Annabrita on the same page shows a stylized version of the Phelps cartridge case bag with military star emblem similar to the one shown in *Women's Wear Daily* on May 7, 1943.[57] The reference to Phelps is clear. The militarism of the cartridge case bag, probably diminished its appeal in the postwar era. Similarly, the Francis Bannerman Sons circular of January 1947 offered for sale "3,000 New Cadet Cartridge Boxes. Made of black leather. Price, 30 cents each."[58] High-priced, custom-made, Revolutionary-era-look cartridge cases must have lost what remained of their luster when the market was suddenly filled with military surplus, very similarly shaped, contemporary cartridge cases for mere cents apiece. In 1955, Francis Bannerman Sons still had not sold all of this lot of cartridge cases.[59]

McCardell's paragraph on Phelps is immediately followed by a section with the subhead "Fashion Survives—When It Deserves To." The harshness of this critique suggests she might have even had a personal conflict with the Phelpses. And of course, McCardell lists herself as the prime example of the designer of fashions that are "dateless because they continue to play the same role and consequently reappear again and again. They stay becoming and comfortable." [60] Ironically, although McCardell seems to dismiss the Phelpses as a flash in the pan (despite that they were the designers of accessories that were paired with her garments many times in the 1940s), the Phelpses' work over the succeeding decades would show them to be, like McCardell, designers for whom "certain basic features reappeared season after season."[61] Regarding dramatic style changes, Elizabeth Phelps said, "Our customers wouldn't stand for" them.[62] A 1960s Phelps shoulder bag was much like one made in the 1940s, minus the military insignia; *Women's Wear Daily* reported in 1964, "The Phelps bag came in a variety of shapes but the one that brings a nostalgic smile to women over 35 years old was a drawstring design with a metal emblem on the flap. It can still be ordered in the Country Clothes Shop at Lord & Taylor for $65 to $135."[63] Like McCardell, the Phelpses created items that a fashion journalist might venture to call "classic."

And in fact, a 1955 *New York Times* article by Elizabeth Harrison was titled "American Classics: Phelps Casual Designs." Harrison reported that each year William introduced five new bag designs, while continuing to keep the old favorites in production. She similarly described Elizabeth's updates to the womenswear line: "Mrs. Phelps occasionally adds new designs to her line while keeping the established favorites. Her principal changes are made with color rather than with her beloved, almost classic separates."[64] McCardell dismisses Phelps's shoulder bags as unfashionable in the 1950s, yet in the 1960s, Phelps would still be producing wrap skirts—just in shorter lengths—and shoulder bags—just in tiny sizes; their basic look did not change significantly in more than thirty years of production.

But as the end of the war and the cycle of fashion lessened the demand for shoulder bags, the Phelpses looked to new opportunities to enhance their brand's offerings. The Phelps Associates business would change and grow in the following years. As William and Elizabeth Phelps branched out in the early postwar period, they initially thought in terms of expanding their handmade offerings: "'Everything,' Phelps summed up, 'that it's logical and better to make by hand.'"[65] This included nonfashion products, such as a cow-horn salad fork and spoon in a leather case, featured in the Museum of Modern Art's *100 Useful Objects of Fine Design 1947* exhibition, and attributed in the catalogue to "W. D. Phelps" only. The exhibition, curated by Edgar Kaufman Jr., focused on everyday objects ranging in price from twenty-five cents to one hundred dollars, and the cow-horn set retailed for fifteen dollars at the Phelps Associates store.[66] Presumably, in the Joanna Furnace workshop, they were far enough away from neighbors to resume their work in cow horn without worrying about the smell being a nuisance. The Museum of Modern Art show would have given the Phelpses publicity outside their normal range of fashion industry connections. The Phelpses also crafted other lifestyle items, including chair seats, luggage stands, gun cases, bone drinking mugs, and wooden items.[67] In the month that the *100 Useful Objects of Fine Design 1947* exhibition opened, *Harper's Bazaar* also featured a Phelps bag that broke with two of the characteristics the label had been so associated with during the war: it was shown as a handbag, rather than a handsfree shoulder bag (although the text noted it came with both long and short straps), and it had a metal frame.[68] Ultimately, none of these new products would prove to be the right way forward for Phelps Associates.

Sportswear

Soon it became clear that women's sportswear was a promising avenue for growth. Textiles entered the Phelps repertoire slowly, originally as a compliment to their leather goods business in their New York City workshop. Elizabeth Phelps's interest in combining leather and fabric in garments probably started with the Phelpses' handbag designs. For example, by 1943 they were combining horse-blanket plaids with leather trim in a series of purses, and a 1944 shoulder bag combined a striped wool fabric with leather, including a red leather lining.[69]

For autumn 1947, Phelps offered leather-trimmed stoles made from converted horse blankets; *Vogue* featured a yellow-and-blue checked one, while *Harper's* showed a rust-and-navy-blue one.[70]

The Phelpses' immersion in the world of a nineteenth-century iron furnace had an impact on their thinking. When Elizabeth Phelps mentioned a stove lid as something an artisan might want to make from start to finish (see chapter 2 for a discussion of artisanship), she was probably thinking of this because ten-plate Joanna Stoves for kitchens and parlors were a product for which Joanna Furnace was known in the early-to-mid-nineteenth century.[71] The Joanna Furnace years also added a layer to Phelps Associates' evolution, from the new production methods at Birdsboro to the introduction of women's sportswear in response to Elizabeth Phelps' lived experience and felt fashion needs as she adjusted to their new life in the country.

As early as 1944, Phelps Associates had been selling custom-made aprons. *Harper's Bazaar* showed one in its March 1944 issue, calling it "the avantgarde apron—the work apron Mrs. Phelps designed for herself—a semicircle of natural crash, wrapped in back, belted in leather."[72] In 1947, socialite Mrs. Howard Hawks (Slim Keith) was shown in *Harper's Bazaar* wearing a "Frontier Apron" of brown-and-white calfskin, which was supposed to be similar to the apron Elizabeth Phelps wore in her workshop. This leather apron was shown worn over pants by Voris, a California-based designer of handmade suede clothing.[73] In October, *Harper's* featured another of these frontier aprons, made of deerskin and worn over custom trousers by Meyers of Philadelphia.[74] The "frontier" description applied to these aprons referenced an Americana similar to that of their bags based on shapes from the Revolutionary period; both relied on an idealized American past as inspiration for twentieth-century American fashion.

It is not surprising that the Phelpses' first foray into clothing was through the apron, an easy-to-construct garment that also referenced their leatherworking artisanship. While as objects, some basic apron forms may appear simple, aprons are weighted with nuances of meaning. Joyce Cheney, curator of popular touring exhibitions of American aprons, argued in 2000, "The power of aprons lies in how they make us feel and what they help us remember. For many, aprons are nostalgic. . . . In the United States, aprons . . . have come to represent the uniform of domesticity, representing the security and sanctity of home and family."[75] In the 1989 Metropolitan Museum of Art exhibition *Apropos Aprons,* curator Beth Alberty analyzed examples across time, geography, and culture and argued that in different contexts, aprons conveyed both sexual meanings and labor associations. In the introduction to the exhibition, she asserted that the work associations of the apron were "particularly with the trades of men and the domestic work of women."[76] The earliest magazine coverage of the Phelps Associates aprons highlighted the fact that Elizabeth Phelps had created the design originally for her own use—not for domestic use, but for her trade as a leatherworker.[77] At least initially, the aprons were promoted for their associations with the Phelpses' leathercraft. The apron as originally designed by Elizabeth Phelps subverted the gender norms and domesticity of women's aprons, by linking the apron to images of strong pioneer women and working artisans.

The first mention of Phelps custom women's separates in *Vogue* was in the October 1948 issue, for a skirt "made of cotton—tough, awning cotton; made to order (no two ever precisely alike)" (Fig. 5.12).[78] *Vogue*'s editorial commentary here focuses on the paradox of tough luxury—the skirt is a luxury good due to its uniqueness as a custom-made garment. Yet at the same time, *Vogue* calls attention to the humble materials used—durable cotton sailcloth.

Elizabeth Phelps relied heavily on sturdy cotton fabrics, such as canvas and denim. She later described her early experimentation with cotton sailcloth:

> When my husband and I first moved to rural Pennsylvania, after having lived in New York City for many years, I became very unhappy about my clothes. They consisted of what I then considered a suitable country wardrobe—freshly starched shirts and skirts. Occasionally, when we were alone, I wore blue jeans; but Jim didn't really approve of these for working hours or trips to the local village. . . . Then, while we were puttering around the workshop one day, I saw some bright-turquoise sailcloth we were using for summer bags. I decided to make an apron. Jim liked the idea of my wearing it over my jeans, and I felt very neat in its bright, pleasant color. During the days that followed, I made more aprons. Then I dyed some old Army slacks of Jim's to match. After that I began making neater-looking, trimmer slacks. And a new costume was born. I loved it, and lived in it, all day long.[79]

In this description, Elizabeth Phelps was writing to the female readership of *Woman's Day,* a few years after she first started experimenting with the apron-and-pants separates combination. Publicist Constance Hope affirmed in her memoir, "Even the

Fig. 5.12. Phelps custom skirt, 1948. "Made for You," *Vogue,* 1 October 1948, 139. (Horst P. Horst, *Vogue,* ©Condé Nast.)

old lady in Dubuque must know that a good many of the stories in our national magazines are publicity inspired. . . . A good many are ghosted, a large part are inspired by the editors (and then ghosted), and a fair share come from the minds of publicity men."[80] Therefore, such articles must be read with caution in attempting to recover the history of the origins of Phelps sportswear. In this account, the textile in colorful and functional sailcloth inspired Elizabeth Phelps to move into creating the apron and pants combinations, although fashion magazine evidence points to her marketing leather aprons before she offered textile examples. She may have shared the sailcloth anecdote, and a ghostwriter may have decided to describe it as the first sportswear, or Phelps herself might have emphasized the sailcloth rather than the leather based on what she was trying to sell in 1953.

Elizabeth Phelps's *Woman's Day* article cites several design inspirations: suitability to location, notions of femininity endorsed by her husband, and finally the textile itself. Fashion media continually reinforced the concept of dressing appropriately for the location, with magazines listing the correct clothing for town versus country, as described in chapter 4. The idea that William Phelps had conservative notions about proper attire—for women and men—accords with Anita Boyer Turner's descriptions of him as always dressed formally and with attention to details like pressing.[81] William Phelps's notions of femininity did not include trousers for women's regular daywear, and this must have had an especially strong impact on Elizabeth, as he was not just her husband but also her co-designer, whose taste and opinions she would have respected. In seeking to please both William and herself, she came upon the apron-and-pants combination as a compromise. This is an important part of their working relationship as a husband-and-wife team. As in the case of the first wide belt, they created to please not just themselves or an imagined client but also each other. William Phelps's ideas regarding gender roles were expressed even in the womenswear separates credited to Elizabeth Phelps individually. It is noteworthy that while Elizabeth Phelps defied certain gendered expectations to become a proficient worker in leather—a material with masculine associations—when out of the workshop she still reinforced traditional notions of femininity regarding dress.

Fig. 5.13. Elizabeth Phelps models her hunting apron. "New Country Aprons . . . Worn by the Designer," *Vogue,* 1 November 1948, 136. (Frances McLaughlin-Gill, *Vogue,* ©Condé Nast.)

The November 1948 issue of *Vogue* featured Elizabeth Phelps's series of aprons worn over pants. The article's opening photograph is a full-page black-and-white photograph of Elizabeth Phelps in her hunting apron, carrying her gun as she strides across a cornfield and looking confident and powerful (Fig. 5.13).[82] Yet, in the late 1940s this image would also have read as very luxurious. Much sporting gear, including hunting boots, had not been manufactured during World War II, as the high-quality leather, especially sole leather, was needed for military applications. Thinking in terms of art historian Michael Baxendall's concept of the "period eye," the 1940s magazine reader would have seen the availability of the materials needed for such an ensemble as a return to plenty and abundance.[83]

Vogue reported, "Mrs. Phelps has quietly revolutionized her wardrobe, worked out a scheme that is wholly new . . . a string of aprons which she wears over the unimprovable country basic: long pants. But long pants which could become more attractive to women by the simple fact of skirt-shaped apron. . . . There is a splashproof fishing apron with a place for a fly-box. A shooting apron with a flick of the hunter's traditional red; two bellows pockets for cartridges, etceteras."[84] The silhouette of Elizabeth Phelps's apron layered over long pants is essentially that of nineteenth-century American reform dress: an updated Bloomer costume. However, the function of the ensemble is not so groundbreaking—Phelps confined her apron and pants look to the country, while reformers like Elizabeth Smith Miller wore trousers and skirt together for street dress.[85] Yet, cultural historian Annemarie Strassel notes that in 1945 a *Vogue* portrait of Broadway actress Celeste Holm, star of *Bloomer Girl,* referenced the Bloomer costume, and its caption drew comparisons "between modern dress and the formal vocabulary of dress reform that saw sturdy, roomy dress as a conduit to women's physical and social liberation."[86] Elizabeth Phelps would have been fully aware of this earlier coverage, which compared her friend Clare Potter's designs to the Bloomer costume, and in creating clothes in this same style Phelps would have been embracing the connotations of dress reform that came with it.[87]

The Phelps aprons are made in a wrap style that overlaps in the back, rather than ending at the sides, thus creating a skirt shape all the way around (Fig. 5.14). One of the photographs shows Elizabeth grooming her dog with her back to the camera, to show the apron's back coverage.[88] Anita Boyer Turner recalled that "Mrs. Phelps loved dogs."[89] The Phelpses' Dalmatian was named Joanna, after the Furnace, and called Jo for short; if William was distracted from his breakfast by a telephone call, Jo was known to eat the eggs from his breakfast plate.[90] They also owned dachshunds, arriving at Joanna Furnace with Puitsy, and later Puitsy's relative Puitskins.[91] Of the several types of aprons for the *Vogue* article, each—described in the text by its purpose, for example, the "dog-grooming apron" in "leatherbound khaki"—is worth noting for its combination of leather trim with fabric.[92] In 1948, Phelps was already using this leather-and-fabric combination. While this may have been difficult to keep neat and clean in a garment meant

Fig. 5.14. Elizabeth Phelps's apron over pants look. "New Country Aprons . . . Worn by the Designer," *Vogue,* 1 November 1948, 137. (Frances McLaughlin-Gill, *Vogue,* ©Condé Nast.)

for pet care, it probably was a luxurious combination for country clothes. Elizabeth Phelps would later take this idea to her work for leather outerwear manufacturer Sills in 1951, as will be discussed later in this chapter.

The multiple types of aprons encouraged customers to buy more than one: There was also a gardening apron in canvas, a fishing apron in turquoise-and-green canvas, and a leather golf apron.[93] The different activities for which the aprons might be used were probably suggested to Elizabeth by activities she enjoyed or saw others enjoying in the country. Helen Hart remembered that Elizabeth Phelps liked to garden—raising flowers, herbs, and vegetables such as asparagus, as well as making herb vinegars and strawberry wine. The gardening apron, as well as later gardening attire that Elizabeth would design, was probably an extension of Elizabeth's own interests and needs in their Joanna Furnace country lifestyle. These aprons were designed for outdoor activities and were shown thusly in *Vogue,* not in the context of the domestic interior. Although Hart recalled that painting was one of Elizabeth Phelps's "hobbies," along with working in her rock garden, there were no aprons for painting.[94] It is doubtful that Elizabeth Phelps, muralist of the 1930s, would have agreed that painting was now just a hobby, even in this stage when her professional artistic output was focused on the accessories and garments of the Phelps brand.

As a result of the November 1948 *Vogue* article, the "demand for pants and aprons put the Phelps in the clothing business."[95] That is to say, that the demand made it clear to the Phelpses that sportswear might form not just a small niche in their custom business but that it might make sense to expand into ready-to-wear. By the following summer, the Phelpses were ready to debut their new clothing line, Phelps Deep Country Clothes. They planned introduce the line through a fashion show and garden party for invited guests at the Joanna Furnace property, on June 4, 1949, from 2:30 to 4:30 P.M.[96] A June 9, 1949, newspaper clipping from Helen Hart's file shows a photograph of eight of the thirty-six models, posed as chatting pairs, lined up outside the western exterior wall of the Mule Stable (Fig. 5.15). The women are wearing various ensembles from the Deep Country Clothes line, including jumpers, skirts and blouses, and the apron-over-pants combination. The clothes are accessorized with wide Phelps leather belts. One shoulder bag is worn crossbody style, and a soft, teardrop-shaped bag is held loosely from a hand.[97] The models ranged from celebrity friends of the Phelpses, including the wife and daughter of movie actor Claude Rains, to local matrons and art students from Philadelphia.[98] The models were given props to carry, such as cutting baskets or potted geraniums, supplied by florist Eleanor Hutchison, emphasizing the purpose of many of the garments as clothing for pursuits like gardening.[99] Not all the ensembles were designed for outdoor activities, however; at least two models wore Elizabeth Phelps's version of a hostess gown, one of magenta blouse and white skirt, and another in black with pink and aqua-blue trim.[100]

Thirty-six models will wear the Phelps Deep Country Clothes at the First Showing at a garden party at Joanna Furnace on Saturday afternoon, the 4th. After selecting the right costume and the right colors for the event eight of the models line up against the stone wall of the work-shops for photographer, Ned Goode. Starting at the left they are Mrs. Everett Hoopes, Mrs. Colin Lofting, Mrs. J. Frederick Bicking, Mrs. W. Burlong Cocks, Mrs. William Rudkin, Mrs. William Bell, Mrs. Horace Spackman, 2nd and Mrs. Robinson McIlvaine.—Courtesy, The Archive, Downing.

Fig. 5.15. Models for first Phelps Deep Country Clothes fashion show, lined up on west side of Mule Stable, newspaper clipping, Helen L. Hart Archives. Joanna Furnace, Hay Creek Valley Historical Association, Berks County, Pennsylvania.)

This fashion show was created by Broadway stage designer Raymond Sovey, known for his work on productions including *Arsenic and Old Lace.*[101] Sovey used the "sloping path from the house to the workshops" as a runway.[102] The Phelpes planned the event to include music from a string quartet, and tea served in the garden from an old Conestoga wagon—a touch of Americana emphasizing the historicism of the surroundings and the leather goods, although the new sportswear looked less aligned with this aesthetic and more focused on modern simplicity.[103]

A key to the fashion show's success was attracting members of the New York fashion press. The local newspaper clipping Helen Hart saved lists the expected members of the press and sounds like a who's who of midcentury American fashion journalism: "The Press will be represented by such notables as Dorothy Roe, of the Associated Press, Alice Richardson, of *Look,* Eve Hatch Holms, *Town and Country,* Virginia Pope, *New York Times,* Editor Carmel Snow and Diana Vreeland, *Harper's Bazaar,* Sally Kirkland, *Life,* Beatrice Simpson, *Vogue,* Wilhela Cushman, *Ladies Home Journal* and Lois Long, *The New Yorker.*"[104] Most of these journalists had already featured the Phelpses' leatherwork prominently, and many had been Coty Award judges. Alice Hughes featured the Phelps Deep Country Clothes fashion show in her syndicated newspaper column, "A Woman's New York," which allowed people across the United States to read about the Phelpses' new project.[105]

Some of the journalists who attended were also Phelps clients. In addition to the Sally Kirkland custom Phelps belt at the Museum at FIT, there is also a belt donated by *Vogue*'s Beatrice Simpson, who attended this fashion show. Simpson's belt is a brown cowhide tooled with a pattern of red diamonds, measuring 30⅝" in overall length by 2¾" wide (Figs. 5.16, 5.17). Here, the classic Phelps buckle shape is produced in red wood. The museum catalogue dates

Fig. 5.16. Detail of belt donated to the Museum at FIT by Beatrice Simpson of *Vogue*. This belt is marked with the Phelps trademark symbol and the words "Phelps-Handmade" stamped into the leather near the buckle. Phelps Associates, belt, leather, wood, metal, circa 1949. (Museum at FIT. Gift of Beatrice Simpson. 74.95.2. Photograph by the author. Courtesy the Museum at FIT.)

Fig. 5.17. Phelps Associates, belt, leather, wood, metal, circa 1949. (Museum at FIT. Gift of Beatrice Simpson. 74.95.2. Courtesy the Museum at FIT.)

the belt to circa 1948, which seems a reasonable date and would put it around the time of colorful first Phelps Deep Country Collection. A belt with a similar wooden buckle was featured in *Women's Wear Daily* in 1952, described as made of "persimmon wood unbreakable and highly polished."[106] Maintaining ties to the New York fashion world was crucial to the Phelps business as a whole and particularly this expansion into ready-to-wear.

Helen Hart recalled that much of the entertaining the Phelpses did was business related. They hosted their friend and early fashion industry contact Clare Potter, who shared their interest in Dalmatians. They also entertained the Robinsons, of New Holland, Pennsylvania, who owned a department store in that town and supplied fabrics for the Phelpses' new sportswear.[107]

The Phelpses initially approached their ready-to-wear line as a project to be designed by Elizabeth but outsourced to a clothing manufacturer elsewhere in Pennsylvania for production. In February 1950, Phelps Deep Country Clothes were being manufactured by a local children's dress manufacturer, Philadelphia Girl.[108] This arrangement was another attempt to expand the Phelps business and profitability, but it meant that the Phelpses had lost control over the production process, with no influence over the working conditions. Outsourcing production to a ready-to-wear manufacturer was a far cry from the egalitarian, artisanal workshop of their ideals. Around this time, *Women's Wear Daily* reported that the Phelps Deep Country Clothes line was being offered in both misses and girls' sizes; however, I have not yet located any extant garments in children's sizes.[109] In a fashion show for the Philadelphia Fashion Group, the Phelpses displayed a ready-to-wear collection that included both leathers and textiles: dark, light, and colored denims, and a buckskin sleeveless jacket with pleated peplum and pouch pocket attached to the waist belt. In early 1950, the Phelpses maintained two showrooms—one at 17 East Forty-Eighth Street in Manhattan and the other at Fifteenth and Mt. Vernon Streets in Philadelphia—showing their divided focus between New York and Pennsylvania.[110]

Elizabeth Phelps's Side Projects

Shortly after the Phelpses' expansion into women's sportswear, Elizabeth Phelps pursued a few side projects. If, as Emma McClendon has argued, her designs in denim and marketing strategy were indebted to Claire McCardell, likewise, Bonnie Cashin's work for Sills might be indebted to Elizabeth Phelps.[111] In December 1951, Elizabeth Phelps designed a suede line for Sills, taking on the role of outside designer for a manufacturer.[112] She only designed for Sills through 1952. In 1953, Bonnie Cashin started working for Sills, but many of the combinations considered hallmarks of Cashin's work for the company, such as suedes and tweeds trimmed in leather, had already been hallmarks under Phelps.[113] Elizabeth Phelps could have created this combination, or the Sills company could have mandated it. The company could have hired a new designer could because Elizabeth Phelps chose to focus on her own company and the Phelps Deep Country Clothes line or because they desired a higher rate of fashion change, not part of the Phelps work style.

Another of Elizabeth Phelps's side projects was a menswear design for the Metropolitan Museum of Art's 1950 *Adam in the Looking Glass* exhibition. Fashion historian Diane Maglio notes that this was "the first exclusively menswear exhibition in America," showcasing six hundred years of the history of menswear and encouraging new ideas in the contemporary American menswear industry, through a section named "Eve Dresses Adam." Maglio notes that this section, in which female fashion designers imagined the menswear of the future, drew both praise and interest from the industry as well as censure from many male visitors and reviewers.[114] Besides Elizabeth Phelps, the "Eve Dresses Adam" section included menswear designs by Claire McCardell, Clare Potter, Lilly Daché, Sophie of Saks, and other prominent female American designers. A *New York Times* journalist described Elizabeth Phelps's contribution as "a collarless suit of faded blue denim with short dickey sewn in. A man's handbag goes with suit."[115] Installation photographs show a mannequin posed with one hand on his hip and the other holding what the *Times* writer had called a handbag but was a variation on the Phelps Associates shoulder bag (Fig. 5.18). The hardware on this bag, including the strap buckle, was similar to that of many bags Phelps

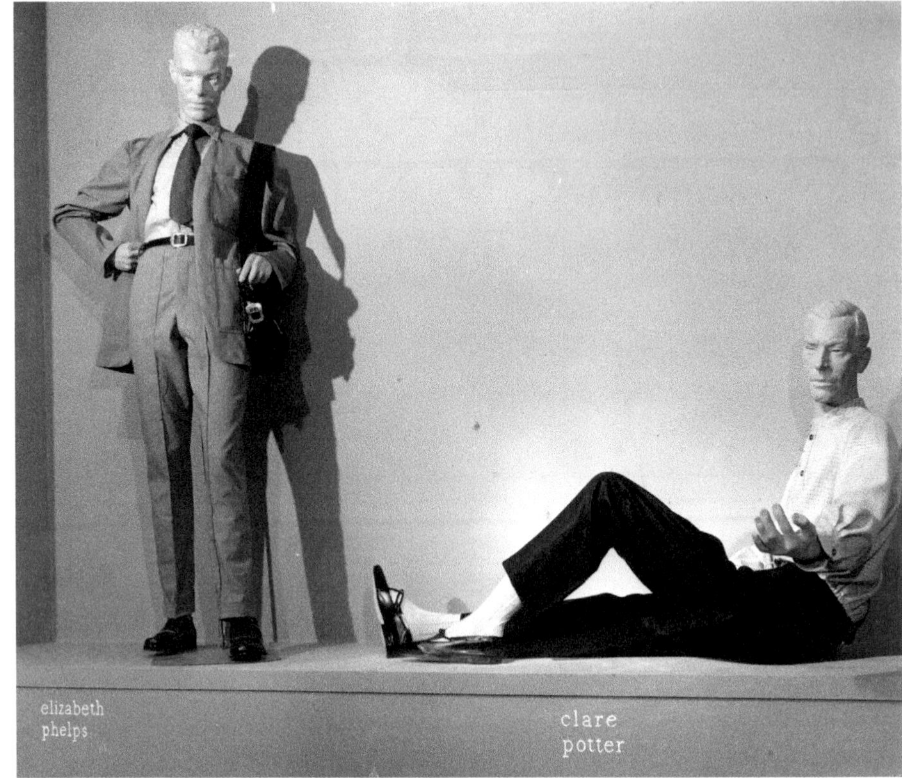

Fig. 5.18. *Left:* Elizabeth Phelps's contribution to the Metropolitan Museum exhibition, *Adam in the Looking Glass,* 1950. (Special exhibition *Adam in the Looking Glass: Men's Fashions from the Fourteenth Century to Tomorrow,* The Metropolitan Museum of Art, The Costume Institute Galleries, January 13–July 30, 1950. View of Tomorrow's Fashion Gallery. Image copyright © The Metropolitan Museum of Art. Image source: Art Resource, NY.)

designed for women. The exhibition checklist notes that the shoulder bag and matching belt were both made of black leather.[116]

Phelps's suit design was meant to make menswear lighter, following criticism from writers like couturiere and critic Elizabeth Hawes that twentieth-century menswear was uncomfortable because men were wearing several pounds more fabric than women.[117] Phelps's interest in removing a layer of textile from menswear also follows the criticisms Bernard Rudofsky posed in his 1947 essay about the 1944 Museum of Modern Art exhibition *Are Clothes Modern?* Rudofsky identified what he termed "the seven veils of the male stomach"—seven layers of fabric covering the abdomen of a man dressed in western fashion of the 1940s, including undershirt, drawers, shirt, trousers, vest, coat, and overcoat, and deemed these multiple layers unnecessary.[118] Elizabeth Phelps's choice of a washable denim for her jacket meant that there would be no need for washable layers of undershirt and shirt underneath the jacket to protect it from perspiration; thus, the design eliminated several layers of heavy textile from the man's body. Fashion historian James Laver's coverage of the exhibition in *Vogue* demonstrated how the layer-eliminating design worked by showing a bare-chested male model slipping on the jacket and dickey, without an undershirt.[119]

The exhibition's promotional material included personal statements from each of the designers; Elizabeth Phelps addressed the issues of textile weight and care:

> In regard to the suit that I made it seemed to me that the one thing men especially wanted was to remove one layer in the summertime and in doing this, to be able to go to their offices and to appear in [r]estaurants. Another very important thing is that with just a shirt and trousers those who are more amply provided present an unattractive silhouette, which is covered up by the loose front of the ordinary jacket. The garment which I made provides ventilation and still gives a slightly formal appearance and could easily be made of all one type lightweight shirting fabric, so that the whole thing can be laundered as a shirt. It is my candid opinion that if men really want lightweight clothes, they will also have to wear shields.[120]

Phelps's statement illuminates some of her beliefs about gender roles and clothing. She shows that her interest in using clothing to obscure parts of the body, and to protect clothes from certain parts of the body, is not limited to womenswear. In her womenswear designs, she used aprons to camouflage hips and bottoms; here a man's protruding stomach creates "an unattractive silhouette." Her design, conservatively retaining the appearance of a jacket form, is intended to cover male figure flaws. In addition, it complies with the requirements of fashion etiquette that dictated men had to wear jackets in restaurants and offices, at a time when a man in shirtsleeves was considered to be in a state of semi-undress. Phelps's aside that she believed that men who embraced lightweight clothes would have to wear shields (she leaves out the feminine associations of the word *dress* from the usual phrase *dress shields*) calls for men to accept a usually hidden item of clothing associated with women's body care and grooming; without heavy jacket layers to hide sweat stains, men will also need strategically placed sweat absorption accessories. It is unclear exactly how these would have been attached—perhaps directly to the armpit of the jacket.

While Elizabeth Phelps seems to have taken the "Eve Dresses Adam" challenge seriously and applied her usual design principles of functionality and appropriateness to the project, she did not introduce a menswear component to her ready-to-wear offerings. Her participation in the exhibition was probably more an exercise in publicity for her name as a designer and to promote Phelps Deep Country Clothes. Phelps's careful and thoughtful approach to rethinking the menswear was also indicative of her approach to womenswear. By participating in the challenge, she made the point that the womenswear she designed was similarly attentive to matters of utility, appropriateness, figure-flattering, and quality.

Near the end of 1950, Elizabeth Phelps also received recognition on her own rather than alongside her husband, through the New York State Women's Council. At an October 15 luncheon for 150 held at Sherry's Restaurant, she was given a citation, or "honor scroll," for outstanding achievement as a woman in business, presented by Governor Thomas E. Dewey of New York State.[121] As Elizabeth was honored alongside other women in fields as varied as journalism, education, packaging, and hospitality, this independent recognition presaged the increasing public role she would take in the Phelps business over the course of the 1950s and 1960s.

End of the Joanna Furnace Years

In 1949, Bethlehem Steel contacted the Phelpses about buying the Joanna Furnace acreage as part of its search for iron ore deposits in the area. The Phelpses sold the steel company two hundred acres of land that year, and the company also made purchases from other local landowners.[122] Historian Suzanne Fellman Jacob states that the Phelpses were "offered a large sum of money for the remaining 3,400 acres of the Joanna Furnace property."[123] They took the offer and moved their workshop to the South.[124]

Perhaps the increased land value due to potential mineral deposits was the primary factor in the decision, or there may have been other issues at work. Anita Boyer Turner recalled, "In retrospect, and in hearing others talking, I really do not think the Phelps[es] had the financial resources to keep up their lifestyle and maintain the mansion and all of the buildings and tenant houses. Before we moved, they were having problems with paying their employees and those who had done contracting work for them, my dad included. Therefore, it was not a surprise when we heard that the property was being sold, along with all of the furniture and antiques."[125] Turner's comments indicate that the Phelpses may have overextended themselves in the Joanna Furnace purchase and the expansion of the business. If Phelps Associates were struggling to pay employees and make ends meet, it is not surprising that they would turn to ready-to-wear and display less concern about the working conditions related to that mode of production.

Bethlehem Steel bought Joanna Furnace as part of a series of land purchases leading up to the founding of the steel company's new iron ore-producing Grace Mine in 1951.[126] The sale was finalized in the summer of 1951.[127] In August, the Phelpses held a public auction at the Ironmaster's Mansion, disposing of most of the house contents, including the furniture they had bought from the previous owners. The mansion they had so painstakingly repaired was abandoned and would only survive about another decade; in the 1960s, Bethlehem Steel tore it down.[128]

The destruction of the mansion seems emblematic of a difficult period for Joanna Furnace and its people. When the Phelpses closed their workshops in Pennsylvania, it was at a cost of local jobs. The Phelpses' employee Helen Hart went on to sew, doing piecework for other factories for many of her working years. However, her eulogy noted, "When the sewing factories closed, she took work cleaning at Holiday Inn—strenuous physical work usually done by younger people. But once again, she gave it her best and did what she had to do to support herself and her parents, a matter of integrity."[129] Hart found herself in a moment when she could no longer find paid work that used her skills and craftsmanship, an experience that must have been true for others in the community as well. In fact, Phelps Associates' move to the South was only one example of a larger postwar trend for businesses to relocate from the Northeast and Midwest, first to the South and West, and then later overseas, where wages were lower, there was less unionization, and new municipalities offered tax breaks and other incentives to companies. We are still dealing with the long-term effects of these shifts today.

In 1975, community members organized the HCVHA, with a mission to promote "an understanding and an appreciation for our local heritage by maintaining and instructing in those crafts, skills, and artifacts that represent our heritage."[130] In 1979, Bethlehem Steel donated a twenty-six acre section of the original Joanna Furnace property, containing surviving buildings such as the Phelpses' former workshop in the Mule Stable.[131] Today, the workshop building still stands and is part of the Historic Joanna Furnace site.[132]

Visiting Joanna Furnace on a brilliantly clear, sunny day in early autumn, everything seems in

Fig. 5.19. The Joanna Furnace Mule Stable, east side, September 21, 2020. The Phelpses added the row of windows on the upper level. (Photograph by the author.)

crisp focus. Turning off Pennsylvania Highway 10 onto old Furnace Road, and then into the Joanna Furnace site, the path winds gently downhill past trees, still wearing summer green, and the remaining stone buildings of the nineteenth-century iron furnace. At the foot of the hill, past a field for parking, there is the elongated rectangular building that was once the Mule Stable, home to the working animals of the furnace in the nineteenth century and for a brief period after World War II home to Phelps Associates workshop (Fig. 5.19).

Currently, the Mule Stable is configured to hold the HCVHA office. The building's north and south ends have small upstairs areas, and its middle is open to the full ceiling height (Fig. 5.20). As of September 2020, the walls in the two upstairs areas were hung with displays of farm implements and paintings of the destroyed Ironmaster's Mansion. The director's office is at the north end, and the south end has a kitchen. The center of the building is arranged with tables and chairs for serving food. Executive director Mark Zerr notes that when the HCVHA took over the site, it had basic restroom facilities, but HCVHA added new ones. When I visited, I was able to study the Helen Hart Phelps accessory set in the very space where the Phelpses once worked. Today the Mule Stable is a place where the many layers of history at the Joanna Furnace site are being preserved, investigated, and recorded.

Conclusion

As William and Elizabeth Phelps sought to expand the Phelps Associates business after World War II, they left New York City and relocated their workshop and residence in rural Pennsylvania. They purchased historic Joanna Furnace and its surrounding acreage and located their custom workshop there. In partnership with retailers, they experimented with a more streamlined non-custom

Fig. 5.20. The Joanna Furnace Mule Stable, interior, September 21, 2020. (Photograph by the author.)

production of fewer models in nearby Birdsboro. Their signature shoulder bag went out of style after the war, prompting the Phelpses to think about other products they could offer. The kinds of clothes that Elizabeth found she needed for a rural lifestyle were the inspiration for a new line of sportswear, first custom-made and then ready-to-wear under the Phelps Deep Country Clothes label. In this sportswear line, Elizabeth balanced pleasing her husband and being in accord with his beliefs about gendered clothing with her own ideas about problem-solving, functional design that addressed what she thought were the needs of middle- and upper-class white women. These characteristics were also evident in her side projects designing for manufacturer Sills and for the "Eve Dresses Adam" section of the Metropolitan Museum of Art's *Adam in the Looking Glass* exhibition. In the Joanna Furnace years, the Phelpses were fruitful in finding new avenues for design, but their attempts to expand the business in Pennsylvania were not ultimately financially successful, and in 1951 they sold Joanna Furnace and relocated to North Carolina.

6

"Mountain Craftsmen" and Ready-to-Wear: Skyland, North Carolina

This chapter examines the third and last Phelps workshop location, in Skyland, North Carolina (just outside of Asheville), which would demonstrate yet another aspect of American identity in the way Phelps products were promoted, as they drew on a tradition of local Appalachian craftsmanship to provide both skilled labor and a new marketing angle for their products. Over the course of the 1950s, Phelps Associates would continue to produce leather goods, but the Phelps Deep Country Clothes ready-to-wear sportswear line would increasingly be the business's focus. Here, Elizabeth Phelps is used as a case study for investigating the interactions between various layers of the American fashion industry, with particular emphasis on the ways textile companies and ready-to-wear designers worked together in mutually beneficial promotion strategies. Relationships with local textile companies and a focus on everyday sportswear that met women's needs and lasted through the years were key factors in the Phelpses' success in this location. In addition, this chapter considers how theories of the everyday apply to Elizabeth Phelps's increasing reach to consumers, both as a designer of ready-to-wear sportswear and creator of paper patterns for home sewing, which allowed an even wider range of people to wear Phelps designs.

Introductory Objects: Two Wrap Skirts

Unlike many of the Phelps Associates leather goods, which stand like small, three-dimensional sculptures, without a wearer's body these two objects from the collection of the Valentine Richmond History Center lie as flat, like yard goods: a Phelps Deep Country Clothes denim wrap skirt and a similar skirt

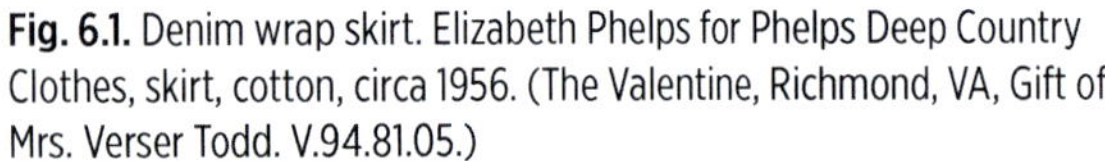

Fig. 6.1. Denim wrap skirt. Elizabeth Phelps for Phelps Deep Country Clothes, skirt, cotton, circa 1956. (The Valentine, Richmond, VA, Gift of Mrs. Verser Todd. V.94.81.05.)

Fig. 6.2. Orange twill wrap skirt. Elizabeth Phelps for Phelps Deep Country Clothes, skirt, cotton, circa 1956. (The Valentine, Richmond, VA, Gift of Mrs. Verser Todd. V.94.81.02.)

orange cotton twill (Figs. 6.1, 6.2). The skirts are from the same donor, Richmond resident Mrs. Verser Todd (Sally Lewis Dickinson Chase Todd, b. 1911?). In the 1990s, Todd donated a collection of garments that she had worn from the 1930s through the 1970s. Todd was also a custom client of French house Balmain and New York firm Fiffi & Elliott, as well as a purchaser of ready-to-wear by American designer Helen Cookman.[1] The Valentine's accession paperwork dates both skirts to circa 1956.

The blue denim skirt is typical of the Elizabeth Phelps wrap style that emerged with her first skirts and aprons and continued throughout her career. Cultural historian Annemarie Strassel argues that wrapping as a construction technique "signified a rejection of architectural elements of dress fabrication such as meticulous tailoring or boning and padding. . . . At the core of the American design movement was a desire to allow women to define for themselves the fit and function of their clothing."[2] Elizabeth's Phelps's wrap skirts would have given Todd this modern flexibility. The front of the skirt has two large patch pockets (7⅜" high by 6¼" wide). The orange skirt has similar pockets (7¾" by 6⅜"). The pockets provide plenty of space for the wearer to tuck in small objects, or assume a hand-in-pocket casual pose. As dress historian Hannah Carlson argues, the concept of the hand-in-pocket pose signifying modern leisure evolved in the twentieth century, "a physical gesture—one that has come to seem natural and unselfconscious, but is learned, culturally specific, and gendered."[3] While in previous centuries considered a breach of etiquette rules against touching the body in public, at the turn of the twentieth century placing hands in pockets came to symbolize "modern ease" for men, and in later decades women appropriated it, as womenswear clothing forms incorporated menswear-inspired construction.[4] In the accession paperwork, Todd also attributed a "snapper" closure to the Phelpses, which, although not accurate, is evidence of the Phelpses' reputation as innovators in functional sportswear design.[5]

The skirts have self-fabric ties. Both use the fabric selvedge, with the white ends of the selvedge at the ends of the ties (Fig. 6.3). This is in accordance with the Phelpses' aesthetic of not wasting anything and making a virtue of careful use of materials. The skirts do not need belts for fit, as the ties make them adjustable; however, the combination of main garment and leather goods accessories is key to the Phelps look. Each skirt has fabric belt loops made

Fig. 6.3. Detail of skirts showing tie incorporating the fabric selvedge. Elizabeth Phelps for Phelps Deep Country Clothes, skirt, cotton, circa 1956. (The Valentine, Richmond, VA, Gift of Mrs. Verser Todd. V.94.81.05, V.94.81.02.)

Fig. 6.4. Detail of denim skirt showing interior labels. Elizabeth Phelps for Phelps Deep Country Clothes, skirt, cotton, circa 1956. (The Valentine, Richmond, VA, Gift of Mrs. Verser Todd. V.94.81.05.)

Fig. 6.5. Detail of denim skirt showing flat felled seams. Elizabeth Phelps for Phelps Deep Country Clothes, skirt, cotton, circa 1956. (The Valentine, Richmond, VA, Gift of Mrs. Verser Todd. V.94.81.05.)

Fig. 6.6 Both skirts can be unfolded for ironing. Elizabeth Phelps for Phelps Deep Country Clothes, skirt, cotton, circa 1956. (The Valentine, Richmond, VA, Gift of Mrs. Verser Todd. V.94.81.05.)

to accommodate a Phelps leather belt. The orange one has belt loops with an overall length of 4¾", which leave space for a belt approximately 3⅛" wide. The denim one has belt loops with an overall length of 4⅞", leaving space for a belt approximately 3¼" wide. Both skirts have similar tags on the interior, including a Deep Country Clothes label with the woven belt buckle symbol (Fig. 6.4). Both skirts are ready-to-wear size medium, marked with a tag reading "M." Both skirts have labels indicating the fiber content is 100 percent cotton.

One construction difference between the two is that the denim skirt has flat felled seams, typical of denim, while the orange skirt does not (Fig. 6.5).[6] The denim skirt is 22¼" long with an 86" sweep of hem, while the orange twill is 22¾" and has a slightly wider, 88", sweep. Both skirts unwrap completely flat for laundering and ironing (Fig. 6.6). This construction with simplicity of care in mind is very similar to that of the plaid Lord & Taylor skirt, which also can unwrap completely for cleaning (Fig. 4.9, 4.10). These skirts from the mid-1950s represent the next era of the Phelps story, as William and Elizabeth Phelps settled into a new home and workshop.

Skyland, North Carolina, Workshop

As Phelps Associates developed their workshop and their business, the Phelpses first sought to expand production of their leather goods, both by reducing overhead by moving out of New York City and through experimentation with less customized products during the Joanna Furnace years. Textile-based garments also were an avenue for expansion: Elizabeth Phelps first created custom-made womenswear separates offerings, then Phelps made a major shift in expanding into ready-to-wear, while continuing the leather goods business.[7] In the small unincorporated community of Skyland, about nine miles outside of Asheville, they built a new workshop and retail store.[8] This move also brought a new name: Phelps Industries, which they were using by 1952.[9]

In the Skyland workshop years, leather goods were still crucial to the brand identity—as the belt-buckle symbol on the Phelps Deep Country Clothes label attests—but media coverage increasingly highlighted Phelps clothing. In the mid-twentieth century, symbiotic relationships between American fashion designers and textile companies promoted both the designers' names and the brands of specific fabrics and suppliers, as Lesley Ellis Miller has demonstrated in the context of the Paris couture.[10] Relationships within the textile industry were key to the Phelpses' ready-to-wear success. Foundationally, the growth of the Phelps brand was built on the supply of materials. Just as the initial New York City workshop produced leather goods drawing on supplies available through New York's historic leather district, in North Carolina the Phelps workshop was in close proximity to textile producers. In their expansion into sportswear, the Phelpses built relationships with American textile companies, such as Crompton and Galey & Lord. The textile suppliers offered promotional opportunities including fashion shows and newspaper and magazine advertising, increasing the visibility of both parties. The fashion designer's name added luster to the textile company's reputation as a fashionable brand, while the textile company had the budget to advertise on a much larger scale than the designer alone.

In the summer of 1951, William and Elizabeth Phelps completed their move to, North Carolina. Their choice of Asheville was serendipitous: while on business in North Carolina, they were forced to stop there when Elizabeth developed an abscessed wisdom tooth and had to be hospitalized for ten days.[11] The trip was likely to visit the facility manufacturing the Phelps Deep Country Clothes ready-to-wear sportswear. By the fall of 1950, they had shifted their manufacturing from Philadelphia to the Perry Manufacturing Company, of Mt. Airy, North Carolina.[12] The couple decided they liked the Asheville area and it would make a suitable location for a new workshop.[13] Outside of Asheville, the Phelpses purchased a twenty-five-acre farm property in Skyland—much smaller than the vast acreage they had owned at Joanna Furnace but probably comparable in terms of the land they had actively used for their home and operations.[14]

Women's Wear Daily reported in August 1951, "Mr. and Mrs. William D. Phelps, a man-and-wife team recognized among the nation's top fashion designers, are building two large studios on Shadowlawn, Hendersonville Road, which they purchased two months ago."[15] The Phelpses bought the Shadowlawn property from the widow of Nicholas Beadles, an Asheville Coca-Cola Bottling Company executive. The property included a log house, garage, and barn.[16] If the Phelpses were "among the nation's top fashion designers," *Women's Wear* did not devote much column space to the article about them—a short piece placed next to an announcement that Macy's had appointed a new umbrella buyer. The short article mentions William Phelps's leatherworking and states that he "works with wood cabinets and carving" and attributes Phelps Associates' 1940s accolades such as the Coty and Neiman Marcus Awards solely to him. Elizabeth Phelps is credited only as "the originator of the wraparound skirt and other fashions for women."[17] The article concludes with the information that the Phelpses were building two separate studios and would each work in his or her own studio. It is strange that this short article emphasizes such division, particularly in the earlier leatherwork, which they clearly did together and for which the Coty Awards jointly recognized them. Perhaps this division could be attributed to the journalist's own ideas about gender, assuming that William would have done "masculine" work such as in leather, especially now that Elizabeth Phelps was becoming more associated with "feminine," fabric-based aprons and other garments.

During the relocation, the Phelpses tried to keep some connection with their New York base. In February 1952, they opened a new, "homelike" space for their custom salon in New York City at 27 East Thirty-Seventh Street, which also included space for selling items Elizabeth was designing for Sills.[18] The store was at least partially staffed by individuals connected to their new hometown of Asheville. For example, in October 1953, *The Asheville Citizen-Times*'s society columnist, Deedie Smith, included an item about a new hire to the Phelps location in New York—herself: "Miss Deedie Smith of the society department of *The Asheville Citizen* left yesterday for New York City where she has accepted a position with Phelps Industries."[19]

At the same time that they moved away from many fashion industry contacts, they moved closer to several important textile industry manufacturers. North Carolina was the leading US state in textile industry employment that year, with more than one-third of the working population employed in textile production.[20] *Miller's Asheville City Directory* for 1954 showed the importance of fiber and textile products in the area, stating that the principle manufactured products of Asheville included "blankets, cotton and yard goods, flour and feed, furniture, leather goods, rice products, . . . rayon yarn, cellophane."[21] The relationships William and Elizabeth Phelps maintained with fabric companies would be crucial to their business in the 1950s.

Despite the plan for the Phelps workshop in Skyland, North Carolina, to be built as two separate studios, it appears that construction happened piecemeal. The building containing the retail shop was erected first. A second building was added that fall.[22] In 1953, the leather workshop was located at the back of the retail store facing US Highway 25 / Hendersonville Road, while Elizabeth Phelps's Deep Country Clothes were manufactured in a wing of the Phelpses' home nearby. The shop was originally located at 1816 Hendersonville Road, but later, the address was listed as 1800 Hendersonville Road.[23]

Women's Wear Daily described the Phelps retail store as a "roadside shop," for its proximity to a popular automobile route to Florida.[24] In choosing this location, the Phelpses were one of many retail businesses moving to reach consumers who were increasingly living in suburbs and driving their cars to participate in activities like shopping. Historian Lizabeth Cohen describes the postwar shifts in the American shopping landscape of the early 1950s:

> Merchandisers also realized that postwar suburbanites were finally living the motorized existence that had been predicted for American society since the 1920s. As consumers became dependent on, virtually inseparable from, their cars, traffic congestion and parking problems discouraged commercial expansion in central business districts of cities and smaller market towns, already hindered by a short supply of developable space. Reaching out to suburbanites where they lived, merchandisers at first built stores along the new highways, in commercial "strips" that consumers could easily reach by car.[25]

It is also noteworthy that the *Women's Wear* article title touted "Roadside Shop Boasts Good Volume, Low Upkeep"; after the Phelpses' struggle to manage a massive property with historic buildings in constant need of renovation and maintenance, a smaller property and more modern space must have been a relief. The workshop building was made of cinderblock and steel, with a brick floor, and the interior was described as having "white walls, open fireplace, and unfinished dark oak fixtures . . . an ideal setting for the colorful deep country separates as well as for the belts and bags."[26] The product displays were described in terms similar to those used for former Phelps showroom at 45 University Place, with belts—and now clothes—draped on tables, and bags shown hanging or on shelves.[27] Over the course of the 1950s, the Phelpses opened additional branded shops. In 1957, they opened the Phelps Shop on Siesta Key, near Sarasota, Florida.[28] By the following year, Phelps Industries was operating four standalone Phelps shops; besides Asheville and Sarasota, these included Charlotte, North Carolina, and Ormond Beach, Florida.[29]

The Phelpses planned for their new workshop to represent a middle ground between largescale mass production and the artist who created one-off crafts. In a 1951 interview with William "Bill" Lindau, William and Elizabeth used the example of a team of geologists who wanted to place a special order for sixty-seven pairs of snake-proof boots. Elizabeth stated, "The factory couldn't produce such a small quantity, economically. On the other hand, an artist-craftsman, if he took the order at all, could produce this quantity—large, for him—at a cost that would be prohibitive. But the small shop could do the job easily, at a reasonable price."[30] The Phelpses also believed that many smaller shops employing people in an area rather than one large factory employer could help avoid the economic depression that followed if that one main employer closed down. They also praised the plethora of small craft shops supporting the French couture system: "'The small shops,' Mrs. Phelps said, 'are where originality starts.'"[31]

In 1958, Lindau wrote an article for *Women's Wear Daily* about the Phelps Industries workshop in Skyland, with a title that emphasized a link between Phelps products and the traditions of Appalachian handcraft: "Mountain Craftsmen: Native Artisans Produce Phelps Style Separates, Accessories."[32] Historian Jane S. Becker notes that beginning in the late nineteenth century, many Americans viewed the Appalachian South as representing a repository of preserved Anglo-Saxon traditions and folkways, including "authentic" handicrafts.[33] In the twentieth century leading up to World War II, many educated, middleclass craft reformers came to the area to try to revive or preserve the local craft traditions; the resulting crafts were shaped not just by local traditions but by reformers, government, and market demands of middleclass consumers from outside the area. Becker argues that these crafts were endowed with constructed meanings of tradition to increase their market value and link them with the past, in the process obscuring the reality of people living in Southern Appalachia in the present.[34] In Lindau's 1951 interview, Elizabeth Phelps referenced some of these ideas of tradition when she described Asheville: "By tradition . . . it's a crafts town. There are still vestiges of this tradition left, and there are a tremendous number of skills in the people."[35] The title of Lindau's 1958 article shows that Phelps products were consciously placed within and marketed as part of this tradition, whether or not the Asheville artisans truly differed in any significant way from the Pennsylvania artisans or even the craftspeople of the New York City workshop. Lindau states in his opening paragraph that Phelps separates and accessories "are produced at Phelps Industries here by traditional Southern mountain artisanship working in the traditional small-shop system of Paris." The article implies that there is value in the local identity of the workers, who are "all natives of the mountains surrounding Asheville."[36] Here, Lindau's emphasis on the rural mountain identity seems key to a presumably passed-down knowledge of Anglo-Saxon tradition and folkways—at least handcraft—that as Becker argues was part of the region's mystique. Becker notes that one of the key debates in the Appalachian craft community was craft as commodity versus as cultural expression; this also came to represent conflict between guilds and government agencies.[37] For their part, the Phelpses clearly celebrated craft as commodity.

The craftspeople of the Skyland workshop were featured in local newspaper coverage of the Phelps Industries workshops, sometimes even by name. The *Asheville Citizen-Times* reported that Aline B. Hollingsworth was the first employee Elizabeth Phelps hired for the Skyland workshops in 1951.[38] By summer of 1952, the Phelpses had moved production of both their ready-to-wear and custom clothing back in house.[39] Journalist Virginia T. Lathrop reported that in the clothing workrooms that year, "The 12 or 15 craftsmen wear the clothes they are making, finding them ideal for working. Wide, sunny windows look out on the mountains."[40] The employees might have been wearing the clothes they were making as a publicity stunt but also as part of the Phelpses' plan to create a workplace where workers were personally invested in, not alienated from, their products. Helen Hart's possession of a Phelps accessory set suggests a possible ongoing practice of encouraging artisans and other employees to have and wear Phelps objects. I have not discovered any evidence of Joanna Furnace workshop employees moving to work in the new North Carolina location; the employees were most likely all new to the Phelps brand, and the Phelpses were probably eager to start this enterprise on a positive note. These new employees would work along with William and Elizabeth Phelps to create the leather goods and sportswear of the Phelps label. With the new location in a textile-producing region, the specific textiles from which the sportswear was produced and relationships with textile companies became more important.

Fabrics and Producers

The following subsections will explore some of these fabrics and producers with which the Phelpses worked after they moved to the South as Phelps Industries.

Cone Mills Denim

Elizabeth Phelps frequently used denim in her sportswear, and many of her separates were available in both canvas and denim. These washable fabrics were typical of her design choices to ensure garments were easy to care for. For example, *Vogue* featured a blue denim sundress with deep patch pockets from the first Phelps Deep Country Clothes collection in its July 1, 1949, issue. The illustration shows a woman wearing the dress, a broad straw hat, and gardening gloves and holding a shovel. The article states that in it, readers will "find one costume for every sort of sudden summer need."[41] Here the "need" is assumed to be new clothes for gardening, in sturdy denim fabric, but in a cut that looks like a resort-worthy sundress. This was also almost instant coverage of the clothing line, with the gardening ensemble appearing in *Vogue* just weeks after the debut showing of Phelps Deep Country Clothes at Joanna Furnace. An extant denim jacket, frayed at the cuffs and neckline, shows evidence of wear—perhaps for gardening or other outdoor activities (Fig. 6.7).

In *Denim: Fashion's Frontier,* MFIT assistant curator Emma McClendon argues that the emergence of a label like Phelps for women's clothing "shows how

Fig. 6.7. Elizabeth Phelps for Phelps Deep Country Clothes denim jacket, cotton, 1950s. (Author's collection. Photograph by the author.)

denim was recoded during the 1950s to align with the more affluent lifestyle of postwar suburbia."[42] Not just denim but Elizabeth Phelps's whole concept of country sportswear separates became recoded thusly. The two wrap skirts that introduce this chapter exemplify this trajectory: Mrs. Todd might have gardened in her denim wrap skirt, but she might also have worn it as casual daywear out and about in suburban Richmond (Fig. 6.1). Similarly, *Women's Wear Daily* noted of Elizabeth Phelps in 1951, "Hitting the big current tide of suburban living in this country, the well-known 'Deep Country' approach of her designs now looks directly applicable to a vast consumer audience."[43] Phelps Associates were able to expand their business by capitalizing on this growing and affluent suburban market.

Along with creating products that appealed to suburban consumers, Phelps Associates needed to be able to market their products—both directly to consumers and to key industry players such as department store buyers. Relationships with their textile suppliers such as Cone, Indian Head, Crompton, and Galey & Lord were important in selling the new separates.

North Carolina-based textile company Cone Mills was one supplier of denim—as well as other fabrics—for Phelps Industries. The Phelpses participated in projects with Cone with an eye to promotional benefits. For example, in 1959, Elizabeth designed a gabardine dress for Miss North Carolina, Judith Lynn Klipfel. Klipfel's official wardrobe was structured around North Carolina manufacturing, and she did a special promotional tour "to plants using Cone fabrics in the design of her wardrobe."[44] As part of Klipfel's time in Western North Carolina, she visited the Phelps Industries facility at Skyland and had tea with Elizabeth Phelps.[45]

Indian Head Woven Cottons

Indian Head Mills was another textile company that helped to advertise Phelps Deep Country Clothes sportswear. The textile firm was founded in 1898 in Cordova, Alabama.[46] The Phelps Deep Country Clothes resort 1950–51 collection included blouses, jackets, and slacks of Indian Head brand woven cotton fabrics.[47] In the spring of 1951, Indian Head ran two small advertisements in *Women's Wear Daily* advertising its link to Elizabeth Phelps. The ad contained a drawing of a metal latch, and the text read, "Want to beat last year? Latch on to Elizabeth Phelps for deep country clothes of Indian Head cotton."[48] This advertisement seems aimed at buyers for retail stores. After the advertisement appeared in *Women's Wear,* the newspaper ran a sketch on page one of an Elizabeth Phelps Deep Country Clothes cropped trouser and panel skirt suit of rayon flannel. While *Women's Wear* did not attribute the flannel to a named producer, it named Indian Head as the producer of the material used for trim on a coordinating cotton jacket.[49] Indian Head may have been credited because it was an advertiser.

Indian Head cotton was also credited in a *New York Times* article on Phelps Deep Country Clothes available at B. Altman and shown in store on May 23, 1951. At Altman's request, Phelps produced Deep Country Clothes in what the *Times* called "large sizes" or "women's playclothes" 18 to 44, a broader size range than the normal misses' offerings.[50] And when Elizabeth Phelps designed two home sewing patterns for *Woman's Day* magazine in 1952, the featured example garments were made up in Indian Head cottons, and the pattern envelopes suggested Indian Head fabrics.[51]

Crompton Pile Fabrics

In building their new line of women's separates, Phelps Associates also relied on their relationship with Crompton, a producer of pile fabrics such as velvets, velveteens, and corduroys. Crompton was founded in 1807 in Rhode Island and followed the larger pattern of American textile manufacturing, moving to the South, where wages were lower and unions were weak. By 1953, Crompton had mills in Georgia, Virginia, and Arkansas; it was the oldest textile company in the United States when it declared bankruptcy in 1984.[52]

Corduroy, such as that produced by Crompton, played a role in both men's and women's casual wardrobes of the 1950s, in what American author Edna Ferber called in 1958, "the careless clothes of the times."[53] Crompton used a combination of print-media advertisements and in-person promotional events to link their fabrics to the glamour of high fashion, reaching both the American fashion industry and consumers. In March 1950 and 1951, Crompton hosted two fashion shows in New York to promote their products that included Elizabeth Phelps designs.

The 1950 Crompton spring showing was held on March 23 at the New York Ritz-Carlton Hotel and included both American and overseas designers.[54] *Women's Wear Daily* reported that the garments shown were about half velvets and half velveteens and corduroys: "A particular effort has been made to show unusual uses for fabrics, and those that have especial application to American fashions."[55] As sportswear separates, Elizabeth Phelps's designs were considered especially American. Fashion historian Rebecca Arnold has argued that although sportswear originated in England in the early twentieth century, it became especially linked with notions of Americanness, modern life, and ease of movement, simultaneously evoking myths of rural America and urban modernity.[56] The March 23 program began with a fashion show of garments that had been made using Crompton fabrics, from dresses, coats, and suits to rainwear and sportswear. *Women's Wear* noted that the fashion show was primarily aimed at "cutters of better-priced garments"; that is, higher quality American ready-to-wear. After the runway show, attending ready-to-wear manufacturers could view the garments again by appointment in the Crompton showrooms.[57]

Much of the advertising for the fashion show was geared toward American ready-to-wear industry. In the lead up to the March showing, Crompton ran a series of advertisements about the show in *Women's Wear.* In February, they bought an ad column that proclaimed "Crompton and [here they listed 27 designers by name] Make It a Year of Creation." Below this was a small sketch of a Parisian street scene, evoking the fashion mystique of the Parisian couture. They included the teaser in the final text at the end: "This paper will announce further details—watch for them."[58] A larger ad, containing a wider view of the street scene sketch, ran about ten days before the fashion show, stating, "Admission will be by invitation only . . . to the designers and manufacturers who will find this advance showing of foremost concern."[59] The goal of an advance showing of fall couture designs was to encourage American ready-to-wear manufacturers to produce their own fall lines in Crompton fabrics, as well. After the fashion show, Crompton ran at least five follow-up advertisements in *Women's Wear Daily.*[60]

In March 1950, Crompton also targeted consumers and ran an advertisement in *Harper's Bazaar.* As did the *Women's Wear* ad, this one included the list of designers and sketch of Paris. The Phelps attribution here and in other Crompton advertisements was "Elizabeth Phelps" rather than "Phelps Associates"—perhaps Elizabeth was asserting her agency in the design partnership, particularly in the context of the womenswear, in opposition to media coverage of the leather goods, which often cast her in the role of supporter or helper to her husband rather. The text of the ad concluded, "Look for Crompton fabrics in fine fashions and by the yard."[61] Crompton also ran a follow-up in *Vogue*'s June issue, with a photograph of a Jacques Fath design in Crompton velvet but also giving an extended listing of other designers, including Elizabeth Phelps, "creating 1950 fashions in Crompton velvets, velveteens and corduroys for evening, cocktail and town types."[62]

Crompton's advertising strategy was to link the prestige of the named couturiers with Crompton velvets, velveteens, and corduroys, to encourage consumers to buy both garments made with their fabrics and Crompton fabrics by the yard, which would have been available in fabric stores and department stores. However, Crompton's advertisements were also helpful to Elizabeth Phelps's business. Phelps Associates and Phelps Deep Country Clothes would not have been able to afford full-page major magazine ads or the long series of ads in *Women's Wear Daily.* The links with the Crompton fabric company kept the Phelps name before the public, both industry and consumer, and served to associate in the minds of magazine and newspaper readers that Elizabeth Phelps's new separates venture was fashionably luxurious, like the work of the Parisian couturiers also featured in the shows; such an association harkened back to times before the war, when the allure of Paris was often a selling point for American fashions.[63]

The 1950 Crompton promotion was successful enough that it was repeated in 1951, with advertisements again directed toward consumers through fashion magazines *Harper's Bazaar* and *Vogue.*[64] For contribution to the 1951 show, Elizabeth Phelps created a lounging costume using a Crompton velvet with the brand name "Vel Bouffant." This at-home ensemble, in a more formal fabric than her usual choices, consisted of olive-green velvet trousers, black velvet coat, and white linen blouse. Phelps's design, alongside those by Elsa Schiaparelli and Robert Piguet, was used after the fashion show to promote Crompton brand velvets by the yard in the fabric departments of department stores.[65] Elizabeth Phelps also used Crompton corduroy in her own fall 1951 line, such as a moss-green jacket and skirt ensemble, which *Vogue* featured in its autumn editorial pages, naming Elizabeth Phelps as designer, Crompton as the fabric company, and Lord & Taylor as the retailer where the outfit could be purchased (jacket $13, skirt $15).[66] Given the close relationship with Crompton, an extant Phelps Deep Country Clothes corduroy jacket is probably made of Crompton fabric (Fig. 6.8). The Museum at FIT has two jackets in brown corduroy (accession numbers 91.134.7 and 91.134.8), one of which reverses to an off-white cotton canvas; these jackets are also quite likely made of Crompton fabric.

Fig. 6.8. This jacket's label notes that it was custom-made, even as much of Phelps's production shifted to ready-to-wear. Elizabeth Phelps for Phelps Deep Country Clothes corduroy jacket, cotton, 1950s. (Author's collection. Photograph by the author.)

Galey & Lord Woven Cottons

By the mid-1950s, Phelps entered into a relationship with Galey & Lord, a member of the Burlington Industries group, which had similar marketing benefits as those Phelps had enjoyed with Crompton. In July 1955, Galey & Lord ran a full-page advertisement in *Women's Wear Daily* featuring Elizabeth Phelps's Deep Country Clothes in Galey & Lord striped cottons. The ad shows two women, lounging on a wooden fence—although no other background is shown, this is enough to evoke the rural setting in which Deep Country Clothes would be appropriately worn. The outfits as sketched, however, are a far cry from Elizabeth Phelps's army-pant–and–apron ensembles of the late 1940s. The woman in front of the fence wears the pants-with-apron combination, but now with the apron so short that the text refers to it as a "separate peplum" rather than an apron.[67] The text advises that this outfit is ideal for the "chic gardener or doit-yourselfer" but the slide-style sandals shown as footwear would make more active pursuits difficult. The woman on the other side of the fence wears a long wrap skirt and matching jacket with stiletto pumps of the type that would sink into the grass before the wearer could even walk to the wooden fence—again this image asserts the luxury of the modern lifestyle of suburban leisure rather than a true "deep country" aesthetic.

In 1957, Galey & Lord ran another full-page ad in *Women's Wear Daily* showing a Phelps dress in striped cotton, worn jumper-style over a short-sleeved sweater. The text reads, "With the nostalgic flavor of life in the deep south, Phelps Associates create an apron dress for barn dance or barbecue—in a black and beige striped cotton by Galey & Lord."[68] The text appeals to its white suburban audience with ideas of a supposedly simpler time in the American past, when barn dances were in barns not local country clubs, and simultaneously perpetuates the myth of the classless American society. The figure of the woman in the dress is highlighted in light colors while her modern-day barbecue guests are shown in silhouette, like the backyard trees. She is grilling hot dogs while wearing her Phelps dress and flat sandals—this leisurely and casual backyard entertaining is a sign of the suburban lifestyle. Phelps Deep Country Clothes are less deep country than suburban planned community, with its implications of white flight from American inner cities. Placed in *Women's Wear Daily,* this cooperative advertisement allowed Phelps to reach out to buyers for suburban department store branches with the support of a well-known fabric company.

The Museum at FIT holds in its collection two examples of Phelps separates made in a navy-and-tan striped fabric, possibly from this period, when Galey & Lord supplied Phelps with striped cottons (Fig. I.6). The first is a skirt in Elizabeth Phelps's signature wrap style, and the second is a pair of shorts. Both pieces are ready-to-wear, with the skirt tagged "S" for small, and the shorts size 14. The skirt has deep patch pockets, fastens with a narrow tie, and has a large belt loop in the back to accommodate a wide Phelps leather belt. The skirt label reads "Phelps New York," with the Phelps trademark symbol. Mason Waters of Georgetown chose this skirt or a very similar model for an ad in *Harper's Bazaar*'s local ad section, "Shopping in Georgetown and Washington," in May 1954. Mason Waters devoted its entire ad space to "Deep Country Clothes by PHELPS; Smart Summer Separates." Skirts were listed as retailing for $12.95 or $14.95, perhaps depending on the hem length or size. Beneath the prices, the text reads, "Send for swatches," which attests to the importance of the textile to potential consumers.[69] In the late 1950s, Phelps separates retailed from about $9.95 to $45, with wholesale prices for stores like Mason Waters from $5.95 to $30, allowing for about a one-third markup. Bags were priced to allow for about a 43 percent markup.[70]

Fabrics Made of Synthetic Fibers

With her November 1955 fall collection Elizabeth Phelps investigated the fabrics made of synthetic fibers, such as Dacron polyester and viscose.[71] Leslie Ellis Miller has observed that Dacron's maker DuPont had actively courted designers, including "Parisian couturiers since the mid-1920s, in the belief that their endorsement swayed even the most recalcitrant women into buying certain textiles."[72] While in some ways working with synthetic rather than natural fibers was a departure for Elizabeth Phelps, given the Phelpses' longstanding interest in natural, "honest" materials, it was in keeping with her interest in performance and easy care. For example, one journalist stated that Phelps's interest in synthetics was to reduce the amount of ironing needed to maintain a crisp appearance: "She thinks women want clothes that can be tossed into a corner and pulled out neat as a pin, and is experimenting with a Dacron and viscose fabric that, she hopes, will make something approximating that possible."[73] Polyester and viscose fabrics were also considered useful for travel because of their wrinkle-resistance and wash-and-wear properties, and the Phelpses' regular vacationing in Florida was another factor in her interest in these fabrics.[74]

Extant garments, advertisements, and documentary material all provide evidence that collaboration with textile suppliers like Indian Head, Crompton, and Galey & Lord was a key element of Phelps Associates' ability to expand their business beyond leather goods and capitalize on the era of American postwar abundance. In the process of promoting both textile companies and Elizabeth Phelps by name, both sides benefitted.

Leather Goods in the 1950s

William Phelps seems to have remained committed to handcrafted leather goods, even as the ready-to-wear garments were made in a more industrial production style. In 1952, Phelps employed about eight men and women in the leather workshop, each producing about one bag per day from start to finish, from cutting to packing for shipment.[75] In 1958, William still designed custom bags for specific clients, with each bag's capacity size and partitions based on the individual's needs. Phelps products were produced in fairly modest numbers. Bags made to fill a retail order were still made by hand, and the largest number of bags they reported making for a single order was 40, with 144 skirts and blouses the largest wholesale separates order. Phelps Industries now employed sixty-eight people, and the Phelpses were careful to assure a *Women's Wear Daily* journalist that "Everything is done at the shops here, except the making of the raw materials and the dyeing. The metal parts for the belts and bags are received in rough form from the manufacturer and are coated, polished and ornamented at the Phelps shops."[76] The Phelpses seem to have clung to the aura of the Washington Square basement workshop even as they desired growth beyond what that model could sustain.

Although the production of Phelps Industries was less artisanal than that of the former Phelps Associates workshop, the Phelpses remained committed to the arts and viewing themselves as artists. They also developed relationships within the Asheville arts community. This was probably an aspect of life that they had missed in their more rural Joanna Furnace location. Elizabeth Phelps made appearances and gave talks at local women's clubs and fashion shows.[77] The Phelpses jointly created the lighting design for a series of outdoor Candlelight Concerts featuring classical music.[78] It is quite likely that the arts community they found in Asheville was part of the area's appeal, along with its proximity to textile companies that were important to the ready-to-wear business. The Phelpses brought their perspective as artists and craftspeople to their production, bringing a functional beauty to all their work, including everyday objects.

Beyond Ready-to-Wear: Paper Patterns and the Everyday

In 1914, one of Edna Ferber's characters noted, "We are apt to forget that those [fashionable] types form only a thin upper crust, and that down beneath there are millions and millions of regular, everyday women doing regular everyday things in regular everyday clothes."[79] One of the ways Elizabeth Phelps sought to expand the Phelps business in the 1950s was by appealing to this consumer group of everyday women. As fashion historians Cheryl Buckley and Hazel Clark have argued in *Fashion and Everyday Life: London and New York,* in everyday wardrobes new and old garments hang side-by-side.[80] Similarly, even within the wardrobes of Phelps's wealthy clients, evening gowns coexisted with seemingly incongruous everyday items such as aprons. Phelps Associates did not transition overnight from their Coty Award–winning custom work into the realm of everyday clothing for a wide range of consumers; the process occurred over several years. By the early 1950s, Phelps was selling ready-to-wear clothing for middleclass women's outdoor activities, housework, and leisure under the Phelps Deep Country Clothes label, and these clothes were more affordable than their custom-made leather goods. Through a relationship with *Woman's Day* magazine, Elizabeth Phelps reached an even wider audience, which might not be able to afford her ready-to-wear clothing but could make "Elizabeth Phelps 'Smart Togs for Action,'" using a series of paper patterns for home sewing.[81] After World War II, William and Elizabeth Phelps had discovered that there was a limited market for custom-made leather goods that lasted a lifetime and might go in and out of fashion. Business growth necessitated evolving from the exclusivity of a high-end workshop creating custom-crafted bags and belts to become a brand that also included designs for everyday women's everyday clothing.

Buckley and Clark have proposed using "theories of everyday life so as to explore the routine elements of fashion," and "understanding fashion as a manifestation of routine daily lives that remains with people over time."[82] In conjunction with this definition of everyday fashion, I add elements from the Edna Ferber quotation above.[83] While Ferber wrote fictional dialogue rather than fashion theory, I return to her words because I argue that Ferber—however unintentionally—offers a helpful three-part theory of the everyday with regard to clothing. Here, I define *theory* as an organized, systematic way of analyzing and thinking through information, and I am interested in broadening the types of writing admitted as sources for fashion theory to include "found theory," such as that in the Ferber novel. Ferber wrote that the everyday included, first, "millions and millions of regular, everyday women." Second, these women were "doing regular everyday things." And finally, they carried out these ordinary activities "in regular everyday clothes."[84] So for Ferber everyday clothes are those worn by the vast majority of women, who are not clients of haute couture or extremely expensive ready-to-wear clothing. They are middle class, working class, or poor—anyone who does not form part of the most fashionable "thin upper crust." These everyday women need clothes for their everyday activities at work, school, or home rather than for gliding down a red carpet or being presented at court. And finally, they wear "regular everyday clothes": the basics that form the backbone of a wardrobe, rather than the standout pieces that so often find their way into museum collections.

Elizabeth Phelps's designs are amenable to this framework in multiple ways. The trajectory this book has already traced shows her evolution from her Phelps Associates work, which was produced slowly, by hand, often for a specific client. After World War II, the Phelpses began to experiment with other modes of production, in addition to maintaining their workshop devoted to handmade and custom leatherwork. Mass-manufactured clothing designs were one way for the Phelpses to reach a broader audience of "regular, everyday women." Second, many of the garments—at least initially—were intended to be worn for everyday, mundane tasks rather than the grand occasions that called for the spectacular expressions of high fashion. Cooking, housework, gardening, childcare, and pet grooming were introduced in magazines as appropriate activities for donning Elizabeth Phelps's designs, as well as more strictly leisure activities, such as hunting, fishing, and travel. Third, the clothing designs were often produced in fabrics that could well be called everyday for the mid-twentieth century—denim and cotton sailcloth, for example, which are also associated with the Americanness of her designs—rather than those that would be higher on what dress historian Lou Taylor has termed the hierarchy of textiles.[85] Finally, in accord with Buckley and Clark's ideas regarding the ways objects remained in a wardrobe, Elizabeth Phelps's designs (as well as the leather goods and other objects produced in partnership with her husband) defied the pace of change normally associated with high fashion. Phelps's wrapped aprons of the late 1940s are basically the same garment as her wrapped miniskirts of the late 1960s. Hem length and purpose might shift, but the basic garment design remained very much the same. Garments were planned to remain in a wardrobe and be worn for multiple years.

Buckley and Clark phrase it succinctly: "The clothes worn by most people going about their daily lives have been typically a synthesis of new and old, bold and mundane."[86] This was probably true even within the wardrobes of Elizabeth Phelps's more wealthy or famous clients. An example of this is found in a 1950 *Vogue* article titled "And She Can Cook, Too," in which Mrs. Richard Rodgers—Dorothy (Feiner) Rodgers, wife the Broadway composer—is shown cooking while wearing one of Elizabeth Phelps's custom trouser with attached apron ensembles, paired with a silk blouse with the sleeves rolled up (Fig. 6.9). This title, lauding Rogers for her seeming ability to do and have it all, still resonates today with debates about the demands placed on women. I argue that Phelps's sportswear designs, while not revolutionary, are important because they helped women navigate these competing demands. Despite the everyday associations of the apron, *Vogue* identifies the Phelps garment as custom, noting in the body of the text rather than a caption, "In the photograph here, she wears slacks with an attached apron, made for her by Phelps Associates."[87]

Fig. 6.9. Dorothy Rodgers wears a custom Phelps apron and slacks ensemble. "And She Can Cook, Too," *Vogue*, 1 April 1950, 145. (Serge Balkin, *Vogue*, ©Condé Nast.)

Dorothy Rodgers had an appreciation of handcraft that made her particularly compatible with the Phelps handmade aesthetic and philosophy. An accomplished interior decorator, writer, and inventor of household goods, for eight years starting in 1935 Rodgers ran her own New York City–based interior repair and decoration business, Repairs, Inc.[88] Rodgers recalled: "Our success was built around and totally dependent on the work of a group of extraordinarily skilled craftsmen. . . . There are few such artisans left. And, while the tooling techniques and design of much mass-produced furniture may have improved immensely in the last few years, they will never completely fill the gap left by the disappearance of things made by people who, from design to finish, were responsible for and took a personal pride in every completed piece."[89]

Rodgers's interest in objects made by a craftsperson from start to finish echoes the Phelpses' statements in interviews. Rodgers's professional contacts included a range of artisans, from cabinetmakers and weavers to clockmakers and tortoiseshell restorers.[90]

Rodgers also had at least some interest in fashion and applied her views about craftsmanship to clothing. In her later writing, Rodgers included her definition of fashion—"Its essence is change"—and her beliefs about its significance in a woman's life.[91] Rodgers told her readers in 1970, "While I am not one of the group that believes that Clothes, with a capital 'C' are worthy of enormous expenditures of money or time, I do think they are important. When a woman knows she is looking her best, she feels better, more self-assured, about everything. And I do think that matters."[92] She emphasized the importance of quality in fashion as well: "When making clothes, it is important to use the best materials."[93] Rodgers spoke out of her own experience as a client of Paris couture houses, including Molyneux.[94] Her interest in craft and quality made her an ideal Phelps client who would appreciate their emphasis on pieces being made start to finish by one person.

Rodgers is photographed in her kitchen, mixing bowl in hand; although clearly staged, the image references Rodgers's participation in the everyday task of cooking—one that many women would relate to. It is worth noting that in 1950, almost a year after the launch of Phelps Deep Country Clothes ready-to-wear, *Vogue* is showing the Phelps apron-and-pants ensemble as appropriate for work in the domestic interior rather than primarily outside. Perhaps this was due to the postwar pressure for women to be primarily homemakers, after the wartime boom in women's employment outside the home. While Rodgers freely credited her household staff for their collaborative contributions to the elegant running of her household, at the time of the *Vogue* article, she had recently taken a Cordon Bleu cooking course and was interested in doing some cooking herself.[95] Rodgers would later include a description and illustration of this kitchen in one of her books about home decorating and entertainment, identifying herself with the everyday when it came to cooking: "My own ideas about kitchens are more those of a wife who likes to cook than those of a decorator."[96]

The *Vogue* article also references Rodgers's talents as an after-theater dinner-party hostess who planned and served crowd-pleasing and elegant meals that could be largely prepped in advance, then quickly served when the guests arrived. Rodgers's dinner parties included famous guests such as novelist Edna Ferber, and the Phelps apron is positioned as an everyday accessory that enables a woman to prepare to host elegantly with a minimum of staff assistance.[97] A client like Rodgers would of necessity have a range of fashionable pieces in her wardrobe, including formal evening gowns that would be appropriate for opening nights; Rodgers later stated that for these occasions, "I always wear a gray dress—one I've worn before."[98] But this *Vogue* article's reference to the mundane demonstrates that even an individual whose lifestyle often required formal, high-fashion garments would also need everyday items, such as a Phelps apron-and-slacks combination. Phelps sportswear serves as a link between the high-quality craftsmanship of couture clothing and everyday dress.

The Phelpses' introduction of Phelps Deep Country clothes in ready-to-wear sizes was an expansion into the everyday wardrobes of an increasingly larger consumer base, which would overshadow their custom clothing operations in the 1950s. A 1949 *Life* magazine article formed a bridge between Elizabeth Phelps's clothing designs as part of the everyday wardrobe of wealthy custom clients and the introduction of Phelps clothes into the everyday wardrobes of middleclass American women.[99] Photography historian Sally Stein argues that the various components of a twentieth-century magazine—text, editorial images, advertisements—should be considered in context. She also draws a parallel between magazine advertising and billboards on the side of the road: both are intended to catch the consumer's attention while she is concentrating on something else.[100] This is very apt in the case of the article, as the photographs and text direct the reader's attention to the center of the page, bracketed on either side by ads, much as billboards bracket a driver's view of the road ahead. The ads are for women's Paradise Shoes, American Greetings Valentines cards, and Sunsweet Prune Juice—items aimed at fashion-conscious young mothers and homemakers. The center of the double-page spread shows a young woman,

Fig. 6.10. Photo with similar pose as that in *Life* magazine editorial coverage of Phelps Deep Country Clothes. *Life,* 7 February 1949, 88–89. (Photograph by Nina Leen. Nina Leen / The LIFE Picture Collection / Shutterstock.)

her right hand on a large wooden buffet, while a preschool-age child braces herself for a strong pull on the woman's denim tunic, revealing the trousers worn below (see Fig. 6.10 for a similar image from this same photo shoot).[101]

The accompanying text reveals that this ensemble is an example of Elizabeth Phelps's "new substitutes for the monotonous house dress[, which] consist of slacks with narrow, tapering legs and, since she like many people does not approve of bulging slacks on women, of concealing apron skirts or tunics as well. All are of plain, practical work fabrics like denim, poplin or sailcloth."[102] The housedress was an item of everyday clothing considered so ordinary that it is dismissed as monotonous by the journalist—who was probably fashion editor Sally Kirkland, a Phelps custom client, and an attendee at the debut fashion show for Phelps Deep Country Clothes. Housedresses could be purchased readymade for less than $2 in the Fall–Winter 1949 Sears catalog. Cultural and fashion theorist Elizabeth Wilson has argued that "in modern western societies no clothes are outside fashion; fashion sets the terms of all sartorial behavior," which would include even the monotonous housedress.[103] Elizabeth Phelps's designs, however, exemplified an intentional engagement between the everyday and high fashion similar to that of Claire McCardell's Popover dress of a few years prior: modernist ideals such as simplicity joined with design principles of functionality in a way that seemed fresh and new but could easily take their place within a woman's everyday wardrobe.

Other outfits from the *Life* article included a garment that combined slacks and skirt fastened together, shown worn for window-washing (Fig. 6.11). It also featured a wrap skirt that could be worn as an apron over a dinner dress by the hostess who served her own guests without the aid of domestic servants.[104] In the 1950s, Elizabeth Phelps sold these everyday clothes for everyday women doing everyday things under the Phelps Deep Country Clothes label, and they were available at large retail stores such as Lord & Taylor in New York, as well as many smaller local stores.

Fig. 6.11. *Life* magazine editorial coverage of Phelps Deep Country Clothes. *Life*, 7 February 1949, 90. (Photograph by Nina Leen. Nina Leen / The LIFE Picture Collection / Shutterstock.)

Phelps Deep Country Clothes were designed to enter and remain part of women's everyday wardrobes. Buckley and Clark discuss everyday fashion as "the ordinary and mundane practices of wearing that draws items from the personal wardrobe in a routine manner."[105] They also discuss the way everyday fashion is composed of layers of garments accumulated over the years, perhaps updated with a new coat or new accessories.[106] This was certainly relevant for Phelps wearers, who were characterized as "collectors" of Phelps garments in a 1954 *Vogue* "Shop Hound" promotion for the Mason Waters store in Washington, DC.[107] The assumption is that pieces were added to the collection each year, but the old garments from previous seasons were not discarded.

Elizabeth Phelps's designs for Phelps Deep Country Clothes were accessible to a wider audience than her custom work, but her aesthetic was available to even more consumers through her paper sewing patterns. Buckley and Clark cite the sewing machine, paper patterns for home sewing, "ready-to-wear systems, and improved methods of distribution, dissemination and retailing" as prompts for fashion assuming a new ubiquity in everyday lives in the twentieth century.[108] While many of these technologies had begun transforming the relationship of ordinary Americans in the nineteenth century, in the mid-twentieth century they became ever more affordable.[109] Phelps's participation in the paper pattern business came at a time when there was wide consumer sewing literacy, bolstered by a combination of knowledge passed between generations of family members, home economics curricula in schools and colleges, and commercial sewing centers such as those run by the Singer sewing machine company.[110]

It was not uncommon for American designers' names to appear on paper patterns for home sewing. For example, *The New York Times*' Fashions of the Times American Designers series, in conjunction with Advance Patterns, included designers like Sophie Gimbel, Tom Brigance, and Emily Wilkens, and Elizabeth Phelps also participated in this series in 1951.[111] A *Times* article by Virginia Pope about the Elizabeth Phelps American Designers pattern credited both spouses of the Phelps partnership with input on the clothing designs: "For though Mr. P does not run up any of the seams on the dresses turned out by Mrs. P., we are convinced his fine judgment goes into much of the general principle of their creating."[112] Pope was probably right that "Mr. P.'s" views were indirectly incorporated into the clothing designs as well as the leatherwork, although with the ready-to-wear being made by an outside manufacturing company at this point, it is doubtful that either "Mr. P." or "Mrs. P." was personally running up seams. With her name alone on the label, it is likely that Elizabeth was the primary designer of the Phelps Deep Country Clothes sportswear; her husband's input would have been limited to the more subtle influence of his tastes and views on women's clothing, with which she was well acquainted. Pope also noted that when Phelps began her Deep Country Clothes collection, "she determined to price her clothes within the reach of the many instead of the few."[113] This "new type of thinking"—a shift from the custom model—was taken to the next logical step in creating sewing patterns for an even broader range of consumers.[114] While the Phelpses had not been as successful as they had hoped in empowering workers on the production side, perhaps these new patterns offered a chance to make a positive difference on the other side, for customers. Sewing patterns would have been more accessible for consumers who could not afford Phelps Deep Country Clothes or were not made welcome in the stores in which Phelps sportswear was sold.

The title of Elizabeth Phelps's "Smart Togs for Action" patterns implied that here were clothes for everyday women going about an everyday active lifestyle. The clothes were featured in color photography in the January 1953 issue of *Women's Day,* which showed a suburban or rural housewife in her everyday tasks.[115] The dress included in pattern 5049 (price 35 cents) could be worn either alone or as a jumper over a blouse, with the two variations both shown in the article and on the pattern envelope (Fig. 6.12). The dress fastens with one button and a series of gripper fasteners (i.e., snaps, or snapper fasteners, an Elizabeth Phelps signature construction technique; see for example, Figs. 6.7, 6.8). Phelps designed this dress to unfold completely flat for ironing, as did her wrap skirts, such as those in the Valentine Richmond History Center (Fig. 6.6). This feature is illustrated in the article, to appeal to the consumer who does her own housework, including laundry. Elizabeth Phelps's careful planning regarding ease of ironing was a way of making women's lives incrementally simpler, as they navigated gender roles that placed the burden on women to ensure a neat, crisp appearance for the whole family.

Fig. 6.12. Elizabeth Phelps's "Smart Togs for Action" home sewing pattern 5049. (Author's collection.)

Phelps also designed patterns for a mix-and-match wardrobe that built on her signature pants and apron combination to provide clothes appropriate for a variety of everyday activities by layering different pieces. Pattern 5048 started with a base layer of coverall jumpsuit, shown in the article as appropriate gear for washing the family car when worn alone (Fig. 6.13). A sewing pattern 5048 from Mark Zerr's collection provides additional information on the reverse side of the envelope, with back views of the coverall and both skirt lengths. This back view demonstrates how the coverall fastens, including the ties for the front and gripper fasteners on the back that create a drop seat (Fig. 6.14). The drop seat feature was Elizabeth Phelps's thoughtful design plan to avoid the common jumpsuit pitfall of the wearer having to completely disrobe to go to the bathroom.

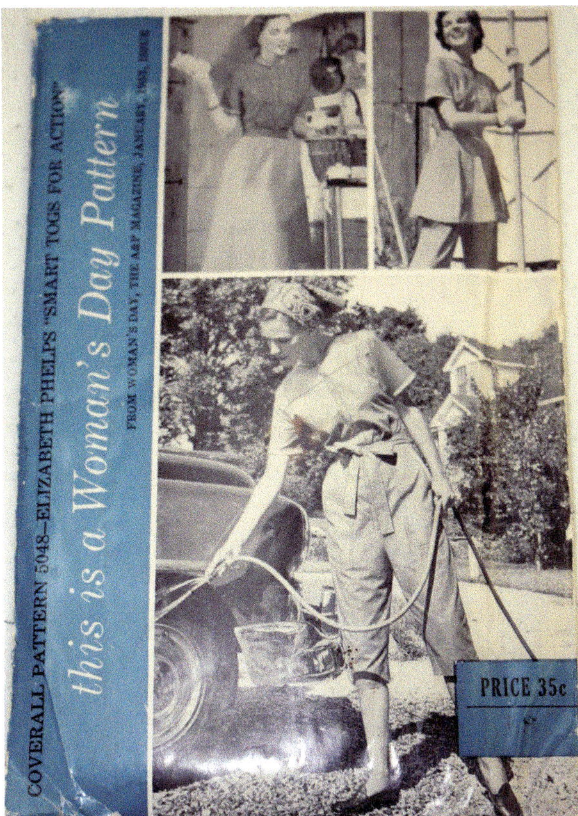

Fig. 6.13. Elizabeth Phelps's "Smart Togs for Action" home sewing pattern 5048. (Collection of Mark Zerr.)

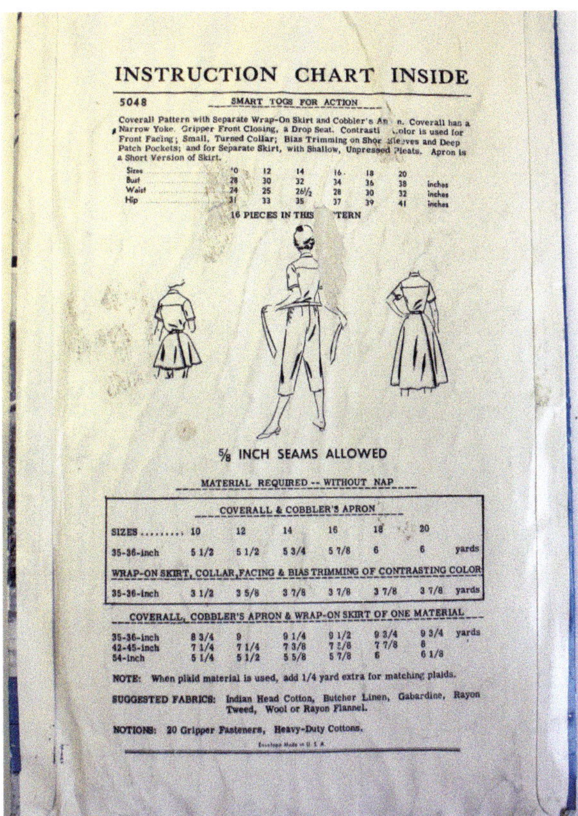

INSTRUCTION CHART INSIDE

5048 SMART TOGS FOR ACTION

Coverall Pattern with Separate Wrap-On Skirt and Cobbler's Ap n. Coverall has a Narrow Yoke, Gripper Front Closing, a Drop Seat. Contrasti Color is used for Front Facing; Small, Turned Collar; Bias Trimming on Shor leeves and Deep Patch Pockets; and for Separate Skirt, with Shallow, Unpressed Pleats. Apron is a Short Version of Skirt.

Sizes	10	12	14	16	18	20	
Bust	28	30	32	34	36	38	inches
Waist	24	25	26½	28	30	32	inches
Hip	31	33	35	37	39	41	inches

16 PIECES IN THIS TERN

⅝ INCH SEAMS ALLOWED

MATERIAL REQUIRED -- WITHOUT NAP

COVERALL & COBBLER'S APRON							
SIZES	10	12	14	16	18	20	
35-36-inch	5 1/2	5 1/2	5 3/4	5 7/8	6	6	yards
WRAP-ON SKIRT, COLLAR, FACING & BIAS TRIMMING OF CONTRASTING COLOR							
35-36-inch	3 1/2	3 5/8	3 7/8	3 7/8	3 7/8	3 7/8	yards
COVERALL, COBBLER'S APRON & WRAP-ON SKIRT OF ONE MATERIAL							
35-36-inch	8 3/4	9	9 1/4	9 1/2	9 3/4	9 3/4	yards
42-45-inch	7 1/4	7 1/4	7 3/8	[illegible]	7 7/8	8	
54-inch	5 1/4	5 1/2	5 5/8	5 7/8	6	6 1/8	

NOTE: When plaid material is used, add 1/4 yard extra for matching plaids.

SUGGESTED FABRICS: Indian Head Cotton, Butcher Linen, Gabardine, Rayon Tweed, Wool or Rayon Flannel.

NOTIONS: 20 Gripper Fasteners, Heavy-Duty Cottons.

Envelope Made in U. S. A.

Fig. 6.14. Reverse, Elizabeth Phelps's "Smart Togs for Action" home sewing pattern 5048, showing coverall drop seat. (Collection of Mark Zerr.)

While the model in the article wore a version with cropped pants extending just below the knee, the text noted, "Trouser legs can be cut shorter or longer, as desired." Further, one could "add a cobbler's apron for a more feminine appearance," in keeping with Elizabeth Phelps's own habits and her husband's preference.[116] The cobbler's apron was shown cut in above knee length, displaying at least twelve inches of the trouser legs. The model is posed as though gardening, holding a rake, with other gardening implements and a basket for carrying produce in the background. (See Fig. 6.13, upper right corner, which reproduces a cropped version of the image from the article.) If one needed to run errands in town, a longer skirt could be layered over the coverall, without the wearer having to get completely changed. The longer skirt example is cut to the same below-knee length as the coverall, and the model is shown in her kitchen, unpacking canned goods that would have been purchased at the grocery store (Fig. 6.13, upper left corner). It is important to note how author Margaret Parker Gary and photographer Leombruno worked to provide context for the reader as to how each permutation of the wardrobe should be worn. Even in the everyday, there was an important etiquette about where different types of garments could be worn with propriety. The model washing her family car in coverall and kerchief would most likely have been met with disapproving looks had she then driven the car to the market without layering on the skirt (Fig. 6.13, main image).

The initial *Woman's Day* paper sewing pattern collaboration led to other Elizabeth Phelps–designed patterns for the magazine released the following year. The first was for boys' playclothes. An article promoting the new pattern, 5077, trumpeted it as "the most exciting news in boys' pattern clothes for a long time."[117] These patterns for boys included functional features that were also signature elements of Phelps Deep Country Clothes, such as expansive, roomy pockets and gripper fasteners. A second pattern, number 5084, was for a simple evening skirt with "only two major pieces, straight sewing, and no fitting—a cinch to make."[118] This simplicity would have allowed women without advanced sewing skills to participate in the craft and have a smart Phelps design on a budget.

Conclusion

While remaining committed to handcraft in Phelps leather goods, Elizabeth Phelps of Phelps Industries reached more broadly into the realm of American everyday dress in the post–World War II period by expanding into ready-to-wear women's clothing and even into paper patterns for home sewing. This allowed a broader range of middleclass women to go about their everyday activities in everyday clothes that bore the stamp of functionality tempered with femininity that were the hallmarks of Elizabeth Phelps's designs. Fashion historian Rebecca Arnold's argument that sportswear became especially linked with notions of Americanness, modern life, and ease of movement, simultaneously evoking myths of rural America and urban modernity, is born out in Elizabeth's designs and the ways her country clothes–type sportswear was promoted.[119] Between Phelps's leather goods, Elizabeth Phelps's experimental designs for men featured in the *Adam in the Looking Glass* exhibition, her paper sewing patterns for boys' clothing, and her ready-to-wear clothing for girls,' misses,' and women's size ranges, Phelps Industries offered ideas for dressing and accessorizing the whole family. Additionally, the exhibition, the articles, and the patterns garnered free publicity for the Phelps brand; as previous chapters have demonstrated, the Phelpses were adept at making the most of this kind of "free advertising."

Paper pattern imagery as well as magazine coverage of Phelps aprons, apron-and-pants ensembles, and other sportswear highlights the number of roles a postwar woman might be expected to fill, all while maintaining an immaculately groomed and fashionable appearance: elegant hostess, patient mother, gourmet cook, gardener, shopper, car washer, and window-washer. Arnold argues that American fashion designers such as Claire McCardell and Clare Potter "rarely, if ever, identified themselves with the feminist movement, but could be said to have 'acted out' the promise of feminism through their careers and promotion of the status of women in the industry."[120] Similarly, Elizabeth Phelps does not appear to have associated herself with feminism, yet her own life was that of a working woman, and her designs consistently offer thoughtful details intended to make women's lives easier. The elements that enabled her to live an active lifestyle while still pleasing and appearing appropriate to her husband and design partner must have helped her clients as well. Thus, not only does Elizabeth Phelps appear to have been concerned with labor, class, and improving the lives of workers, but also her work responds to the needs of both wealthier and less affluent women as they navigated the demands of everyday life and cultural expectations during a time of societal change.

7

Elizabeth Phelps Leads

Elizabeth Phelps continued running Phelps Industries singlehandedly when William Phelps retired at the end of the 1950s, even after his death in 1962.[1] She kept the label going long enough to capitalize on the 1960s resurgence of the shoulder bag. That decade, it became more acceptable for women to wear one of Elizabeth's signature items—trousers—and this encouraged her to experiment with new styles of pants, which she patented. The 1960s would be the final decade of Phelps Deep Country Clothes, with Elizabeth increasingly interested in a return to her painting, which had been sidelined for many years while she was active in craft, business management, and clothing design.

Introductory Object: Phelps Deep Country Clothes Trews

Although trousers were one of Elizabeth Phelps's signature offerings in the Phelps Deep Country Clothes line, this is not reflected in museum holdings. Perhaps because curators and potential donors considered trousers items of everyday dress, and/or consumers used them until they wore out, trousers do not generally appear in collections. A notable exception is a light gray-brown pair now in the collection of the North Carolina Museum of History, dated about 1960–64 (Figs. 7.1, 7.2). The museum catalog entry describes the slacks with "narrow tapered leg, contoured and faced waistline, long narrow belt carriers anchored with silver-toned studs at lower edge, curved patch pockets at sides, 8" heavy metal zipper hidden in left side pocket, two sets of heavy "gripper" snaps above zipper, all seams and edges top stitched . . . called 'trews.'" These trousers differ from Elizabeth Phelps's initial offerings at Joanna Furnace back in 1949. First, rather

Fig. 7.1. Front view of trousers. Elizabeth Phelps for Phelps Deep Country Clothes, trousers, Dacron polyester and rayon, 1960–64. (North Carolina Museum of History, Gift of Louise Thomas. H.1993.434.19. Photograph by the North Carolina Museum of History.)

Fig. 7.2. Reverse view of trousers. Elizabeth Phelps for Phelps Deep Country Clothes, trousers, Dacron polyester and rayon, 1960–64. (North Carolina Museum of History, Gift of Louise Thomas. H.1993.434.19. Photograph by the North Carolina Museum of History.)

Fig. 7.3. Brand, fiber content, and ready-to-wear size labels of the trousers. Elizabeth Phelps for Phelps Deep Country Clothes, trousers, Dacron polyester and rayon, 1960–64. (North Carolina Museum of History, Gift of Louise Thomas. H.1993.434.19. Photograph by the North Carolina Museum of History.)

Fig. 7.4. Detail of proper left side of trousers, opened to show fastenings. Elizabeth Phelps for Phelps Deep Country Clothes, trousers, Dacron polyester and rayon, 1960–64. (North Carolina Museum of History, Gift of Louise Thomas. H.1993.434.19. Photograph by the North Carolina Museum of History.)

unlike the early designs in various cotton fiber fabrics, by the 1960s Phelps was experimenting with synthetic fibers like Dupont's Dacron polyester. Three labels inside the slacks state, "Phelps Deep Country Clothes," "65% Dacron Polyester / 35% rayon," and the ready-to-wear size, "12" (Fig. 7.3). Even more significantly, here is a pair of trousers meant to be worn without a skirt or apron covering.

The trousers' first noticeable feature are the large patch pockets on the fronts. These are 13" high and 6⁵⁄₁₆" wide, with the bottom center corners squared off toward the center front of the pants, then gently curving back toward the side seams. The upper outside corners of the pockets are cut away to create hand openings; these 8¼" high side openings are also curved. These pants allow for a hands-in-pockets pose, similar to that provided by the wrap skirts in the Valentine collection (Figs. 6.1, 6.2). The waistband fastenings for the trousers are hidden behind the fabric that contains the pocket on the proper left side of the garment (Fig. 7.4). Instead of having a zippered fly at the center front, this pair of pants zips on an overlapping side flap. This design shows that Elizabeth Phelps's thinking in producing pants was similar to her wrapping skirts: wrap and snap. Earlier pant-and-skirt combination garments probably fastened similarly. This also gives the front of the trousers a smooth look, much like the front of Phelps's wrap skirts. The side flap conceals an 8" metal zipper on a brown tape. Extending down the center front of each pant leg there is a very narrow, ¹⁄₁₆", seam that stands up to create a fine outward pleat. The pleat begins just below the pocket on each side and extends the rest of the length of the pants—about 26³⁄₁₆" The bottom hem of each leg is approximately 1⅛" deep.

The museum catalog description highlights several long-established characteristics of Phelps Deep Country Clothes, such as gripper fasteners and patch pockets. Above the zipper, two metal gripper fasteners hold the waistband in place. These are riveted through the fabric. On the front side, they read, "Gripper Gripper," in words encircling the center. On the reverse, the name brand "Scovill" appears. The Scovill company—now called Morito Scovill—was founded in 1802 in Waterbury, Connecticut, as a button maker, producing gilt buttons. In 1930, the company introduced the Gripper® snap fastener.[2] While many Phelps skirts eschew zippers altogether in favor of the imagined ease of snaps, these trousers incorporate both.

The second most prominent feature of the exterior of the trousers are the belt loops. There are five altogether: one on each side, and three at the back. The back loops are clustered together, one at the center back and the other two approximately two inches apart from it on either side. Each is ornamented at its bottom with a metal rivet approximately ¼" in diameter. The "long narrow belt carriers" would have allowed for a wide Phelps leather belt to be worn with the slacks. The belt loops are about 3¾" long, and the opening would allow for a leather belt approximately 2½" wide to be worn. This is not wide enough for the more dramatic Phelps belts, but it could certainly hold the standard-width Phelps belt.

The original museum catalog entry for these trousers notes that they were "called 'trews.'" Elizabeth Phelps had been designating her tapered trousers as *trews* at least as early as 1951.[3] According to Webster's Dictionary, *trews* are "tightfitting trousers, usually of tartan" or "close-cut tartan shorts worn under the kilt in Highland dress."[4] Fashion editorial coverage of Phelps Deep Country Clothes also included similar information: "The fall series features the Scottish-inspired tapered slacks known as 'trews.'"[5] While it was not uncommon for women's sportswear to borrow from menswear, Elizabeth Phelps's use of the word *trews* connects to other aspects of the Phelpses' work. Here, she imbued an item of contemporary women's sportswear with associations of historical menswear, tying this ready-to-wear to Phelps Associates' modern yet historicizing work in leather.

This terminology was probably provided by the donor, (Myrtle) Louise Thomas (1922–2013), showing that she was familiar with the marketing term Elizabeth Phelps gave her trousers. The catalog also notes that the pants are "casual with narrow tapered leg." When I studied them in December 2020, the fashionable look of the past decade had included extremely formfitting jeans and leggings, which leave no space between the pants and the body, so it is important to contextualize how narrow was considered narrow. The proper right leg opening is about 14⅜" in circumference, and the proper left leg opening is about 14½" in circumference. A pair of jeggings from the author's personal wardrobe circa 2015 has a 13" leg opening circumference, so Thomas's trews would have been slightly less fitted but still fairly narrow for a trouser without spandex fiber. The pants are relatively short: the inseam of the proper left leg is 27¼" and the inseam of the proper right leg is 27½". The pants do not appear to have been altered to make them shorter, so this fractional difference must have been original to the garment.

The reverse of the trousers shows a design consistent with Elizabeth Phelps's belief that a woman's bottom was if not to be hidden at least to be deemphasized visually (Fig. 7.2). There are no pockets on the back; the trousers are gently shaped to the curves of the body, with one dart on each cheek extending down from the waist. Otherwise, the seat is left smooth. The reverse side of the trousers has a vertical crease, but it is not stitched in as a pleat.

RaeLana Poteat, North Carolina Museum of History's curator of social history, notes that these Phelps trousers were part of a larger gift that primarily includes suits and dresses that were part of Thomas's wardrobe while she worked for the North Carolina retailers Ivey's and Thalhimers.[6] In her memoir, *Dear Emily: A Memoir: My Life in the Fine Stores,* published nearly twenty years after the donation, Thomas wistfully writes, "Often I regret that I gave most of my designer clothes to the North Carolina History Museum, for I am still the same size. After shopping for hours, I usually come home and appreciate a Gloria Sachs, a Bill Blass, or an Ellen Tracy more than when it was purchased. With fabric the first component of any garment, there is little hope for improvement in what's being offered in fashion today."[7] This short statement reveals much about the donor of the Phelps garment, a fashion industry professional who, at the age of eighty-nine when her book was published, still took pride in retaining her figure, relished shopping as an immersive activity, and valued quality in fashion. The main thesis of Thomas's book is that a combination of corporate greed, mismanagement, and offshoring led to the decline of "the fine stores"—exclusive department and specialty stores offering a high quality, inventive, and locally relevant product assortment, as well as a special mix of entertainment and service.[8] To put this in context, in the mid-1950s only 5 percent of women's and children's apparel in the United States was imported, but by the 1980s over half was manufactured elsewhere.[9]

Thomas began her working life as a mathematician for NACA (later NASA), before moving to New York City in the late 1940s and embarking on her retail career. In her memoir, she glowingly describes Lord & Taylor and credits executives Walter Hoving and Dorothy Shaver with Lord & Taylor's creativity and excitement in the 1940s and 1950s. Thomas also notes that during her time working at Lord & Taylor she embraced American designers, including purchasing a black Claire McCardell dress.[10] This is notable because, as in the case of Seymour Laughon Rennolds (chapter 3), it shows some overlap between McCardell and Phelps clients, although Thomas might not have purchased Phelps contemporaneously with McCardell. Thomas was likely familiar with the Phelps label at this time, however. As she entered the Lord & Taylor store, she would have passed the main-floor accessories area where Phelps bags were sold.

When Thomas returned to North Carolina in 1948, she went to work as an assistant to the accessories buyer at the fashion-conscious Ivey's department store. Thomas notes that jewelry and handbags were her favorite of all the departments. Again, her knowledge in the handbag field must have made her aware of Phelps. Thomas subsequently was promoted to juniors buyer at Ivey's, and she noted that her experience at Lord & Taylor had made her aware of what some of the most exciting postwar American labels, including Anne Fogarty and Anne Klein for Junior Sophisticates. Thomas recalled: "I bought and wore all the styles I loved."[11] In 1957, she was named to a North Carolina best-dressed list.[12]

In 1958, Ivey's changed its compensation structure for buyers, and Thomas moved to work with Thalhimer's in Winston-Salem.[13] Thomas would work with Thalhimer's first in Winston-Salem, then in Richmond, Virginia, until her retirement in 1986, becoming both the first female executive at the company and the first female officer of their Associated Merchandising Corporation buying office.[14] Thomas acquired the Phelps trousers during her early years with Thalhimer's. She does not mention Phelps in her memoir, and she lists two French designers—Gabrielle "Coco" Chanel and Yves St. Laurent—as her favorite designers.[15] However, she expresses her strong feelings about quality and innovation in design, whether from the United States or Europe: "I think that when the public gets tired of 'throw away' merchandise, we will see more 'made in America.'"[16] The Phelps trousers most likely fit this interest in quality, long-lasting clothing. Thomas also wore trousers when traveling abroad on buying trips, and she included in her memoir a photo of herself wearing trousers in Athens in 1965.[17]

The wear patterns, alterations, and repairs to this pair of trousers indicate that this was a garment the owner wore and loved for many years before donating it. The fabric shows wear in several places that tend to experience damage: the knees, the seat, and the edge of the pants hem. These areas all show pilling consistent with the polyester fiber. There are also some whitish stains on the front of the trousers, 14" above the proper left hem and 5⅜" above the proper right hem.

Before seeing this object in person, having read in the catalog description that the sides of the garment had been taken in and the crotch seam repaired, my initial thought was that Thomas must have used the professional seamstresses at her work to do the alterations. Through Thalhimers, she had access to "capable fitters and seamstresses who could and did perform miracles."[18] I anticipated that these professionals might have done the original alterations, although she might have had the later repair done elsewhere. However, examining the trousers in person changed my mind and underscored yet again how crucial it is for the fashion historian to examine objects personally. The work is not done to a professional standard as would have been offered by a fine specialty store or department store, so Thomas herself most likely did it. Looking at the interior of the trousers, it is clear that they were taken in slightly at the side seams from a point starting just below the belt loop studs to about 8" above the hems (8¼" proper left side; 7⅞" proper right side) (Fig. 7.5). The stitching was done in

Fig. 7.5. Detail of side seam alteration. Elizabeth Phelps for Phelps Deep Country Clothes, trousers, Dacron polyester and rayon, 1960–64. (North Carolina Museum of History, Gift of Louise Thomas. H.1993.434.19. Photograph by the North Carolina Museum of History.)

Fig. 7.6. Detail of trouser interior, showing crotch repair. Elizabeth Phelps for Phelps Deep Country Clothes, trousers, Dacron polyester and rayon, 1960–64. (North Carolina Museum of History, Gift of Louise Thomas. H.1993.434.19. Photograph by the North Carolina Museum of History.)

brown thread, apparently with a home sewing machine that had some thread tension issues—the threads are tangled about 18" down from the waist at the proper left side, but the sewer left them that way and charged ahead with the seam. The side seams are regular, pressed open seams, but after making the alteration the sewer left the original seam intact and did not rip it out and press the fabric open to the new one. A professional seamstress would not have done an alteration in such a haphazard fashion, so, again, this alteration must have been done by the wearer—perhaps in response to weight loss through the hips.

A repair to the crotch at the upper portion of the inseam shows that Thomas both used the trousers enough to wear out the seams and liked the pants enough to repair them so she could continue wearing them (Fig. 7.6). The crotch of a garment is an area at which the seams are under strain as the wearer's legs move back and forth while walking. The interior of the trousers reveals a 2⅝" area of handsewn backstitching to repair this part of the garment. The repair shows that Thomas continued to wear the trousers long enough for them to show major signs of wear—a long-term approach to clothing of which the Phelpses would have approved.

The patterns of usage and repair in these trousers demonstrate that at least one client bought and lovingly used her Phelps garment in a long-term pattern consistent with the Phelpses' philosophy of classic rather than disposable fashion. To use today's terminology, Phelps fashions were created with sustainability in mind: quality and a slower pace of fashion change that would enable years of use. They are also consistent with the Phelps pattern of drawing on historical forms and creating sportswear designed to make women's lives a bit easier. At the same time, these trousers represent one significant change in

Elizabeth Phelps's designs for the 1960s: as trousers for women gained greater acceptance, Phelps trousers were offered without a tunic or apron covering.

Elizabeth Phelps on Her Own

The 1960s saw Phelps Industries firmly ensconced in the South. The 1960 North Carolina Directory of Manufacturing Firms listed "W. D. and Elizabeth Phelps" as owners of "Phelps Industries, P. O. Box 44, Skyland." They were among twenty-one manufacturers listed under "Leather and Leather Products." Phelps Industries also continued to benefit from close proximity to textile manufacturing, with Asheville's Buncombe County also home to rayon makers America Enka Corporation.[19]

Although William Phelps was still listed as one of the owners of Phelps Industries in the 1960 North Carolina Directory of Manufacturing Firms, by the beginning of the decade he had begun stepping back from actively running the business. He may have been suffering from declining health.[20] In 1959, Elizabeth Phelps filed articles of incorporation with the office of North Carolina's secretary of state, Thad Eure. The information stated, "Phelps Industries, Inc., Asheville, to manufacture and deal in ladies' wearing apparel and leather goods. Authorized capital $1,000 no par value; to begin business with $100. By Elizabeth H. Phelps, J. G. Adams, Jr., Joel B. Adams, all of Asheville."[21] J. G. Adams Jr. and Joel B. Adams were a father and son, both local Asheville attorneys.[22] It is unclear why William and Elizabeth Phelps chose to incorporate their business at this point; perhaps they were thinking in terms of succession planning or limiting liability as they moved toward retirement.

William and Elizabeth Phelps's attention had shifted away from New York City over the course of the 1950s. While Phelps Industries expanded into additional Phelps-branded retail stores during the decade, these were in North Carolina and Florida, their main state of residence and the location of their vacation home. At least by 1960, Phelps Industries had closed its year-round New York City showroom. They now embarked on a schedule of seasonal hotel-room showings in the City to present their latest designs to buyers, rather than incurring the expense of keeping up a fulltime presence. Elizabeth Phelps chose the Sheraton-Russell Hotel at Park Avenue and Thirty-Seventh Street for her showings from 1960 through 1969.[23] Three times per year (February, June, and October), she traveled from North Carolina to show to buyers, while her friend and industry mentor Clare Potter also traveled into the City from her Nyack home, Timbertop, to display her designs to buyers at the same hotel.[24]

Elizabeth Phelps also made personal appearances at stores that carried Phelps products. Out of state, she traveled to stores such as Neiman Marcus in Dallas and Houston.[25] In North Carolina, she visited retailers such as Ivey's—where Louise Thomas had worked in the previous decade. On March 9, 1961,

Ivey's advertised a showing of Phelps Deep Country Clothes and Phelps leather accessories in their second floor Country Clothes Shop, with informal modeling of the spring collection in morning and afternoon segments. The advertisement promised that Phelps would be present: "Mrs. Elizabeth Phelps, designer of these dashing casuals will be here to assist in your selections."[26] Its illustration showed pastel floral blouses worn tucked into shorts or a skirt with deep patch pockets, belted with Phelps leather belts with pointed buckles in the shape of the Phelps trademark symbol.

1961 was a year that saw Elizabeth Phelps recognized by the American fashion industry for her work in sportswear. In January, Lord & Taylor gave her an award "for creative contributions to the continuing traditions of American design."[27] She did still occasionally attend New York City gatherings, and in November she was again honored, this time at a Fashion Group event celebrating American sportswear designers. The guests of honor included Phelps along with other designers such as Bonnie Cashin, Tom Brigance, Vera Maxwell, Tina Leser, and Phelps's friend Clare Potter.[28] The Fashion Group archives at the New York Public Library include two photographs that may both be from this event. The first is marked "Phelps Nov. 3, 1961—Sportswear" on the back and shows a white model in a trouser ensemble of collarless jacket, blouse, and cropped corduroy pants. The second shows a Black model in a tennis dress and sweater ensemble; the dress has patch pockets in an immediately recognizable Phelps style.[29] This is the first instance of a Black model wearing Phelps clothing that I have uncovered in my research.

On January 20, 1962, just two over months after her recognition by the Fashion Group, William Drown Phelps died at the Phelpses' vacation home in Ormond Beach, Volusia County, Florida.[30] Both *The New York Times* and *Women's Wear Daily* ran obituaries.[31] The *Times* headline celebrated William for his handwork as a leather craftsman, a characterization that certainly would have pleased the Phelpses: "William Phelps, Designer, Was 71; Leather Craftsman Noted for Hand-Made Items Dies." The cause of death was stated to be a heart attack. Unlike some articles published in the 1950s, both obituaries noted that the couple had jointly won honors such as the Coty Award. Both also stated that on William's retirement "a few years ago," the firm name was changed to Phelps Enterprises, with Elizabeth Phelps heading the company.[32] Perhaps in the 1960s, with Elizabeth taking a greater leadership role in the business, the fashion industry was willing to give her greater recognition for her earlier achievements. Or perhaps she simply drafted the press release for the obituary to include her contributions. An obituary in the newspaper of Wilkes-Barre, Pennsylvania, Phelps's childhood hometown, added that he was also survived by his son Walter James Phelps, an officer in the British Army stationed in Cyprus, which suggests that William's first wife, Jean, took the children and went back to the United Kingdom to live after their divorce. This paper also stated that Phelps would be buried in Wilkes-Barre.[33] After William's passing, Elizabeth

Fig. 7.7. Elizabeth Phelps for Phelps Deep Country Clothes, blouse, cotton, circa 1963. (Author's collection. Photograph by the author.)

would carry on the Phelps Industries business for the remainder of the decade.

Elizabeth Phelps continued to design ready-to-wear under the Phelps Deep Country Clothes label throughout the 1960s. A Phelps Deep Country Clothes yellow floral blouse from the author's collection, circa 1963, is made in 100 percent cotton (Fig. 7.7). In a May 1960 article, "Permanent Weekend Clothes-List," *Vogue* showed a blouse in a similar floral print for wear in the country, advising, "The Phelps people, who invented [the] Rolls Royce of country skirts, have ideas of their own about what looks wonderful with it. Their thin cotton shirts are small-sleeved and flowered—but flowered with vast restraint, and the tailoring, as you'd expect, is impeccable."[34] The phrase "the Phelps people" suggests that Elizabeth was not the sportswear's only designer; perhaps the *Vogue* journalist was still thinking of William being actively involved, or perhaps the phrasing came from some statement Elizabeth made to include her workers in the credit. The blouse shown in *Vogue* had a standard pointed collar, but in the summer of 1963, *New York Times* journalist Charlotte Curtis, profiling Elizabeth Phelps, noted of Phelps's current collection, "There are blouses with peter pan or Byron collars."[35] The blouse's floral print and cut is also very similar to one worn by a college student in the 1964 Disney film *The Misadventures of Merlin Jones.*[36] It seems likely that the yellow floral blouse was produced sometime between the initial *Vogue* coverage and the Disney movie.

Phelps Deep Country Clothes of the 1960s were still best accessorized with Phelps belts or bags, as the *Vogue* "Permanent Weekend Clothes-List" article demonstrated. Its first photograph in showed a model in what the article described as a pink Phelps wrap skirt and matching pink Phelps belt, worn with a polo-style knit shirt, palm leaf hat, and straw basket bag (Fig. 7.8). The skirt has deep patch pockets in front and looks similar to those in the Valentine Richmond History Center collection (Figs. 6.1, 6.2). A similar Phelps belt was described in *Women's Wear* that year, noting the coordination of color between Phelps Deep Country Clothes main garments and matching accessories: "Dyed to match scalloped leather belts finished by two grommets are tied by the ends of drawstringed skirt belt."[37]

A similarly constructed belt in the author's collection is a scalloped orange leather with grommets in front to hold fabric ties (Fig. 7.9). The leather section of this belt is 23⅜" long and is 1⅞" wide at the widest part of the scallops. The ties are 34½" long. Another belt with ties (in red leather) was shown in *The New York Times* a few years before, in a style that drew the two leather sections almost to meet in front.[38] In the *Vogue* article, however, the belt is shown tied to leave approximately a two-inch gap between the leather ends, which means, if tied similarly, the orange belt could accommodate a 24"-to-25" waist. However, the fabric ties do give the belt flexibility, so it could be worn by someone with a slightly smaller or large waist; the dress form in Fig. 7.9 has a 23" waist, and the belt is drawn in tighter than as illustrated in *Vogue*.

The matching belt and skirt shown in *Vogue* were described as part of a plan for clothes to be left at one's country or beach home or quickly packed for a weekend getaway: "Now for the plan itself: it involves the kinds of clothes described on these ten pages—in a word, staples. You buy them and—because timelessness is the forte of fashion staples—you buy them over and over again."[39] Just as Elizabeth Harrison's article of the previous decade had described the Phelpses' work as "American Classics," *Vogue*'s viewpoint in the 1960s was that the line comprised classic clothes and accessories that would stand the test of time.[40]

Fig. 7.8. Pink Phelps skirt accessorized with matching pink scalloped leather belt. "Permanent Weekend Clothes-list." *Vogue*. 1 May 1960, 173. (*Vogue*, ©Condé Nast.)

Fig. 7.9. Phelps Industries, belt, leather, fabric, metal, circa 1960. (Author's collection. Photograph by Elizabeth Grace Matheson.)

A Phelps Deep Country Clothes black-and-white scroll-and-floral-print wrap skirt in the author's collection is probably also from the 1960s (Fig. 7.10). It contains tags stating "Phelps Deep Country Clothes" and "100% Cotton." Unlike many of Elizabeth Phelps's wrap skirts, this one has pockets set into the seams rather than patch pockets. This skirt is longer than wrap skirts in the Museum at FIT and Valentine Richmond History Center collections and may have been intended for a hostess to wear while entertaining in her own home in the evening. Phelps advertised Elizabeth Phelps's designs for "THE ULTIMATE IN FEMININE SPORTSWEAR; Phelps Classic Deep Country Clothes; Town and Travel Wear; Evening Separates," in *Women's Wear* to promote her 1965 Sheraton-Russell Hotel showings.[41] The extant evening skirt is 40" long at the center front seam, which must have fit the garment's first owner. However, a

Fig. 7.10. Elizabeth Phelps for Phelps Deep Country Clothes, skirt, cotton, late 1960s. (Author's collection. Photograph by the author.)

later owner or user appears to have attempted to shorten it with a "no-sew" hem of glue, folding the hem over twice and gluing it to a center front length of 37½", perhaps to use as a costume.

In the 1960s, Elizabeth Phelps was assisted by a team of local artisans and other employees, some of whom had been with the workshop since its relocation to Skyland. In a 1964 article in an Asheville newspaper, Elizabeth shared the credit for her work with her team of craftspeople and other employees, who were photographed at work. Her direct assistant was Jean Salmon. Cutters included Donald Merrill, James West, and Clyde W. Roberts.[42] A year later, W. M. Cook and Reggie Coxe were listed as cutters, along with Roberts.[43] Mildred Franklin, Lorraine Hughes, Ruth McMahan, Bessie Lee Jenkins, and Barbara Ingle were seamstresses, along with Aileen B. Hollingsworth, who had been the Phelpses' first hire for the Skyland workshop.[44] Hollingsworth was a multitalented craftsperson who also sometimes assisted with finishing handbags.[45]

The Skyland, North Carolina, workshop method, while still stressing handwork, incorporated more elements of division of labor and factory production than the original workshop plan of one artisan making an object from start to finish. Some of the job titles sound like those of a small factory rather than the egalitarian Washington Square workshop: Velda Drucker was forewoman, and Ellsworth Ard was plant superintendent.[46] At Skyland, too, there were three different departments involved with leather-good production: metalworking, leather cutting and polishing, and sewing and finishing. By 1965, the metalwork elements on Phelps bags and belts were no longer primarily vintage. Instead, metalworker Roger Frazier crafted new bag frames and metal ornaments copied

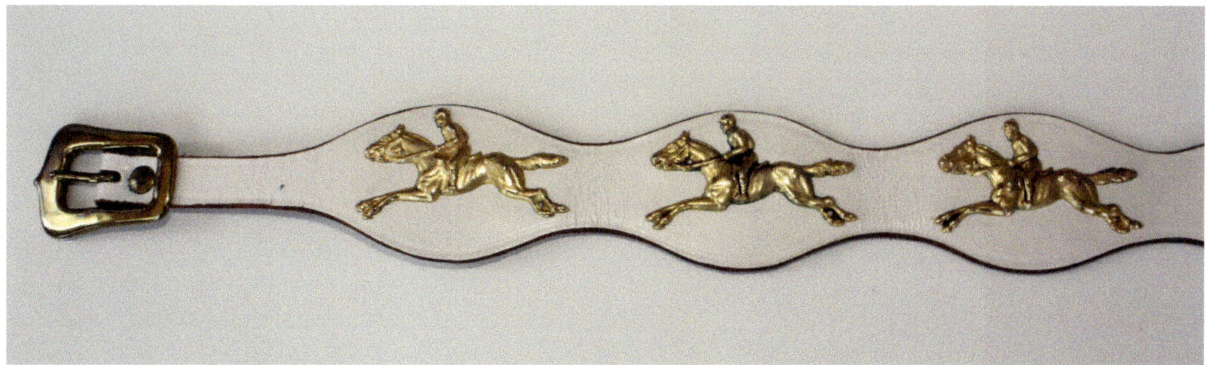

Fig. 7.11. Detail of a scalloped white leather belt with horseracing motifs. Phelps Industries, belt, leather, metal, circa 1960s. (Author's collection. Photograph by the author.)

from vintage horse brass, as well as ornaments that were "chiefly from nature, ranging from leaves and life-size cicadas to tiny ladybugs and stars."[47] They might have hired a metalworker as a means for obtaining a more reliable supply of ornaments, out of a desire to support that branch of craft. An example from this period is a white leather scalloped belt, ready-to-wear size 26, which has seven scallops, each decorated with a metal motif of a jockey riding a racehorse (Fig. 7.11). These motifs are less directly related to the themes of the Phelps vintage metalwork of the past, such as heraldry, military Americana, and traditional horse harness motifs, and this belt may date from the 1960s, when Phelps produced new metalwork.

In February 1964, Elizabeth Phelps applied for a patent on a garment that could be worn as either shorts or long trousers, demonstrating her continuing interest in convertible clothing that could be changed based on what was appropriate for the location and activity (Fig. 7.12). In US Patent 3,266,057, dated August 16, 1966, Phelps protected her intellectual property in her invention: "The shorts have the appearance of ordinary walking or Bermuda shorts and may be worn on any occasion when shorts are appropriate dress. However, if a change in climate, environment, or protocol makes it desirable to convert the shorts into slacks or trousers, this may be readily accomplished by attaching a pair of elongated tubular members . . . to the leg portions."[48] Phelps did not claim to have been the first to create a convertible shorts-to-trousers garment, but she emphasized that "in modern trousers the shape is very important and the outward appearance of the garment drastically affects its commercial practicability and its overall usefulness."[49] In other words, she was claiming the fashionable look as part of her invention. This look included a vertical "continuous pleat extending from the leg portion of the shorts throughout the respective tubular extension members," and the fact that each tubular leg matched a specific shorts leg.[50] The continuous vertical pleat was very similar to the pleat she used in normal trousers, such as the Louise Thomas trousers at the North Carolina Museum of History (Fig. 7.1). To match right tube to right shorts leg and left tube to left shorts leg, Phelps envisioned color-coded looped tabs (which could be used to hang up the tube when not in use), although she also noted that "left"

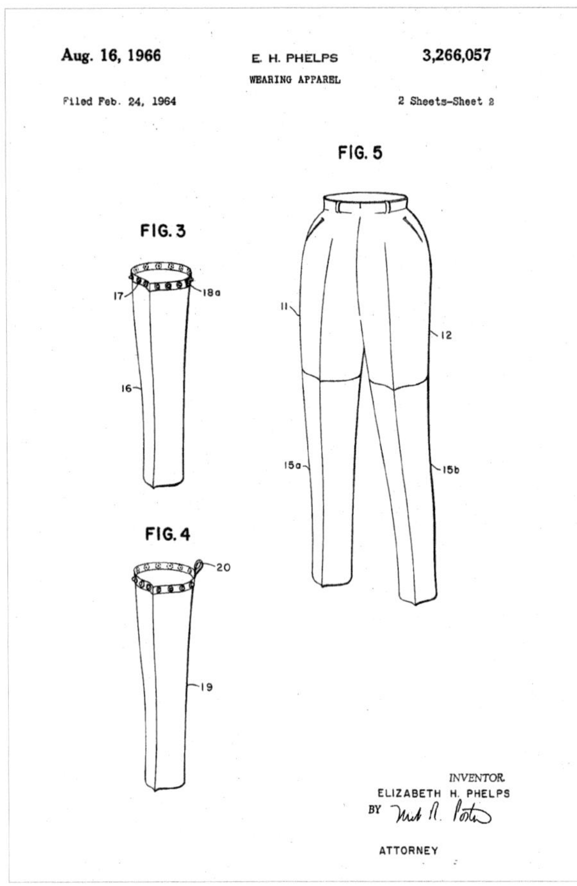

Fig. 7.12. Elizabeth H. Phelps, design patent for convertible trousers to shorts, patented 1966. (Author's collection. Photograph by the author.)

and "right" labels, metallic disks, bar-tacking, or woven shapes could accomplish the same ends. The segments attached via a series of gripper fasteners, as in so many of Elizabeth Phelps's earlier designs.[51]

In the patent filing, Elizabeth Phelps stressed the importance of wearing the right item for the right occasion, and her design made it easier for women to dress appropriately according to prevailing norms, just as her paper patterns for *Woman's Day* had addressed the same concerns. Phelps imagined her convertible shorts being used in traveling and for negotiating the needs of private versus public spaces. "For example, in slacks form, the apparel may be worn on the street for marketing and converted into shorts when returning home."[52] The fact that Phelps argues that trousers are acceptable for streetwear in the 1960s, and it is now shorts that must be kept in the privacy of home, shows how the etiquette of casualwear had changed since her 1953 *Woman's Day* collection, when a skirt was deemed necessary for marketing, and it was trousers that were worn at home.[53] Phelps's change of viewpoint may also be related to the absence of her husband's influence, as William Phelps seemed to retain strong views as to the importance of a skirt or skirtlike outer garment for women. The private-versus-public divide was also cited as a reason to wear Phelps's invention while traveling: "The shorts may be worn in an automobile for comfort and converted into slacks when entering public places or stopping for meals."[54] Phelps also imagined that her invention might serve utilitarian functions in the outdoors, such as adding the trouser legs for protection from insects, sun, wind, or cold or to facilitate wading. While Elizabeth Phelps was successful in this patent application, she does not seem to have pursued other patents. It is unclear whether this design was put into production.

During the 1960s, Elizabeth Phelps also designed shorts that were not convertible. A pair in the author's collection are extremely similar to the Louise Thomas trousers and might have been part of a collection of coordinating separates (Fig. 7.13). Three labels inside the shorts state: "Phelps Deep Country Clothes," "65% Dacron Polyester / 35% rayon," and the ready-to-wear size "10." The fiber content is the same as the Thomas trousers, and it appears to be the exact same fabric. The Scovill Gripper fasteners are also the same. Like the Thomas trousers, these shorts have a side opening and large belt loops that could have accommodated a wide leather Phelps belt (Fig. 7.14, 7.15).

Some of Elizabeth Phelps's work in the 1960s brought her back full circle to the sturdy clothing for outdoor activities that first brought demand for Phelps Deep Country Clothes in the late 1940s. In the 1960s, the Phelps workshop sometimes produced small projects for other designers or companies. In 1964, Elizabeth designed a collection of women's

"field clothes" for Abercrombie & Fitch, including "trousers, shirts, and jackets in earthy colors of rust, woods shades of green," which were promoted as being more attractive than khaki and as practical as camouflage.[55] Conversely, in 1965 Phelps also produced a collection of shooting clothes for women designed by big-game hunter Fred Palmer.[56] My research has not uncovered examples of Phelps Associates, Phelps Industries, or Phelps Enterprises producing items designed by someone outside their workshops previous to these examples. The following year, Elizabeth Phelps advertised her own designs for women's hunting and shooting attire, "No kooky clothes for her ladies that hunt, shoot, and go for deep country walks. FOR THE HUNT . . . the authentic hunting suit in hunting green or natural Dacron with quilted suede trim. . . . ELIZABETH PHELPS KNOWS ABOUT REAL SPORTSWEAR."[57] An accompanying illustration showed a tunic-length top, with the quilted suede sections positioned at the shoulders to absorb the kickback force of the gun—another example of the way Phelps designed functional and elegant clothing and accessories to make women's lives easier or more pleasant. A tunic top now covered the top of the pants, rather than an apron, but the design still calls to mind the 1948 *Vogue* image of Elizabeth Phelps striding across the Joanna Furnace property in her hunting apron (Fig. 5.13).

Fig. 7.13. Elizabeth Phelps for Phelps Deep Country Clothes, shorts, Dacron polyester and rayon, 1960–64. (Author's collection. Photograph by the author.)

Fig. 7.14. Reverse view of shorts, showing belt loops. Elizabeth Phelps for Phelps Deep Country Clothes, shorts, Dacron polyester and rayon, 1960–64. (Author's collection. Photograph by the author.)

Fig. 7.15. Detail of shorts, showing side opening, with both zipper and Scovill Gripper® fasteners. Elizabeth Phelps for Phelps Deep Country Clothes, shorts, Dacron polyester and rayon, 1960–64. (Author's collection. Photograph by the author.)

Revival of Styles

In the 1960s and 1970s, there was a revival of interest in Phelps shoulder bags, belts, and belt bags. Journalist Marilyn Bender reported for *The New York Times* in 1964 that the World War II–style shoulder bag was back in style again, including examples by Phelps. "The Phelps bag came in a variety of shapes, but the one that brings a nostalgic smile to women over 35 years old was a drawstring design with a metal emblem on the flap. It can still be ordered in the Country Clothes Shop at Lord & Taylor for $65 to $135." Bender noted that shoulder bags were useful for the modern woman's adventures, whether riding a motorcycle "or dancing the frug in a discothèque."[58]

The group of leather goods in the collection of the Valentine Richmond History Center exemplifies how some 1940s-era Phelps objects enjoyed a second season of fashionable use. The Valentine's provenance notes in its curatorial recommendation for accession for this group of objects that this belt and these bags were used by Seymour Rennolds, mother of the donors and that "the donors also wore this belt in the 1960s and 1970s."[59] This note of use pattern is repeated in the entries for the two belt bags.[60] This confirms fashion media reports, from Bender's example in *The New York Times,* to coverage in fashion magazines such as *Vogue,* that Phelps belts and waist bags came back into style in the late 1960s and early 1970s, in essentially the same shapes as their 1940s predecessors. That fashionable young women of the 1960s and 1970s would be able to wear their mother's (or even their grandmother's) Phelps belt fits with the Phelps's design philosophy of creating objects that were usable over many years of wear and persisted despite changes in fashion.

Fashion historian Caroline Rennolds Milbank recalls that as a teenager she enjoyed wearing her mother's vintage Phelps belts: "We liked to go 'attic shopping' and wear what we found there."[61] Milbank remembers wearing vintage clothes as well as sewing some of her clothes for herself. The dress code for students at Milbank's school in Richmond required the girls to wear skirts or dresses rather than trousers. She recalls that a classic style was popular: "the dominant look at that place and time was Ladybug, Villager, John Meyer of Norwich, Aigner, Bermuda Bags and Pappagallo."[62] Around 1970 and 1971, Milbank sewed her own dirndl skirts and accessorized them with Phelps belts.[63]

Milbank did not wear the Phelps belt bags, but her sister, architect Amie Rives Rennolds, did. According to Milbank, her sister remembers wearing a bag with a belt "and possibly even wearing out the belt and replacing it. She loved the attached belt/bag for going out and having a place to put a key."[64] Just as women in the World War II period enjoyed the handsfree simplicity of Phelps bags that hung from the body rather than being carried in the hands, some women in the late 1960s and early 1970s found the freedom of a Phelps belt bag enabled them to carry the minimal items necessary for their active lifestyles.

Winding Down Phelps Industries

At the end of the 1960s, Elizabeth Phelps closed the Phelps workshop. A *Women's Wear Daily* article tantalizingly describes her as having been offered a consultant-designer's role at Hanes in August 1969 and mentions her plans to wind down the Phelps Industries business, yet Phelps designs were still featured in *Vogue* in 1970.[65] Several North Carolina newspapers also reported Phelps's new role with Hanes.[66] According to *Women's Wear,* Phelps was "closing the business to devote full time to her job with Hanes."[67] Richard B. Port, Hanes's vice president of merchandising, was quoted as indicating that Phelps's role would be to increase the fashion appeal of Hanes's mass-produced products: "We are directing greater emphasis to fashion at Hanes, and we are pleased to have someone of Mrs. Phelps' stature with us. She will work directly with our various divisions in providing new ideas and fashion intelligence for our hosiery and knitwear products."[68]

In some ways, it is understandable what might have appealed to Phelps about the Hanes role. She might have been growing tired of running Phelps Enterprises by herself. Her responsibilities as head of the company most likely took tremendous time away from the work of designing and making, and Phelps would not be the first creative mind to wish for less time spent on management and more time spent on her artistic interests. At sixty, nearing retirement age, Phelps might have decided this was a good time to reevaluate her commitments. However, consulting for Hanes, while remunerative, was also potentially fraught for the designer who had long preferred smaller operations. She had chosen to take her Deep Country Clothes ready-to-wear back in house after briefly working with a larger scale manufacturer in the early 1950s, and her design collaboration with leather manufacturer Sills in the same period was similarly short-lived. Additionally, from the point of view of the manufacturer, Phelps seems an odd choice for injecting a more fashionable viewpoint into the Hanes product line. First, her experience was not in knitwear but in working with woven textiles and leather. Perhaps even more surprisingly, she was known for classic designs that changed very slowly or not at all from year to year. Finally, she was of a very different generation than that of the youthquake exerting such fashion influence in the 1960s.

Elizabeth Phelps quickly wound down the business. Beginning in August, just a few days after her new role with Hanes was announced, Phelps ran a closing sale. Clothing was on sale August 18 through September 13, and September 3 through 13 fabric yardage went on sale.[69] By October 1969, part of the property containing the Phelps Enterprises Skyland workshop had been purchased by Holcombe and Kerstin McDaniel to be used as a factory for producing their new childrenswear line, Gildafrox. They planned to be open for business by October 15.[70]

After the closure of Phelps Enterprises, Elizabeth Phelps seems to vanish from the national fashion scene. Her clothes were still shown in magazines the following year, but where would they have been produced with the factory and workshop sold? Since Phelps designs did not change drastically from year to year, the most likely explanation is that these items were leftover stock.

Elizabeth Phelps appears to have retained part of the original Shadowlawn property—including the house—for four more years, then sold off additional real estate and chattels as she moved away from the Asheville area. In May 1973, she sold additional acreage to Fairfax Enterprises.[71] In October, Phelps ran a series of ads in the local newspaper announcing a final sale of Phelps clothing and fabrics. The ad advised, "Clothes mostly in sample sizes eight to 14. Fabrics—corduroy, denims, assorted cottons, prints, zippers, and so-forth. Also ask Elizabeth Phelps about valuable antiques. Driveway left, past Gerber's Outlet, at back of Factory Building."[72] This sale was followed on November 3 by a public auction of the "remaining contents of the former home of Elizabeth Phelps at 1860 Hendersonville Road."[73] The auction, managed by Robert Bunn auction service, included mostly antiques such as a "carved Duncan Phyfe sofa" and "poster bed, circa 1810" but also items of more recent vintage, such as a 1955 Rambler station wagon, a television, and office furniture.[74]

It is unclear how long Elizabeth Phelps remained in the consulting role with Hanes after winding down Phelps Enterprises, or how active she was in the Hanes business. No longer carrying the heavy responsibility of running her own business, Phelps was free to return her focus to painting. In 1956, while still designing her Phelps Deep Country Clothes line, she had written to Jimmie Booth, "Got a large watercolor bloc and I hope I can do something with those inks. It'll be fun to try."[75] By the mid-1960s, she had become an exhibiting member of the Associated Artists of North Carolina.[76] By 1977, Elizabeth Phelps had relocated to the coastal town of Ocean Springs, Mississippi, where she participated in local juried art exhibitions.[77] In 1978, she also had her own show at the Ocean Springs Library. She was pictured in the newspapers with one of her paintings of a flock of geese.[78] This example of her late-career artwork brought together her interests in painting and birdwatching; in 1964, Elizabeth Phelps had been profiled by a local journalist, not for her fashion designs but for the "birdwatching bar" she had arranged in her living room, with bar stools lined up in front of a plate glass window and birding reference books below.[79]

In the 1980s, Elizabeth Phelps continued to paint and exhibit her work in Mississippi. In 1981, she won a $100 cash prize from the Mississippi Chemical Company for her contribution to the Seventeenth Annual LaFont Art Workshop exhibition in Pascagoula.[80] The LaFont, built in 1960, was a hotel that local television news reported was "for decades . . . synonymous with fine dining and hospitality in Jackson County" (Fig. 7.16).[81] In 1982, Phelps had another solo exhibition, this time at the Municipal Art Gallery in Jackson.[82] Two years later, she again showed at the LaFont, contributing to a two-artist exhibition,

Fig. 7.16. Postcard: *LaFont Inn on US 90, Pascagoula, Mississippi,* circa 1960. (Author's collection.)

along with Mary Layacano.[83] Newspaper coverage of the show stated, "Mrs. Phelps says she paints from memory and imagination. . . . After the death of her husband and her retirement from the fashion world she returned to her first career and now, as a resident of Ocean Springs, she enjoys the arts groups in the area, attends workshops, and hangs exhibitions of her work."[84] Painting provided a fulfilling artistic outlet for Phelps during her retirement years.

Elizabeth Phelps died on November 17, 1987, less than two weeks before her seventy-eighth birthday, according to the Social Security Death Index, but I have not yet been able to discover additional information, such as the cause of death or whether she was still living independently.[85] Unlike her husband, she had no obituary in *The New York Times* or *Women's Wear Daily*—or even in the local Mississippi or North Carolina newspapers, as far as I have been able to locate. But this absence seems an important part of the narrative, and part of the reason it is so important to reclaim her story. How does an important American woman designer just disappear? Did Elizabeth Heintges Phelps simply not have anyone close enough to her when she died to send the details to the newspaper, or did she not wish for publicity?

Today, the Phelps name is continued in a leather goods brand owned by a family member, but producing a different range of products than the original Phelps Associates, Phelps Industries, and Phelps Enterprises accessories and sportswear. William Phelps's grandnephew Thomas Bates started his leather accessories company in 1989 under his own name and still sells belts and other accessories under the Thomas Bates brand. Many of these items are manufactured in Haverhill, Massachusetts, in a former tannery, and "Made in the USA" is an important aspect of the marketing.[86] Bates later added the T. B. Phelps line, pairing his own initials with the Phelps name. The fall 2020 T. B. Phelps retail catalog included primarily leather goods for men, such as shoes, wallets, and belts, in leathers including elk and bison.[87] The T. B. Phelps brand uses a shield-shaped symbol in green outlined in gold that is slightly reminiscent of the original Phelps belt buckle symbol turned upside down. In the center of the shield there is a monogram with the initials TPB, and the words "Est. 1938."[88] In 2017, Bates told the *Boston Voyager,* "Our newest marketing development is offering hand sewn men's shoes under the T. B. PHELPS brand. Phelps is an old family brand name of mine, it is also my middle name. My great uncle had a leather accessories brand in the 1940's, making women's belts and bags under that name Phelps name [*sic*]. In 2015, we purchased one of our customers (a small footwear company) and combined the product lines to include men's leather shoes, bags and wallets."[89] In this version of the brand identity, Elizabeth Phelps and her contributions to the Phelps workshop from the very beginning were erased, but by October 2021, the T. B. Phelps website included both Phelpses in a blurb on the origin of the T. B. Phelps brand:

> T. B. PHELPS™ celebrates *Classic American Style.* Our footwear and accessories feature the highest quality materials and craftsmanship while highlighting traditional, classic designs. Since 1938, the Phelps name has been associated with leather products. Elsie and Bill Phelps started Phelps Leather in New York City featuring leather bags. Their innovative design of a women's leather messenger bag was adopted by the US Army as standard issue for all women in the service. Today, Thomas Phelps Bates, grandnephew, has 35 years making quality leather products and continues the same attention to innovation, design and quality with our T. B. PHELPS footwear and accessories line.[90]

Conclusion

In the 1960s, Elizabeth Phelps took on increasing responsibility for leading the Phelps business. After William's death in 1962, Elizabeth Phelps continued designing the Phelps Deep Country Clothes sportswear line and leading the leathergoods workshops. With trousers increasingly acceptable as womenswear, Elizabeth Phelps designed pants made to be worn without an apron or tunic over them and even patented a design for trousers convertible to shorts. Meanwhile, a new generation of women discovered the freedom of movement offered by Phelps shoulder bags and belts with waist bags, and Phelps leather goods were embraced by youthful wearers, who either purchased new products or wore vintage examples. By the close of the 1960s, she retired, turning first to work as a consultant for Hanes. In the last years of Elizabeth Phelps's life, her artistic interests came full circle, with a return to painting.

Conclusion

William and Elizabeth Phelps positioned themselves and their products to connect with American patriotism, history, and craft, resulting in great critical acclaim during World War II. The story of their workshop, Phelps Associates, begins with the personal and family histories of this husband-and-wife design team, and the ways they selectively included elements of their histories in their creation of the Phelps brand. William Phelps, a white, Anglo-Saxon Protestant craftsman, descended from generations of New England craftsmen and later capitalist factory owners. Elizabeth Phelps was a first-generation German immigrant, but this was obscured during the war. Wartime marketing efforts by both the broader fashion industry and the Phelpses themselves focused on Americana and American history, as well as local Manhattan leather-production history, and not on Elizabeth Phelps's immigrant status. The Phelpses created leather goods that referenced historical forms of horse harness and military uniform, domesticating and making these forms seem particularly "American." Their shoulder bags, made without metal frames, were a solution to the metal shortage plaguing bag manufacturers and time offered women handsfree mobility. Together, William and Elizabeth Phelps forged a fashion brand that drew on their strengths and interests as a couple and outlasted the exigencies of the war that brought their accessories to national fame.

The Phelpses were forward-looking, creative, and unusual among American fashion designers in their attempts to reimagine how American fashion was produced. Their struggle to create a mode of production that was different from largescale mass-production in impersonal factories, yet still was economically feasible, shows the difficulty that entrepreneurs faced when departing from the typical business model. They sought to revive the artisan workshop and empower workers, continuing on from their 1930s involvement in Works Progress Administration (WPA) projects. Phelps Associates' history points to the opportunities and the challenges for working artists and artisans trying to succeed financially. The Phelpses illustrate the blurry line between practitioners of "fine art," like painting, and handcraft in the 1930s, as they participated in WPA projects. Like many others in the design field during that decade, the Phelpses connected art and craft in the search for American design based on American history and carried this perspective as they moved into fashion creation in the 1940s. With the fall of Paris, the American fashion industry, previously more focused on mass-market ready-to-wear reproduction of French couture, sought American craftsmanship to replace the lack of access to French artisanship, in order to bolster the industry's image while encouraging consumers to make fewer, higher quality purchases. This was the American fashion industry's moment to shine, for both propaganda and economic purposes.[1] Phelps Associates offered accessories that perfectly fit the mood of the moment as the United States went to war.

The Phelpses looked to American history for inspiration for their initial leather goods. Conceiving of themselves as artisans, the Phelpses moved between craft, fashion, and fine art. Their swift entry into the field of custom leathercraft, in which they started leatherworking as amateurs making individual pieces and built their skills along with the workshop, points to their talent for design and publicity, and their effective leveraging of fashion industry connections. At the same time, the Phelpses' experiences point to the difficulty of running a small-shop model of production in a country based on the large factory, mass-production, and assembly-line method. The Phelpses desired and worked toward a production model that balanced competing needs for their own pleasure in creating, the well-being of their team of artisans, and profitability. This was an ongoing struggle. The Phelpses' experiments in Pennsylvania in splitting production between a quasi-mass-produced small-scale factory and the custom workshop do not appear to have been profitable, and they lasted only a short time. Their North Carolina workshop and small-batch factory seem to have been more successful, and Phelps ultimately was based outside of Asheville longer than it had been in New York or Pennsylvania.

Phelps Associates' story points to the centrality of accessories to our understanding of the fashions of a given time period, especially in the mid-twentieth century, when the etiquette of fashion meant that accessories set the tone for an ensemble and determined where, when, and for what activities a main garment was appropriate. Understanding the accessories is crucial also to understanding how an ensemble would have been read and understood by viewers. Research on Phelps' clients has shown the importance of accessories to creating the right look for a particular time and place—albeit one that might have been different from the way the accessories were originally shown in magazines. A point that has been underscored by this object-based research is that accessories were often bought and conceptualized by their owners as sets. Clients with larger wardrobe budgets might have worn their custom-made belt and bag ensembles for country casual, for example. Clients with smaller budgets used items differently; a Joanna Furnace employee might see her Phelps bag and belt ensemble as her Sunday best. A fashion-forward 1940s teenage client carefully saved her Phelps accessories to be used and enjoyed by her own daughters a generation later. Coordination was key, from accessory sets in the 1940s to accessories that were color-toned to the main garments of the 1960s. Additionally, object-based research reveals other insights, such as the way people loved their Phelps pieces so much that they wore them over and over, repairing them when they became worn, rather than discarding them.

William and Elizabeth Phelps offer a case study of one husband-and-wife design team's working method, and how, like any relationship, this evolved over time. The objects they created also gave women sartorial tools to navigate wartime and postwar gender roles. The flow of ideas between the partners, and each individual's desires to please the other, other make it difficult to attribute specific ideas within the partnership, especially in the early work. In the initial Washington Square workshop, they worked closely together in physical space. Early 1940s media coverage often portrayed William Phelps as the primary designer and Elizabeth Phelps a subordinate or helper. Together, they crafted leather goods, including bags and belts that gave women the ability to move about with hands free, which was needed during World War II, as women carried their own packages and pursued active lifestyles. As the Phelps workshop expanded, workspaces became more separated, and the partners moved to supervise separate teams on different floors of the University Place workshop, and, later, even in different buildings in Skyland.

After World War II, William Phelps's conservative views on fashion and gender roles, particularly women wearing trousers, inspired Elizabeth Phelps to create compromise sportswear that pleased both partners. These clothes generated opportunities for more women to wear pants that still read as feminine. Moreover, Elizabeth Phelps designed elegant and functional clothing solutions that made postwar American women's demanding lives easier, from a drop-seat jumpsuit, to a wrap skirt that opened completely flat for ironing, to a pair of shorts that converted to trousers. Phelps Deep Country Clothes gave women freedom of mobility without fear of impropriety, which was empowering. That young women of the late 1960s and early 1970s again embraced the handsfree styles of Phelps leathergoods suggests that both the accessory forms and the national symbols that adorned them could be reinterpreted and repurposed by a new generation with very different views of gender roles and national identity.

While Elizabeth Phelps and most of her mid-twentieth-century fashion-design did not engage with feminism directly, it remains important to recover the stories of these women and their work. As William Phelps approached retirement, and the Phelps Deep Country Clothes ready-to-wear became increasingly important to the business, Elizabeth took over leadership of the workshops and was more often the public face of the brand. She continued running the business after her husband's death, but she did later list his loss as a contributing factor in her decision to wind down Phelps Industries and return to painting.

Even after much discovery, there are still more avenues to be explored in the story of Phelps Associates. Some of the key outstanding questions raised by this research include: Were any of the workshops ever unionized? Were there Phelps clients from racially diverse backgrounds? How did the Phelpses' close relationship with Lord & Taylor come about, and what was buyer Jimmie Booth's role in that? I would also like to find out more about the Skyland workshop and the workers there, who were credited by name in articles about Phelps Industries.

The materiality of Phelps Associates' products points to their prescient sustainability. While the Phelpses do not seem to have had the environment foremost in mind, their practices of reusing materials, making things to last, caring for craftspeople as people, and slowing the pace of fashion change are familiar elements in twenty-first-century dialogues on sustainable or slow fashion. Early Phelps leatherwork designs were built on ideas of reusing and reimagining things past their initial use, such as the vintage military and horse harness metalwork they incorporated into early bags and belts—"upcycling," in today's terminology. They believed in creating high-quality and longwearing items. Accordingly, they challenged the speed of fashion change and were slow to alter shapes and silhouettes, allowing for the same accessories or main garments to be worn year after year.

William and Elizabeth Phelps believed that both materials and labor were important aspects of value. The Phelpses cared about materials, whether leather or fabric. However, they cared equally about the ways their designs were produced, and the quality of life of the people who worked for them. The Phelps story shows the difficulty of labor relations, even with the best of intentions. The sequential moves of the Phelps workshop demonstrate the challenges of finding the right balance of labor expenses and overhead, and the cost of the final product at retail. Yet today's sustainability organization Fashion Revolution's **#whomademyclothes?** campaign question could have been answered by a Phelps client who read newspaper or fashion magazine articles about the Phelps Associates workshop and saw pictures of the Phelps Associates artisans at work.[2] Long before sustainability was an industry buzzword, the Phelpses defied the frantic pace of fashion obsolescence by crafting objects that were meant to be investments, collected over time and worn for years, as well as celebrating the people who made the objects and the process of making.

Acknowledgments

I am extremely grateful to everyone who has provided support, assistance, guidance, or all of the above over the course of this project.

First, I thank everyone involved in transforming this research into book form. I am very grateful for the enthusiasm and work of Kelly Reddy-Best, Costume Society of America series editor. At Kent State University Press, thank you to the whole team, including Clara Totten, interim director and acquisitions editor; Mary D. Young, assistant director and editorial manager; Christine Brooks, design and production manager; Darryl M. Crosby, design and marketing associate and designer; Katherine Saunders, associate editor; and Erin Holman, copyeditor. Thank you to the Costume Society of America (CSA), its leadership team, and Executive Director Kristen Miller Zohn for arranging funding for many of the images and permissions for the book.

I am also grateful to the CSA for generously funding travel and image photography earlier in my research, through the Stella Blum Student Research Grant. Thank you to Abby Lillethun, chair of the Blum Grant Committee, who met me in Central Park to present the grant award, as it was 2020 during the COVID-19 pandemic! The research funded by CSA was subsequently published as the Stella Blum Grant Report in *Dress: The Journal of the Costume Society of America,* with thanks to Editor in Chief Ingrid Mida, and forms parts of chapters 5, 6, and 7 of this book.

The book is derived in part from an article published in *Dress* 49, no. 1 (2023), copyright Costume Society of America, available online: https://doi.org/10.1080/03612112.2023.2165330.

This book originated as my doctoral dissertation at the Bard Graduate Center, and I thank my dissertation advisors Michele Majer and Meredith Linn.

They were immense help and sources of wisdom. Thank you also to committee member Catherine Whalen. I have been very blessed to have the opportunity to study with and learn from Michele, Meredith, and Catherine, and I so appreciate you all! While they were not involved in this project, I owe a huge debt of gratitude to Lourdes Font and Denyse Montegut at the Fashion Institute of Technology (FIT,) and Judith Keeling at Texas Tech University Press, who have been mentors and were crucial to my early career development.

Thank you so much to all the individuals and institutions who made research appointments and images available: Art Students League of New York: Stephanie Cassidy; Center for Creative Photography: Leigh Grissom; Condé Nast: Marianne Brown and Páton Hardy; Costume Institute, the Metropolitan Museum of Art and Art Resource: Tae In Ahn, Marci Morimoto, Bethany Gingrich, Joyce Fung, Julie Zeftel, and Sophie Jones; Coty, Inc.: Hannah Adkins; East Texas Research Center, R.W. Steen Library, Stephen F. Austin State University, Nacogdoches: Kyle Ainsworth and Linda Reynolds; Fashion Group International: Karen Young; FIT, Gladys Marcus Library, Special Collections and College Archives: Karen Trivette, April Calahan, and Tiffany Nixon; Fraunces Tavern Museum: Christian Sabharwal; Hay Creek Valley Historical Association: Mark Zerr; Hearst: Wendy Israel; Estate of André Kertész: Victor Gurbo; Library of Congress: Jonathan Eaker and Tomeka Myers; Massachusetts Historical Society: Hilde Perrin; Museum at FIT: Valerie Steele, Melissa Marra-Alvarez, Elizabeth Way, Michelle McVicker, Eileen Costa, Faith Cooper, and Frida McKeon Loyola; National Museum of American History, Smithsonian Institution: Alison Oswald, Kay Peterson; New-York Historical Society Museum and Library: Erin Weinman and Eleanor Gillers; New York Public Library, Brooke Russell Astor Reading Room for Rare Books and Manuscripts, Manuscripts, Archives, and Rare Books: Tal Nadan; North Carolina Museum of History: RaeLana Poteat, Paige Myers, Eric N. Blevins and Kent Thompson; Irving Penn Foundation: Matthew Krejcarek; Valentine Richmond History Center: Kristen Stewart, Meg Hughes, Kelly Kerney, and Michael Kaliris; Virginia Museum of Fine Arts: Katie Domerat; Wadsworth Atheneum: Ned Lazaro and Jordan Fenn; *Women's Wear Daily* / Wright's Media: Benjamin Shepard. I owe an extra debt of gratitude to Kristen Stewart for her hospitality and encouragement during this research.

This research and writing would not have been possible without the support of Christine Childs, Leah Cravenho, Hannah Silver McKnight, and Emma Roberts Bortins, who provided childcare during the years when that was essential. Thank you to Jennifer Farley Gordon and Colleen Terrell for wisdom and advice on grant writing. In FIT's MA Program in Fashion and Textile Studies, thank you to Hilary Davidson, Marjorie Phillips, and all my colleagues.

Thank you to the incredibly talented fashion historian Caroline Rennolds Milbank for generously sharing information about her family history relating to the Valentine Richmond History Center's Phelps leather goods.

I am also grateful for the time of two talented contemporary craftsmen: Joe Collmorgen of CollmorgenLeather in Lufkin, Texas, for generously sharing his knowledge and expertise in leatherworking—and for the gorgeous bracelet!—and Matt Christie of GreenRiverWoods and his wife, Stephanie Hellert, for welcoming my parents into his Asheville workshop.

I have been blessed by the faithful, essential prayer support of many people. Thank you to all the women of my Tuesday Bible Study throughout the years (especially Cindy Paulus and Clara Park, who have been there the whole time!); everyone from Friday evening Community Group (especially Gretchen Bennett and Bethany Martin); and my one-to-one Bible reading and prayer partners Abena Frempong, Joanna Justice, and Angela Shirey.

I would like to acknowledge all my family as partners in this project. Thank you and so much love to you all. Thank you to Rachel Jumper Kimbrell and Bruce Kimbrell, hosts extraordinaire during the long months of COVID. My parents, Jack Jumper and the late Dana Rusk Jumper, have always enthusiastically supported my research and writing passion, even when I was a preteen researching the Loch Ness Monster. Dana always thought that whatever I did was wonderful, which was an incredible foundation of security to build on. Thank you also to Team Matheson, aka our "Four Family": Big thank you hugs and love to Elizabeth Grace Matheson and Priscilla Leah Matheson, and more thanks and love than I can express to my awesome and amazing husband, Dan Matheson, for endurance and loving support throughout this project.

Above all, I give all thanks and glory to God—Father, Son and Holy Spirit. "Not to us, O Lord, not to us, but to your name give glory, for the sake of your steadfast love and your faithfulness!" Psalm 115:1 (ESV).

Notes

Introduction

1. Here and throughout, I use the word *American* to indicate things and people of the United States of America.

2. "Home Dressmaking," *Harper's Bazaar,* Oct. 1942, 104.

3. 1940 US Census, New York County, New York, population schedule, Manhattan, dwelling 42, household 113, William and Elizabeth Phelps, roll *m-t0627-02645,* p. *3B,* available via Ancestry.com.

4. Truth to materials means allowing a material's natural look to show through and using the material appropriately for its functional properties. See chapter 3 for a discussion of the Phelpses' use of "honest" leather.

5. See Rebecca Jumper Matheson, *Young Originals: Emily Wilkens and the Teen Sophisticate* (Lubbock, TX: Texas Tech University Press, 2015), 75–93.

6. Bernice G. Chambers, *Fashion Fundamentals* (Prentice-Hall, 1947), 398.

7. "About FGI: Our History," Fashion Group International website, https://www.fgi.org/system/about-fgi/, accessed 2 Oct. 2021; Chambers, *Fashion Fundamentals,* 398.

8. The American Fashion Critics Awards, sponsored by Coty and popularly known as the Coty Awards, sought to promote American fashion and fashion designers. DLW, "Phelps Associates Win Design Award," *Women's Wear Daily,* 4 Feb. 1944, 20; Mary Braggiotti, "Leather-Bound Love," *New York Post,* 20 Sept. 1947; Jessie Stuart, *The American Fashion Industry* (Prince School of Retailing, Simmons College, 1951), 73.

9. Dorothy Rodgers and Mary Rodgers, *A Word to the Wives* (Alfred A. Knopf, 1970), 285.

10. See, for example, Sara B. Marcketti and Jean Parsons, *Knock It Off: A History of Design Piracy in the US Women's Ready-to-Wear Apparel Industry* (Texas Tech Univ. Press, 2016); Cheryl Buckley and Hazel Clark, *Fashion and Everyday Life: London and New York* (Bloomsbury, 2017).

11. "This Half Century," *Vogue,* Jan. 1950, 93.

12. On 1950s fashion and gender roles, see Valerie Steele, *Fifty Years of Fashion: New Look to Now* (Yale Univ. Press, 1997), 28–26.

13. Museum of Modern Art, *100 Useful Objects of Fine Design 1947: Available Under $100* (Museum of Modern Art, 1947), 4.

14. Rebecca Arnold, *The American Look: Fashion, Sportswear and the Image of Women in 1930s and 1940s New York* (I. B. Taurus, 2009), 4; Richard Martin, *American Ingenuity: Sportswear 1930s–1970s* (Metropolitan Museum of Art, 1988), 11, 17.

15. The first fashion photographs that I have found showing Black models wearing Phelps clothing were taken in the 1960s, under the auspices of the Fashion Group.

16. "Suggests Store Clinics to Seek Out Latent Designing Talents," *Women's Wear Daily,* 7 Feb. 1950, 2.

17. For more on the Eames and the Knolls, see Pat Kirkham, *Charles and Ray Eames: Designers of the Twentieth Century* (MIT Univ. Press, 1995); Earl Martin ed., *Knoll Textiles, 1945–2010* (Bard Graduate Center and Yale Univ. Press, 2011).

18. Hazel Clark, "SLOW + FASHION—an Oxymoron—or a Promise for the Future . . . ?" *Fashion Theory* 12, no. 4 (2008): 428.

19. Lourdes M. Font and Trudie A. Grace, *The Gilded Age: High Fashion and Society in the Hudson Highlands*

1865–1914 (Putnam County Historical Society and Foundry Museum, 2006), 26.

20. Elizabeth Wilson, *Adorned in Dreams: Fashion and Modernity*. Rev. ed. (I. B. Taurus, 2003), 3.

21. Buckley and Clark, *Fashion and Everyday Life,* 4; "Permanent Weekend Clothes-List," *Vogue,* 1 May 1960, 169, 171.

22. Jane Bradbury and Edward Maeder, *American Style and Spirit: Fashions and Lives of the Roddis Family, 1850–1995* (V & A Publications, 2016).

23. Charlotte Nicklas and Annabella Pollen, eds., *Dress History: New Directions in Theory and Practice* (Bloomsbury Academic, 2015).

24. Ingrid Mida, *Reading Fashion in Art* (Bloomsbury, 2020), 42.

25. Anne Hollander, *Seeing Through Clothes* (Viking, 1978; repr., Univ. of California Press, 1993), xi–xii.

26. Sally Stein, "The Graphic Ordering of Desire: Modernization of a Middle-Class Women's Magazine, 1919–1939," in *The Contest of Meaning: Critical Histories of Photography,* ed. Richard Bolton (MIT Press, 1989).

27. Marilee Boyd Meyer, foreword to *Inspiring Reform: Boston's Arts and Crafts Movement,* ed. Marilee Boyd Meyer et al. (Davis Museum and Harry N. Abrams, 1997), 14; Pat Kirkham and Amy F. Ogata, "Europe 1830–1900," in *History of Design,* ed. Pat Kirkham and Susan Weber (Bard Graduate Center and Yale Univ, Press, 2013), 427; Elizabeth Stillinger, *A Kind of Archeology: Collecting American Folk Art, 1876–1976* (Univ. of Massachusetts Press, 2011), 4–5, 12–13; Catherine L. Whalen, "Collecting as Historical Practice and the Conundrum of the Unmoored Object," in *The Oxford Handbook of History and Material Culture,* ed. Ivan Gaskell and Sarah Anne Carter (Oxford Univ. Press, 2020), 2.

28. Lou Taylor, *The Study of Dress History* (Manchester Univ. Press, 2002), 3. The other two areas, conservation and display, will not be as relevant to this project.

29. "The Small Shop," *Fortune,* Nov. 1945, 158.

30. "TFC: Bridging Academic and Popular Understandings of Fashion History Through Research and Programming," Texas Fashion Collection website, Univ. of North Texas, accessed 2 Oct. 2021, https://tfc.cvad.unt.edu/.

31. Valerie Steele, *Women of Fashion: Twentieth-Century Designers* (Rizzoli, 1991), 108, quoting "This Half Century," *Vogue,* Jan. 1950, 93.

32. Annalee Gold, *One World of Fashion,* 4th ed. (Fairchild, 1987), 184.

33. Caroline Rennolds Milbank, *New York Fashion: The Evolution of American Style* (Harry N. Abrams, 1989), 162–63.

34. Richard Martin, "All-American: A Sportswear Tradition," *All-American: A Sportswear Tradition,* by Fashion Institute of Technology (Fashion Institute of Technology, 1985), 38–39.

35. Kohle Yohannan and Nancy Nolf, *Claire McCardell: Redefining Modernism* (Abrams, 1998), 53, 54–55, 57, 116–17.

36. Emma McClendon, *Denim: Fashion's Frontier* (Yale Univ. Press and FIT, 2016), 84–85.

37. Wadsworth Atheneum, *Designing Women: American Style 1940–1960,* Labels and Gallery Guide, box 1, ser. 1, folder 11, Virginia "Jimmie" Booth Collection, NMAH. AC.0729, Archives Center, National Museum of American History, Smithsonian Institution.

38. Chambers, *Fashion Fundamentals,* 397–98.

39. DLW, "Phelps Associates Win Design Award," 20.

1. Craft Connections and Early Careers

1. "Big Bags and Belts," *Life,* 19 Nov. 1945, 85.

2. The size 12 is 31½" from end to end, with 27½" from the end of the belt strap to the middle belt notch. The size 10 is 29½" from end to end, with 24½" from the end of the belt strap to the middle belt notch; wear patterns on this belt indicate that this was the notch at which the owner usually wore it. Both belts are 2⅜" wide, with buckles 3¼" high by 2" wide.

3. "What Clinches New Fashions," *Vogue,* 1 May 1962, 68; "For Hot Springs and All Points," *Vogue,* 1 Oct. 1944, 136–37; "Ready for Anything," *Harper's Bazaar,* Jan. 1943, 59.

4. Braggiotti, "Leather-Bound Love."

5. Chambers, *Fashion Fundamentals,* 397.

6. "Small Shop," 158.

7. DLW, "Phelps Associates Win Design Award," 20.

8. William Drown Phelps's hometown, as he knew it, no longer exists. In 1915, miners accidentally started a fire in the seam of the anthracite coal underneath Laurel Run. The fire continued to smolder for decades and in the 1960s the Appalachian Regional Commission deemed the town of Laurel Run unsafe for human occupation. Laurel Run's residents were relocated, and its buildings were razed. Ben Swenson, "Laurel Run, Pennsylvania; Fire Beneath the Mountain," *Abandoned Country: Disappearing History and the Natural World Reclaiming It* (blog), 12 May 2015, http://www.abandonedcountry.com/2015/05/12/laurel-run-pennsylvania-fire-on-the-mountain/.

9. US Passport Applications, 1795–1925, database with images, available via FamilySearch.org; William Drown Phelps, 1920, citing Passport Application, Pennsylvania, United States, source certificate #92600, Passport Applications, Jan. 2, 1906–Mar. 31, 1925, 1363, NARA microfilm publications M1490 and M1372, National Archives and Records Administration, Family History Library microfilm 1,651,093;William Drown Phelps and Elizabeth Heintges Von Mevis, 31 Dec. 1934, Pennsylvania, Marriages, 1852–1968, database online, Original data: Marriage Records, Pennsylvania Marriages, Various County Register of Wills Offices, Pennsylvania, available via Ancestry.com.

10. Pennsylvania Society of Sons of the Revolution, *Annual Proceedings: Pennsylvania Society of Sons of the Revolution, 1913–1914* (Pennsylvania Society, 1914), 44.

11. "Death of Francis Phelps," *Wilkes-Barre Record,* 7 July 1911.

12. "Pennsylvania Strike Riot; Superintendent of Parish Coal Company Assaulted Near Wilkes-Barre—More Trouble Feared," *New York Times,* 10 May 1900.

13. Pennsylvania Society of Sons of the Revolution, *Annual Proceedings,* 44.

14. Virginia Pope, "American Inspiration," *New York Times,* 6 Feb. 1944.

15. Braggiotti, "Leather-Bound Love," 3.

16. Shem Drowne, *Native American Archer Weathervane,* circa 1716, information available at Massachusetts Historical Society, Collections Online, accessed 11 Sept. 2019, http://www.masshist.org/database/1769.

17. Nathaniel Hawthorne, *Mosses from an Old Manse* (1846; repr., A. L. Burt, n.d.), 248–60.

18. Hawthorne, *Mosses from an Old Manse,* 252, 259.

19. Hawthorne, *Mosses from an Old Manse,* 253.

20. Hawthorne, *Mosses from an Old Manse,* 259.

21. Hawthorne, *Mosses from an Old Manse,* 259; Drowne, *Native American Archer Weathervane.*

22. Virginia T. Lathrop, "Abscessed Tooth Brought Asheville New Industry," *Charlotte (NC) Observer,* 28 Dec., 1952; Ernest Hexamer, "Wm. A. Drown & Co., Umbrella and Parasol Factory," *Hexamer General Surveys,* vol. 21, 1887, available through Greater Philadelphia GeoHistory Network, https://www.philageohistory.org/rdic-images/view-image.cfm/HGSv21.2049-2050.

23. Hexamer, "Wm. A. Drown & Co."

24. Fashion designer Emily Wilkens, who studied nineteenth-century Costume Institute objects as inspiration for her work, included parasols as accessories to her spring-summer 1944 collection, almost immediately after Phelps's 1943 donation. See Matheson, *Young Originals,* 71–72, 81.

25. "Academy Commencement," *Wilkes-Barre (PA) Record,* 12 June 1901.

26. *Catalogue of Yale University 1909–1910* (Tuttle, Morehouse & Taylor, 1909), 704; Braggiotti, "Leather-Bound Love," 3.

27. "Death Claims Francis Phelps at Laurel Run," *Evening News* (Wilkes-Barre, PA), 6 July 1911.

28. Pennsylvania Society of Sons of the Revolution, *Annual Proceedings,* 44.

29. Braggiotti, "Leather-Bound Love," 3.

30. "William Drown Phelps," World War I Veterans Service and Compensation File, 1917–19, 1934–48. RG 19, ser. 19.91, Pennsylvania Historical and Museum Commission, Harrisburg, available via Ancestry.com.

31. "Phelps-Ross," *New York Herald,* 7 Jan. 1921.

32. William D. Phelps, Arrival Date 29 Sept., 1924, *Passenger Lists of Vessels Arriving at Philadelphia, Pennsylvania, Records of the Immigration and Naturalization Service, 1787–2004;* Record Group *85,* ser. *T840,* FHL microfilm 2,312,478, NARA, available via Ancestry.com.

33. William Phelps, 1916–1930, Belgique, Anvers, index de police de l'immigration, 1840–1930, database with images, citing reference 42, Stadsarchief Antwerpen, Belgie (Municipal Archives, Antwerp); FHL microfilm 2,234,923, available via FamilySearch.

34. "Big Bags and Belts," 85; William D. Phelps, arrival date 21 Oct. 1927, *Passenger and Crew Lists of Vessels Arriving at New York, New York, 1897–1957,* microfilm publication T715, 8892 rolls, NAI: 300346, Records of the Immigration and Naturalization Service, NARA, available via Ancestry.com; William D. Phelps, Arrival Date 29 Sept. 1924.

35. "Workshop on Washington Square," *Harper's Bazaar,* June 1942, 22.

36. Caroline Evans, *The Mechanical Smile: Modernism and the First Fashion Shows in France and America, 1900–1929* (Yale Univ. Press, 2013), 57, 58, 74; Richard Sennett, *The Craftsman* (Yale Univ. Press, 2008), 47.

37. "Workshop on Washington Square," 22.

38. "New York City: The Leather Trade; The Swamp—Hide and Leather Dealers—Capital Employed—Brokers," *New York Times,* 31 Mar. 1856.

39. "Workshop on Washington Square," 22.

40. Braggiotti, "Leather-Bound Love."

41. "Small Shop," 158. According to the US Bureau of Labor Statistics, the average weekly salary for a man employed in hand-carving furniture in 1931 was $37.03. See *Wages and Hours of Labor in the Furniture Industry, 1910–1931* (GPO, 1932), 3.

42. "Elizabeth H. Phelps," Social Security Administration, Washington DC, *Social Security Death Index, Master File,* available via Ancestry.com. *U.S., Social Security Death Index, 1935–2014,* available via Ancestry.com. Phelps and Von Mevis, 31 Dec. 1934, Pennsylvania, Marriages, 1852–1968.

43. Braggiotti, "Leather-Bound Love," 3.

44. Pat Kirkham and Lynne Walker, "Women Designers in the USA, 1900–2000: Diversity and Difference," in *Women Designers in the USA, 1900–2000: Diversity and Difference,* ed. Pat Kirkham (Bard Graduate Center and Yale Univ. Press, 2000), 58.

45. "Conversations with Joanna Furnace Area Residents," Hay Creek Valley Historical Association *Journal* (2010), 24.

46. Virginia T. Lathrop, "Fashion-Award Winners Move Home-Shop to Asheville," *News and Observer* (Raleigh, NC), 28 Dec. 1952.

47. Beverly Gordon, *The Saturated World: Aesthetic Meaning, Intimate Objects, Women's Lives, 1890–1940* (Univ. of Tennessee Press, 2006), 1. 48.

48. Eleanor Lambert, "Phelps Associates," press release, circa 1944, 1–2, SC.214.3.10, Eleanor Lambert Collection, Special Collections and College Archives, Gladys Marcus Library, Fashion Institute of Technology; "Award-Winning Designer Joins Hanes Corporation," *Asheville (NC) Citizen-Times,* 15 Aug. 1969.

49. Braggiotti, "Leather-Bound Love," 3.

50. "Around Asheville," *Asheville (NC) Citizen-Times,* 15 Mar. 1964.

51. Braggiotti, "Leather-Bound Love"; Lathrop, "Abscessed Tooth Brought Asheville New Industry."

52. Enrollment Records: Elsie Heintges, 1932–33 term, Art Students League of New York.

53. Nancy Deihl, introduction to *The Hidden History of American Fashion,* ed. Nancy Deihl (Bloomsbury, 2018), 3.

54. Enrollment Records: Elsie Heintges, 1932–33 term; Art Students League of New York, *Course Catalogue, 1932–1933 Winter Season* (Art Students League of New York, 1932), 9–11.

55. Enrollment Records: Elsie Heintges, 1933–34 term, Art Students League of New York; Art Students League of New York, *Course Catalogue, 1933–1934 Winter Season* (Art Students League of New York, 1933), 9.

56. Stephanie Cassidy, manager, editorial services, Art Students League of New York, email message to author, 14 Aug. 2019.

57. Elizabeth Heintges, arrival date 8 Sept. 1933, *Passenger and Crew Lists of Vessels Arriving at New York, New York, 1897–1957.*

58. "William Drown Phelps," World War I Veterans Service and Compensation File, 1934–48, RG 19, ser. 19.91, Pennsylvania Historical and Museum Commission, Harrisburg, available via Ancestry.com.

59. Phelps and Von Mevis, 31 Dec. 1934, Pennsylvania, Marriages, 1852–1968. "Amy Sturdevant Barber," obituary originally published in *Wilkes-Barre Record,* 1 Feb. 1934, available via *Find A Grave,* https://www.findagrave.com/memorial/155347014/barber.

60. Braggiotti, "Leather-Bound Love"; "Workshop on Washington Square," 22.

61. "Small Shop," 158.

62. Braggiotti, "Leather-Bound Love."

63. Lambert, "Phelps Associates," 2; Braggiotti, "Leather-Bound Love.

64. "Dr. J. S. Taylor Speaker to League," *Kingston (NY) Daily Freeman,* 23 Mar. 1939.

65. 1940 US Census, available via Ancestry.com.

66. Braggiotti, "Leather-Bound Love," 3.

67. Barbara McMartin, *Hides, Hemlocks, and Adirondack History: How the Tanning Industry Influenced the Region's Growth* (North Country Books, 1992), 5; Charles H. McDermott, *A History of the Shoe and Leather Industries of the United States, Together with Historical and Biographical Notices,* vol. 2 (John W. Denehy & Co., 1920), 258.

68. Frank W. Norcross, *A History of the New York Swamp* (Chiswick Press, 1901), 7. These tanneries were located slightly further north, one on James Street, and one at the corner of Bowery and Canal.

69. McMartin, *Hides, Hemlocks and Adirondack History,* 31; "New York City: The Leather Trade," 3; Tanner's Council of America, *The Romance of Leather: A Brief History of Leather and a Description of Tanning* (Tanner's Council of America, 1937), 12.

70. "New York City: The Leather Trade," 3.

71. Council of the Citizens' Association of New York, *Report of the Council of Hygiene and Public Health of the Citizens' Association of New York upon the Sanitary Condition of the City* (D. Appleton & Company, 1865), vii–ix, lxx.

72. Gergely Baics, *Feeding Gotham: The Political Economy and Geography of Food in New York, 1790–1860* (Princeton Univ. Press, 2016), 225; New York Metropolitan Board of Health, *Third Annual Report of the Metropolitan Board of Health for the State of New York* (Charles Van Benthuysen & Sons, 1868), 38, 157.

73. "Historic Buildings Torn Down," *New York Times,* 6 Mar. 1878.

74. "Relics of an Old Street," *New York Times,* 7 Mar. 1880.

75. "Relics of an Old Street."

76. "Warehouses Under the Bridge," *New York Times,* 20 Apr. 1884.

77. Braggiotti, "Leather-Bound Love."

78. "Tanning Industry Goes Back to Earliest Colonial Days," *New York Times,* 12 Aug. 1934.

79. Tanner's Council of America, *Romance of Leather,* 36. In 2021, the New York City Department of Housing Preservation and Development occupies a 1960s-era office building at this address. "100 Gold Street," New York City Citywide Administrative Services website, accessed 22 Oct. 2021, https://www1.nyc.gov/site/dcas/business/dcasmanagedbuildings/100-gold-street.page.

80. M. B. Levick, "'Swamp' Has New Dean to Maintain Traditions," *New York Times,* 12 Oct. 1924.

81. Jane Butzner, "Leather Shocking Tales," *Vogue,* Mar. 1936, 139.

82. Elizabeth Harrison, "American Classics: Phelps Casual Designs: A Designing Couple Now Experiment with Fabric," *New York Times,* 9 Nov. 1955.

83. Braggiotti, "Leather-Bound Love"; DLW, "Phelps Associates Win Design Award," 20; Beryl Williams, *Fashion Is Our Business* (J. B. Lippincott, 1945), 20, 28.

84. Tiffany Webber-Hanchett, "Dorothy Shaver: Promoter of 'The American Look,'" *Dress* 30, no. 1 (2003): 84.

85. Harrison, "American Classics," 38.

86. Williams, *Fashion Is Our Business,* 22.

87. William Drown Phelps, 1942, *Selective Service Registration Cards, World War II: Fourth Registration,* Records of the Selective Service System, Record Group 147, NARA, St. Louis, MO, available via *Ancestry.com.*

88. Lambert, "Phelps Associates," 2, 1.

89. Chambers, *Fashion Fundamentals,* 398.

90. DLW, "Phelps Associates Win Design Award," 20.

91. Other craftspeople they admired included Charles Millward, who made salad bowls for Hammacher Schlemmer, and Jack Miller, a tailor who made riding clothes. "Small Shop," 161.

92. Kirkham and Walker, "Women Designers in the USA," 68.

93. "Workshop on Washington Square," 22.

94. Betty Dougherty, *Your Leatherwork* (1947; repr., Sylvan, 1948), 35.

95. Kirkham and Walker, "Women Designers in the USA," 68.

96. Wilhela Cushman, "You're at Liberty to Make," *Ladies Home Journal,* Feb. 1943, 30.

97. Braggiotti, "Leather-Bound Love."

98. Kirkham and Walker, "Women Designers in the USA," 64.

99. Harrison, "American Classics," 38.

100. William Lindau, "Mountain Craftsmen: Native Artisans Produce Phelps Style Separates, Accessories," *Women's Wear Daily,* 29 Jan. 1958, 45.

2. Workshop on Washington Square to University Place

1. Paul Martineau, "Style in the Face of Crisis, 1930–1946," in *Icons of Style: A Century of Fashion Photography,* ed. Paul Martineau (J. Paul Getty Museum, 2018), 86.

2. Bernadine Morris, "Sally Kirkland, 77, Editor at Life; Brought Readers European Styles," *New York Times,* 3 May 1989.

3. "Designs for Dressmaking: Make a Skirt Wardrobe," *Vogue,* 15 Sept. 1944, 159; Bettina Ballard, *In My Fashion* (David McKay, 1960), 158, 297; "Work Clothes: New Substitutes for House Dress Are Rugged, Trim, and Tailored," *Life,* 7 Feb. 1949, 88–90.

4. Sally Kirkland, "Sportswear for Everywhere," in *All-American: A Sportswear Tradition,* by Fashion Institute of Technology (Fashion Institute of Technology, 1985), 39.

5. Eleanor Lambert, "Phelps Associates," press release, circa 1944, 1, Eleanor Lambert Collection, SC.214.3.10, Special Collections and College Archives, Gladys Marcus Library, Fashion Institute of Technology.

6. Claudia Kidwell, *Suiting Everyone: The Democratization of Clothing in America* (Smithsonian Institution Press, 1974), 15; Sandra Ley, *Fashion for Everyone: The Story of Ready-to-Wear* (Charles Scribner's Sons, 1975), 106, 137, 147; Nancy MacDonell, *Empresses of Seventh Avenue: World War II, New York City, and the Birth of American Fashion* (St. Martin's Press, 2024), 5, 91–94.

7. Fashion Group International, "Los Angeles and San Francisco Groups Present Fashion Futures; Stress on Craftsmanship," *Fashion Group Bulletin* 7, no. 1 (1941): 3. The extensive archives of the Fashion Group International are held in the New York Public Library's Manuscripts, Archives, and Rare Books collection and include many issues of the *Fashion Group Bulletin,* in MSS Col. 908, boxes 144–50.

8. Fashion Group International, "Quality, New Fashions in Unions Discussed at April and May Luncheons," *Fashion Group Bulletin* 7, no. 3 (1941): For more on Pennoyer, see Rebecca Jumper Matheson, "Sara Pennoyer: Twentieth-Century Retail and Advertising Executive and Her Creation, Polly Tucker, Merchant," *Fashion, Style & Popular Culture* 5, no. 1 (2018): 59–79.

9. Fashion Group International, "Fashion Availables for a Wartime Autumn; A Realistic Report Keyed to Government Orders, Necessity for New Advertising, Promotion Techniques," *Fashion Group Bulletin* 8, no. 5 (1942): 7.

10. Fashion Group International, "Morale—Inventory for Fashion Industry and Individual, 'Take the Folly Out of Fashion; Make Quality and Value the Sales Points,' Advises Edna Woolman Chase," *Fashion Group Bulletin* 8, no. 1 (1942): 3, 4.

11. Winifred Raushenbush, *How to Dress in Wartime* (Coward-McCann, 1942), 119, 167–72, 120, 101.

12. American Fashion Critics' Award Program 1944, 2, SC.214.3.9, Lambert Collection.

13. Wilson, *Adorned in Dreams,* 60–61.

14. Edward S. Cooke Jr., "Modern Craft and the American Experience," *American Art* 21, no. 1 (2007): 2.

15. Lambert, "Phelps Associates," 2.

16. Sennett, *Craftsman,* 53, 54.

17. "Workshop on Washington Square," 22; "United States Census, 1940," available via Ancestry.com.

18. "Workshop on Washington Square," 22.

19. "Museum History," Merchant's House Museum website, 2013 http://merchantshouse.org/about/museum-history/.

20. Lathrop, "Abscessed Tooth Brought Asheville New Industry."

21. Frank L. Walton, *Thread of Victory* (Fairchild, 1945), 155.

22. "The Market Basket," *Vogue,* 1 July 1941, ii.

23. "Fastenings and Embellishments," Oct. 28, 1942–Jan. 22, 1943, Thomas J. Watson Library Digital Collections, Metropolitan Museum of Art, b1752635_001, b1752635_007, https://libmma.contentdm.oclc.org/digital/collection/p16028coll1/id/17038.

24. "Small Shop," 161.

25. Workshop on Washington Square," 22.

26. "Small Shop," 161.

27. Ferber, *Giant,* 201.

28. Edna Ferber, *Fanny Herself* (1917; repr., CreateSpace, n.d.), 67.

29. Edna Ferber, *Giant* (1952; repr, Harper Perennial, 2019), 108.

30. McMartin, *Hides, Hemlocks, and Adirondack History,* 12.

31. Tanner's Council of America, *Romance of Leather,* 20.

32. Phyllis Hobson and Steven Edwards, *Tan Your Hide! Home Tanning Leathers and Furs* (Garden Way/Storey, 1977), 25, 48.

33. Gideon Lee, *Two Lectures on Tanning Delivered Before the Eclectic Fraternity* (Eclectic Fraternity, 1838), 16.

34. Tanner's Council of America, *Romance of Leather,* 10.

35. Tanner's Council of America, *Romance of Leather,* 22.

36. Lee, *Two Lectures on Tanning Delivered Before the Eclectic Fraternity,* 16–18.

37. Hobson and Edwards, *Tan Your Hide!*, 82.

38. Tanner's Council of America, *Romance of Leather*, 10.

39. McMartin, *Hides, Hemlocks, and Adirondack History*, 30.

40. Lee, *Two Lectures on Tanning Delivered Before the Eclectic Fraternity*, 8; American Pharmaceutical Association, *Yearbook of the American Pharmaceutical Association 1913* (American Pharmaceutical Association, 1915), 2:102.

41. Lee, *Two Lectures on Tanning Delivered Before the Eclectic Fraternity*, 19–20.

42. Hobson and Edwards, *Tan Your Hide!*, 19.

43. Tanner's Council of America, *Romance of Leather*, 10, 19.

44. Hobson and Edwards, *Tan Your Hide!*, 46, 59, 63.

45. Gertrude McAllister, "Fashion Jury Names Leading American Designers," *Brooklyn Eagle*, 4 Feb. 1944.

46. "Big Bags and Belts," 88.

47. "Small Shop," 160.

48. Tanner's Council of America, *Romance of Leather*, 16–17.

49. Matthew Dalton, "Louis Vuitton Makes a Home on the Range," *Wall Street Journal*, 18 Oct. 2019.

50. "Small Shop," 160.

51. McDermott, *History of the Shoe and Leather Industries*, 399.

52. Tanner's Council of America, *Romance of Leather*, 29.

53. Tanner's Council of America, *Romance of Leather*, 28. One type of cattlehide leather is sole leather, strong but flexible, abrasion-resistant, breathable, and thus much in demand for footwear during World War II; however, it was rationed during because it was needed to supply the military (25). Phelps Associates would not have worked with sole leather, as it was too tough for their purposes, but they did work with other types of cowhide.

54. "What Animals Are These?," *Harper's Bazaar*, Nov. 1942, 61.

55. "Ready for Anything," 59.

56. Tanner's Council of America, *Romance of Leather*, 29.

57. "Fur Belts," *Harper's Bazaar*, Aug. 1943, 105.

58. Dougherty, *Your Leatherwork*, 23; Tanner's Council of America, *Romance of Leather*, 29.

59. "Something in Wool and Leather: Something Half and Half," *Harper's Bazaar*, Aug. 1943, 66.

60. "Big Bags and Belts," 86.

61. "Paid Notice: Deaths: Messinesi, Despina (Nee Plakias)," *New York Times*, 28 July 2003.

62. Tanner's Council of America, *Romance of Leather*, 30.

63. "What Animals Are These?," 60.

64. "Historic Sources Inspire Bags," *Women's Wear Daily*, 7 May 1943, 20.

65. Dougherty, *Your Leatherwork*, 23.

66. Tanner's Council of America, *Romance of Leather*, 30.

67. "Spring Paraphernalia," *Harper's Bazaar*, Mar. 1943, 60.

68. Tanner's Council of America, *Romance of Leather*, 31; "How Leather Is Imitated," *Compton's Pictured Encyclopedia*, vol. 4, ed. Guy Stanton Ford (F. E. Compton, 1922), 1977.

69. "Junior Bazaar," *Harper's Bazaar*, Mar. 1943, 126.

70. Walton, *Thread of Victory*, 158.

71. Dougherty, *Your Leatherwork*, 23.

72. "Selling Handbags," *Women's Wear Daily*, 21 Apr. 1944, 22.

73. "Historic Sources Inspire Bags," 20.

74. Pope, "American Inspiration."

75. "Threading Your Way Through the Labeling Requirements Under the Textile and Wool Acts," Federal Trade Commission website, ed. Jan. 2024, https://www.ftc.gov/tips-advice/business-center/guidance/threading-your-way-through-labeling-requirements-under-textile.

76. R[aphael]. A[rthur]. Salaman, "Handbag and Purse Maker," *Dictionary of Leather-Working Tools, c. 1700–1950* (George Allen & Unwin, 1986), 218.

77. McDermott, *History of the Shoe and Leather Industries*, 247.

78. McDermott, *History of the Shoe and Leather Industries*, 248. McDermott was the former editor of the *Boot and Shoe Recorder* (283).

79. Braggiotti, "Leather-Bound Love," 3.

80. McDermott, *History of the Shoe and Leather Industries*, 249.

81. *American Fashion Critics' Award Program 1944*, 2.

82. Harrison, "American Classics," 38.

83. Harrison, "American Classics," 38.

84. Jennifer L. Roberts, "Things: Material Turn, Transnational Turn," *American Art* 31, no. 2 (2017): 65.

85. Salaman, *Dictionary of Leather-Working Tools*, 225.

86. Peter C. D. Brears, *Horse Brasses* (Country Life Books, 1981), 17.

87. Virginia Lathrop, "Fashion-Award Winners Move Home-Shop to Asheville," *News and Observer* (Raleigh, NC), 28 Dec. 1952.

88. The leather strap of this belt is 28¾"and the length including the buckle is 29¾".

89. "Small Shop," 159.

90. "Workshop on Washington Square," 22.

91. Sennett, *Craftsman*, 20.

92. "Small Shop," 158, 160, 161; "Big Bags and Belts," 88.

93. "Small Shop," 159.

94. Goffman, *Presentation of Self in Everyday Life*, 106, 107–8, 113, 114, 134.

95. Goffman, *Presentation of Self in Everyday Life*, 109, 124.

96. *The March of Time*, 1947, available through Getty Images, clip 510560825, object name 4932538356_013, uploaded Sept. 3, 2014, https://www.gettyimages.com/detail/video/salesman-adjusting-leather-handbags-on-rack-designer-news-footage/510560825?adppopup=true.

97. Stephen E. Bowles, "And Time Marched On: The Creation of *The March of Time*," *Journal of the University Film Association* 29, no. 1 (1977): 7, 11.

98. "March of Time Fashion Film Set to Be Released Tomorrow," *Women's Wear Daily*, 20 Feb. 1947, 22.

99. *March of Time*.

100. According to color theorist and historian Elizabeth Burris-Meyer, the years 1937 to 1942 "saw the introduction of the dirndl from the Tyrol to American women. Taken to the heart of all college girls, for campus or parties, by the matron for lounging, country or evening, this fashion made possible the attractive mother and daughter fashions because both looked so young, fresh, and American in the full skirts." Elizabeth Burris-Meyer, *This Is Fashion* (Harper & Bros., 1943), 62.

101. "Small Shop," 159.

102. "Historic Sources Inspire Bags," 20.

103. Lambert, "Phelps Associates," 2.

104. "Small Shop," 160.

105. Elizabeth Etnier, "Ten Families Who Abandoned the Cities," *Harper's Bazaar,* Apr. 1947, 213.

106. Dougherty, *Your Leatherwork,* 18.

107. Cooke, "Modern Craft and the American Experience," 6.

108. Edna Ferber, "Long Distance," in *One Basket* (Chicago: People's Book Club, 1947), 92, 89.

109. For a WAC's first-person account of the work of theatre as therapy, see Clarice F. Pollard, *Laugh, Cry, and Remember: The Journal of a G. I. Lady* (Journeys Press, 1991), 182–83.

110. Lambert, "Phelps Associates," 2.

111. "Small Shop," 159.

112. Nell Znamierowski, *Dorothy Liebes: Retrospective Exhibition, March 20–May 20, 1970, Museum of Contemporary Crafts of the American Crafts Council* (Museum of Contemporary Crafts, 1970), 5, 34, 5.

113. "Portrait of America—No. 53: American Red Cross Helps Rehabilitate U.S. Servicemen," LOT 4081 (F) [P&P], Prints and Photographs Division, Library of Congress.

114. Fashion Group International, "Home Furnishings—Craftsmanship," *Fashion Group Bulletin* 10, no. 1 (1945): insert 1–2.

115. "Portrait of America—No. 53."

116. Znamierowski, *Dorothy Liebes,* 5.

117. "Small Shop," 159. In 2022 US dollars, this is the equivalent of about $210 to $1,257 for bags and $50 to $518 for belts, rate via "Inflation Calculator," at Smart Asset website, accessed 9 Feb. 2022, https://smartasset.com/investing/inflation-calculator#WnVZQKjy4o.

118. "Town and Country Counter Points," *Town and Country,* Jan. 1944, 98.

119. "Historic Sources Inspire Bags," 20.

120. "Bold—Not Bitsy," *Vogue,* 15 Aug. 1944, 120.

121. "Bold—Not Bitsy," 120.

122. "Designs for Dressmaking," 159.

123. "Paid Notice: Deaths Tanner, Dorelle M," *New York Times,* 26 June 2001.

124. Greenwich Garden Club, *The Greenwich Garden Club Celebrates 100 Years: 1914–2014* (Greenwich Garden Club, 2014), 70.

125. William Searle, *The Garden Club of America: One Hundred Years of a Growing Legacy* (Smithsonian Books, 2012), appendix 2. Tanner also appears to have been an alumna of Sarah Lawrence College. The alumni magazine text is not available online, but she appears in the finding aid: "College Archives: Collections: Search Alphabetically," Sarah Lawrence College website, accessed 18 June, 2019, https://www.sarahlawrence.edu/archives/collections/magazine/alpha/?letter=T.

126. The bag is 24½" in overall length (including the strap) x 7¼" wide; the pouch alone is 9¼" long.

127. The realism of the cicada ornament is somewhat reminiscent of a silver writing casket by Renaissance-era Nuremberg goldsmith Wenzel Jamnitzer (1507/08–1585), also decorated with a cicada. See "Writing Utensils," Kunsthistorisches Museum, Vienna, accessed 18 June, 2019, https://www.khm.at/en/objectdb/detail/919688/?offset=16&lv=list.

128. Dilys E. Blum, *Shocking! The Art and Fashion of Elsa Schiaparelli* (Philadelphia Museum of Art and Yale University Press, 2003), 184–85.

129. "Phelps Collection at Lord & Taylor," *Women's Wear Daily,* 13 May 1955, 10.

130. "Hattie Carnegie Original Two-Piece Dress," National Museum of American History, Smithsonian Institution, accessed 18 June 2019, https://www.si.edu/object/nmah_372245.

131. The dimensions of the bag are 23¼" overall length (including strap) by 8¾" wide x 1¾" deep (at thickest part).

132. This brown leather bag is 8¾" high by 10⅝" wide, without the shoulder strap.

133. Hawes, *Fashion Is Spinach* (Random House, 1938), 200.

134. Claire McCardell, *What Shall I Wear?* (Simon & Schuster, 1956), 37.

135. Lambert, "Phelps Associates," 2.

136. Fashion Group International, "Regional Groups—Recent Activities. Philadelphia," *Fashion Group Bulletin* 16, no. 1 (1950): 5; "Suggests Store Clinics to Seek Out Latent Designing Talents," 2.

137. Fashion Group International, "Regional Groups—Recent Activities." 5.

138. "Suggests Store Clinics to Seek Out Latent Designing Talents," 2.

139. "Suggests Store Clinics to Seek Out Latent Designing Talents," 2.

140. "Suggests Store Clinics to Seek Out Latent Designing Talents," 2.

141. "Small Shop," 159.

142. Cooke "Modern Craft and the American Experience," 5.

143. "The Small Shop," 160, 158.

144. "Small Shop," 159.

3. Shortages and Shapes

1. While the vast majority of the Phelpses' work was for women, they did occasional menswear projects (see chapter 6).

2. Caroline Rennolds Milbank, telephone conversation with the author, 10 Oct. 2020.

3. 1940 US Census, Ann Seymour Laughan in household of David C Laughan, Ward 2, Pulaski, Pulaski Magisterial District, Pulaski, VA, Enumeration District 78–12, sheet 13B, line 67, family 303, available via Ancestry.com. Note that the "Laughon" name was misspelled in the census.

4. "Caroline K. Rennolds to Wed," *New York Times,* 20 Mar. 1983.

5. Milbank, telephone conversation.

6. Edwin Slipek Jr., "The Valentine's Latest Exhibit Remembers the Stores That Once Kept the City Bustling," *Style Weekly,* Richmond, 1 Jan. 1980.

7. Milbank, telephone conversation.

8. Milbank, telephone conversation.

9. Stuart Hall School, *The Inlook* Yearbook (McClure, 1947), n.p. A scanned copy, which additionally has a note to the owner by Seymour Laughon beside her photo, is available via Ancestry.com.

10. The overall dimensions of the belt are 30¼" long by 2½" wide.

11. The buckle is 3⅜" high by 2⅛" wide, and there are no marks on the buckle.

12. Its dimensions are 6¾" high by 6¼"wide at the widest point, and it is wider at the top than at the bottom.

13. This bag measures 12⅝" high by 7¼" wide overall.

14. The interior of the bag appears to be in good condition, with no visible rot.

15. The overall dimensions of this bag are 10⅜" high by 10¼" wide.

16. Fashion Group International, "Morale—Inventory for Fashion Industry and Individual," 3.

17. "Dress as the War Production Board Wants You To," *Harper's Bazaar,* 15 Mar. 1942, 60–61.

18. Raushenbush, *How to Dress in Wartime,* 38; Jacqueline Field, "Dyes, Chemistry, and Clothing: The Influence of World War I On Fabrics, Fashions and Silk," *Dress* 28, no. 1 (2001): 77.

19. Fashion Group International, "Rules We Work By," *Fashion Group Bulletin* 9, no. 4 (1943): 4, 3. The extensive archives of the Fashion Group International are held in the New York Public Library's Manuscripts, Archives, and Rare Books collection and include many issues of the *Fashion Group Bulletin,* in MSS Col. 908, boxes 144–50.

20. Evans Case Company, "The Newest Mode . . . Evans Fitted Handbags," advertisement, *Vogue,* 1 Oct. 1939, 20.

21. Rolfs LaGarde Originals, "Journey's End," advertisement, *Vogue,* 1 Dec. 1939, 159.

22. Chambers, *Fashion Fundamentals,* 398.

23. Of the Phelps objects I have studied, this seems to refer to seashell-shaped metalwork rather than the case for ammunition. "Workshop on Washington Square," 22.

24. "Historic Sources Inspire Bags," 20.

25. "Historic Sources Inspire Bags," 20.

26. American Fashion Critics' Award Program 1944, 2, SC.214.3.9, Eleanor Lambert Collection, Special Collections and College Archives, Gladys Marcus Library, Fashion Institute of Technology.

27. DLW, "Phelps Associates Win Design Award," 20.

28. "Big Bags and Belts," 88.

29. "Big Bags and Belts," 85.

30. "Small Shop," 160.

31. *Francis Bannerman Sons, 84th Anniversary January 1949 De Luxe Edition Military Goods Catalogue* (Francis Bannerman Sons, 1949), 108, author's collection.

32. Francis Bannerman Sons, Jan. 1955 Circular, 1, box 4, folder 1, Bannerman Family Papers, 1788–2001, Patricia D. Klingenstein Library, Manuscripts Division, New-York Historical Society Museum and Library.

33. Francis Bannerman Sons, 80th Anniversary Circular, Jan. 1947, 1, box 4, folder 1, Bannerman Family Papers.

34. *Francis Bannerman Sons, 84th Anniversary Catalogue.*

35. Francis Bannerman Sons, 80th Anniversary Circular, 2 (emphasis in original).

36. Francis Bannerman Sons, 80th Anniversary Circular, 6.

37. Francis Bannerman Sons, 1954 Circular, 6, box 4, folder 1, Bannerman Family Papers,

38. "American Tricks for Suits," *Vogue,* 1 Sept. 1939, 111.

39. See, for example, "Say Red, Say White, Say Blue," *Harper's Bazaar,* Feb. 1945, 108–9.

40. "Small Shop," 160.

41. Francis Bannerman Sons, 80th Anniversary Circular, 10, 11.

42. "Add a Belt," *Harper's Bazaar,* Nov. 1943, 105.

43. *Francis Bannerman Sons, 84th Anniversary Catalogue,* 182, 203.

44. Pope, "American Inspiration," 2.

45. "Historic Sources Inspire Bags," 20.

46. "Junior Bazaar," 126.

47. DLW, "Phelps Associates Win Design Award," 20.

48. US Department of Commerce, *Index of Trademarks Issued from the United States Patent Office* (GPO, 1945), 187, 239.

49. Harold Koda and Andrew Bolton, *Poiret* (Metropolitan Museum of Art and Yale University Press, 2007), 14; Lourdes M. Font and Trudie A. Grace, *Summer Afternoon: Fashion and Leisure in the Hudson Highlands, 1850–1950* (Putnam History Museum, 2012), 30.

50. Arnold, *American Look,* 40–42.

51. Ann Marguerite Tartsinis, *An American Style: Global Sources for New York Textile and Fashion Design, 1915–1928* (Bard Graduate Center, 2013), 13, 14, 16; Lauren D. Whitley, "Morris De Camp Crawford and the 'Designed in America'

Campaign, 1916–1922," *Textile Society of American Symposium Proceedings* 6 (1998): 412.

52. M[orris]. D[e]. C[amp]. Crawford, *The Ways of Fashion* (Fairchild, 1948), 284.

53. Marylin Bender, "Shoulder Bags Are Back from the War," *Women's Wear Daily,* 10 July 1964, 32.

54. "Home Dressmaking," 104–5; "What Animals Are These?" 61.

55. "Big Bags and Belts," 85.

56. DLW, "Phelps Associates Win Design Award," 20.

57. DLW, "Phelps Associates Win Design Award," 20.

58. "Spring Paraphernalia," 60.

59. Grace Herrick, "Fashion Notes," *New York Times,* 7 Oct. 1945. The Phelpses' interest in Poland is probably related to the war; Anne Hollander notes, "It has always been fashionable to copy certain elements of dress that have public timeliness, such as military motifs in wartime or foreign motifs while the public is focused on the foreigners in question." Hollander, *Seeing Through Clothes,* 313.

60. "Big Bags and Belts," 85.

61. Helene Maddock, "Buying," in *Keys to a Fashion Career,* ed. Bernice Gertrude Chambers (McGraw-Hill, 1946), 10.

62. *Francis Bannerman Sons, 84th Anniversary Catalogue,* 222–23.

63. "Handbags Become Functional and Attractive Accessories," *New York Times,* 5 Apr. 1944.

64. "Big Bags and Belts," 86.

65. "Work or Play Attire Made in Large Sizes," *New York Times,* 24 May 1951.

66. Marcel Mauss, "Techniques of the Body," in *Incorporations,* ed. Jonathan Crary and Sanford Kwinter (1934; repr., Zone, 1992), 455.

67. Mauss, "Techniques of the Body," 455, 473, 465, 467, 468, 469.

68. Mauss, "Techniques of the Body," 457–58; Hollander, *Seeing Through Clothes,* 311.

69. Mauss, "Techniques of the Body," 458.

70. Chambers, *Fashion Fundamentals,* 398.

71. Dougherty, *Your Leatherwork,* 25.

72. DLW, "Phelps Associates Win Design Award," 20.

73. Eleanor Lambert, "Phelps Associates," press release circa 1944, 1, SC.214.3.10, Lambert Collection.

74. DLW, "Phelps Associates Win Design Award," 20.

75. McAllister, "Fashion Jury Names Leading American Designers," 8.

76. Erna Risch, *A Wardrobe for the Women of the Army,* QMC Historical Studies no. 12, (Historical Section, General Administrative Services Division, Office of the Quartermaster General, 1945), 75.

77. This branch of the service was originally established as the WAACs, but in September 1943, WAACs were offered the choice to be discharged or join the army proper, in a newly constituted Women's Army Corps (WACs). On October 1, 1943, per an act of Congress, those servicewomen who chose to stay were sworn in as WACs. See Clarice F. Pollard, *Laugh, Cry and Remember* (Journeys Press, 1991), 89.

78. Risch, *Wardrobe for the Women of the Army,* 76.

79. Pollard, *Laugh, Cry and Remember,* 121, 175.

80. McCardell, *What Shall I Wear?,* 13.

81. By the time the Office of Defense Transportation enacted regulations requiring delivery services to be dramatically reduced in June 1942, many department stores, including Macy's, had already cut back on deliveries and conducted effective campaigns to persuade customers to carry their own packages. See "Store Deliveries Cut Drastically: Bread, Laundry, Newspapers, Other Daily Services Reduced to Save Rubber and Oil," *New York Times,* 2 June 1942.

82. James Laver, *Taste and Fashion,* 2nd ed. (1945; repr., George G. Harrap & Co., 1948), 202.

83. Fashion Group International, "Accessories," *Fashion Group Bulletin* 7, no. 2 (1941): insert 1.

84. Chambers, *Fashion Fundamentals,* 398.

85. Fashion Group International, "Fashion Availables for a Wartime Autumn," 7.

86. Fashion Group International, "Accessories," insert 1.

87. Fashion Group International, "Fashion Editors' Choice—Advance News—All About the Way We'll Look This Spring," *Fashion Group Bulletin* 12, no. 1 (1946): 1

88. This is based on examination of copies of the *Fashion Group Bulletin* from 1941–to 1947, in boxes 144 and 145 of the Fashion Group International Records.

89. Fashion Group International, "Welcome to Membership," *Fashion Group Bulletin* 12, no. 2 (1946): 4.

90. Fashion Group International, "New Trend Fall Accessories," *Fashion Group Bulletin* 12, no. 2 (1946): 4.

91. Fashion Group International, "Preview of Spring Accessories," *Accessories Meeting Report,* 6 Nov. 1947, 1, box 145, folder 2, in Fashion Group International Records.

92. Fashion designer Emily Wilkens later recalled, "The war had been over for a year, and we wanted to forget it had happened. The days of rationing were past, and we celebrated their passing with indulgences." Emily Wilkens, *More Secrets from the Super Spas* (Dembner, 1983), 103.

93. Fashion Group International, "Rules We Work By," 5.

94. Mary Ellen Snodgrass, *World Clothing and Fashion: An Encyclopedia of History, Culture and Social Influence,* vols. 1 and 2 (Routledge, 2014), 2:369.

95. Dominique Veillon, *Fashion Under the Occupation,* Trans. Miriam Kochan (Berg, 2002), 49.

96. Florence S. Richards, *The Ready-to-Wear Industry, 1900–1950* (Fairchild, 1951), 29.

97. Geraldine Howell, *Wartime Fashion: From Haute Couture to Homemade, 1939–1945* (Berg, 2012), 89.

98. "Shoe Rationing Touches Off Rush for Bags, Particularly Leathers," *Women's Wear Daily,* 12 Feb. 1943, 12.

99. "What They Bought This Week: EVERYTHING. . . . . . but Particularly Pumps, Ties," *Women's Wear Daily, Women's Foot Wear,* 12 Feb. 1943, 1.

100. Tanner's Council of America, *Romance of Leather,* 27.
101. "Shoe Retailers WPB Talks End Differences," *Women's Wear Daily,* 13 Mar. 1944, 18.
102. Fashion Group International, "Rules We Work By," 4.
103. "Curb's End Raises Question of Making Calfskin Handbags for Christmas," *Women's Wear Daily,* 31 Aug. 1945, 11.
104. "Shopping Bazaar: Leather and Fur," *Harper's Bazaar,* July 1943, 8g.
105. Raushenbush, *How to Dress in Wartime,* 127; Risch, *Wardrobe for the Women of the Army,* 25, 72–75.
106. Colin McDowell, *Forties Fashion and the New Look* (Bloomsbury, 1997), 58.
107. Risch, *A Wardrobe for the Women of the Army,* 25, 72–73.
108. Risch, *Wardrobe for the Women of the Army,* 75.
109. Risch, *Wardrobe for the Women of the Army,* 110.
110. Pollard, *Laugh, Cry and Remember,* 47.
111. Pollard, *Laugh, Cry and Remember,* 48.
112. Pollard, *Laugh, Cry and Remember,* 46.
113. Pollard, *Laugh, Cry and Remember,* 90, 212.
114. Pollard, *Laugh, Cry and Remember,* 58.
115. Risch, *Wardrobe for the Women of the Army,* 73.
116. Braggiotti, "Leather-Bound Love," 3.
117. "Selling Handbags," 22.
118. "Expects Tight Leather Basis for Some Time," *Women's Wear Daily,* 28 July 1944, 13.
119. "Curbs Lifted to Speed Output of Leather Bags and Footwear," *Women's Wear Daily,* 29 Aug. 1945, 1.
120. "Curb's End Raises Question of Making Calfskin Handbags for Christmas," 11.

4. Promoting and Selling Phelps Associates' Products

1. The pouch is 11½" high and 11½" wide, excluding the strap, and with a gusset that gives it a 3⅓" depth.
2. The belt is 29" in overall length and 3⅛" wide at the widest point; the length from the end of the belt to the first notch that shows use is 25".
3. For example, Emily Wilkens, designer of teenage fashions, donated items from her spring–summer 1945 collection to the Museum of Costume Art after she was awarded a Coty. On the history of the Costume Institute, see "The Costume Institute: History of the Department," Metropolitan Museum of Art website, accessed 25 Oct. 2021, https://www.metmuseum.org/about-the-met/collection-areas/the-costume-institute.
4. Wilson, *Adorned in Dreams,* 14.
5. Constance Hope, *Publicity Is Broccoli* (Bobbs-Merrill, 1941), 12. The name is obviously a play on Elizabeth Hawes's 1938 *Fashion Is Spinach,* but Hope never explains the title in her text, and her stance towards publicity is positive, versus Hawes's primary intention to critique.
6. Hope, *Publicity Is Broccoli,* 106–18.
7. Matheson, "Sara Pennoyer," 60–61. See also Bernice Fitz-Gibbon, *Macy's, Gimbels, and Me* (Simon & Schuster, 1967), and Estelle Hamburger, *It's a Woman's Business* (Vanguard, 1939).
8. Hope, *Publicity Is Broccoli,* 201.
9. Lilly Daché, *Talking Through My Hats* (Coward-McCann, 1946), 177–78; Rebecca Jumper Matheson, "'A House That Is Made of Hats': The Lilly Daché Building, 1937–1968," in *The Places and Spaces of Fashion: 1800–2006,* ed. John Potvin (Routledge, 2008), 217–18.
10. "Small Shop," 160.
11. Eleanor Lambert, *World of Fashion* (R. R. Bowker/Xerox, 1976), 271.
12. Lambert's extensive archives and files were housed adjacent to the Costume Institute's Irene Lewisohn Reference Library when I worked at the Costume Institute, first as an intern and later as a staff member, from 2003 to 2007. In May 2009, the Eleanor Lambert collection, 1943–2003, was donated to Special Collections and College Archives of the Gladys Marcus Library at the Fashion Institute of Technology (FIT) in New York City. Processed from 2009 to 2016, the collection today comprises some fifty-six linear feet of material. Collection SC.214: Eleanor Lambert Collection, 1943–2003, *FIT SPARC Connect,* FIT Library's Special Collections and Archives, accessed 24 Mar. 2025, https://atom-sparc.fitnyc.edu/sc-214.
13. Sandra Stansbery Buckland, "Promoting American Designers, 1940–44," in *Twentieth-Century American Fashion,* ed. Linda Welters and Patricia A. Cunningham (Berg, 2005), 116.
14. Lambert, *World of Fashion,* 284.
15. Eleanor Lambert, press release, 4 Feb. 1944, 1–2, SC 214.3.8 Lambert Collection.
16. Lambert, press release, 4 Feb. 1944, 1–2.
17. Chambers, *Fashion Fundamentals,* 398; American Fashion Critics' Award Program 1944, 4, SC.214.3.9, Lambert Collection.
18. "Agencies," *Broadcast: The Weekly Newsmagazine of Radio Broadcast Advertising,* 3 Sept. 1945, 56.
19. "Fashion Group Luncheon: 2 Authors Are Heard and New Officers Are Announced," *New York Times,* 24 Nov. 1948; Shelley Spector, "75th Anniversary: Proud to Be in PR: The Story of Denny Griswold, Founder of *PRNews,*" *PRNews,* Apr. 2019, 10, https://www.prnewsonline.com/wp-content/uploads/2019/04/prn-2019-04-01.pdf.
20. Lambert, press release, 4 Feb. 1944, 2.
21. American Fashion Critics' Award Program 1944, 1–4.
22. Lambert, press release, 4 Feb. 1944, 1.
23. American Fashion Critics' Award Program 1944, 2.
24. Lambert, press release, 4 Feb. 1944, 2.
25. Lambert, press release, 4 Feb. 1944, 2.
26. Lambert, press release, 4 Feb. 1944, 3.
27. American Fashion Critics' Award Program 1945, SC.214.3.11, Lambert Collection.

28. Eleanor Lambert, wall text for *Seven American Wars* exhibition, 1943, available at Metropolitan Museum of Art, Thomas J. Watson Library Digital Collections, b1752638_013, http://library.metmuseum.org/record=b1752638. Today, the lion rampant bag has conservation issues that are likely the result of its being displayed hanging for an extended period in the exhibition. Conservator Barbara Appelbaum writes, "Leather objects are easily distorted and torn by long-term hanging, even for pieces which appear to be strong enough to withstand such treatment." Barbara Appelbaum, *Guide to Environmental Protection of Collections* (Sound View Press, 1991), 188. The shoulder strap on the lion rampant shoulder bag is broken on the proper right side—completely sheared off just past the metal hardware connecting the strap to the body of the bag. This appears to be the area that bore the weight of the bag while it was displayed.

29. Roland Barthes, *The Fashion System*, trans. Matthew Ward and Richard Howard (1983; repr., Univ. of California Press, 1990), 5.

30. "Made for You," *Vogue*, 1 Oct. 1948, 136–41.

31. "Custom-Made for American Women," *Harper's Bazaar*, Oct. 1945, 88–101.

32. "What Animals Are These?" 60.

33. "What Animals Are These?" 61.

34. "Ready for Anything," 59.

35. "See That You're Born in Texas," *Harper's Bazaar*, Apr. 1943, 87.

36. Lesley Ellis Miller, "Perfect Harmony: Textile Manufacturers and Haute Couture 1947–57," in *The Golden Age of Couture: Paris and London 1947–57*, ed. Claire Wilcox (V & A Publications, 2008), 128.

37. Milbank, *New York Fashion*, 162.

38. *The Street*, in *Ann Petry: "The Street," "The Narrows,"* ed. Farah Jasmin Griffin (1946; repr., Library of America, 2019), 27.

39. Petry, *The Street*, 36–37.

40. Gertrude Warburton and Jane Maxwell, *Fashion for a Living* (McGraw-Hill, 1939), 227.

41. "A Suit for Everyone," *Harper's Bazaar*, Sept. 1942, 85.

42. "Home Dressmaking," 104–5.

43. "Something in Wool and Leather," 66.

44. Grace Herrick, "Accessories Were Specially Made to Dramatize Outfits in the Show," *New York Times*, 26 Oct. 1945.

45. "Suits with Two Lives," *Vogue*, 15 Jan. 1944, 68–69.

46. "Suits with Two Lives," 68–69.

47. Kimberly Chrisman-Campbell, *Fashion Victims: Dress at the Court of Louis XVI and Marie-Antoinette* (Yale Univ. Press, 2015), 9.

48. Petry, *The Street*, 36.

49. "Long Island Autumn," *Vogue*, 1 Oct. 1947, 206.

50. Anne Fogarty, *Wife Dressing: The Fine Art of Being a Well Dressed Wife* (Julian Messner, 1959), 21, 22, 51, 60.

51. Phelps, "For Country or Suburban Living," advertisement, *New York Times*, 9 Sept. 1951.

52. "Incorporations," *Women's Wear Daily*, 1 Mar. 1928, 18; "Mrs. James Stewart: Her Kind of Clothes," *Vogue*, 15 Apr. 1953, 82–83.

53. "Historic Sources Inspire Bags," 20.

54. "Small Shop," 159.

55. Margaretta Byers, *Help Wanted—Female* (Julian Messner, 1941), 128–29; Susan Porter Benson, *Counter Cultures: Saleswomen, Managers, and Customers in American Department Stores, 1880–1940* (Univ. of Illinois Press, 1986), 12.

56. Benson, *Counter Cultures*, 12, 16.

57. "New York Store Presents Phelps Bags and Belts," *Women's Wear Daily*, 17 May 1946, 16.

58. Jan Whitaker, *Service and Style: How the American Department Store Fashioned the Middle Class* (St. Martin's Press, 2006), 197.

59. Benson, *Counter Cultures*, 44.

60. "New York Store Presents Phelps Bags and Belts," 16.

61. Harrison, "American Classics," *New York Times*, 9 Nov. 1955.

62. "Fashions Go Round the Clock," *Philadelphia Inquirer*, 11 Oct. 1956.

63. Webber-Hanchett, "Dorothy Shaver," 82, 83.

64. Tom Mahoney and Rita Hession, *Public Relations for Retailers* (Macmillan, 1949), 204–6.

65. Linda Guica, "Jimmie Booth: The Artistic Force Behind Golden Lamb Buttery," *Hartford Courant*, 2 Oct. 2011.

66. "Phelps Designs Separates Group That Is 2-Faced," *New York Times*, 8 May 1956.

67. "Week-End Wardrobe Plan: Bag and Baggage," *Vogue*, 1 May 1956, 158.

68. Arnold, *American Look*, 132; Matheson, *Young Originals*, 30–31.

69. "Phelps Designs Separates Group That Is 2-Faced," 36; "Week-End Wardrobe Plan," 158.

70. "Phelps Summer Collection 1964," advertisement, *Women's Wear Daily*, 12 Feb. 1964, 34.

71. Phelps, "For Country or Suburban Living."

72. William Lindau, "Mountain Craftsmen: Native Artisans Produce Phelps Style Separates, Accessories," *Women's Wear Daily*, 29 Jan. 1958, 45.

5. Postwar Expansion

1. "Helen L. Hart," obituary, *Reading (PA) Eagle*, 1 Jan. 2020.

2. "Helen L. Hart."

3. Eulogy for Helen L. Hart, 9 Jan. 2020, Harmony United Methodist Church, Helen L. Hart Archives, Joanna Furnace, HCVHA, Berks County, PA.

4. Helen Hart's Phelps belt is 30½" by 3", at the widest point on scallop.

5. The buckle is 2¼" long by 1¾" wide.

6. The bag's overall height with strap extended is 19½".

The bag without the strap measures 5¼" high by 9" wide and 2" deep.

7. I have consistently seen this green oxidation on the brass hardware of Phelps bags, particularly on bag interiors.

8. Valerie Reich Hunt, "Composite Objects: Materials and Storage Conditions," in *Conservation Concerns: A Guide for Collectors and Curators,* ed. Konstanze Bachmann (Cooper-Hewitt and Smithsonian Institution Press, 1992), 132–33.

9. "Fantasy and Modernism Combined in Array of Fashion Accessories for Day and Night," *New York Times,* 2 Apr. 1946.

10. "Helen L. Hart."

11. Eulogy for Helen L. Hart.

12. "Conversations with Joanna Furnace Area Residents," "Conversations with Joanna Furnace Area Residents." HCVHA *Journal,* 2010, 23.

13. "Conversations with Joanna Furnace Area Residents," 23; eulogy for Helen L. Hart.

14. Suzanne Fellman Jacob, *The History of Joanna Furnace, 1791–1999* (HCVHA, 1999), 243.

15. "Conversations with Joanna Furnace Area Residents," 23.

16. Helen L. Hart and Gail Karahuta. Layout of the Joanna Furnace Mansion House as Occupied by the Phelpses, circa 2019, Hart Archives.

17. "Conversations with Joanna Furnace Area Residents," 24.

18. Eulogy for Helen L. Hart.

19. "Conversations with Joanna Furnace Area Residents," 21–24.

20. "Small Shop," 159.

21. "Bethlehem Steel Purchases Joanna Furnace, Acreage," 1 June 1951, newspaper clipping, Hart Archives.

22. Braggiotti, "Leather-Bound Love," 3.

23. "Small Shop," 160.

24. HCVHA, "Historic Joanna Furnace: An 18th and 19th Century Iron Making Community," brochure, n.d.

25. Jacob, *History of Joanna Furnace,* 89–95, 233, 242, 282.

26. "Big Bags and Belts," 85; Jacob, *History of Joanna Furnace,* 243.

27. "Big Bags and Belts," 85; "Small Shop," 158.

28. "Small Shop," 158, 161.

29. Many thanks to my husband, Dan Matheson, for sharing his insights as to the advantages of the Birdsboro corporate structure.

30. "Small Shop," 161.

31. Cooke "Modern Craft and the American Experience," 5.

32. "Small Shop," 161.

33. "Small Shop," 160–61. The governing federal minimum wage enacted October 24, 1945, was $.40 per hour, which, assuming a forty-hour work week, would give the $16 lower end of the scale for a week's wages, versus the highest rate of approximately $1.13 per hour in New York City. "History of Federal Minimum Wage Rates Under the Fair Labor Standards Act, 1938–2009," US Department of Labor, Wage and Hour Division website, accessed 15 Mar. 2021 https://www.dol.gov/agencies/whd/minimum-wage/history/chart.

34. HCVHA, Mule Stable didactic labels, Joanna Furnace.

35. Jacob, *History of Joanna Furnace,* 243.

36. Braggiotti, "Leather-Bound Love," 3.

37. Anita Boyer Turner, "Two Personal Looks Back," HCVHA *Journal,* 2010, 24.

38. "Conversations with Joanna Furnace Area Residents," 23–24.

39. Jacob, *History of Joanna Furnace,* 104.

40. "Small Shop," 161.

41. Jane S. McIlvanie, "'Deep Country' Clothes Attract Great Interest," *Philadelphia Inquirer,* 20 May 1949.

42. Turner, "Two Personal Looks Back," 24.

43. Turner, "Two Personal Looks Back," 24.

44. Turner, "Two Personal Looks Back," 25.

45. Turner, "Two Personal Looks Back," 25.

46. Braggiotti, "Leather-Bound Love," 3.

47. HCVHA, "Historic Joanna Furnace."

48. These are measurements based on my own 21 September 2020 site visit, generously funded by the Costume Society of America's Stella Blum Student Research Grant.

49. "Big Bags and Belts," 88.

50. "People Are Talking About . . . in Fashion," *Vogue,* 1 Aug. 1947, 94.

51. Francis Bannerman Sons, Jan. 1954 Circular, 1, box 4, folder 1, Bannerman Family Papers, 1788–2001, Patricia D. Klingenstein Library, Manuscripts Division, New-York Historical Society Museum and Library.

52. Brook Kindred, *McCall's,* to Eileen, circa 1956, author's collection. The full text reads, "Dear Eileen: McCall's fashion editor, Estelle Brent, had a little finger in this book—being somewhat of an expert. It was condensed in our November issue—too. I thought you might like to have a copy. It's a first for Claire McCardell, as well as a first for McCall's. As we hope McCall's does throughout the year, maybe this book can be of some use, and enjoyment to you. My best wishes for a happy holiday season, Brook."

53. McCardell, *What Shall I Wear?,* 12.

54. McCardell, *What Shall I Wear?,* 12–13.

55. McCardell, *What Shall I Wear?,* 13.

56. McCardell, *What Shall I Wear?,* 13.

57. "Historic Sources Inspire Bags," 20; McCardell, *What Shall I Wear?,* 13.

58. Francis Bannerman Sons, 80th Anniversary Jan. 1947 Circular, 8, box 4, folder 1, Bannerman Family Papers.

59. Francis Bannerman Sons, Jan. 1954 Circular, 7.

60. McCardell, *What Shall I Wear?,* 13.

61. McCardell, *What Shall I Wear?,* 13.

62. Lindau, "Mountain Craftsmen," 45.

63. Bender, "Shoulder Bags Are Back from the War," 32.

64. Harrison, "American Classics," 38.

65. Braggiotti, "Leather-Bound Love," 3.

66. Museum of Modern Art, *100 Useful Objects of Fine Design,* 4; "Museum of Modern Art Opens 1947 Useful Objects Exhibition," 1, Sept. 17, 1947, available at Museum of Modern Art website, https://assets.moma.org/documents/moma_press-release_325578.pdf?_ga=2.223119128.2068047290.1602796583-199212535.1602796583.

67. Braggiotti, "Leather-Bound Love," 3.

68. "New Ways with Flannel," *Harper's Bazaar,* Sept. 1947, 255.

69. "Historic Sources Inspire Bags," 20; Zelma Bendure, Director, Fairchild Retail Selling Division, "Selling Handbags," *Women's Wear Daily,* 21 Apr. 1944, 22.

70. "Long Island Autumn," 206; "Tweeds Against the Wind," *Harper's Bazaar,* Nov. 1947, 210–11.

71. Braggiotti, "Leather-Bound Love," 3; Jacob, *History of Joanna Furnace,* 118. Jacob notes that "the phrase 'ten-plate' referred not to the actual number of pieces needed to assemble a stove but to the number of molds, or forms, needed for the castings."

72. "One Thing at a Time," *Harper's Bazaar,* Mar. 1944, 116–17. *Crash* is a category of fabrics with a rough texture due to coarse, uneven yarns.

73. "Leather Takes a Good Tan," *Harper's Bazaar,* Apr. 1947, 227; Helen P. Wulbern, "Voris of Hollywood: Designer for Sheer Suedes," *Women's Wear Daily,* 18 Mar. 1938, 11, 14.

74. "To the Springs: Sporting Life," *Harper's Bazaar,* Oct. 1947, 228–29.

75. Joyce Cheney, *Aprons: Icons of the American Home* (Running Press, 2000), 10, 15. Cheney curated an apron exhibition that toured in the late 1990s, and a more recent exhibition, *Apron Strings: Ties to the Past,* toured from 2014 to 2022.

76. Beth Alberty, "Apropos Aprons: Wall and Label Text for an Exhibition at The Metropolitan Museum of Art, June 6–September 3, 1989: Introduction," Thomas J. Watson Library Digital Collections, Metropolitan Museum of Art, b1158065_002, accessed 19 Oct. 2020, https://libmma.contentdm.oclc.org/digital/collection/p15324coll10/id/230619.

77. "One Thing at a Time," 116–17; "Leather Takes a Good Tan," 227.

78. "Made for You," 139.

79. Elizabeth Phelps, "Have Fun with the Colors You Wear," *Woman's Day,* July 1953, 69.

80. Hope, *Publicity Is Broccoli,* 175.

81. Turner, "Two Personal Looks Back," 24.

82. "New Country Aprons . . . Worn by the Designer," *Vogue,* Nov. 1948, 136.

83. Michael Baxandall, *Painting and Experience in Fifteenth-Century Italy* (Clarendon, 1972), 29–108.

84. "New Country Aprons," 137.

85. Patricia A. Cunningham, *Reforming Women's Fashion, 1850–1920* (Kent State Univ. Press, 2003), 38–39.

86. Annemarie Strassel, "Designing Women: Feminist Methodologies in American Fashion," *Women's Studies Quarterly* 41, nos. 1–2 (2012): 41.

87. "Celeste Holm, Star of 'Bloomer Girl,'" *Vogue,* 1 Jan. 1945, 56–57.

88. "New Country Aprons," 137.

89. Turner, "Two Personal Looks Back," 25.

90. "Conversations with Joanna Furnace Area Residents," 24; Turner, "Two Personal Looks Back," 25.

91. Turner, "Two Personal Looks Back," 25.

92. "New Country Aprons," 137.

93. "New Country Aprons," 137.

94. "Conversations with Joanna Furnace Area Residents," 24.

95. Harrison, "American Classics," 38.

96. "Phelps Fashion Show Saturday, June 4th," newspaper clipping, 2 June 1949, Hart Archives.

97. "Thirty-Six Models," newspaper clipping, 4 June 1949, Hart Archives.

98. "Phelps Fashion Show Saturday."

99. "Broadway Stage Designer to Direct Phelps Fashion Show," newspaper clipping, 26 May 1949, Hart Archives.

100. "Phelps Fashion Show Saturday."

101. Alice Hughes, "A Woman's New York," column, *Muncie (IN) Star,* 15 June 1949.

102. "Broadway Stage Designer to Direct Phelps Fashion Show."

103. "Phelps Fashion Show Saturday 4th."

104. "Broadway Stage Designer to Direct Phelps Fashion Show."

105. Hughes, "Woman's New York." See also, for example, *Journal Herald* (Dayton, OH), 16 June 1949; *Daily Oklahoman* (Oklahoma City), 15 June 1949; *Fort Worth (TX) Star-Telegram,* 17 June 1949.

106. "Fall Belts: Reversibles and High-Low Effects," *Women's Wear Daily,* 16 May 1952, 11.

107. "Conversations with Joanna Furnace Area Residents," 24.

108. "Suggests Store Clinics to Seek Out Latent Designing Talents," 2

109. "Denim, Sailcloth Coordinates Adapted from Custom-Mades," *Women's Wear Daily,* 30 Jan. 1950, 32; Phelps Deep Country Clothes, "Now it Can Be Sold (By You)," advertisement, *Women's Wear Daily,* 29 Mar. 1950, 32.

110. "Now It Can Be Sold," 32.

111. McClendon, *Denim,* 84.

112. "Mrs. Phelps Designing New Suede Group," *Women's Wear Daily,* 31 Dec. 1951, 3.

113. "Bonnie Cashin to Design for Sills," *Women's Wear Daily,* 14 Apr. 1953, 29.

114. Diana Maglio, "A Brief Historical Overview of the First Major Menswear Exhibition in the United States—Adam in the Looking Glass at the Metropolitan Museum of Art, New York, 1950," *Critical Studies in Men's Fashion* 4 no. 1 (2017): 80, 85–86, 83, 85.

115. GM, "Adam in the Looking Glass," *New York Times,* 8 Jan. 1950.

116. Metropolitan Museum of Art, "Tomorrow's Fashions—Adam in the Looking Glass," [press releases, installation photographs, wall text] Jan.–July 1950, Thomas J. Watson Library Digital Collections, b1756982_056. b1756982_068, accessed 24 Mar. 2025, https://libmma.contentdm.oclc.org/digital/collection/p16028coll11/id/18828/.

117. Elizabeth Hawes, *Men Can Take It* (World, 1941), 5, 136.

118. Bernard Rudofsky, *Are Clothes Modern?* (Paul Theobald, 1947), 125.

119. James Laver, "Clothes and the Man," *Vogue,* 15 Feb. 1950, 63.

120. Metropolitan Museum of Art, "Tomorrow's Fashions."

121. "Women in Business Get Honor Scrolls," *New York Times,* 17 Oct. 1950.

122. "Bethlehem Steel Purchases Joanna Furnace."

123. Jacob, *History of Joanna Furnace,* 245.

124. Harrison, "American Classics," 38.

125. Turner, "Two Personal Looks Back," 25.

126. Jacob, *History of Joanna Furnace,* 246; Suzanne Fellman Jacob and Ron Schlegel, "Joanna Furnace, Then and Now," *Pennsylvania Folklife* 45, no. 3 (1996): 135.

127. "Bethlehem Steel Purchases Joanna Furnace."

128. Jacob, *History of Joanna Furnace,* 246

129. Eulogy for Helen L. Hart.

130. HCVHA, "Historic Joanna Furnace," back cover and interior.

131. HCVA, "Historic Joanna Furnace," back cover.

132. "Historic Joanna Furnace," HCVHA website, accessed 25 Mar. 2025, https://haycreek.org/history/.

6. "Mountain Craftsmen" and Ready-to-Wear

1. "Curatorial Recommendation for Accession, Accession #: V.94.81," 9 Dec. 1994, 1. Valentine Richmond History Center.

2. Strassel, "Designing Women," 51.

3. Hannah Carlson, "Idle Hands and Empty Pockets: Postures of Leisure," *Dress* 35, no. 1 (2008): 10.

4. Carlson, "Idle Hands," 10, 24.

5. "Curatorial Recommendation for Accession," 6.

6. My thanks to former Valentine curator Kristen Stewart for her observation of this construction detail and her insightful supervision of my research appointment.

7. Harrison, "American Classics," 38; "New Country Aprons," 137.

8. Lindau, "Mountain Craftsmen," 45.

9. "Phelps Industries Opens New Quarters," *New York Times,* 6 Feb. 1952.

10. In this, I am indebted to Lesley Ellis Miller's investigation of similar relationships between the Paris couture and the French textile industry. Miller, "Perfect Harmony," 113–34.

11. Lathrop, "Fashion-Award Winners Move Home-Shop to Asheville," 38.

12. "'Cotton Covert' and Tunic-Line Jacket in New Playclothes Line," *Women's Wear Daily,* 2 Nov. 1950, 34.

13. Lathrop, "Fashion-Award Winners Move Home-Shop to Asheville," 38.

14. "Bethlehem Steel Purchases Joanna Furnace, Acreage." 1 June 1951, newspaper clipping, Helen L. Hart Archives, Joanna Furnace, Hay Creek Valley Historical Association, Berks County, PA.

15. "Phelps Building Studios in South," *Women's Wear Daily,* 24 Aug. 1951, 12.

16. "Top Fashion Designers Buy Shadowlawn," *Asheville (NC) Citizen-Times,* 14 Aug. 1951.

17. "Phelps Building Studios in South," 12.

18. "Phelps Industries Opens New Quarters," 32.

19. Deedie Smith, "In & Out: Celebration and Excitement Are Always Part of Weddings," *Asheville (NC) Citizen-Times,* 25 Oct. 1953

20. George E. Linton, "Textile Highlights of 1952," *American Fabrics* 24 (Winter 1952–1953): 75.

21. *Miller's Asheville City Directory, 1954* (Piedmond Directory Co., 1954).

22. Lathrop, "Abscessed Tooth Brought Asheville New Industry."

23. "Design Award Is Received by Mrs. Phelps," *Asheville (NC) Citizen-Times,* 27 Jan. 1961; Phelps, "Closing Sale," advertisement, *Asheville (NC) Citizen-Times,* 17 Aug. 1969.

24. Jane Cahill, "Roadside Shop Boasts Good Volume, Low Upkeep," *Women's Wear Daily,* 5 June 1953, 6.

25. Lizabeth Cohen, "From Town Center to Shopping Center: The Reconfiguration of Community Marketplaces in Postwar America," *American Historical Review* 101, no. 4 (1996): 1052.Ab

26. Cahill, "Roadside Shop Boasts Good Volume, Low Upkeep," 6.

27. Cahill, "Roadside Shop Boasts Good Volume, Low Upkeep," 6.

28. "Phelps Opens New Shop," *Women's Wear Daily,* 19 Feb. 1957, 13.

29. Lindau, "Mountain Craftsmen," 45.

30. Bill Lindau, "Asheville Is Seen as Perfect Location for Developing Small Craftsmen's Shops," *Asheville (NC) Citizen-Times,* 2 Sept. 1951.

31. Lindau, "Asheville Is Seen as Perfect."

32. William Lindau, "Mountain Craftsmen," 45.

33. Jane S. Becker, *Selling Tradition: Appalachia and the Construction of an American Folk, 1930–1940* (Univ. of North Carolina Press, 1998), 5. Note that while some historians have categorized the Scotch-Irish as Celts, David Hackett Fischer argues that the (mostly eighteenth-century) immigrants themselves resented this label and association, preferring Anglo-Irish or Saxon-Scotch. They were mostly from the lowlands of Scotland and north of England and

had little contact with Celtic culture. Fischer writes, "They gradually became the dominant English-speaking culture in a broad belt of territory that extended from the highlands of Appalachia through much of the Old Southwest." David Hackett Fischer, *Albion's Seed: Four British Folkways in America* (Oxford Univ. Press, 1989), 633–34; 618, 620.

34. Becker, *Selling Tradition,* 7.

35. Lindau, "Asheville Is Seen as Perfect."

36. Lindau, "Mountain Craftsmen," 45.

37. Becker, *Selling Tradition,* 74.

38. "Deep Country Clothes Are a Way of Life," *Asheville (NC) Citizen-Times,* 6 Sept. 1964.

39. "Phelps Industries Making Own Lines," *Women's Wear Daily,* 25 July 1952, 32.

40. Lathrop, "Fashion-Award Winners Move Home-Shop to Asheville," 38.

41. "To Buy in July," *Vogue,* 1 July 1949, 101.

42. McClendon, *Denim,* 84.

43. "Tunic-Shirts over Trousers in Fall Deep-Country Clothes," *Women's Wear Daily,* 17 May 1951, 3.

44. "A Queenly Wardrobe," *Asheville (NC) Citizen-Times,* 6 Aug. 1959.

45. "Queenly Wardrobe."

46. James P. Kaetz, "Cordova," in *Encyclopedia of Alabama* online, Auburn Univ., last updated 24 Jan. 2024, http://encyclopediaofalabama.org/article/h-3297.

47. "'Cotton Covert' and Tunic-Line Jacket," 34; Virginia Pope, "Beach Togs," *New York Times,* 31 Dec. 1950.

48. Indian Head, "Want to Beat Last Year?" advertisement, *Women's Wear Daily,* 4 Apr., May 1951.

49. "One-Piece Trouser Suit, Suburban or Country," *Women's Wear Daily,* 17 May 1951, 1.

50. "Work or Play Attire Made in Large Sizes," *New York Times,* 24 May 1951.

51. Margaret Parker Gary, "Smart Togs for Action," *Woman's Day,* Jan. 1953, 19–20.

52. Timothy J. Minchin, "The Crompton Closing: Imports and the Decline of America's Oldest Textile Company," *Journal of American Studies* 47 (2013): 231, 233, 239.

53. Edna Ferber, *Ice Palace* (Doubleday, 1958), 29.

54. "Fall Ideas of 'Name' Designers in Inspirations Velvet Show," *Women's Wear Daily,* 24 Mar. 1950, 38.

55. "Crompton Sets March 23 for Fashion Show," *Women's Wear Daily,* 21 Feb. 1950, 27.

56. Arnold, *American Look,* 4, 11, 13, 16.

57. "Crompton Sets March 23 for Fashion Show," 27.

58. Crompton Richmond Co., "Crompton and . . . Make it a Year of Creation," advertisement, *Women's Wear Daily,* 28 Feb. 1950, 10.

59. Crompton Richmond Co., "Crompton and," 10–11.

60. Crompton Richmond Co., advertisements, *Women's Wear Daily,* 28 Mar. 1950, 5; 4 Apr. 1950, 7; 18 Apr. 1950, 14; 2 May 1950, 9; 9 May 1950, 16.

61. "Crompton Makes It a Year of Creation," advertisement, *Harper's Bazaar,* 15 Mar. 1950, 18c.

62. Crompton Richmond Co., "Parisian Event in Crompton Velvet," advertisement, *Vogue,* 1 June 1950, 8.

63. Marcketti and Parsons, *Knock It Off,* 55.

64. Crompton-Richmond Co., "Crompton Has Invited . . . ," advertisement, *Harper's Bazaar,* Mar. 1951, 96; Crompton-Richmond Co., "Crompton Has Invited . . . ," advertisement, *Vogue,* 15 Mar. 1951, 32.

65. Edyth Radom, "Famous Designers Interpret Fashions in Velvet," *Hartford (CT) Courant Magazine,* 15 July 1951.

66. "Interview: Deep Country," *Vogue,* 1 Nov. 1951, 137.

67. Galey & Lord, "Pick a Pocket," advertisement, *Women's Wear Daily,* 14 July 1955, 44.

68. Galey & Lord, "With the Nostalgic Flavor," advertisement, *Women's Wear Daily,* 5 Sept. 1957, 76.

69. Mason Waters Georgetown, "Deep Country Clothes by PHELPS," advertisement, *Harper's Bazaar,* May 1954, 63.

70. Lindau, "Mountain Craftsmen," 45.

71. Harrison, "American Classics," 38.

72. Miller, "Perfect Harmony," 125.

73. Harrison, "American Classics," 38.

74. Harrison, "American Classics," 38.

75. Lathrop, "Fashion-Award Winners Move Home-Shop to Asheville," 38.

76. Lindau, "Mountain Craftsmen," 45.

77. "Mrs. Phelps Is Speaker at Workshop," *Asheville (NC) Citizen-Times,* 10 Feb. 1966; "Mrs. Phelps Will Talk," *Asheville (NC) Citizen-Times,* 9 Mar. 1966.

78. Gertrude Ramsey, "Transylvania Orchestra, Cass Give Outdoor Concert," *Asheville (NC) Citizen-Times,* 20 July 1954.

79. Edna Ferber, *Personality Plus* (1914; repr., Univ. of Illinois Press, 2002), 82.

80. Buckley and Clark, *Fashion and Everyday Life,* 7.

81. Gary, "Smart Togs for Action," 19–20.

82. Buckley and Clark, *Fashion and Everyday Life,* 4.

83. I have previously used this found theory in analysis of women's everyday fashions in rural Texas. Rebecca Jumper Matheson, "'Smart Togs for Action': Everyday Clothes for Rural Women in Texas in the 1950s," in *Fashion in American Life,* ed. Hazel Clark and Lauren Downing Peters (Bloomsbury, 2024), 60–61.

84. Ferber, *Personality Plus,* 82.

85. Lou Taylor, "De-Coding the Hierarchy of Fashion Textiles," in *The Textile Reader,* ed. Jessica Hemmings (Bloomsbury, 2012), 420–21.

86. Buckley and Clark, *Fashion and Everyday Life,* 9.

87. "And She Can Cook, Too," *Vogue,* 1 Apr. 1950, 145.

88. "And She Can Cook, Too," 145; William Grimes, "Dorothy Rodgers Is Dead at 83; Writer, Inventor and Decorator," *New York Times,* 18 Aug. 1992; Dorothy Rodgers, *My Favorite Things* (Avenel, 1964), 4, 46.

89. Rodgers, *My Favorite Things,* 46.

90. Rodgers, *My Favorite Things,* 4.

91. Rodgers and Rodgers, *A Word to the Wives,* 277.

92. Rodgers and Rodgers, *Word to the Wives,* 277.

93. Rodgers, *My Favorite Things,* 73.

94. After starting as a client, Rodgers was still in touch with Molyneux as a friend in the late 1960s. Dorothy Rodgers, *The House in My Head* (Avenel, 1967), 33; Dorothy Rodgers, *A Personal Book* (Harper & Row, 1977), 46–48, 66.

95. "And She Can Cook, Too," 145; Rodgers, *My Favorite Things,* xv.

96. Rodgers, *My Favorite Things,* 28.

97. Eliza McGraw, *Edna Ferber's America* (Louisiana State Univ. Press, 2013), 25.

98. Rodgers, *My Favorite Things,* 228.

99. "Work Clothes, 88–90.

100. Stein, "Graphic Ordering of Desire," 146.

101. "Work Clothes," 88–89.

102. "Work Clothes," 89.

103. Wilson, *Adorned in Dreams,* 3. For more on housedresses and the wash dress industry, see Matheson, "Smart Togs for Action," 66–68.

104. "Work Clothes," 90.

105. Buckley and Clark, *Fashion and Everyday Life,* 4.

106. Buckley and Clark, *Fashion and Everyday Life,* 7.

107. "Shop Hound," *Vogue,* 15 Oct. 1954, 65.

108. Buckley and Clark, *Fashion and Everyday Life,* 4.

109. By the late twentieth century, a combination of increased mechanization in factories and exploitative overseas labor practices produced the opposite effect with regard to home sewing, making ready-to-wear clothing cheaper than ever—so cheap, in fact, that a middleclass American home sewer could not reproduce a factory produced garment at the same price—the fabric alone cost more at retail, and once the sewer's time was factored in it became economically unfeasible other than as a leisure activity.

110. In 1948, a Singer Sewing Centers brochure advertised classes in home dressmaking and home decoration, as well as classes specifically for teenage girls aged twelve to seventeen. Singer Sewing Machine Company, *The Secret of Beautiful Clothes and a Beautified Home* (Singer Manufacturing, 1948), 4.

111. Virginia Pope, "Patterns of the Times: American Designer Series: A Typical Phelps Idea: 2 Piece Costume for Town, Country," *New York Times,* 4 June 1951; Macy's, "Macy's Salute to the American Designers," advertisement, *New York Times,* 2 Mar. 1952.

112. Pope, "Patterns of the Times," 40.

113. Pope, "Patterns of the Times," 40.

114. Pope, "Patterns of the Times," 40.

115. Gary, "Smart Togs for Action," 18–20, 82, 84.

116. Gary, "Smart Togs for Action," 19.

117. *Woman's Day* Fashion Department, "At Last: It Makes Sense to Make Boys' Clothes," *Woman's Day,* July 1954, 38.

118. Margaret Parker Gary, "One Wonderful Evening Skirt," *Woman's Day,* Dec. 1954, 79.

119. Arnold, *American Look,* 4, 11, 13, 16.

120. Arnold, *American Look,* 206.

7. Elizabeth Phelps Leads

1. "William Phelps," Social Security Administration, Washington DC, *Social Security Death Index, Master File,* available via Ancestry.com.

2. "History," Morito Scovill website, accessed 1 Dec. 2020, http://www.scovill.com/about-us/history/.

3. Phelps, "For Country or Suburban Living," advertisement. *New York Times,* 9 Sept. 1951.

4. *Webster's Ninth New Collegiate Dictionary* (1990), under "trews."

5. "Fashions Go Round the Clock," *Philadelphia Inquirer,* 11 Oct. 1956.

6. RaeLana Poteat, email message to author, 27 Apr. 2020; Louise Thomas, *Dear Emily: A Memoir: My Life in the Fine Stores* (Running Angel, 2011), 5, 7; Miss Myrtle Louise Mar Thomas, North Carolina, United States, 21 Feb. 2013, obituary, from Recent Newspaper Obituaries (1977—Today), database, *GenealogyBank.com,* citing *Winston-Salem Journal* 21 Feb. 2013.

7. Thomas, *Dear Emily,* 3.

8. Thomas, *Dear Emily,* 191–92, 237–39, 249.

9. Minchin, "Crompton Closing," 233.

10. Thomas, *Dear Emily,* 20–21, 25, 30, 39–40.

11. Thomas, *Dear Emily,* 48, 49, 40, 51–52.

12. Thomas, *Dear Emily,* 52.

13. Thomas, *Dear Emily,* 71, 82.

14. Thomas, *Dear Emily,* 83, 179, 152.

15. Thomas, *Dear Emily,* 92.

16. Thomas, *Dear Emily,* 103.

17. Thomas, *Dear Emily,* 104.

18. Thomas, *Dear Emily,* 147.

19. Division of Statistics, North Carolina Department of Labor, *North Carolina Directory of Manufacturing Firms* (North Carolina Department of Labor, 1960), 142, 423, 368.

20. "W. D. Phelps Death Victim: Wilkes-Barre Native Succumbs in Florida," *Wilkes-Barre (PA) Record,* 28 Jan. 1962.

21. "New Corporations," *The News & Observer* (Raleigh, NC), 3 May 1959.

22. "Joel Adams, Civic Leader, Lawyer, Dies," *Ashville (NC) Citizen-Times,* 17 Oct. 1972.

23. "Functional Country Clothes in Pretty Pastels," *Women's Wear Daily,* 2 Feb. 1960, 31; Phelps, "Deep Country Clothes and Leather Accessories for 'City-Country Any Country' by Elizabeth Phelps Now Showing," advertisement, *Women's Wear Daily,* 5 Feb. 1969, 68.

24. "The Gang at the Sheraton Russell," *Women's Wear Daily,* 10 Oct. 1962, 38; Phelps, "Designer Elizabeth Phelps," advertisement, *Women's Wear Daily,* 10 Mar. 1965, 44.

25. "Around Asheville."

26. Ivey's of Charlotte, "Showing of Phelps 'Deep Country Clothes,'" advertisement, *Charlotte (NC) Observer,* 9 Mar. 1961.

27. "Design Award Is Received by Mrs. Phelps," 6.

28. "Sportswear Designers Are Honored," *New York Times,* 4 Nov. 1961.

29. Photographs, "Phelps," box 11, folder 20, Fashion Group International Records, MSS Col 908, "American Design Collections" files, Manuscripts, Archives, and Rare Books, New York Public Library.

30. "William Phelps," *U.S., Social Security Death Index;* "William Phelps, Designer, Was 71; Leather Craftsman Noted for Hand-Made Items Dies," *New York Times,* 24 Jan. 1962.

31. "William Phelps, Designer, Was 71"; "William D. Phelps," *Women's Wear Daily,* 25 Jan. 1962, 43.

32. "William Phelps, Designer, Was 71"; "William D. Phelps," 43.

33. "W. D. Phelps Death Victim," 12.

34. "Permanent Weekend Clothes-List," 173.

35. Charlotte Curtis, "Designer Seeks to Feminize Country Clothes," *New York Times,* 11 June 1963.

36. *The Misadventures of Merlin Jones,* directed by Robert Stevenson (Disney, 1964), DVD.

37. "Functional Country Clothes in Pretty Pastels," 31.

38. Virginia Pope, "Style with a Country Air," *New York Times,* 30 May 1954.

39. "Permanent Weekend Clothes-list," 169.

40. Harrison, "American Classics," 38.

41. Phelps, "Phelps Fall-Winter Collection 1965," advertisement, *Women's Wear Daily,* 2 June 1965, 47.

42. "Deep Country Clothes Are a Way of Life."

43. Gertrude Ramsey, "Phelps Leather," *Asheville (NC) Citizen-Times,* 18 July 1965.

44. "Deep Country Clothes Are a Way of Life

45. Ramsey, "Phelps Leather,"

46. "Deep Country Clothes Are a Way of Life,"

47. Ramsey, "Phelps Leather."

48. Elizabeth Heintges Phelps, "Wearing Apparel," US Patent 3,266,057, filed Feb. 24, 1964, and issued Aug. 16, 1966, column 1.

49. Phelps, "Wearing Apparel," column 1.

50. Phelps, "Wearing Apparel," column 2.

51. Phelps, "Wearing Apparel," columns 1–3.

52. Phelps, "Wearing Apparel," column 2.

53. Gary, "Smart Togs for Action," 18–20.

54. Phelps, "Wearing Apparel," column 2.

55. "Around Asheville."

56. John C. Dills, "Fred Palmer, Big Game Hunter, Is Teaching Women to Shoot," *Asheville (NC) Citizen-Times,* 17 Jan. 1965.

57. Phelps, "Deep Country," advertisement, *Women's Wear Daily,* 25 Oct. 1966.

58. Bender, "Shoulder Bags Are Back from the War," 32.

59. "Curatorial Recommendation for Accession, Accession #: V95.46," 1, Valentine Richmond History Center.

60. "Curatorial Recommendation for Accession," 7, 8,

61. Caroline Rennolds Milbank, email message to author, 12 Oct. 2020.

62. Milbank, email.

63. Caroline Rennolds Milbank, telephone conversation with the author, 10 Oct. 2020; Milbank, email.

64. Milbank, email.

65. "Name Mrs. Phelps to Hanes Post," *Women's Wear Daily,* 14 Aug. 1969, 12; "The Girls of Today in the Look of Today," *Vogue,* 1 Aug. 1970, 72–73.

66. "Award-Winning Designer Joins Hanes Corporation," *Asheville (NC) Citizen-Times,* 15 Aug. 1969; "Mrs. Elizabeth Phelps," *Charlotte (NC) Observer,* 17 Aug. 1969; Ray Hubbard, "Business Notes," *High Point (NC) Enterprise,* 17 Aug. 1969.

67. "Name Mrs. Phelps to Hanes Post," 12.

68. "Name Mrs. Phelps to Hanes Post," 12.

69. Phelps, "Closing Sale," advertisement, *Asheville (NC) Citizen-Times,* 17 Aug.1969.

70. "Gildafrox Children's Line Started as a Family Project," *Women's Wear Daily,* 6 Oct. 1969, 27.

71. "Real Estate Transfers," *Asheville (NC) Citizen-Times,* 2 May 1973, 12.

72. Phelps, "Final Sale," advertisement, *Asheville (NC) Citizen-Times,* 11 Oct. 1973; see also Phelps, "Final Sale," advertisement, *Asheville (NC) Citizen-Times,* 7 Oct. 1973.

73. "Auction," *Asheville (NC) Citizen-Times,* 27 Oct. 1973; "Auction," *Asheville (NC) Citizen-Times,* 31 Oct. 1973.

74. "Auction," 31 Oct. 1973.

75. Elizabeth Phelps to Jimmie Booth, 7 May 1956, box 4, folder 7, Virginia "Jimmie" Booth Collection, Archives Center, National Museum of American History, Smithsonian Institution.

76. "Award Winners Named at Open Exhibition," *Asheville (NC) Citizen-Times,* 2 Oct. 1966.

77. "LaFont Workshop Show," *Clarion-Ledger* (Jackson, MS), 13 Nov. 1977.

78. "On the Coast," *Clarion-Ledger* (Jackson, MS), 9 Apr. 1978; "Painting Again," *Asheville (NC) Citizen-Times,* 16 Apr. 1978.

79. Gertrude Ramsey, "Nothing Beats This Plan for Watching Bird Life," *Asheville (NC) Citizen-Times,* 22 Mar. 1964, 20.

80. "LaFont Art Winners Announced," *Clarion-Ledger* (Jackson, MS), 22 Nov. 1981.

81. Steve Phillips, "Hundreds Line Up for a Piece of Pascagoula History," *WLOX News* (Biloxi, MS), 9 Dec. 2010, https://www.wlox.com/story/13644492/buy-a-piece-of-pascagoula-history-at-la-font-inn/; Cherie Ward, "LaFont Inn Coming Down, Owners and City Leaders Excited About Prospects," *GulfLive.com,* Apr. 24, 2010, https://www.gulflive.com/mississippi-press-news/2010/04/lafont_inn_coming_down_owners_and_city_leaders_excited_about_prospects.html.

82. "Happenings," *Northside Sun* (Jackson, MS), 23 Sept. 1982.

83. "Ninety Artists Join Forces for Gallery's First Reunion Show," *Clarion-Ledger* (Jackson, MS), 3 June 1984.

84. "McCravey Paintings on Display at LaFont," *Scott County Times* (Forest, MS), 6 June 1984. Forest was McCravey's hometown, presumably the reason Phelps goes unmentioned in the headline.

85. "Elizabeth H. Phelps," Social Security Administra-

tion; Washington D.C, *Social Security Death Index, Master File,* available via Ancestry.com.

86. "Our Story," Thomas Bates website, 2022, https://thomasbates.com/index.php/our-story/.

87. *T. B. Phelps Footwear and Accessories, Fall 2020 Retail Pricing,* vol. 10, https://tbphelps.com/index.php/retail-catalog/, accessed 1 Mar. 2021, page discontinued as of 28 Mar. 2025.

88. "Home," T. B. Phelps website, accessed 1 Mar. 2021, https://tbphelps.com/index.php/.

89. "Meet Thomas Bates of Haverhill," *Boston Voyager,* 18 Sept. 2017, http://bostonvoyager.com/interview/meet-thomas-bates-t-b-phelps-thomas-bates-northeast-haverhill/.

90. See "About Us," T. B. Phelps website, accessed 28 Mar. 2025, https://tbphelps.com/about-us/.

Conclusion

1. See, for example, "America Delivers the Goods," *Vogue,* 1 Feb. 1941, 110–11, 158; "American Fashion on Its Own," *Vogue,* 1 Feb. 1941, 78, 160.

2. For more about the organization that has coordinated campaigns including #whomademyclothes, see "About," Fashion Revolution website, accessed 28 Mar. 2025, https://www.fashionrevolution.org/about/.

Bibliography

Primary Sources

Asheville (NC) Citizen-Times. "Around Asheville." 15 Feb. 1964.
Asheville (NC) Citizen-Times. "Auction." 27 Oct. 1973.
Asheville (NC) Citizen-Times. "Award Winners Named at Open Exhibition." 2 Oct. 1966.
Asheville (NC) Citizen-Times. "Award-Winning Designer Joins Hanes Corporation." 15 Aug. 1969.
Asheville (NC) Citizen-Times. "Deep Country Clothes Are a Way of Life." 6 Sept. 1964.
Asheville (NC) Citizen-Times. "Design Award Is Received by Mrs. Phelps." 27 Jan. 1961.
Asheville (NC) Citizen-Times. "Mrs. Phelps Is Speaker at Workshop." 10 Feb. 1966.
Asheville (NC) Citizen-Times. "Mrs. Phelps Will Talk." 9 Mar. 1966.
Asheville (NC) Citizen-Times. "Painting Again." 16 Apr. 1978.
Asheville (NC) Citizen-Times. "A Queenly Wardrobe." 6 Aug. 1959.
Asheville (NC) Citizen-Times. "Real Estate Transfers." 2 May 1973.
Asheville (NC) Citizen-Times. "Top Fashion Designers Buy Shadowlawn." 14 Aug. 1951.
Broadcast: The Weekly Newsmagazine of Radio Broadcast Advertising, "Agencies." 3 Sept. 1945, 56.
Art Students League of New York. *Course Catalogue, 1932–1933 Winter Season.* Art Students League of New York, 1932.
Art Students League of New York. *Course Catalogue, 1933–1934 Winter Season.* Art Students League of New York, 1933.
Ballard, Bettina. *In My Fashion.* David McKay, 1960.
Bender, Marylin. "Shoulder Bags Are Back from the War." *Women's Wear Daily,* 10 July 1964, 32.
Boston Voyager. "Meet Thomas Bates of Haverhill." 18 Sept. 2017, http://bostonvoyager.com/interview/meet-thomas-bates-t-b-phelps-thomas-bates-northeast-haverhill/.
Braggiotti, Mary. "Leather-Bound Love." *New York Post,* 20 Sept. 1947.
Burris-Meyer, Elizabeth. *This Is Fashion.* Harper, 1943.
Butzner, Jane. "Leather Shocking Tales." *Vogue.* Feb. 1936, 139.
Byers, Margaretta. *Help Wanted—Female.* Julian Messner, 1941.
Cahill, Jane. "Roadside Shop Boasts Good Volume, Low Upkeep." *Women's Wear Daily.* 5 June 1953, 6.
Chambers, Bernice G. *Fashion Fundamentals.* Prentice-Hall, 1947.
Chambers, Bernice G., ed. *Keys to a Fashion Career.* McGraw-Hill, 1946.
Clarion-Ledger (Jackson, MS). "LaFont Art Winners Announced." 22 Nov. 1981.
Clarion-Ledger (Jackson, MS). "LaFont Workshop Show." 13 Nov. 1977.
Clarion-Ledger (Jackson, MS). "Ninety Artists Join Forces for Gallery's First Reunion Show." 3 June 1984.
Clarion-Ledger (Jackson, MS). "On the Coast." 9 Apr. 1978.
Council of the Citizens' Association. *Report of the Council of Hygiene and Public Health of the Citizens' Association of New York upon the Sanitary Condition of the City.* D. Appleton & Company, 1865.
Crawford, M[orris]. D[e]. C[amp]. *The Ways of Fashion.* Fairchild, 1948.

Curtis, Charlotte. "Designer Seeks to Feminize Country Clothes." *New York Times.* 11 June 1963.
Cushman, Wilhela. "You're at Liberty to Make." *Ladies Home Journal.* Feb. 1943, 30–31, 150.
Daché, Lilly. *Talking Through My Hats.* Coward-McCann, 1946.
Dalton, Matthew. "Louis Vuitton Makes a Home on the Range." *Wall Street Journal.* 18 Oct. 2019.
Dills, John C. "Fred Palmer, Big Game Hunter, Is Teaching Women to Shoot." *Asheville (NC) Citizen-Times.* 17 Jan. 1965.
DLW. "Phelps Associates Win Deign Award." *Women's Wear Daily.* 4 Feb. 1944, 20.
Etnier, Elizabeth. "Ten Families Who Abandoned the Cities." *Harper's Bazaar.* Apr. 1947, 213.
Evening News (Wilkes-Barre, PA). "Death Claims Francis Phelps at Laurel Run." 6 July 1911.
Fashion Group International. "Accessories." *Fashion Group Bulletin* 7, no. 2 (1941): insert 1.
Fashion Group International. "Accessories." *Fashion Group Bulletin* 12, no. 1 (1946): insert 1.
Fashion Group International. "Fashion Availables for a Wartime Autumn; A Realistic Report Keyed to Government Orders, Necessity for New Advertising, Promotion Techniques." *Fashion Group Bulletin* 8, no. 5 (1942): 1, 3–8.
Fashion Group International. "Fashion Editors' Choice—Advance News—All About the Way We'll Look This Spring." *Fashion Group Bulletin* 12, no. 1 (1946): 1, 3.
Fashion Group International. "Home Furnishings—Craftsmanship." *Fashion Group Bulletin* 10, no. 1 (1945): insert 1–2.
Fashion Group International. "Los Angeles and San Francisco Groups Present Fashion Futures; Stress on Craftsmanship." *Fashion Group Bulletin* 7, no. 1 (1941): 3–4.
Fashion Group International. "Morale—Inventory for Fashion Industry and Individual, 'Take the Folly Out of Fashion; Make Quality and Value the Sales Points,' Advises Edna Woolman Chase." *Fashion Group Bulletin* 8, no. 1 (1942): 1, 3–5.
Fashion Group International. "New Trend Fall Accessories," *Fashion Group Bulletin* 12, no. 2 (1946): 4.
Fashion Group International. "Preview of Spring Accessories." *Accessories Meeting Report,* 6 Nov. 1947, 1.
Fashion Group International. "Quality, New Fashions in Unions Discussed at April and May Luncheons." *Fashion Group Bulletin* 7, no. 3 (1941): 1, 9–12.
Fashion Group International. "Regional Groups—Recent Activities. Philadelphia." *Fashion Group Bulletin* 16, no. 1 (1950): 5.
Fashion Group International. "Rules We Work By." *Fashion Group Bulletin* 9, no. 4 (1943): 3–5.
Fashion Group International. "Welcome to Membership." *The Fashion Group Bulletin* 12, no. 2 (1946): 4.
Ferber, Edna. *Fanny Herself.* 1917. Reprint. CreateSpace, n.d.
Ferber, Edna. *Giant.* 1952. Reprint. Harper Perennial, 2019.
Ferber, Edna. *Ice Palace.* Doubleday, 1958.
Ferber, Edna. *One Basket.* People's Book Club, 1947.
Ferber, Edna. *Personality Plus.* 1914. Reprint. Univ. of Illinois Press, 2002.
Fitz-Gibbon, Bernice. *Macy's, Gimbels, and Me.* Simon & Schuster, 1967.
Fogarty, Anne. *Wife Dressing: The Fine Art of Being a Well-Dressed Wife.* Julian Messner, 1959.
Fortune. "The Small Shop." Nov. 1945, 158–61.
Gary, Margaret Parker. "One Wonderful Evening Skirt." *Woman's Day.* Dec. 1954, 78–79, 96.
Gary, Margaret Parker. "Smart Togs for Action." *Woman's Day.* Jan. 1953, 18–20, 82, 84.
GM. "Adam in the Looking Glass." *New York Times.* 8 Jan. 1950.
Grimes, William. "Dorothy Rodgers Is Dead at 83; Writer, Inventor and Decorator." *New York Times.* 18 Aug. 1992.
Guica, Linda. "Jimmie Booth: The Artistic Force Behind Golden Lamb Buttery." *Hartford Courant.* 2 Oct. 2011.
Hamburger, Estelle. *It's a Woman's Business.* Vanguard Press, 1939.
Harper's Bazaar. "Add a Belt." Nov. 1943, 104–5.
Harper's Bazaar. "Custom-Made for American Women." Oct. 1945, 88–101.
Harper's Bazaar. "Dress as the War Production Board Wants You To." 15 Feb. 1942, 60–61.
Harper's Bazaar. "Fur Belts." Aug. 1943, 104–5.
Harper's Bazaar. "Leather Takes a Good Tan." Apr. 1947, 226–27.
Harper's Bazaar. "Home Dressmaking." Oct. 1942, 104–5.
Harper's Bazaar. "Junior Bazaar." Feb. 1943, 126.
Harper's Bazaar. "New Ways with Flannel." Sept. 1947, 255.
Harper's Bazaar. "One Thing at a Time." Mar. 1944, 116–17.
Harper's Bazaar. "Ready for Anything." Jan. 1943, 59.
Harper's Bazaar. "Say Red, Say White, Say Blue." Feb. 1945, 108–9.
Harper's Bazaar. "See That You're Born in Texas." Apr. 1943, 87.
Harper's Bazaar. "Shopping Bazaar: Leather and Fur." July 1943, 8f–8g.
Harper's Bazaar. "Something in Wool and Leather: Something Half and Half." Aug. 1943, 66.
Harper's Bazaar. "Spring Paraphernalia." Mar. 1943, 60–61.
Harper's Bazaar. "A Suit for Everyone." Sept. 1942, 85.
Harper's Bazaar. "To the Springs: Sporting Life." Oct. 1947, 224–31.
Harper's Bazaar. "Tweeds Against the Wind." Nov. 1947, 210–11.
Harper's Bazaar. "What Animals Are These?" Nov. 1942, 60–61.
Harper's Bazaar. "Workshop on Washington Square." June 1942, 22.
Harrison, Elizabeth. "American Classics: Phelps Casual Designs: A Designing Couple Now Experiment with Fabric." *New York Times.* 9 Nov. 1955.
Hawes, Elizabeth. *Fashion Is Spinach.* Random House, 1938.
Hawes, Elizabeth. *Men Can Take It.* World, 1941.
Hawthorne, Nathaniel. *Mosses from an Old Manse.* 1846. Reprint. A. L. Burt, n.d.

Hay Creek Valley Historical Association. "Conversations with Joanna Furnace Area Residents." *Journal,* 2010: 21–24.

Herrick, Grace. "Accessories Were Specially Made to Dramatize Outfits in the Show." *New York Times.* 26 Oct. 1945.

Herrick, Grace. "Fashion Notes." *New York Times.* 7 Oct. 1945.

Hope, Constance. *Publicity Is Broccoli.* Bobbs-Merrill, 1941.

Hubbard, Ray. "Business Notes." *High Point (NC) Enterprise,* 17 Aug. 1969.

Hughes, Alice. "A Woman's New York" Column. *Muncie (IN) Star.* 15 June 1949.

Kingston (NY) Daily Freeman. "Dr. J. S. Taylor Speaker to League." 23 Feb. 1939.

Lathrop, Virginia T. "Abscessed Tooth Brought Asheville New Industry." *Charlotte (NC) Observer.* 28 Dec. 1952.

Lathrop, Virginia T. "Fashion-Award Winners Move Home-Shop to Asheville." *News and Observer* (Raleigh, NC). 28 Dec. 1952.

Laver, James. "Clothes and the Man." *Vogue.* 15 Feb. 1950, 60–65, 117.

Lee, Gideon. *Two Lectures on Tanning Delivered Before the Eclectic Fraternity.* Eclectic Fraternity, 1838.

Life. "Big Bags and Belts." 19 Nov. 1945, 85–86, 88.

Life. "Work Clothes: New Substitutes for House Dress Are Rugged, Trim and Tailored." 7 Feb. 1949, 88–90.

Lindau, William [Bill]. "Asheville Is Seen as Perfect Location for Developing Small Craftsmen's Shops." *Asheville (NC) Citizen-Times.* 2 Sept. 1951.

Lindau, William [Bill]. "Mountain Craftsmen: Native Artisans Produce Phelps Style Separates, Accessories." *Women's Wear Daily.* 29 Jan. 1958, 45.

Linton, George E. "Textile Highlights of 1952." *American Fabrics* 24 (Winter 1952–53): 74–75.

Mahoney, Tom, and Rita Hession. *Public Relations for Retailers.* Macmillan, 1949.

Mason Waters. "Deep Country Clothes by PHELPS." *Harper's Bazaar.* May 1954, 63.

McAllister, Gertrude. "Fashion Jury Names Leading American Designers." *Brooklyn Eagle.* 4 Feb. 1944.

McCardell, Claire. *What Shall I Wear?* Simon & Schuster, 1956.

McIlvanie, Jane S. "'Deep Country' Clothes Attract Great Interest." *Philadelphia Inquirer.* 20 May 1949.

"Mrs. Elizabeth Phelps." *Charlotte (NC) Observer,* 17 Aug. 1969.

Museum of Modern Art. *100 Useful Objects of Fine Design 1947: Available Under $100.* Museum of Modern Art, 1947.

New York Herald. "Phelps-Ross." 7 Jan. 1921.

New York Times. "Caroline K. Rennolds to Wed." 20 Feb. 1983.

New York Times. "Fantasy and Modernism Combined in Array of Fashion Accessories for Day and Night." 2 Apr. 1946.

New York Times. "Fashion Group Luncheon: 2 Authors Are Heard and New Officers Are Announced." 24 Nov. 1948.

New York Times. "Handbags Become Functional and Attractive Accessories," 5 Apr. 1944.

New York Times. "New York City: The Leather Trade; The Swamp—Hide and Leather Dealers—Capital Employed—Brokers." 31 Mar. 1856.

New York Times. "Paid Notice: Deaths: Messinesi, Despina (Nee Plakias)." 28 July 2003.

New York Times. "Paid Notice: Deaths: Tanner, Dorelle M." 26 June 2001.

New York Times. "Pennsylvania Strike Riot; Superintendent of Parish Coal Company Assaulted Near Wilkes-Barre—More Trouble Feared." 10 May 1900.

New York Times. "Phelps Designs Separates Group That Is 2-Faced." 8 May 1956.

New York Times. "Phelps Industries Opens New Quarters." 6 Feb. 1952.

New York Times. "Sportswear Designers Are Honored." 4 Nov. 1961.

New York Times. "Store Deliveries Cut Drastically: Bread, Laundry, Newspapers, Other Daily Services Reduced to Save Rubber and Oil." 2 June 1942.

New York Times. "William Phelps, Designer, Was 71; Leather Craftsman Noted for Hand-Made Items Dies." 24 Jan. 1962.

New York Times. "Women in Business Get Honor Scrolls." 17 Oct. 1950.

New York Times. "Work or Play Attire Made in Large Sizes." 24 May 1951.

New York Metropolitan Board of Health. *Third Annual Report of the Metropolitan Board of Health for the State of New York.* Charles Van Benthuysen & Sons, 1868.

Norcross, Frank W. *A History of the New York Swamp.* Chiswick Press, 1901.

Northside Sun (Jackson, MS). "Happenings." 23 Sept. 1982.

Pennsylvania Society of Sons of the Revolution. *Annual Proceedings: Pennsylvania Society of Sons of the Revolution 1913–1914.* Pennsylvania Society, 1914.

Petry, Ann. *The Street.* In *Ann Petry: "The Street," "The Narrows,"* edited by Farah Jasmin Griffin. Library of America, 2019.

Phelps, Elizabeth. "Have Fun with the Colors You Wear." *Woman's Day.* July 1953, 69.

Philadelphia Inquirer. "Fashions Go Round the Clock." 11 Oct. 1956.

Pollard, Clarice F. *Laugh, Cry, and Remember: The Journal of a G.I. Lady.* Journeys Press, 1991.

Pope, Virginia. "American Inspiration." *New York Times.* 6 Feb. 1944.

Pope, Virginia. "Beach Togs." *New York Times.* 31 Dec. 1950.

Pope, Virginia. "Patterns of the Times: American Designer Series: A Typical Phelps Idea: 2 Piece Costume for Town, Country." *New York Times.* 4 June 1951.

Pope, Virginia. "Style With a Country Air." *New York Times.* 30 May 1954.

Radom, Edyth. "Famous Designers Interpret Fashions in Velvet." *Hartford (CT) Courant Magazine,* 15 July 1951.

Ramsey, Gertrude. "Nothing Beats this Plan for Watching Bird Life." *Asheville (NC) Citizen-Times.* 22 Mar. 1964.

Ramsey, Gertrude. "Phelps Leather." *Asheville (NC) Citizen-Times.* 18 July 1965.

Ramsey, Gertrude. "Transylvania Orchestra, Cass Give Outdoor Concert." *Asheville (NC) Citizen-Times.* 20 July 1954.
Raushenbush, Winifred. *How to Dress in Wartime.* Coward-McCann, 1942.
Risch, Erna. *A Wardrobe for the Women of the Army.* QMC Historical Studies No. 12. Historical Section, General Administrative Services Division, Office of the Quartermaster General, 1945.
Rodgers, Dorothy. *The House in My Head.* Avenel, 1967.
Rodgers, Dorothy. *My Favorite Things.* Avenel, 1964.
Rodgers, Dorothy. *A Personal Book.* Harper & Row, 1977.
Rodgers, Dorothy, and Mary Rodgers. *A Word to the Wives.* Alfred A. Knopf, 1970.
Scott County Times (Forest, MS). "McCravey Paintings on Display at LaFont." 6 June 1984.
Searle, William. *The Garden Club of America: One Hundred Years of a Growing Legacy.* Smithsonian Books, 2012.
Singer Sewing Machine Company. *The Secret of Beautiful Clothes and a Beautified Home.* Singer Manufacturing, 1948.
Smith, Deedie. "In & Out: Celebration and Excitement Are Always Part of Weddings." *Asheville (NC) Citizen-Times.* 25 Oct. 1953.
Stuart, Jessie. *The American Fashion Industry.* Simmons College, 1951.
Thomas, Louise. *Dear Emily: A Memoir: My Life in the Fine Stores.* Running Angel Books, 2011.
Town and Country. "Town and Country Counter Points." Jan. 1944, 98.
Turner, Anita Boyer. "Two Personal Looks Back." *Journal,* Hay Creek Valley Historical Association. 2010: 24–26.
US Bureau of Labor Statistics. *Wages and Hours of Labor in the Furniture Industry, 1910–1931.* GPO, 1932.
US Department of Commerce. *Index of Trademarks Issued from the United States Patent Office.* GPO, 1945.
Walton, Frank L. *Thread of Victory.* Fairchild, 1945.
Warburton, Gertrude and Jane Maxwell. *Fashion for a Living.* McGraw-Hill, 1939.
Wilkens, Emily. *More Secrets from the Super Spas.* Dembner, 1983.
Woman's Day Fashion Department. "At Last: It Makes Sense to Make Boys' Clothes." *Woman's Day.* July 1954, 38.
Vogue. "America Delivers the Goods." 1 Feb. 1941, 110–11, 158.
Vogue. "American Tricks for Suits." 1 Sept. 1939, 111.
Vogue. "American Fashion on Its Own." 1 Feb. 1941, 78, 160.
Vogue. "And She Can Cook, Too." 1 Apr. 1950, 144–45.
Vogue. "Bold—Not Bitsy." 15 Aug. 1944, 120–21.
Vogue. "Celeste Holm, Star of 'Bloomer Girl.'" 1 Jan. 1945, 56–57.
Vogue. "Designs for Dressmaking: Make a Skirt Wardrobe." 15 Sept. 1944, 156–61.
Vogue. "For Hot Springs and All Points." 1 Oct. 1944, 134–41.
Vogue. "The Girls of Today in the Look of Today." 1 Aug. 1970, 56–75.
Vogue. "Interview: Deep Country." 1 Nov. 1951, 136–37.
Vogue. "Long Island Autumn." 1 Oct. 1947, 202–7, 246.
Vogue. "Made for You." 1 Oct. 1948, 136–41.
Vogue. "The Market Basket." 1 July 1941, ii.
Vogue. "Mrs. James Stewart: Her Kind of Clothes." 15 Apr. 1953, 82–83.
Vogue. "New Country Aprons . . . Worn by the Designer." Nov. 1948, 136–37.
Vogue. "People Are Talking About . . . In Fashion." 1 Aug. 1947, 94.
Vogue. "Permanent Weekend Clothes-List." 1 May 1960, 168–77, 226.
Vogue. "Shop Hound." 15 Oct. 1954, 64–65.
Vogue. "Suits with Two Lives." 15 Jan. 1944, 68–69.
Vogue. "This Half Century." Jan. 1950, 86–94.
Vogue. "To Buy in July." 1 July 1949, 100–103.
Vogue. "Week-End Wardrobe Plan: Bag and Baggage." 1 May 1956, 158.
Vogue. "What Clinches New Fashions." 1 May 1962, 68.
Wilkes-Barre (PA) Record. "Academy Commencement."12 June 1901.
Wilkes-Barre (PA) Record. "Death of Francis Phelps." 7 July 1911.
Women's Wear Daily. "Bonnie Cashin to Design for Sills." 14 Apr. 1953, 29.
Women's Wear Daily. "'Cotton Covert' and Tunic-Line Jacket in New Playclothes Line." 2 Nov. 1950, 34.
Women's Wear Daily. "Crompton Sets March 23 for Fashion Show." 21 Feb. 1950, 27.
Women's Wear Daily. "Curb's End Raises Question of Making Calfskin Handbags for Christmas." 31 Aug. 1945, 11.
Women's Wear Daily. "Curbs Lifted to Speed Output of Leather Bags and Footwear." 29 Aug. 1945, 1.
Women's Wear Daily. "Denim, Sailcloth Coordinates Adapted from Custom-Mades." 30 Jan. 1950, 32.
Women's Wear Daily. "Expects Tight Leather Basis for Some Time." 28 July 1944, 13.
Women's Wear Daily. "Fall Belts: Reversibles and High-Low Effects." 16 May 1952, 11.
Women's Wear Daily. "Fall Ideas of 'Name' Designers in Inspirations Velvet Show." 24 Feb. 1950, 38.
Women's Wear Daily. "Functional Country Clothes in Pretty Pastels." 2 Feb. 1960, 31.
Women's Wear Daily. "The Gang at the Sheraton Russell." 10 Oct. 1962, 38.
Women's Wear Daily. "Gildafrox Children's Line Started as a Family Project." 6 Oct. 1969, 27.
Women's Wear Daily. "Historic Sources Inspire Bags." 7 May 1943, 20.
Women's Wear Daily. "Incorporations." 1 Feb. 1928, 18.
Women's Wear Daily. "March of Time Fashion Film Set to Be Released Tomorrow." 20 Feb. 1947, 22.
Women's Wear Daily. "Mrs. Phelps Designing New Suede Group." 31 Dec. 1951, 3.
Women's Wear Daily. "Name Mrs. Phelps to Hanes Post." 14 Aug. 1969, 12.
Women's Wear Daily. "New York Store Presents Phelps Bags and Belts." 17 May 1946, 16.

Women's Wear Daily. "One-Piece Trouser Suit, Suburban or Country." 17 May 1951.
Women's Wear Daily. "Phelps Collection at Lord & Taylor." 13 May 1955, 10.
Women's Wear Daily. "Phelps Building Studios in South." 24 Aug. 1951, 12.
Women's Wear Daily. "Phelps Industries Making Own Lines." 25 July 1952, 32.
Women's Wear Daily. "Phelps Opens New Shop." 19 Feb. 1957, 13.
Women's Wear Daily. "Selling Handbags." 21 Apr. 1944, 22.
Women's Wear Daily. "Shoe Rationing Touches Off Rush for Bags, Particularly Leathers." 12 Feb. 1943, 12.
Women's Wear Daily. "Shoe Retailers WPB Talks End Differences." 13 Mar. 1944, 18.
Women's Wear Daily. "Suggests Store Clinics to Seek Out Latent Designing Talents." 7 Feb. 1950, 2.
Women's Wear Daily. "Tunic-Shirts over Trousers in Fall Deep-Country Clothes." 17 May 1951, 3.
Women's Wear Daily. What They Bought This Week: EVERYTHING...... But Particularly Pumps, Ties." 12 Feb. 1943, 1.
Women's Wear Daily. "William D. Phelps." 25 Jan. 1962, 43.
Wulbern, Helen P. "Voris of Hollywood: Designer for Sheer Suedes." *Women's Wear Daily,* 18 Mar. 1938, 11, 14.
Yale Univ. *Catalogue of Yale University 1909–1910.* Tuttle, Morehouse & Taylor, 1909.

Secondary Sources

American Pharmaceutical Association. *Yearbook of the American Pharmaceutical Association 1913.* Vol. 2. American Pharmaceutical Association, 1915.
Appelbaum, Barbara. *Guide to Environmental Protection of Collections.* Sound View Press, 1991.
Arnold, Rebecca. *The American Look: Fashion, Sportswear and the Image of Women in 1930s and 1940s New York.* I. B. Tauris, 2009.
Baics, Gergely. *Feeding Gotham: The Political Economy and Geography of Food in New York, 1790–1860.* Princeton Univ. Press, 2016.
Barthes, Roland. *The Fashion System,* translated by Matthew Ward and Richard Howard. 1983. Reprint. Univ. of California Press, 1990.
Baxandall, Michael. *Painting and Experience in Fifteenth-Century Italy.* Clarendon, 1972.
Becker, Jane S. *Selling Tradition: Appalachia and the Construction of an American Folk, 1930–1940.* Univ. of North Carolina Press, 1998.
Benson, Susan Porter. *Counter Cultures: Saleswomen, Managers, and Customers in American Department Stores, 1880–1940.* Univ. of Illinois Press, 1986.
Blum, Dilys E. *Shocking! The Art and Fashion of Elsa Schiaparelli.* Philadelphia Museum of Art and Yale Univ. Press, 2003.
Bowles, Stephen E. "And Time Marched On: The Creation of *The March of Time.*" *Journal of the University Film Association* 29, no. 1 (1977): 7–13.
Bradbury, Jane, and Edward Maeder. *American Style and Spirit: Fashions and Lives of the Roddis Family, 1850–1995.* V & A Publications, 2016.
Brears, Peter C. D. *Horse Brasses.* Country Life Books, 1981
Buckland, Sandra Stansbery. "Promoting American Designers, 1940–44." In *Twentieth-Century American Fashion,* edited by Linda Welters and Patricia A. Cunningham. Berg, 2005.
Buckley, Cheryl and Hazel Clark. *Fashion and Everyday Life: London and New York.* Bloomsbury, 2017.
Burrows, Edwin G. and Mike Wallace. *Gotham: A History of New York City to 1898.* Oxford Univ. Press, 2000.
Carlson, Hannah. "Idle Hands and Empty Pockets: Postures of Leisure." *Dress* 35, no. 1 (2008): 7–27.
Cheney, Joyce. *Aprons: Icons of the American Home.* Running Press, 2000.
Chrisman-Campbell, Kimberly. *Fashion Victims: Dress at the Court of Louis XVI and Marie-Antoinette.* Yale Univ. Press, 2015.
Clark, Hazel. "SLOW + FASHION—an Oxymoron—or a Promise for the Future . . . ?" *Fashion Theory* 12, no. 4 (2008): 427–46.
Cohen, Lizabeth. "From Town Center to Shopping Center: The Reconfiguration of Community Marketplaces in Postwar America." *American Historical Review* 101, no. 4 (1996): 1050–81.
Cooke, Edward S. Jr. "Modern Craft and the American Experience." *American Art* 21, no. 1 (2007): 2–9.
Cunningham, Patricia A. *Reforming Women's Fashion, 1850–1920.* Kent State Univ. Press, 2003.
Deihl, Nancy, ed. *The Hidden History of American Fashion: Rediscovering 20th-Century Women Designers.* Bloomsbury, 2018.
Dougherty, Betty. *Your Leatherwork.* 1947. Reprint. Sylvan, 1948.
Ellsworth, Lucius F. "Craft to National Industry in the Nineteenth Century: A Case Study of the Transformation of the New York State Tanning Industry." *Journal of Economic History* 32 no. 1 (1972): 399–402.
Evans, Caroline. *The Mechanical Smile: Modernism and the First Fashion Shows in France and America, 1900–1929.* Yale Univ. Press, 2013.
Fashion Institute of Technology. *All-American: A Sportswear Tradition.* Fashion Institute of Technology, 1985.
Fischer, David Hackett *Albion's Seed: Four British Folkways in America* Oxford Univ. Press, 1989.
Goffman, Erving. *The Presentation of the Self in Everyday Life.* Doubleday, 1959.
Gordon, Beverly. *The Saturated World: Aesthetic Meaning, Intimate Objects, Women's Lives, 1890–1940.* Univ. of Tennessee Press, 2006.

Field, Jacqueline. "Dyes, Chemistry and Clothing: The Influence of World War I On Fabrics, Fashions and Silk." *Dress* 28, no. 1 (2001): 77–91.

Font, Lourdes, M. and Trudie A. Grace. *The Gilded Age: High Fashion and Society in the Hudson Highlands 1865–1914.* Putnam County Historical Society and Foundry Museum, 2006.

Font, Lourdes, M. and Trudie A. Grace. *Summer Afternoon: Fashion and Leisure in the Hudson Highlands, 1850–1950.* Putnam History Museum, 2012.

Ford, Guy Stanton, ed. *Compton's Pictured Encyclopedia.* Vol. 4. F. E. Compton, 1922.

Gold, Annalee. *One World of Fashion,* 4th ed. Fairchild, 1987.

Greenwich Garden Club. *The Greenwich Garden Club Celebrates 100 Years: 1914–2014.* Greenwich Garden Club, 2014.

Hobson, Phyllis, and Steven Edwards. *Tan Your Hide! Home Tanning Leathers and Furs.* Garden Way / Storey, 1977.

Hollander, Anne. *Seeing Through Clothes.* Viking, 1978. Reprint. Univ. of California Press, 1993.

Howell, Geraldine. *Wartime Fashion: From Haute Couture to Homemade, 1939–1945.* Berg, 2012.

Hunt, Valerie Reich. "Composite Objects: Materials and Storage Conditions." In *Conservation Concerns: A Guide for Collectors and Curators,* edited by Konstanze Bachmann. Cooper-Hewitt and Smithsonian Institution Press, 1992.

Jacob, Suzanne Fellman. *The History of Joanna Furnace, 1791–1999.* Hay Creek Valley Historical Association, 1999.

Jacob, Suzanne Fellman and Ron Schlegel. "Joanna Furnace, Then and Now." *Pennsylvania Folklife* 45, no. 3 (1996): 134–40.

Kidwell, Claudia. *Suiting Everyone: The Democratization of Clothing in America.* Smithsonian Institution Press, 1974.

Kirkham, Pat. *Charles and Ray Eames: Designers of the Twentieth Century.* MIT Univ. Press, 1995.

Kirkham, Pat. *Women Designers in the USA, 1900–2000: Diversity and Difference.* Bard Graduate Center for Studies in the Decorative Arts and Yale Univ. Press, 2000.

Kirkham, Pat and Amy F. Ogata. "Europe 1830–1900." In *History of Design,* ed. Pat Kirkham and Susan Weber. Bard Graduate Center and Yale Univ. Press, 2013.

Leach, William. *Land of Desire: Merchants, Power, and the Rise of a New American Culture.* Pantheon, 1993.

Koda, Harold and Andrew Bolton. *Poiret.* Metropolitan Museum of Art and Yale Univ. Press, 2007.

Kopytoff, Igor. "The Cultural Biography of Things." In *The Social Life of Things: Commodities in Cultural Perspective,* edited by Arjun Appadurai. Cambridge Univ. Press, 1986.

Lambert, Eleanor. *World of Fashion.* R. R. Bowker/Xerox, 1976.

Laver, James. *Taste and Fashion.* 2nd ed. 1945. Reprint. George G. Harrap & Sons, 1948.

Ley, Sandra. *Fashion for Everyone.* Charles Scribner's Sons, 1975.

MacDonell, Nancy. *Empresses of Seventh Avenue: World War II, New York City, and the Birth of American Fashion.* St. Martin's Press, 2024.

Maglio, Diane. "A Brief Historical Overview of the First Major Menswear Exhibition in the United States—Adam in the Looking Glass at the Metropolitan Museum of Art, New York, 1950." *Critical Studies in Men's Fashion* 4, no. 1 (2017): 79–88.

Marcketti, Sara B. and Jean L. Parsons. *Knock It Off: A History of Design Piracy in the US Women's Ready-to-Wear Apparel Industry.* Texas Tech Univ. Press, 2016.

Martin, Ann Smart. "Magical, Mythical, Practical, and Sublime: The Meanings and Uses of Ceramics in America." *Ceramics in America,* vol. 1, no. 1 (2001): 29–46.

Martin, Ann Smart. "Ribbons of Desire: Gendered Stories in the World of Goods." In John Styles and Amanda Vickery, eds. *Gender, Taste, and Material Culture in Britain and North America, 1700–1830.* Yale Center for British Art and the Paul Mellon Centre for Studies in British Art, 2006.

Martin, Earl, ed. *Knoll Textiles, 1945–2010.* Bard Graduate Center and Yale Univ. Press, 2011.

Martin, Richard. *American Ingenuity: Sportswear 1930s–1970s.* Metropolitan Museum of Art, 1998.

Martineau, Paul, ed. *Icons of Style: A Century of Fashion Photography.* J. Paul Getty Museum, 2018.

Mauss, Marcel. "Techniques of the Body." In. *Incorporations,* edited by Jonathan Crary and Sanford Kwinter. 1934 Reprint. Zone, 1992.

Matheson, Rebecca Jumper. "'A House That Is Made of Hats': The Lilly Daché Building, 1937–1968." In *The Places and Spaces of Fashion: 1800–2006,* edited by John Potvin. Routledge, 2008.

Matheson, Rebecca Jumper. "Sara Pennoyer: Twentieth-Century Retail and Advertising Executive and Her Creation, *Polly Tucker, Merchant.*" *Fashion, Style & Popular Culture* 5, no. 1 (2018): 59–79.

Matheson, Rebecca Jumper. "'Smart Togs for Action': Everyday Clothes for Rural Women in Texas in the 1950s." In *Fashion in American Life,* edited by Hazel Clark and Lauren Downing Peters. Bloomsbury, 2024.

Matheson, Rebecca Jumper. *Young Originals: Emily Wilkens and the Teen Sophisticate.* Texas Tech Univ. Press, 2015.

McClendon, Emma. *Denim: Fashion's Frontier.* Yale Univ. Press and FIT, 2016.

McDermott, Charles H. *A History of the Shoe and Leather Industries of the United States Together with Historical and Biographical Notices.* Vol. 2. John W. Denehy & Co., 1920.

McDowell, Colin. *Forties Fashion and the New Look.* Bloomsbury, 1997.

McGraw, Eliza. *Edna Ferber's America.* Louisiana State Univ. Press, 2013.

McMartin, Barbara. *Hides, Hemlocks, and Adirondack History: How the Tanning Industry Influenced the Region's Growth.* North Country Books, 1992.

Meinig, D[onald]. W[illiam]., ed. *The Interpretation of Ordinary Landscapes.* Oxford Univ. Press, 1979.

Meyer, Marilee Boyd et al. *Inspiring Reform: Boston's Arts and Crafts Movement.* Davis Museum and Harry N. Abrams, 1997.

Mida, Ingrid. *Reading Fashion in Art.* Bloomsbury, 2020.

Milbank, Caroline Rennolds. *New York Fashion: The Evolution of American Style.* New York: Harry N. Abrams, 1989.

Miller, Lesley Ellis. "Perfect Harmony: Textile Manufacturers and Haute Couture 1947–57." In *The Golden Age of Couture: Paris and London 1947–57,* edited by Claire Wilcox. V & A Publications, 2008.

Minchin, Timothy J. "The Crompton Closing: Imports and the Decline of America's Oldest Textile Company." *Journal of American Studies* 47 (2013): 231–60.

Nicklas, Charlotte, and Annabella Pollen, eds. *Dress History: New Directions in Theory and Practice.* Bloomsbury Academic, 2015.

Prown, Jules David. "Mind in Matter: An Introduction to Material Culture Theory and Method." *Winterthur Portfolio* 17, no. 1 (1982): 1–19.

Richards, Florence S. *The Ready-to-Wear Industry 1900–1950.* Fairchild, 1951.

Roberts, Jennifer L. "Things: Material Turn, Transnational Turn." *American Art* 31, no. 2 (2017): 64–69.

Rudofsky, Bernard. *Are Clothes Modern?* Paul Theobald, 1947.

Salaman, R[aphael]. A[rthur]. *Dictionary of Leather-Working Tools, c.1700–1950.* George Allen & Unwin, 1986.

Sennett, Richard. *The Craftsman.* Yale Univ. Press, 2008.

Slipek, Edwin Jr. "The Valentine's Latest Exhibit Remembers the Stores That Once Kept the City Bustling." *Style Weekly* (Richmond, VA). 1 Jan. 1980.

Snodgrass, Mary Ellen. *World Clothing and Fashion: An Encyclopedia of History, Culture and Social Influence.* Vols. 1 and 2. Routledge, 2014.

Spector, Shelley. "75th Anniversary: Proud to Be in PR: The Story of Denny Griswold, Founder of *PRNews.*" *PR News.* Apr. 2019, 9–10, https://www.prnewsonline.com/wp-content/uploads/2019/04/prn-2019-04-01.pdf.

Steele, Valerie. *Fifty Years of Fashion: New Look to Now.* Yale Univ. Press, 1997.

Steele, Valerie. *Women of Fashion: Twentieth-Century Designers.* Rizzoli, 1991.

Stein, Sally. "The Graphic Ordering of Desire: Modernization of a Middle-Class Women's Magazine, 1919–1939." In *The Contest of Meaning: Critical Histories of Photography,* edited by Richard Bolton. MIT Press, 1989.

Stillinger, Elizabeth. *A Kind of Archeology: Collecting American Folk Art, 1876–1976.* Univ. of Massachusetts Press, 2011.

Strassel, Annemarie. "Designing Women: Feminist Methodologies in American Fashion." *Women's Studies Quarterly* 41, nos. 1–2 (2012): 35–59.

Tanner's Council of America. *The Romance of Leather: A Brief History of Leather and a Description of Tanning.* Tanner's Council of America, 1937.

Tartsinis, Ann Marguerite. *An American Style: Global Sources for New York Textile and Fashion Design, 1915–1928.* Bard Graduate Center, 2013.

Taylor, Lou. "De-Coding the Hierarchy of Fashion Textiles." In *The Textile Reader,* edited by Jessica Hemmings. Bloomsbury, 2012.

Taylor, Lou. *The Study of Dress History.* Manchester Univ. Press, 2002.

Veillon, Dominique. *Fashion Under the Occupation.* Trans. Miriam Kochan. Berg, 2002.

Webber-Hanchett, Tiffany. "Dorothy Shaver: Promoter of 'The American Look.'" *Dress* 30, no. 1 (2003): 80–90.

Whalen, Catherine L. "Collecting as Historical Practice and the Conundrum of the Unmoored Object." In *The Oxford Handbook of History and Material Culture,* edited by Ivan Gaskell and Sarah Anne Carter. Oxford Univ. Press, 2020.

Whitaker, Jan. *Service and Style: How the American Department Store Fashioned the Middle Class.* St. Martin's Press, 2006.

Whitley, Lauren D. "Morris De Camp Crawford and the 'Designed in America' Campaign, 1916–1922." *Textile Society of American Symposium Proceedings* 6 (1998): 410–19.

Williams, Beryl. *Fashion Is Our Business.* J. B. Lippincott, 1945.

Wilson, Elizabeth. *Adorned in Dreams: Fashion and Modernity.* Rev. ed. I. B. Taurus, 2003.

Yohannan, Kohle, and Nancy Nolf. *Claire McCardell: Redefining Modernism.* Abrams, 1998.

Znamierowski, Nell. *Dorothy Liebes: Retrospective Exhibition, March 20–May 20, 1970, Museum of Contemporary Crafts of the American Crafts Council.* Museum of Contemporary Crafts, 1970.

Index

NOTE: Page numbers in *italics* refer to illustrative material.